BRITISH MILITARY INTELLIGENCE, 1870-1914

The Development of a Modern Intelligence Organization

Thomas G. Fergusson

ARMS AND ARMOUR PRESS
London Melbourne Cape Town

Published in 1984 by Arms and Armour Press.
Lionel Leventhal Limited, 2-6 Hampstead High Street,
London NW3 1QQ.
Australasia: 4-12 Tattersalls Lane, Melbourne,
Victoria 3000.
South Africa: Sanso Centre, 8 Adderley Street,
P.O. Box 94, Cape Town 8000.

© 1984 Thomas G. Fergusson
Frederick, Maryland

1 2 3 4 5 6 7 8 9 0

ISBN 0-85368-641-6

BRITISH MILITARY INTELLIGENCE, 1870-1914

The Development of a Modern Intelligence Organization

To the Memory of
Major Thomas Taylor Galloway, U.S. Army Air Corps,
killed in action, Tourouvre, France, 24 July 1944
and
Captain Edward Mallory Almond, Jr., U.S. Army,
killed in action, Wattweiler, Germany, 19 March 1945.

CONTENTS

ILLUSTRATIONS

Plates

Following Page 74

Following Page 170

Organizational Charts

Maps

FOREWORD

Like any good intelligence officer, Tom Fergusson was his own owl and mole. His owl got the big picture. His mole dug into a paper mountain that covered forty-four years of military awakening, after fifty-five years of slumber. At the end of the Napoleonic era, the British Army clearly understood the principles of overseas military intelligence. "No general," Charles James remarked in the 1802 edition of his *New and Enlarged Military Dictionary*, "can be said to be in any degree qualified,...unless, like an able minister of state, he be constantly prepared...to obtain the best intelligence respecting the movements and the designs of the enemy.... It is not possible to conceive a greater crime than that of affording [information about one's own army] to an enemy, and thereby bringing about the overthrow and destruction of a whole army." All of the modern terms for intelligence, except that of a special military office of intelligence, were already in use. "There is not," James concluded, "a more dangerous ground to tread on than that of secret intelligence.... A wise general will consequently hear everything and say nothing.... *Private assassinations*, the *use of poison*, or the *disregard of paroles of honour*" will only gain a general "infamy" and expose him "to all the melancholy casualties of retaliation."

Colonel Fergusson's story is that of the successful establishment "of a permanent agency in the War Office for the collection, processing, and dissemination of information." As any issue of the *Foreign Intelligence Literary Scene* newsletter will suggest, it is unusual in its systematic coverage of a prewar era, in a field where people have concentrated on wartime problems and the mechanization of the intelligence machinery to match the mechanization of twentieth-century life.

Colonel Fergusson's admiration for the British Army's expertise in that later era got him to study its roots, as it jumped from the Napoleonic era to that of the Prussian General Staff. Here the modernization of the army's intelligence machinery preceded the establishment of either the British, the Imperial, or the American General Staffs. But until we have a history of American intelligence as expert as Fergusson's, it will be hard to know how deliberate American parallels were, and how many were unconscious reactions to similar conditions and threats. What we do know, as Fergusson notes, is how well the systems meshed in wartime, even in their political naiveté about treason by members of the establishment.

In scientific and economic matters, navies tended to be ahead of armies, with the United States and Japanese navies being better informed on technological matters than the Royal Navy. Both outside navies were trying to out-Britain Britain, and the British shipbuilding industry was doing an expert job of selling the latest technology. Armies were doing the same things, but here the Germans were equally complacent about their capabilities and products, so that the British Army could not be seen as responsible for their failure to foresee the trench deadlock of World War I. As trading nations, all the major industrial powers were reasonably well informed about their competitors. As first in the field, and facing the dangers of an old-fashioned cruiser war against an island dependent on food imports, the British were well informed about that naval problem. But, not expecting a long war, they were no better informed about a blockade than were the Germans. But here again, no army was well informed about problems of war production.

Long experience in colonial wars, where tactical and even strategic intelligence had to be the responsibility of the local commander, gave the British and particularly the Indian Army great intelligence capabilities. Where British Army intelligence did very badly in World War I was in amphibious operations, where intelligence responsibilities were no clearer than they had been during the Crimea, and in internal political intelligence where, again, responsibilities were as divided as they had been during the American Revolution. And, except in dealing with Ireland, where political intelligence was excellent, metropolitan Britons were quite unaware of the skill with which colonials, who had admired and studied the British system, knew how to exploit its respect for what Charles James called "those laws of nations which are founded upon the wise basis of humanity." That George Washington, or Mohandas Gandhi, or Jan Christiaan Smuts were, in some ways, more English than the English was a great advantage for leaders of a movement with many supporters in England. This led to few cases of treason, but political intelligence officers were constantly baffled by it. As far as Colonel Fergusson's story goes, however, the lack of clear guidelines within the intelligence community absolved the army from most of its wartime failures.

In similar situations, for example during the Philippine Insurrection, American Army intelligence officers deliberately copied Indian Army methods. It was only when they became involved in more sophisticated "wars of national liberation" that the American intelligence community managed to repeat most of the British mistakes during the American Revolution. The Americans' mistakes in dealing with Quebec showed the same problems of local knowledge and languages that would occur in Vietnam. Our bizarre failure to consult French colonials because they were losers was a reaction, albeit unconscious, to the British establishment's over-trusting French exiles during the Revolution. As Fergusson remarks, this was the original reason for the militarization of British intelligence. For both intelligence communities, mobilization shortages of professional and reserve intelligence officers forced them to depend heavily on reservists and volunteers. This proved to be a blessing in disguise. The Germans did not make as good use of the reservists they had, particularly at higher levels, partly because of their professionals' well-founded reputations and confidence in themselves.

The moral—since Colonel Fergusson simply asserts his reasons for respecting the professional performance of British intelligence—may be that a new and untried peacetime professional organization may perform best when it is forced by crisis to do the best it can with what assets it has. There is no time for doubts, discussions of first principles, or second-guessing. This was surely the story of those first generation Prussian military reformers whose principles, but not all of whose methods, the British were belatedly forced to copy. The nineteenth-century Prussian military machine rested on the feudal concepts of loyalty and honor, enlightened despotism's ideas of hard work and discipline (even for the nobility), the Age of Reason's use of reason to discover and then to apply first principles. The successes of the British and Americans depended on the same concepts. They, however, rejected the idea that "necessity knows no law," except in retaliation. Since the English and American Revolutions, it may not be politically possible for French-style Committees of General Security and Public Safety to operate with full public support, except in cases of foreign invasion. Politically we have been willing to take the word of the most unstable monarchs and egregious tyrants until they attack or betray us. But in these revolutions, political, internal, and military intelligence functions were so carefully sepa-rated that army intelligence could not be charged with failures like those, say, of the Indian Mutiny.

These introductory comments on Colonel Fergusson's splendid history are meant to indicate its importance. It opens other windows to the history of intelligence as a modern military managerial art and science. The successes of wartime intelligence are being intensely studied, now that more documents are available, or perhaps because of the gross failures of intelligence in limited wars in Korea, Egypt, and Vietnam. And, wartime "dirty tricks" carried over into peacetime have brought public dishonor on the whole intelligence community. But Colonel Fergusson drew his guidelines and bounded his study so neatly that he was able to write a highly illuminating and fascinating study of what he wanted to study. It explains to anyone who wants to know how the past relates to the present of British, American, and Free World—since the Empire was already "dissolving" into an alliance—military intelligence. In following Lord Acton's famous advice to "Study problems, not periods," he has managed to do both in showing what British professionals did, and why and how a small group of reformers did it. The result is a story of which any professional intelligence officer and professional historian can be proud.

Durham, North Carolina
March 25, 1983

Theodore Ropp
Emeritus Professor of History
Duke University

PREFACE

My own experiences as a military intelligence officer in the United States Army, together with an interest in the history of military intelligence, the British Army, and the British Empire, have been important motivations for undertaking the investigation of the strategic and tactical intelligence systems of the British Army during the forty-five years from the eve of the Franco-Prussian War to the beginning of World War I. My particular curiosity about the development of British military intelligence during the half century before 1914 has been inspired by a deep admiration for the remarkable accomplishments of British intelligence during both world wars, and, further, by the conviction that American intelligence organizations during and since these great conflicts have accumulated a considerable debt to their British counterparts. The World War II forerunner of the Central Intelligence Agency, the Office of Strategic Services, was, after all, the American offspring of two famous British organizations, MI 6 and the Special Operations Executive.

The record of British intelligence since 1914 is far from unblemished. There have been spectacular, highly publicized failures, especially in the post-World War II period. The unmasking in 1979 of Sir Anthony Blunt, the Queen's art advisor, as a former Russian spy shocked the British public and Britain's friends abroad and brought to mind the earlier defections of three notorious traitors—H.A.R. "Kim" Philby, Guy Burgess, and Donald Maclean—to the Russians. Still more recently, in 1982, Geoffrey Prime, a Russian linguist formerly employed as a translator by GCHQ (the British equivalent to our National Security Agency), was convicted of passing some of the innermost secrets of Britain's communications intelligence effort to the Russians over a period of many years. Nevertheless, the notion persists that, at least until 1945 and probably well beyond, to include even the present, British intelligence, particularly the secret services, has known no equal among the world's intelligence services. The fascinating story of Britain's codebreaking successes during World War II and the crucial role they played in the Allied victory over the Axis powers, as told in F.W. Winterbotham's *The Ultra Secret* (London, 1974), and Ronald Lewin's *Ultra Goes to War* (London, 1978), have served to enhance further still the lofty reputation of British intelligence.

If British intelligence was as outstanding during the two world wars as we Americans generally believe, and if our military commanders and intelligence organizations received more from the British in the way of timely, reliable intelligence and assistance than they gave in return, as the evidence seems to indicate, the development of British military intelligence before 1914, including its secret service branches, is a topic worthy of careful examination. It was upon this general premise that I began to explore the history of British military intelligence in the pre-World War I era, focusing initially upon the South African War (1899-1902). From the period of the South African War, I widened the chronological scope of my investigation back to 1870 and the birth of a permanent intelligence organization at the War Office, and forward to the eve of the Great War. I discovered that this was an eventful, indeed crucial, era in the history of British intelligence. During these years, the foundations were laid for Britain's intelligence successes between 1914 and 1945. At the War Office, a tiny, practically defunct topographical department was transformed into an efficient and highly respected intelligence organization and, eventually, into a large and important branch of the British General Staff. In the field, the traditional British Army system of tactical intelligence underwent significant change during and after the South African War. By 1914, British military intelligence, on both the strategic and tactical levels, had developed many of the characteristics of intelligence organizations or systems as we know them today.

There are many to whom I owe special thanks for advice, assistance, and inspiration during the course of my work. First, I am deeply grateful to Professors Theodore Ropp and Richard Preston of Duke University for their wise guidance, encouragement, and admirable patience. The genesis of my work began to take shape in the fall of 1972 during a seminar on the history of the British Empire conducted by Professor Preston. It was he who guided me in the direction of the South African War as a possibly fruitful period for a study of British military intelligence. Professor Ropp's helpful criticisms and penetrating insights were a regular source of inspiration. One could not have asked for more from one's thesis supervisor.

Others to whom I am indebted for having read and offered their comments on all or part of this work are: Professors R. Taylor Cole, Joel Colton, William E. Scott, and I.B. Holley of Duke University; Professor A.M.J. Hyatt of the University of Western Ontario; Professor Don Higginbotham of the University of North Carolina; Professor Edward M. Coffman of the University of Wisconsin; two former fellow graduate students at Duke University, Lt. Cols. Richard M. Swain II and Robert H. Scales, Jr.; and two officers with whom I served in the Third Armored Cavalry Regiment, Lt. Col. Eric K. Shinseki and Capt. Mark S. Partridge. For their kind assistance in helping me locate and gain access to valuable documentary materials, I want to thank the following individuals: Lt. Col. W.W. Leary, curator of the Intelligence Corps Museum at Templer Barracks, Ashford, Kent; J.C. Andrews (chief librarian), C.A. Potts, and David Bradley of the Ministry of Defence Library (Central and Army) in Whitehall, London; and Col. James Shepard, formerly acting director of the U.S. Army Military History Institute, Carlisle Barracks, Pennsylvania. Also, I would like to express my appreciation to the entire staffs of the following institutions for aiding my research: Perkins Library, Duke University; the United States Military Academy Library, West Point, New York; the Public Records Office, London; the Liddell Hart Centre for Military Archives, King's College, University of London; and the U.S. Army Command and General Staff College Library, Fort Leavenworth, Kansas.

Finally, I would like to recognize the unique and valuable contributions of several family members. Without the patience and understanding of my wife, Beverly, and my daughter, Robin, particularly over the past several years, when the demands of challenging military assignments and my research and writing have left precious little time for family activities, I doubt that I would have finished the dissertation which has now been transformed into this book.

Through the years, my parents, Col. and Mrs. Charles M. Fergusson, Jr., USA Ret., of Austin, Texas, have inspired my efforts through their continuing interest in and encouragement for my professional and academic pursuits. In addition, my father read several chapters and offered helpful comments. My grandfather, Lt. Gen. Edward M. Almond, USA Ret., passed away in 1979 before I was able to finish my dissertation. To him I owe many things, not the least of which is an interest in military history. The study of military history was an important part of his own self-education for a long and distinguished military career. His easy familiarity with the campaigns of Napoleon and the American Civil War and his vivid personal recollections of World Wars I and II and the Korean War stirred my interest in the history of the military art early in life.

Thomas G. Fergusson
Würzburg,
Federal Republic of Germany
6 March 1983

ABBREVIATIONS

AAG	Assistant Adjutant General
ADMO	Assistant Director of Military Operations
AG	Adjutant General
AQMG	Assistant Quartermaster General
B.E.F.	British Expeditionary Force
C.I.D.	Committee of Imperial Defence
C.O.	Colonial Office Archives
COMINT	Communications Intelligence
DAAG	Deputy Assistant Adjutant General
DAG	Deputy Adjutant General
DAQMG	Deputy Assistant Quartermaster General
DGMI	Director General of Mobilization and Military Intelligence
DMI	Director of Military Intelligence
DNI	Director of Naval Intelligence
DQMG	Deputy Quartermaster General
F.I.D.	Field Intelligence Department
F.O.	Foreign Office Archives
F.S.R.	Field Service Regulations
GOC	General Officer Commanding
GSO	General Staff Officer
HUMINT	Human Intelligence
IMINT	Imagery Intelligence
I.O.	India Office Archives
M.O.D.	Ministry of Defence
N.I.D.	Naval Intelligence Department
QMG	Quartermaster General

R.F.C.	Royal Flying Corps
R.U.S.I.	Royal United Services Institution
SIGINT	Signals Intelligence
SIS	Secret Intelligence Service
T&S Department	Topographical and Statistical Department
W.O.	War Office Archives

NOTE ON SOURCES

The documentation of the history of a modern military intelligence organization or system is nearly always difficult, since secrecy normally surrounds intelligence operations, especially in wartime. Often, the most sensitive (and therefore, valuable) intelligence estimates, reports, and other products are destroyed as soon as they have lost their immediate value, so as not to fall into the hands of the enemy, or in some other way compromise a valuable source. This is particularly true in the field in time of war, but is also likely to occur in peacetime at the national level. The historian is fortunate indeed if he can locate official manuals on intelligence operations or the administration of secret service funds. It is also true, understandably, that those who have participated in intelligence activities are often extremely reticent about their pasts. They are frequently reluctant to write their memoirs, or if they do write them, to include in them any details of their experiences in intelligence.

I have had to contend with all of these problems in my research on British military intelligence before the First World War. Yet, I have also been fortunate to find a good deal of material of both an official and private nature. The work of several others before me has aided my work immensely. Most important in this regard have been Lt. Col. W.V.R. Isaac's "The History of the Development of the Directorate of Military Intelligence, the War Office, 1855-1939," an unpublished paper prepared in 1955, and Brig. Gen. B.A.H. Parritt's *The Intelligencers: The Story of British Military Intelligence up to 1914*. Though neither of these works include footnotes, both authors list the principal sources from which most of their material was drawn, which is helpful to the researcher. Though there are some minor discrepancies, both have proven to be factually reliable. Colonel Isaac provides valuable charts depicting the organization of War Office intelligence at various points in time. General Parritt includes lengthy excerpts from primary material, also of special interest to the historian. Jock Haswell's *British Military Intelligence*, published in 1973, several years after *The Intelligencers*, is not well documented and offers little on the pre-1914 era that Parritt and Isaac have not already said. Other important secondary works dealing with various aspects of intelligence upon which I have relied are: Richard Deacon's *A History of the British Secret Service*, David Kahn's monumental classic, *The Code-breakers*, and Alfred Vagts's *The Military Attaché*.

A veritable mountain of documents on both strategic and tactical intelligence was located at the Ministry of Defence Library (Central and Army). Particularly useful were the MOD Library's large and well-preserved holdings of War Office intelligence products—handbooks on foreign armies, the military resources of foreign powers series, annual reports on foreign maneuvers, and so on—some of which date from the mid-1870s. Various manuals, regulations, and instructions for intelligence officers were also found at the MOD Library, including David Henderson's *Field Intelligence*. A wealth of additional primary material was reviewed at the Intelligence Corps Museum at Templer Barracks in Ashford, Kent. The single most valuable document located there was Capt. E.H.H. Collen's *Report on the Intelligence Branch* of 1878, which provides a fascinating description of the Intelligence Branch in London at that time. Some extremely useful material on War Office intelligence between 1899 and 1910 was found in the Edmonds Papers at the Liddell Hart Centre for Military Archives, Kings College. Among the most useful material found in British public documents were the *Report* and *Minutes of Evidence* (*I* and *II*) of the Royal Commission on the War in South Africa, the *Report* of the Hardwicke Committee, and the *Report of the War Office (Reconstitution) Committee*.

Often, the memoirs of former intelligence officers or attachés were an excellent source on the internal operations of War Office intelligence, the methods of secret service and covert collection, or the activities of military attachés. The most useful were those of William R. Robertson, Edward Gleichen, Charles Callwell, Charles à Court Repington, George Aston, James E. Edmonds and W.H.H. Waters.

Secondary works not already mentioned which have been of particular value to me were: Brian Bond's *The Victorian Army and the Staff College 1854-1914*, John Gooch's *The Plans of War: The General Staff and British Military Strategy 1900-1916*, W.S. Hamer's *The British Army: Civil Military Relations, 1885-1905*, Jay Luvaas's *The Education of an Army*, Zara Steiner's *The Foreign Office and Foreign Policy 1898-1914*, and Samuel R. Williamson's *The Politics of Grand Strategy: Britain and France Prepare for War 1904-1914*.

Chapter I

Introduction: Intelligence and Empire

The practical monopoly of ocean cables that we possess, the sensibility of our mercantile and financial systems, whose preservation has become almost a cosmopolitan interest, our consular and diplomatic agencies, and the sharp watch upon events now maintained by our Naval and Military Intelligence Departments and Attachés abroad, have reached this stage, that the world has become a vast Anglo-Saxon whispering gallery, and that the centre of the Empire at once responds to the smallest shock experienced at any one of its extremities.

Major Charles à Court Repington
The Military Resources of France, 1895

Without really trying, nineteenth-century Britain possessed a superb and constantly improving capability for the collection of political, economic, military, naval, geographic, and scientific-technical information throughout the world. The British Empire, including the "informal empire,"[1] grew almost continually from 1815 to 1899, and as it expanded so did Britain's ability to collect strategic intelligence.[2] No other power—neither France before 1815, nor Germany or Russia in the final quarter of the century—could challenge the superiority of this gigantic and marvelously efficient antenna, on a worldwide basis. For the most part, the rulers of the British Empire took this advantage for granted. This was, after all, the age of the Pax Britannica. Between the final defeat of Napoleon Bonaparte at Waterloo and the beginning of the Second Anglo-Boer War in 1899, Britain was the wealthiest and most powerful nation on earth. In retrospect, it is not surprising that the nineteenth century's superpower had the world's premier strategic intelligence system and that her leaders were well-informed about events in virtually every corner of the globe. Even on the Continent, where the French, the Germans, and particularly the Russians were spending huge sums of money on secret service during the closing decades of the century,[3] the British still managed to excel in gathering information, relying primarily on their diplomats in European capitals, including military and naval attachés, and ordinary commercial and tourist contacts. Throughout the rest of the world, Britain far outdistanced the competition.

The advantage enjoyed by the British in strategic intelligence collection during the last century was, of course, a function of the strength and dimensions of the Empire. The tentacles of British power were far-reaching and durable; they also served admirably as collectors and conduits of information. At the same time, the system by which information was gathered all over the world and funneled back to decision makers in London was an important, indeed essential, element of the power and stability of the Empire. Throughout most of the nineteenth century, Britain's diplomatic position with respect to the European great powers was one of "splendid isolation." In these circumstances, the maintenance of British naval supremacy was vital. So, too, was the regular acquisition of information from a variety of sources overseas. The ascendancy of the Royal Navy on the high seas was complemented by the less visible, but nonetheless significant, pre-eminence of the British in strategic intelligence collection, particularly in the non-European areas of the world.

The current heads of the CIA and the KGB, were they to give the matter some thought, surely would be envious of the relative ease with which Whitehall kept abreast of developments inside and outside the Empire during the nineteenth century. It mattered not that Britain habitually spent less than any other great power of the day on secret service, that her covert intelligence organization, the Secret Intelligence Service (SIS), was almost continously bogged down with operations in Ireland to the exclusion of the rest of the world, nor that she failed to adopt the general staff system until the early years of the twentieth century.[4] From the end of the Napoleonic Wars in 1815 until at least the 1880s, the flow of strategic intelligence to London from overseas was not dependent upon covert sources or methods of collection. Nor, until after the Franco-Prussian War (1870-71), did either the War Office or the Admiralty decide that it was necessary to appoint a head of military or naval intelligence in peacetime.[5]

During the nineteenth century, the methods of intelligence collection changed somewhat, or, more accurately, some new means of gathering information were added, and the advent of the electric telegraph greatly increased the speed with which data reached Whitehall. The British experienced little difficulty in adjusting to these changes. By and large, they turned them to their own advantage. Collection was the principal strength of the British strategic intelligence system in the nineteenth century, but the acquisition of information is only one, albeit vital, function of an intelligence organization or system. Until the 1870s, the notable British proficiency in collection more than compensated for a lack of organization and centralized direction in British strategic intelligence. Weaknesses in Britain's intelligence system, particularly those which made reform imperative in military intelligence, were generally not in the collection of information, but in two other major functional areas, processing-analysis and dissemination-reporting.

How did the British Empire manage to function so effectively in the acquisition of strategic information? Let us briefly examine the structure and operation of Britain's strategic intelligence system in the nineteenth century, prior to 1873. Admittedly, the late-twentieth-century notion of a national or strategic intelligence system, as it is used here, was, in all probability, foreign to the minds of British civilian and military leaders of the nineteenth century. Similarly, the "structure" of British national intelligence, in the broad sense that is implied, was for the most part an unplanned consequence of the administrative framework of the British government in London and of the various instruments it employed overseas to conduct its foreign policy and to administer and protect its vast empire. Nevertheless, from a late-twentieth-century perspective, it is both possible and instructive to try to comprehend nineteenth-century British intelligence in these terms.

Since the British intelligence system in the nineteenth century functioned most effectively as a collector of information, the system's organization and operation are best viewed through an examination of the various parts of its collection machinery. All of the individual instruments of this machinery may be assigned to one of three general categories: (1) nonmilitary overt collection, (2) covert collection, and (3) military and naval collection. There was some overlap between the second and third categories, but until the closing decades of the nineteenth century the British fighting services normally became involved in covert intelligence operations only in time of war.[6]

An understanding of the first category, nonmilitary overt collection, is more easily achieved after a review of some basic historical facts about the nineteenth-century British Empire. Although the British Empire expanded almost continually between the Congress of Vienna and the end of the century, many British citizens, including members of Parliament, maintained an attitude of indifference toward the Empire during much of the period. The precise beginning and ending dates may be debated, but historians generally agree that Britain experienced an anti-imperialist era during the mid-nineteenth century, which was related to the free-trade school of thought in England.[7] Only in the final decades of the century did the indifference vanish and a new enthusiasm for empire and the expansion of the Empire appear among the majority of Britons. Regardless of the waxing and waning of support for imperial adventure among the populace at home, more and more territories overseas found themselves under the Union Jack as the nineteenth century progressed. The expansion of the Empire was often unplanned and piecemeal, but the process was seemingly relentless. At the same time, British

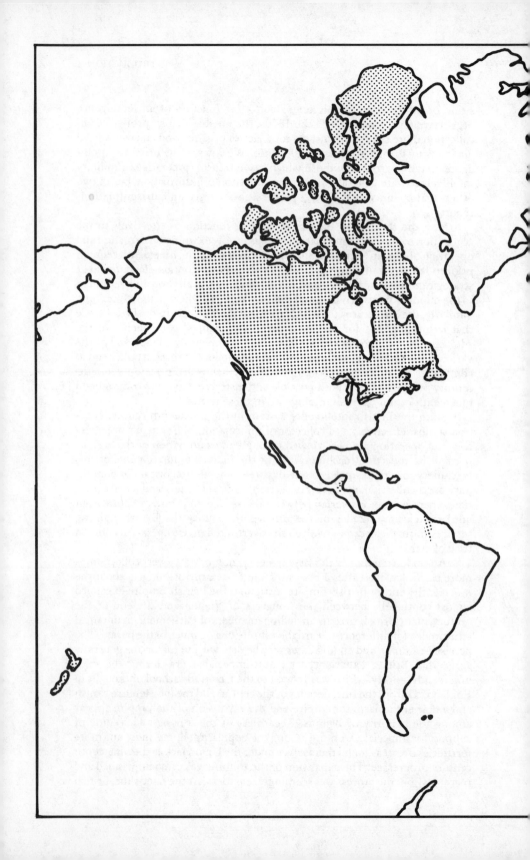

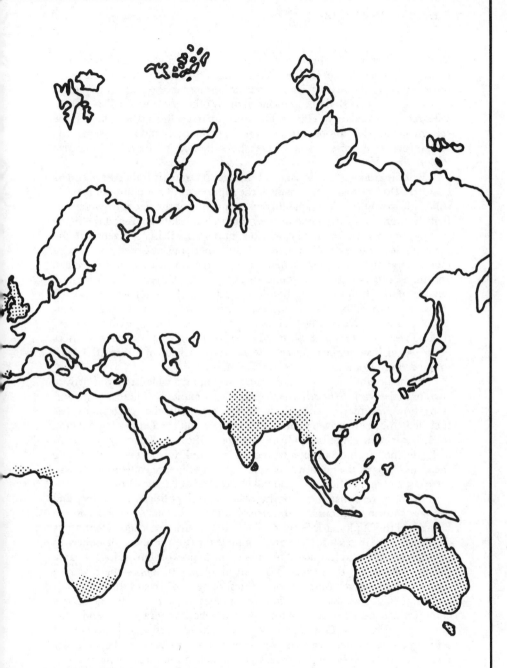

THE BRITISH EMPIRE IN 1870

influence in other non-European areas of the world was growing steadily through the extension of trade and economic, rather than political, ties. In the broadest sense, the British Empire was not limited to the areas of the world which flew the British flag, but included many other areas where Britain held a degree of ascendancy. The Empire encompassed India, the colonies, the self-governing dominions, various other dependencies and possessions, and an "informal empire," whose members looked to Britain for world leadership.

Britain attained her decisive advantage in strategic intelligence collection after 1815 primarily as a result of the superiority of her nonmilitary overt collection capability. This capability was a function of the size and diversity of British interests overseas and of the thousands of individuals and the many institutions, private and public, which kept it going. British citizens—in the form of governors, local administrators, diplomats, businessmen, civil service members, scientists, explorers, newspaper correspondents, private travelers, and many others—could be found in every part of the world, inside and outside of the Empire. Even before the advent of the telegraph and the transoceanic cable in the mid-nineteenth century, the unchallenged supremacy of the Royal Navy, together with the fact that both British naval and trading vessels were constantly moving between England and the far corners of the world, insured the timely and secure transmission of information back to the center of power on the River Thames.

In the nonmilitary sphere, Britain relied upon a wide variety of private citizens and government officials to gather information. A number of institutions, however, played particularly important intelligence collection roles. Included among these were the Foreign Office and the Diplomatic Service, the Colonial Office, the India Office, the Post Office, the Treasury, the Board of Trade, the East India Company, and the Bank of England. Foremost among these, in terms of the quantity and quality of intelligence collected overseas, were the Foreign Office, the Colonial Office, and the India Office.

Primary responsibility for the collection of political, economic, and military information outside the British Empire belonged to the Foreign Office and the Diplomatic Service. The Foreign Office was dependent on its diplomats abroad both for information and for the execution of policy. In addition to ambassadors and their staffs in the major foreign capitals—Paris, Berlin, Vienna, St. Petersburg, Constantinople, and others—there were a number of diplomatic missions of the first or second class in the capitals of less important nations. Each embassy or mission staff usually included a commercial consul. In many countries, consuls would operate independently, but in any case, the Consular Service functioned as a major collector of economic intelligence overseas, which was funneled back to the Consular Department of the Foreign Office. Considerable economic intelligence was also collected by the Board of Trade, which, among other things, maintained statistics on British overseas investments. In contrast to their ample ability to gather political and economic information in foreign countries, British diplomatic and consular missions were notably ill-equipped to collect military intelligence until the Foreign Office began appointing military attachés to the major European capitals in the mid-nineteenth century.[8]

During the first half of the nineteenth century, colonial and military affairs were united under the secretary of state for war and the colonies. After the end of the Napoleonic Wars in 1815, the colonial section of this department began to assume a leading role in the handling of colonial matters, a role which it maintained for the rest of the century. The Colonial Office became the main channel of communication between the British government and the governments of most British colonial areas around the world. It was, therefore, the primary collector of massive amounts of political, economic, and military information from throughout the Empire, excluding India. When the department split into the Colonial Office and the War Department in 1854, it not only brought increasing friction between colonial governors and the commanders of British Army units stationed in the Colonies, but it also cut the War Department off from direct access to information reaching London from colonial governments.[9]

The one colonial area which was never within the range of the Colonial Office's responsibilities was India. Until the Great Mutiny of 1857, India was ruled by Britain through the instrument of the East India Company. The reform engendered by the mutiny included the creation of a new office, the Secretary of State for India, which was responsible to Parliament. The India Office directed the affairs of India through its chief administrator, the governor general, later known as the viceroy. He, in turn, was assisted by subordinate governors of the provinces of India and political advisors assigned to the governors and to the various "native states." The real backbone of the Indian administrative structure, however, was the Indian Civil Service. Also, there was the British-officered Indian Army, which had units stationed throughout the subcontinent. The Foreign Department was the Indian government's equivalent to the Foreign Office. To represent the Indian government at the courts of the native states of India and in the capitals of India's neighbors, the Foreign Department had its own Political Service, similar in purpose to the British Diplomatic Service. Yet another valuable source of intelligence for the British rulers of India was the Survey Department, whose officers conducted both topographical and revenue surveys of India. The Indian Civil Service, the Foreign Department, and the Survey Department were probably the most important nonmilitary, overt collectors of information inside India and on her frontiers. The Indian Army collected some nonmilitary information of interest to the Indian government and to the authorities in London, but it was primarily involved in the acquisition of military intelligence.[10]

Between 1815 and 1873, the second major category of Britain's strategic collection apparatus, covert intelligence, played a minor and, at times, virtually nonexistent role in the overall collection of information for national level decision makers. This revelation may come as a shock to a generation fascinated with the world of espionage and double agents and conditioned by the sensational novels of Ian Fleming and the infinitely more believable ones of John le Carré, not to mention the famous exploits of British intelligence during the two world wars. Some explanation of the actual condition of British secret intelligence during the period 1815-73 is, therefore, in order.

Although spies and informants were employed by Britain's army and navy during the Napoleonic Wars in the early years of the nineteenth century, their major purpose was the acquisition of tactical, not strategic, intelligence. Perhaps the best example is the excellent spy network which served the Duke of Wellington in the Peninsular War. Such military-oriented intelligence organizations were of little or no value once the fighting was over and British troops were withdrawn from the Continent. Consequently, neither civilian nor military leaders gave much thought to maintaining them after the final defeat of Napoleon in 1815. After all, even if these organizations could have been reoriented to a strategic intelligence mission and perhaps turned over to civilian control, of what value would they have been to London when the chances of British military involvement on the Continent appeared to be so remote, and the government's requirements for political, economic, and military intelligence within Europe could have been adequately supplied to the Foreign Office by the Diplomatic and Consular Services?

The absence of a major strategic intelligence collection role for Britain's secret service during much of the nineteenth century was the exception and not the rule, however, when one considers the history of British national intelligence over the last four centuries. England's secret intelligence organizations have appeared in several forms and were, at various times, under the control of the Crown, the Privy Council, the Foreign Office, the Post Office, and the military departments. Excluding the nineteenth century, they traditionally have enjoyed a prominent, if well-concealed, place in the shaping of British foreign policy in peace and war, from the reign of Elizabeth I (1558-1603) down to and including the present century, when the prestige of the British secret service has been raised high once more by MI 5, MI 6, and the SOE.[11]

To fully appreciate the lowly position of clandestine operations in the structure of British national intelligence in the years before 1873, it is necessary to review the historical development of two distinct, although frequently interrelated, modes of collection common to all secret services in the nineteenth century and, indeed, well before 1800: espionage and the interception of correspondence/communications. The British government was still involved in both areas after 1815, but it so neglected them that by the outbreak of the Crimean War in 1854, it depended entirely on noncovert collection at the strategic level, even for military intelligence.

National espionage systems in time of peace first appeared in Europe during the Middle Ages, when Venice employed ambassadors and envoys as spies. The English were slow to accept the need for this sort of activity, but beginning at least as early as the reign of William the Conqueror in the eleventh century, English monarchs built royal counterespionage organizations to keep them informed of court intrigues and domestic political matters. Not until the reign of Elizabeth I, however, was there an effort to set up a permanent overseas spy network. At first this was financed and controlled by the English ambassador in Paris, but, during the 1580s, a London-directed national secret service was established by Sir Francis Walsingham for the purpose of collecting political and military intelligence in Europe, independent of the spy networks organized by ambassadors. Sir Francis profoundly distrusted ambassadors as espionage operatives. Walsingham's small but efficient organization, following the instructions provided by its chief in the spring of 1587, played no small part in the early detection and subsequent defeat of the Spanish Armada in 1588. Thus was born the Secret Intelligence Service (SIS).[12]

As the power of the English Parliament grew in the seventeenth and eighteenth centuries, the control of the SIS shifted from the Crown to the prime minister and the Parliament.[13] The SIS remained a small civilian organization, from its creation in the sixteenth century through its decline in the nineteenth century and its resurgence early in the twentieth century. In the first half of the eighteenth century, the SIS reverted to an almost entirely domestic role; its main task was keeping track of Jacobites in England and Scotland. After the elder Pitt became head of the government in 1757, however, he took a personal part in reorganizing the SIS and employing it once again as a worldwide secret service, targeted mainly on political, and secondarily on military information. It appears that in the eighteenth and nineteenth centuries, money for the operation of the SIS was provided by Parliament, within the budget for the Diplomatic Service. It is not clear how much of the money for "secret service" actually went to the SIS and how much of it went to ambassadors for their own private collection efforts.[14]

Whether temporarily diverted into domestic intelligence or employed in its traditional role of espionage overseas, throughout its history the SIS was a collector of information and was not, as a rule, concerned with or capable of detailed analysis of the reports its agents produced. The head of the SIS likely had very little, if any, assistance in evaluating the accuracy of agent reports and in collating them with information obtained overtly by other institutions or by the SIS itself.[15] It was, therefore, very seldom that he was able to produce a comprehensive intelligence estimate on a particular country or situation. More often, his procedure merely was to disseminate undigested intelligence reports to key government leaders or at least to his immediate supervisor, who might have been, depending on the era in question, the King, the prime minister, the foreign secretary, or the entire cabinet. Time permitting, the SIS chief might have prepared a brief summary to call attention to information he judged to be of special importance and of high reliability.

From the days of Sir Francis Walsingham, the British secret service relied on the interception of diplomatic and other correspondence for intelligence, in addition to the information gathered by spies. This was intimately connected with espionage, since good spies obtained intelligence not only from personal observation of and conversation with highly placed foreign officials, but also from the theft of documents or from the illegal opening of mail and official correspondence. If a message was of any real consequence, it was likely to be enciphered or encoded. Walsingham, therefore, set up a cipher department of the SIS in his London home, not only for deciphering intelligence reports from his own agents, but also for the deciphering of intercepted foreign correspondence as well. According to one recent historian of the SIS, "Walsingham, without question, had the best cryptographic organization in Europe."[16] Although removed from SIS control during the seventeenth century, interception and deciphering continued as an important source of political intelligence through the eighteenth century.

Government mail-opening and deciphering units, more popularly known as "black chambers," were considered essential by most European powers of the late seventeenth and eighteenth centuries; England was no exception. The statute of 1657, which established the English Postal Service, included the observation that the "best means of discovering dangerous and wicked designs against the commonwealth" was through the interception of the mail. This was reinforced by the Post Office Act of 1711, which permitted government officials to open mail under warrants that they themselves issued. Operating in complete secrecy and enjoying full legality, the English "black chamber" was founded in the late seventeenth century by a brilliant mathematician, John Wallis. In 1703, the young grandson of Wallis became the first Englishman to bear the official title "Decypherer" and to be paid a regular salary for cryptanalysis. As the workload for deciphering grew and the head "Decypherer" found the need to have several assistants, the men employed by the government for cryptanalysis became known collectively as the Decyphering Branch. These men did not do the actual intercepting of the mail; instead, they received the foreign correspondence, which had been encrypted, from a subdivision of the Post Office appropriately known as the Secret Office. Intercepted diplomatic correspondence of interest, which had not been enciphered, was copied before being resealed, and the copy was sent directly from the Secret Office to the King.[17]

Men of affairs in England and elsewhere were aware of the practice of opening private letters by eighteenth-century governments, but not until after the French Revolution and the Napoleonic Wars did the general public in Europe perceive this sort of activity as an infringement of their personal liberty. In England, the government came under public and parliamentary pressure to reduce, and, ultimately, to discontinue the surreptitious opening of letters. Finally, in 1844, England stopped the interception of diplomatic correspondence and permanently dissolved the once powerful Decyphering Branch.[18]

Unlike the Decyphering Branch, the SIS survived as a national espionage organization through the turbulence of nineteenth-century reforms, but was only a mere shell of its former self by 1873. During the French Revolution and the wars against Napoleon, the SIS was weakened by its increasing reliance upon reactionary aristocrats as agents. In comparison with Napoleon's brilliantly efficient espionage organization, the SIS of the early nineteenth century was inept and amateurish. Furthermore, the SIS in this period was under Foreign Office control, and, unfortunately, that institution, especially under Baron Grenville in the last decade of the eighteenth century, was so inefficient that "many intelligence reports went unread for years."[19] As the SIS faded, the army and the navy were forced by the necessities of the long struggle against Napoleon to build up intelligence services of their own, and although these generally were disbanded after 1815, their solid wartime achievements did little for the already sagging morale of the SIS. Then, too, in the nineteenth century, there was a growing attitude of disdain for secret service; it was a subject not to be mentioned in polite society. Not unlike the public clamor over the opening of the mails, this outlook regarded espionage as something indecent and out of keeping with British traditions. After 1815 the SIS concentrated its major efforts on Irish insurrectionists. As the British government grew more fearful of Irish revolutionaries in the late eighteenth century, a special branch of the SIS was set up in Dublin. Its mission was to keep London informed of the plans of Irish terrorists and to uncover Irish links with French espionage. There is strong evidence that the SIS was mesmerized with Ireland after 1815, while almost entirely neglecting the Continent and the rest of the world.[20]

And, finally, what contribution was made to Britain's collection of strategic intelligence by military and naval intelligence? The British Army's strategic intelligence system in the nineteenth century, prior to 1873, is examined in the next chapter. As for the Royal Navy, it was an important collector and conveyor of intelligence from overseas. The Royal Navy was, in the words of one well-known historian of the British Empire, "the most obvious and impressive of the elements of power of the nineteenth-century Pax Britannica."[21] Although it was cut sharply in personnel strength and number of ships in commission after 1815,[22] the navy remained a magnificent fighting force, far superior to any other navy. Throughout the century, it played a vital role in the defense of the Empire and in the protection of imperial trade routes across the seas. With its ships deployed all over the world, it was able to obtain valuable economic intelligence, as well as naval, and, on occasion, political and military intelligence. The Royal Navy, and, to a lesser extent the vast British merchant navy, not only reported on the dispositions and activities of foreign fighting ships and merchant vessels on the high seas, but also gathered additional information while visiting foreign ports. In an age when the vast majority of trade between Europe and other continents was by sea, a careful monitoring of the destinations and cargoes of foreign merchant ships was perhaps the most reliable and timely source of strategic economic intelligence.

Between 1815 and 1873, the combined contribution of the army and the navy to the collection of strategic intelligence throughout the Empire and the world—economic, political, and military—was certainly of far more consequence than that of the SIS, thanks, mainly, to the Royal Navy. At the same time, the contribution clearly was less significant than the combined output of Britain's nonmilitary overt collectors. The fighting services should be forgiven for their parochial but understandable emphasis on gathering information about foreign armies and navies. Nevertheless, even in the area of purely military and naval intelligence, the collection effort, especially by the army, was surprisingly haphazard, considering Britain's status as a first-class world power. The establishment of the Topographical and Statistical Department of the War Office in 1855 offered a ray of hope for the future, but the rapid decay of that embryonic military intelligence organization following the

Crimean War left a void that was unfilled until 1870. The improvement in Britain's ability to collect strategic military intelligence after 1864, owing to the appointment of military attachés to five European capitals, only worsened the problem. Quite simply, British military intelligence lacked central direction and management. Furthermore, there was no office or agency to process the information collected. Prior to the Franco-Prussian War, neither the War Office nor the Admiralty had been able to establish and maintain a functioning, permanent department in London for the systematic analysis and production of intelligence at the national level. The establishment of such an agency within the War Office betwen 1870 and 1873 constituted the crucial first step toward the development of a modern military intelligence organization in Great Britain.

NOTES

1. The "informal empire" of the nineteenth century refers to numerous communities in the world not under the British flag or with ties to the British Crown, but in which Britain held a degree of ascendancy, "communities which were part of what has been spoken of as the informal empire of trade, or which were related in other forms of association, not all of them commercial." Donald C. Gordon, *The Moment of Power*, p.30.

2. Strategic intelligence is that intelligence required at the national level by strategic planners and government policy makers or high-level military commanders. Normally, it includes political, economic, military, geographic, sociological, and scientific-technical intelligence which bears on national strategy. Tactical intelligence, also known as combat intelligence or field intelligence, is that intelligence needed by tactical commanders in the field, usually concerning the enemy, the weather, and the terrain in the area of operations.

3. In the 1890s the Russians spent more than £1,000,000 per year on secret service (for both domestic and foreign operations). According to Richard Deacon, this figure approached £1,700,000 at the turn of the century. Estimates for British expenditure on secret service in this same period range from £50,000 to £60,000 per year. Richard Deacon, *A History of the British Secret Service*, p. 137.

4. The British General Staff was not established on a permanent basis throughout the army until 1906, exactly one hundred years after Colonel von Massenbach had completed his reorganization and expansion of the quartermaster general's staff in Prussia. Beginning in 1806, "quartermaster-general's staff" and "general staff" were synonymous in Prussia. The general staff system was adopted in Russia (1863), France (1874), Austria-Hungary (1875), Japan (1879), and Italy (1882) long before it was in Britain.

5. The Intelligence Branch of the War Office was established on 1 April 1873. The Foreign Intelligence Committee of the Admiralty was established in the fall of 1882.

6. Likewise, British covert collection operations in peacetime sometimes obtained information of value to the War Office or the Admiralty. Individual officers of the two fighting services were loaned to the Secret Intelligence Service for a tour of duty or a particular assignment, a practice that continued through both world wars and is alive and well today. The direction and funding of the Secret Intelligence Service in the nineteenth century emanated from the Foreign Office, however, not from the War Office or the Admiralty.

7. Gordon, *The Moment of Power*, pp. 36-37. See also John Gallagher and Ronald Robinson, "The Imperialism of Free Trade," *Economic History Review*, 2d ser., no. 1 (August 1953), pp. 1-15, and Oliver Macdonagh, "The Anti-Imperialism of Free Trade," *Economic History Review*, vol. 16, no. 3 (April 1962), pp. 489-501.

8. The complete amalgamation of the Foreign Office and the Diplomatic Service did not occur until after the end of World War I. Throughout the nineteenth century, the two services were regarded as separate, though interchanges of personnel between them were fairly common. Ray Jones, *The Nineteenth Century Foreign Office*, pp. 136-42. See also Alfred Vagts, *The Military Attaché*, pp. 28-29.

9. Gordon, *The Moment of Power*, pp. 57-59. See also Charles Jeffries, *The Colonial Office*.

10. Ibid., pp. 65-67. See also Phillip Mason, *A Matter of Honour*, and L.S.S. O'Malley, *The Indian Civil Service* (London: John Murray, 1931).

11. MI 5 and MI 6 are Britain's counterespionage and espionage organizations, respectively. The Special Operations Executive directed covert operations behind enemy lines and in Nazi-occupied areas during World War II. For the history of the British secret service, see Deacon, *A History of the British Secret Service* and Bernard Newman, *Spy and Counter-Spy*. Caution must be exercised with both these works, as neither is thoroughly documented.

12. Richard Deacon, *A History of the British Secret Service*, pp. 9-15.

13. It is a near certainty that Britain's espionage organization was not actually called the Secret Intelligence Service during the sixteenth, seventeenth, eighteenth, and nineteenth centuries. The actual title of the SIS probably changed almost as often as its subordination within the British government.

14. Secret service efforts of ambassadors in the eighteenth century consisted mainly of attempts to gain confidential information from host country officials and other diplomats through bribery.

15. This contrasts sharply with a modern intelligence agency, such as the CIA, which employs approximately one half of its personnel in analysis-production.

16. Deacon, *British Secret Service*, p. 27.

17. David Kahn, *The Codebreakers*, pp. 163, 166-73. Kahn writes that the security surrounding the Decyphering Branch was so tight that in all England, "probably only 30 people knew that diplomatic correspondence was being read at any given moment."

18. Ibid., p. 97.

19. Deacon, *British Secret Service*, p. 97.

20. Ibid., pp. 122-23.

21. Gordon, *The Moment of Power*, p. 78.

22. In 1815 the Royal Navy had 140,000 men and 700 ships in commission. By 1818 the figures were 19,000 men and only 130 ships. David Howarth, *Sovereign of the Seas*, p. 296.

Chapter II

The Origins of the Intelligence Branch at the War Office

During the Crimean War, a great want was felt of some Department in the War Office whose duty it should be to procure maps and statistical information of the seat of war. It was therefore determined to establish a "Topographical and Statistical Department of the War Office." . . . The intention was to consolidate the collections of plans, maps, and military documents, scattered throughout the various departments, and to place in the same establishment the Topographical Depot then existing in the Quarter-Master-General's Department, Horse Guards.

> Captain E.H.H. Collen,
> *Report on the Intelligence Branch,*
> *Quarter-Master-General's*
> *Department, Horse Guards*, 1878

On 24 February 1873, British war minister Edward Cardwell made a speech to the House of Commons, in which he announced his plans to establish an intelligence department in the War Office under the direction of a general officer. The Intelligence Branch, as this new department of the War Office was called for the first fifteen years of its existence, was activated on 1 April 1873. Headed by a major general and staffed by a grand total of twenty-seven military and civilian personnel,[1] the Intelligence Branch was tiny and, seemingly, unequal to its worldwide responsibilities, when compared with the military intelligence staffs in London, Washington, and Moscow of today, and was small, even in its own day, when measured against staff sections performing similar functions in Berlin, Vienna, and Paris. Recent history, however, is replete with evidence that the efficiency of intelligence organizations is not necessarily proportional to the size of their staffs! In any case, the size of the War Office's Intelligence Branch in 1873 in no way diminishes the significance of its creation, not only in the development of British military intelligence, but in the growth of the country's national intelligence system, as well. The establishment of a permanent agency in the War Office for the collection, processing, and dissemination of information about the geography and military forces of foreign countries indicated a recognition, within the highest circles of government, of the requirement for a less haphazard method of producing strategic military intelligence for national decision makers and for the army itself. Despite the importance of this event in the history of British intelligence, the birth of the Intelligence Branch at the War Office has generally not been regarded by historians as one of Edward Cardwell's major accomplishments at the War Office. Instead, it has been overshadowed by the major reforms of the British Army and the War Office, for which Cardwell is best known.

In the nineteenth century, and, indeed, throughout the history of the British Army and the War Office, Edward Cardwell was unquestionably one of the great war ministers. A Liberal statesman who entered Parliament in 1842 at the age of twenty-nine, Cardwell demonstrated his considerable intellectual powers early in life by earning degrees in classics and mathematics at Balliol College, Oxford. He had already served in a number of important posts[2] before joining the first government of William Gladstone, in 1868, as the secretary of state for war. As Gladstone's war minister, he carried out sweeping reforms with such long-range impact—most notably, the reorganization of the War Office, the abolition of the purchase of commissions, the institution of shorter terms of service for enlisted soldiers, and the establishment of a system to provide an equal number of army battalions for service at home and overseas—that the Cardwell years at the War Office (1868-74) have often been seen as a major turning point in British military history. These years witnessed, in the view of some historians, the most radical change within the army between Waterloo and the beginning of the twentieth century.[3] Other historians, although recognizing the importance of Cardwell's work, have argued that more fundamental modifications were made during and immediately following the Crimean War, and that "Cardwell's ministry is in some ways the culmination rather than the initiation of a period of military reform."[4] Few would disagree, however, with W.S. Hamer, that, "Between 1854 and 1871 the administration and command of the British Army was completely revolutionized."[5] Furthermore, most would contend that Edward Cardwell made a major contribution to this era of change.

To those who feel Cardwell's reforms completed, rather than inaugurated, a period of reform in the British Army, his actions in reorganizing the

War Office during his six years as secretary for war were only the concluding phase of a process of departmental reconstruction which began in 1855, during the Crimean War.[6] The multiple reorganizations of the War Office during the Crimean War, and in the fifteen years following it, transferred control of the army from the Crown to the cabinet and the secretary of state for war. In other words, an army which had been directly responsible to the British monarch was, by 1871, legally responsible to Parliament, although the civilians were still far from achieving absolute control over the army.[7] As was usual in British constitutional practice, the cabinet had already controlled many aspects of British Army administration, although representatives of the Crown continued to exercise what some reformers saw as an unduly conservative influence long after the legal turning point.

Edward Cardwell was a resolute and talented individual who succeeded in putting controversial reforms through, despite powerful and determined opponents of change in the army and Parliament, particularly the Duke of Cambridge, then the commander-in-chief. After giving clear notice to Prime Minister Gladstone, in December 1868, of his intention to take vigorous action to improve the efficiency of the army,[8] Cardwell moved boldly to bring the administration of the army under his control. This he achieved primarily through the War Office Act of 1870 and an Order in Council of 4 June the same year, in which he rearranged the numerous separate offices and branches of the army into three major offices subordinate to the secretary of state for war: the Supply Department, the Finance Department, and the Military Department. Even more remarkable, although primarily symbolic in nature, was Cardwell's show of strength in forcing the move of the head of the Military Department, the commander-in-chief, from his traditional head-quarters at the Horse Guards to the War Office in Pall Mall.

In the remaining years of the Cardwell War Office, 1870-74, administrative reorganization took a back seat to other major issues of reform in the army: short service, abolition of purchase, and the linking of line regiments and militia regiments in territorial districts throughout Britain.[9] Indeed, the next major reorganization of the War Office did not occur until 1887-88.[10] In early 1873, near the end of Cardwell's reign as secretary, in the course of his continuing, but less heralded actions of restructuring the War Office, he decided to authorize the establishment of the Intelligence Branch within the War Office.

Although Great Britain has had a military intelligence staff at the national level without interruption since the Cardwell ministry at the War Office, 1873 was not the first time an attempt had been made to form such an organization in the British Army. The first official recognition of the need to collect and assemble data for the army in time of peace occurred after the suppression of the rebellion in Scotland in 1745. Capt. David Watson, deputy quartermaster-general in North Britain, decided that a good map of the Scottish Highlands ought to be prepared for future contingencies. He assigned his assistant, Lt. W. Roy, to perform the task. Roy's work, which eventually extended into the Lowlands of Scotland, was the first large military survey undertaken in Great Britain. Due to the disruption brought about by the Seven Years War, the map was never completed. The future Major General Roy conducted a determined, individual campaign for over twenty years, beginning in 1763, to convince the country's leaders of the need for a topographical survey of all of Great Britain. Finally, in 1784, General Roy's efforts were rewarded with powerful support from the Royal Society and financial assistance from King George III, and he was authorized to begin the Ordnance Survey. The work of the Ordnance Survey was more sharply defined in 1791, when the master-general of the ordnance ordered the preparation of a military map of the United Kingdom.[11]

Thus, the first permanent organization established within Great Britain to collect geographical or military information for the army in time of peace had mapmaking as its primary mission. The story of topographical organizations is inseparable from the development of a national military intelligence organization in Great Britain. For a long time, indeed, down to the eve of the birth of the Intelligence Branch in 1873, the organization of the peacetime British Army at the highest echelons reflected greater interest in matters of geographic intelligence than in any other aspect of strategic intelligence.

The establishment of the Ordnance Survey in the late eighteenth century insured accurate maps of the United Kingdom for military purposes, but it did nothing to provide the army with maps of the Empire or of foreign countries. Furthermore, the survey had no mission to collect information about the armed forces of other nations.[12] Not until the early years of the nineteenth century did the authorities recognize the need for a department to collect information about the armed forces of other nations as well as the topography of the colonies and foreign countries.

On the eve of the Napoleonic Wars, British political and military leaders suddenly awakened to the scarcity of reliable information in London about Napoleon's strength and capabilities. The commander-in-chief of the army, the Duke of York, and his staff were frequently embarrassed by their inability to provide up-to-date briefings on the European military situation and the plans of Napoleon. During a brief interval of peace between the Treaty of Amiens in March 1802 and England's declaration of war against France in May of the following year, the Duke of York was under particularly intense pressure to present a more accurate description of developments on the Continent.[13]

Fortunately, a solution was offered to the commander-in-chief in a paper prepared by his quartermaster-general in March 1803. Gen. Sir Robert Brownrigg proposed the creation of a new branch of his own office, to be called the Depot of Military Knowledge. The collection and study of intelligence in peacetime, thought Brownrigg, would be of great value in preparing the army for war. The Duke of York was enthusiastic about the idea, and, when he submitted it to the secretary of state for war, added that "the most valuable books and maps concerning the enemy are printed by the enemy themselves and that the period of war is not favourable to their being collected."[14] Thus, the Depot of Military Knowledge came to life in April 1803, only weeks before the British again found themselves at war with Napoleon.

Modeled along the lines of Napoleon's Dépôt de la Guerre in Paris, the Depot had four departments: a plans branch, to collect military information overseas and prepare contingency plans; a movements branch, to make plans for troop movements; a military library, to study operations of the past; and a topographical branch, to collect topographical information and prepare maps of the colonies and of foreign countries. Initially it flourished and even expanded under the sponsorship of the Duke of York.[15] Though it was subordinate to the quartermaster-general, the ease with which the Depot obtained funds for its operation, and the very fact that its budget was distinct from the quartermaster-general's[16] were indicative of favored status.

Clouds, however, were soon to darken the horizon. Almost from its very inception in 1803, the Depot of Military Knowledge was plagued by a personnel problem that only worsened with time. It proved very difficult to retain competent officers for any length of time. Capable and ambitious young officers assigned to the infant intelligence organization lost no time in pulling every possible string to be reassigned to their regiments. After all, the country was at war, and the real action—along with the best chance for promotion—was on the battlefield and not in a dusty room on the top floor of the Horse Guards. More damaging still, and perhaps the crowning blow, was the fall from grace of the Duke of York. A great scandal arose in 1809, when the public learned that the venerable duke had an "arrangement" by which he compensated his young mistress for her favors by helping her obtain army commissions for those men she recommended. The commander-in-chief resigned and everything connected with him, including the Depot of Military Knowledge, fell into disrepute.[17] In addition to the declining caliber of officers in the Depot and the blow suffered by the loss of its patron, the prevalent attitude of the day among army officers was that once the country had an army in the field in wartime, the commander's own headquarters staff and local intelligence organization were of far greater value to him than a repository of outdated information hundreds or thousands of miles away in London. The experience of the long but victorious struggle against Napoleon seemed to bear this out.

In the final analysis, the Depot of Military Knowledge played an insignificant role in the Napoleonic Wars. Somehow, the sound principles upon which it had been founded in 1803 were obscured with the passage of time, and less and less intelligence work was accomplished in both topography and the collection of information about foreign armies. No help of consequence was afforded the Duke of Wellington in either the Peninsular War (1808-14) or the Waterloo campaign.[18] His own well-trained and efficient intelligence service far outshone anything that the Depot was able to do. Interestingly, of the four departments within the Depot, the library seems to have accomplished the most.[19]

The final defeat of Napoleon at Waterloo in 1815 was not followed by a revival of the ill-fated Depot of Military Knowledge, despite the fact that it no longer had to face the competition of Wellington's intelligence apparatus. During the Great Peace of 1815-54, the general lack of interest in military affairs in England affected the Depot, as it did the entire army. During these forty years "the Depot petered out, used by nobody though remembered by a few."[20] Technically, it remained in existence, but for all practical purposes it was merely a neglected and useless appendage of the Quartermaster General's Department. It produced almost nothing in the way of new maps or information about the armies of foreign powers. The Depot even lost its original name and became known as the "Topographical Department of the Quartermaster-General."

Between Waterloo and the Crimean War, Britain engaged in no wars on the European continent. The British Isles were not threatened by invasion, and the Royal Navy ruled the seas. Mindful of all this, and either unaware of or indifferent to their country's colonial affairs, some Englishmen of the day spoke proudly of an era of peace. Although Britain may have enjoyed peaceful relations with other European nations, she was hardly at peace in various non-European areas of the globe. In fact, Great Britain was involved in a seemingly endless series of small colonial wars between 1815 and 1854. For the first time in its history, the British Army was largely a colonial army; up to three-fourths of its infantry battalions were deployed overseas. The army's duties included not only defending the existing frontiers of the British Empire, but also serving as the cutting edge in an unplanned, piecemeal process of expansion. Its campaigns were conducted in such places as southern Africa, India, Burma, New Zealand, Malaya, and China. While the Royal Navy maintained the vital lines of communication by sea from the mother country, the army did the actual fighting. Despite the attitude of indifference that many at home showed toward its sacrifices and accomplishments, the army generally fought well and almost always emerged victorious.[21] It seemed equally unaffected by the chronic inability of the War Department[22] to provide it with useful information about new theaters of operations and about the native forces, sometimes quite formidable, that it would have to fight. Who could argue with success? Did it really matter that the Depot of Military Knowledge was all but dead?

One man was concerned enough about the situation at the War Department and in the government in general to try to do something about it eight years before the Crimean War began. Unfortunately, he was only a retired Indian Army major, and men of power paid little attention to him. Maj. Thomas Best Jervis had retired in 1836 after thirty years in the Bombay Engineer Corps. Before sailing to India at the outset of his army career, Jervis had worked briefly on the Ordnance Survey in England where he acquired the great interest in cartography which was to last his entire life. He saw little combat action with the Bombay Engineers, occupying himself almost solely with topographical work on behalf of the Indian Survey Department.[23] Major Jervis built himself an excellent reputation in the Survey Department and nearly reached its top position. Considering his future role as one of the founding fathers of British military intelligence, it is fortunate that he failed. Bitterly disappointed when he was not offered the post of surveyor general of India upon his retirement in 1836, Jervis returned to England and involved himself in a variety of public service activities.

Major Jervis's interest in cartography never wavered, and in 1846 he wrote to Lord Aberdeen, the secretary of state for foreign affairs, urging him to set up a topographical department at the Foreign Office. In the letter, he reminded the secretary that

> Great Britain is the only country of note which has no *geographer* attached to the government and no national depot of geographical maps and plans. The Ordnance Survey is exclusively directed to British territories, the Hydrographic Office to nautical charts.[24]

Major Jervis also referred to the "acknowledged want of geographical information in many well known and recent cases," and pointed out that in the future the government could expect neither the accuracy nor the secrecy it might desire if it continued to depend on the assistance of private individuals, or worse yet, on chance. One of Aberdeen's subordinates wrote a letter of thanks to Jervis, assuring him that the plan for a map depot would receive full consideration. Apparently, nothing more was done by the Foreign Office.[25] One can only speculate why Thomas Jervis did not try to persuade the War Department as well, but it is likely that his plea would have fallen upon deaf ears there, too.

A less-determined man might have given up in the face of such official apathy, but Major Jervis would not abandon his crusade. His great chance finally came just after the outbreak of the Crimean War in early 1854. During a holiday journey through Belgium, Jervis obtained copies of two rare and valuable military maps which were virtually impossible for a private citizen to acquire anywhere in Europe: the Russian General Staff's map of the Crimea and the Austrian Army's map of Turkey-in-Europe. Not only were these maps closely guarded by the Russian and Austrian governments, respectively, but they were much better than any the British government had in its possession.[26]

Jervis, certain that the War Department wanted to place the best possible maps in the hands of its army commanders preparing to depart for the Crimea, offered both maps to the Duke of Newcastle, then the secretary of state for war. He was shocked to learn that the government was interested in using them only if he, personally, would pay for the reproduction of the maps. Since Jervis had already gone to the trouble of preparing an English version of the Russian map, this was asking a great deal. Undaunted, however, he quickly set up an office and was able to make several copies of the Crimean map in time to provide them to the headquarters staff of the British expeditionary force before it landed in the Crimea.[27] The War Department bought only a few copies at first, but the map proved so valuable in the theater of war that eventually large numbers were bought.[28]

Throughout 1854, Major Jervis petitioned the government to establish a topographical department. In a letter to the secretary for war in July 1854, Jervis wrote candidly,

> The fact is palpable and notorious, that this great, intelligent, powerful commercial country . . . is entirely dependent for good maps on the Continent for German, French, and other maps. What else we have are, in truth, but school atlases. We have an admirable hydrographical office for nautical surveys and charts, and another for the Tithe Commissioners' surveys; but for our colonial, commercial, or war purposes we have no resource but foreign information.[29]

The enthusiasm which his Crimean map generated in the field among British and French officers, as well as the high-level recognition of his work—Emperor Napoleon III invited Jervis to Paris and presented him with a massive gold snuff box—helped Major Jervis move the British government to action. What satisfaction he must have felt when a letter arrived in February 1855 from the War Department, telling him of the Treasury's approval of the creation of a Topographical and Statistical Department in the War Department and offering him the post of superintendent.[30]

If judged by the cramped physical environment in which its offices were first established, the beginnings of the Topographical and Statistical Department[31] in March 1855 were hardly impressive, except for the fact that it was situated close to the center of power. The department initially was housed in converted stables and a coach house at 9 Adelphi Terrace in Whitehall. After little more than a year it was moved to a more suitable location.[32] Under its newly promoted chief, Lieutenant Colonel Jervis, the T&S Department produced several books and some excellent maps in its first two years.[33] An even brighter and more productive future appeared to be in store when, in 1856, Jervis won the support of one of his superiors, namely Lord Panmure, the secretary of state for war, for a plan to send a small team of soldiers and civilians to the Middle East to engage in "scientific geographical exploration."[34]

Much has been made of the creation of the T&S Department in 1855. In an unpublished historical paper written to help commemorate "the centenary year of Military Intelligence in the British Army, 1955," Lt. Col. W.V.R. Isaac states, matter-of-factly, "this event has always been regarded as the beginning of the service of intelligence in the British Army."[35] Brian Bond, a leading authority on the British Army in the latter half of the nineteenth century, feels that it was "the first tentative step towards a future British general staff," and he is not alone in this opinion.[36] Lt. Col. B.A.H. Parritt sees an "unbroken line" from the T&S Department of 1855 to the Joint Service Directorate of Intelligence in the British Ministry of Defence today.[37] An even bolder claim is asserted by Jock Haswell, a retired British Army major employed for many years as an author at Britain's School for Service Intelligence. Haswell finds in the T&S Department the origins of both the British General Staff and the Joint Service Directorate of Intelligence.[38]

Did the establishment of the T&S Department in 1855 represent, as Isaac, Parritt, and Haswell suggest, the birth of a permanent intelligence department at the War Office? The acceptance of this idea has led some to the conclusion that the Crimean War was the primary cause of the emergence of such an organization in Great Britain. After all, it was the Crimean War experience which brought about a great wave of reform in the British Army. More specifically, it was the war that made possible the personal triumph of Thomas Jervis in winning official support for his national topographical depot in 1855. But can an "unbroken line" be traced from the T&S Department of 1855 to the Intelligence Branch of the 1870s and its successors?

From its earliest days under Thomas Jervis, until 1870, the T&S Department was heavily oriented toward the "topographical" as opposed to the "statistical"[39] side of its title. Its first director was, after all, a geographer by training and experience, and his principal objective in petitioning various government officials before 1855 had been to create a map depot or topographical department. Why Lord Panmure decided to add "statistical" to the title of the new organization he placed under Jervis in 1855 is not clear. He may have been influenced by the historical precedent of the defunct Depot of Military Knowledge, or perhaps he aimed at setting up an organization along the lines of the Dépôt de la Guerre in France, which had been a repository for both topographical and statistical information. Then, too, early nineteenth-century geographers like Thomas Jervis were both mapmakers and statisticians. Prior to his transfer to the general staff in 1833, Helmuth Karl von Moltke (the Elder) spent a number of years in the Prussian Topographical Bureau, where his talent for drawing was fully exploited. Moltke's first studies involved both topography and statistics.

Letters written by Thomas Jervis during the years 1854-56 show his admiration for the Dépôt de la Guerre and his understanding of the statistical function of the T&S Department. Writing to the secretary for war in March 1854, Jervis pointed out that no other major European nation was so ill-informed as Great Britain, not only in the area of geographical information, but also in

> statistical information which we ought by rights to possess, when we might have been expected from the habitual tastes of the people for adventure, commerce, and exploration to have accumulated the largest and most valuable stores of such information. . . .[40]

Now that the country was at war, Jervis added, the demand grew daily for information about the military and naval forces of the enemy as well as of the geography and climate of the theater of war.

> The public, the legislature, and very Ministers themselves, and the Sovereign, above all, desire to be perfectly informed with respect to the minutest details of the statistics and geography of the seat of war. . . .[41]

But did the T&S Department, especially in its first two years under Thomas Jervis, accomplish much useful work outside the area of cartography? The answer appears to have been no, despite the director's professed interest in "statistics." Considering that twenty-six of the twenty-eight men who worked in the T&S Department under Jervis in 1855-56 were civilian lithographers,[42] it is not surprising that the principal product of the office was maps. The excellent reputation that the T&S Department enjoyed during the Crimeran War was based entirely upon the high quality and usefulness of these maps and on the immense personal achievements of its widely acclaimed founder, Thomas Jervis, the geographer. In fact, the Depot of Military Knowledge of 1803 bore a much greater resemblance to the Intelligence Branch of 1873 than did the T&S Department of 1855-57. Unlike the T&S Department, both the depot and the Intelligence Branch were organized and manned to collect and process information about foreign armies as well as to produce maps. Also overlooked, or at least downplayed, by those who consider 1855 to be the great watershed in the history of British military intelligence, is the decline and near collapse of the T&S Department in the thirteen years between 1857 and 1870.[43] This development, even more than the topographical bias of the Department in the Jervis years, weakens the argument for continuity between 1855 and 1873.

Soon after the death of Thomas Jervis in 1857, the secretary for war, Lord Panmure, appointed a committee to look into the efficiency of the T&S Department and its relationship to other government agencies.[44] The recommendations of this committee were followed, almost to the letter, by Panmure. To unify all government mapmaking agencies and save money, he placed the Ordnance Survey and the Topographic Depot of the QMG (the surviving remnant of the Depot of Military Knowledge) under the T&S Department. This enlarged T&S Department was directed to maintain close relations with topographical agencies of the self-governing colonies and to coordinate the mapping of the Crown colonies and other dependencies.[45]

Rather than breathing life into the "statistical" half of the T&S Department, these changes served to reinforce the already near-total dominance of the "topographical" side. The new director of the Department, Lt. Col. Henry James of the Royal Engineers, a veteran of many years in the Ordnance Survey, had little interest in military intelligence.[46] As in the first several years under Jervis, the efforts of the T&S Department "seem to have been devoted to studying the topography of foreign countries. The nature and strength of their armies were treated as minor matters, relegated to the background."[47]

By the mid-1860s, even the topographical mission was being slighted, and the Department was being assigned such odd and sundry tasks as producing the illustrations for the dress regulations, compiling a volume on the organization and composition of the British Army, and publishing "that portion of the army equipment series relating to the Royal Artillery."[48] Here was a situation analogous to that of the Depot of Military Knowledge after 1815. Sir George Aston's description seems particularly apt:

> . . . the department enjoyed a long slumber from the time when the memory of the Crimean scandals faded into the past until a certain amount of public interest was awakened by the conspicuous successes of the German Army against Austria in 1866 and against France in 1870.[49]

An even more damning indictment of the T&S Department was contained in the initial report of a young officer who replaced Colonel James as director in April 1870. Capt. Charles W. Wilson prepared a memorandum decrying the unsatisfactory condition of the department which soon reached the desk of Secretary for War Cardwell. According to Wilson's firsthand assessment, the map collection of foreign countries was "very incomplete," there was a shameful lack of information on hand about foreign armies, and there were "no means for keeping the office supplied with information from abroad."[50] In retrospect, Wilson was not entirely correct on the third point, but there is no reason to doubt the accuracy of the first two. Thirteen years after the death of Jervis, the T&S Department had reached an all-time low in usefulness, even in its traditionally strong topographical function.

Beginning early in 1871, however, and continuing for several years until it was absorbed by the newly established Intelligence Branch in April 1873, the T&S Department underwent a remarkable transformation. So complete was its metamorphosis that the T&S Department of June 1871 appeared to be only distantly related to the Department of 1855-70. It was during this eventful two-year period that the T&S Department began to pay attention to its neglected statistical function. Information about foreign armies was collected, processed, and reported. On the topographical side, the emphasis returned to the production of maps useful in strategic planning and overseas military operations.

Just as Thomas Jervis deserves much of the credit for the birth of the T&S Department in 1855, so one man played a decisive role in reviving and transforming it, a matter which will receive more attention in the next chapter. Once again, as in both 1803 and 1855, war or the threat of war provided a powerful incentive for improving national military intelligence. This time, however, Great Britain was not a participant. As Sir George Aston correctly observed, the T&S Department and, he might have added, the entire War Office, were rudely awakened from their peacetime complacency by the spectacular victories of the Prussian Army against Austria in 1866 and France in 1870-71. A third significant factor which may be counted among immediate causes of the 1871-73 transformation was discussed at the outset of the chapter: the atmosphere of reform which descended on the War Office with the arrival of Edward Cardwell in 1868 and which continued until his departure in 1874. But the individual efforts of Charles Wilson, the rise of German military power evident in the Austro-Prussian and Franco-Prussian Wars, and the encouragement given by Cardwell to War Office reform do not account entirely for the reconstruction of the T&S Department and the birth of the Intelligence Branch.

It ought not to be forgotten that India was the main reservoir of British power outside of the British Isles in the nineteenth century. Adrian Preston has argued that the Russian threat to British India, "complex, protean, and conjectural as that was . . . accounted for the late nineteenth-century renaissance of official British strategic thought and policy."[51] Well before 1870, the Anglo-Russian rivalry and the struggle of the two empires for control of West and Central Asia had begun to surface. In 1870, the Russian threat to India was perceived more clearly in London as a result of a sudden ominous shift in Russia's Turkish policy. The government of Tsar Alexander II took advantage of the Franco-Prussian War to announce that Russia no longer considered herself bound by the Black Sea articles of the Treaty of Paris (1856). To the Admiralty, the Foreign Office, and the British Embassy at Constantinople, Russia's new policy promised to affect the future control of the recently opened Suez Canal, the vital lifeline to India.[52] The Indian Army had no Intelligence Department at this time. In London, neither the War Office, the India Office, nor the Foreign Office had a Central Asian bureau responsible for collecting information and advising the government on foreign and military policy.[53] The "crisis of 1870" forced a

> grudging official awareness that if strategic policy was to be realistic in
> an age of rapid technical and political change, then intelligence must be
> acquired and interpreted on a regular and systematic basis.[54]

Although Adrian Preston's underlying premise concerning the "Indianisation" of imperial defense policy,[55] as well as his concept of "imperial defence,"[56] are arguable, his point about the role of Indian affairs in exposing the weaknesses of the existing strategic intelligence system is worthy of serious consideration.

Causes of a longer range are also relevant. The imprints left by the French Dépôt de la Guerre on the British Depot of Military Knowledge, and, less directly, on the T&S Department, have been mentioned. In a more general sense, one cannot omit the effect on Britain, and indeed on all of Europe, of the development of the Prussian Great General Staff or the "capital staff," the central military organ which assisted the supreme military authority of the state. One of the main distinguishing characteristics of the general staff was the "systematic and extensive collection in time of peace of specific information which may be important to the future conduct of operations."[57] Strategic intelligence collection and production was an important function of the Prussian General Staff from its earliest days. One of the routine but vital duties performed by Prussian General Staff officers in peacetime was to make trips abroad in order to reconnoiter the terrain over which possible future battles would be fought and to collect information about the armies of potential enemies.[58] Although the British did not duplicate the Prussian General Staff system, they were not unaware of its existence before 1870 and, when significant change came beginning in 1871, they were clearly influenced by the Prussian model. The reorganization of the T&S Department in 1871 was spurred not only by the success of Prussian armies in the field, but also by the existence and remarkable efficiency of the Prussian General Staff.

Another component of the Prussian General Staff system was a staff school which provided elementary training in staff duties, scientific training for cartographical work, and some training in the higher conduct of war. The establishment of a staff college of this sort did not occur in England until 1857, much later than was the case in Prussia (1810), France (1818), Russia (1832), or even Austria (1852).[59] When this occurred, however, the Staff College at Camberley began turning out officers who were far better prepared to perform strategic intelligence duties (as well as other staff duties) than British officers were before. The very presence of trained staff officers in the British Army made the establishment of an intelligence department in London more likely and provided that department, once established, with most of the officers who helped it grow in the 1870s and 1880s.

The example provided by the Prussian General Staff system affected, in varying degrees, the methods used by every European power in strategic planning and the higher direction of war in the latter half of the nineteenth century, particularly after 1871. The general staff system proved to be one of the answers to the challenges posed by enormous change in the nature of war, change brought about by the Industrial Revolution and scientific invention. The impact of rapid technological change was apparent in the wars of the mid-nineteenth century in the use of the steam engine, railways, breech-loading rifles, rifled breech-loading artillery, armored ships, and the telegraph. The speed with which this revolution in war was taking place presented the military intelligence systems of the various European states with a special challenge. Governments and military leaders wanted not only accurate and timely information about the latest innovations in tactics, weapons, and so on, but also expert reporting of technical information.

A partial solution to the problem of staying abreast of foreign military developments was found in the publication and wide circulation of military journals. In France, *Spectateur militaire* served such a purpose beginning in 1826; in mid-century it was supplemented by *Revue militaire des armées étrangères*. *Militärwochenblatt*, which had been published in Prussia as early as the 1840s, continued to serve the German officer corps after 1871 and was joined by *Deutsche Heereszeitung*. In Britain, the *United Service Magazine* first appeared in 1829, followed in 1858 by the *Journal of the Royal United Services Institution*.

Neither the *United Service Magazine* (the *Army Quarterly* after 1920) nor the *Journal of the R.U.S.I.* limited their contributors solely to topics dealing with foreign military and naval developments. Historical articles were common, especially in the *United Service Magazine*. Many pieces in the *Journal of the R.U.S.I.* focused on contemporary issues of tactics or strategy within the British services. In its very first issue, however, the *Journal* included an article entitled "The Regimental Schools of the French Army," and in the 1859 edition followed with one comparing the "rifled small arms" of England, France, and the United States. The number of articles per issue devoted to foreign, especially continental, military affairs increased in the late 1860s and reached a peak in the mid- to late-1870s, when an average of six to eight per issue was the norm.[60]

More specialized publications began to appear, as well. For example, beginning in 1858, *The Proceedings of the Royal Artillery Institution* gave artillery officers of the British Army a regular source of information of new artillery weapons and doctrine. "New ideas, particularly those from foreign writers and critics, were freely and frankly discussed and occasionally bitterly debated in the pages of *The Proceedings. . . .*"[61] While the military journals of the mid-nineteenth century performed a valuable function, they could not fulfill the need for systematic military intelligence collection.

A second method employed by European governments to gather military information in this era was to send military officers, individually or in teams, as official observers to wars in which their own countries remained neutral. Jay Luvaas has amply documented this practice during the American Civil War, when France, Germany, and Britain all sent observers. Many of these officers were well qualified to collect, analyze, and report on technical military matters, but in the final analysis, they (or their superiors back in Europe) misinterpreted what was reported.[62] Of the most significance, however, is that these officers were sent to observe a war in progress. When peace came they were to return home. Therefore, they were not the solution to the increasing requirement for peacetime military intelligence collection.[63]

The most significant advance toward the improvement of Britain's peacetime strategic military intelligence effort overseas prior to 1871 occurred in 1864 when, rather reluctantly, the Foreign Office bowed to the desires of the Duke of Cambridge and appointed military attachés to Berlin, Vienna, and St. Petersburg. In his capacity as commander-in-chief of the British Army, the duke had been pressing the foreign secretary since 1860 to station a military attaché in Berlin. He was motivated by the idea that the Prussian military buildup required close observation and by the conviction that, in a time of growing technical complexity in military developments, civilian ambassadors alone were no longer able to cope with reporting on military affairs.[64]

The military attaché was yet a third response developed by Europeans in the nineteenth century in their efforts to satisfy the growing appetite for news of military and naval advances and of the readiness of rival and friendly powers for war. Prior to the nineteenth century, the main function of the modern military attaché—to observe the armed forces of a foreign country, its general state of preparation for war, and the country's overall war capability—had been performed by ambassadors and other diplomats. As military and naval developments grew more complex in the nineteenth century, governments sent out military officers as ambassadors or provided civilian ambassadors with military or naval attachés as expert assistants. One of the first true modern military attachés, in all but name, was a French Army captain appointed second secretary of the Vienna Embassy in 1806 and given the task of "*constant* systematic observation of the potential enemy." The first Prussian military attaché was a captain posted in 1830 as "military expert" with the Paris legation. During the late 1830s, four officers were detached from the French Army and admitted to the foreign service for duty as military attachés. The number of military attachés throughout Europe grew slowly from the 1830s through the 1850s. Great Britain, despite the presence of a small corps of military attachés in London beginning in the late 1840s, remained coldly aloof from this trend until 1854.[65]

It was the Crimean War which brought about England's first tentative step toward acquiring her own military attachés. "Commissars of the Queen," actually liaison officers, were sent to the headquarters of Britain's allies at Paris, Turin, and Constantinople, and also to the French headquarters in the Crimea. After the war, Britain had no strong desire to continue these attachments, although officers did continue on at Paris and Turin. They were called military attachés beginning in 1857; in 1860 the British added a naval captain to the Paris Embassy, their first naval attaché.[66]

The presence of her military attachés at five European capitals in the late 1860s[67] enhanced Britain's ability to collect strategic military intelligence. Unfortunately, no matter how efficient these attachés were at acquiring information, their product was sharply diminished in value by the lack of an adequate processing system in London. The reports of military attachés were forwarded directly to the undermanned Foreign Office, where there was no one qualified to analyze raw information pertaining to purely military developments.[68] The T&S Department at the War Office was in a state of disarray until 1871, and it was concerned with making maps, if it did anything at all. Where could the Foreign Office send reports containing technical military information in which it had no interest? The answer seems to have been that the Foreign Office simply did the best it could, which meant that large quantities of potentially usable information were left undigested. This sad state of affairs lay behind the recommendation made by the director of the T&S Department in 1870 that the military attachés be brought under control of the War Office and that the Department make better use of their reports.[69]

Military journals, official military observers sent by neutral nations to war zones, and military attachés were utilized by European powers of the mid-nineteenth century, including Great Britain, to improve their strategic intelligence systems so that they could keep up with technological innovations affecting warfare as well as with the overall strength of potential enemies. Interestingly, one of the technological innovations of the century gave intelligence organizations in European capitals the ability to receive reports from distant locations far more quickly than ever before and thereby enhanced considerably their value to their governments. Long distance telegraphy first was used in wartime during the Crimean War in 1854, but only within the theater of war. The telegraph was used effectively on a large scale by military forces for the first time in the American Civil War,[70] and immediately after the war, in 1866, the first permanently successful transatlantic telegraph cable was laid. By the time of the Franco-Prussian War in 1870-71, the potential impact of the telegraph on strategic as well as tactical military intelligence systems was obvious. The British Army set up a signal division at the School of Military Engineering in 1869 to teach electric as well as visual signalling.[71] One suspects that a growing awareness in London of the remarkable potential of the telegraph was at least a small factor in the acceptance of the notion in the early 1870s that an Intelligence Branch at the War Office might be useful.

Lastly, in accounting for the transformation of the T&S Department and the establishment of the Intelligence Branch between 1871 and 1873, it is possible to show a relationship with certain developments within the British Empire and the administrative machinery of the Empire. In India, the Sepoy Mutiny of 1857 was crushed by the British, thanks, in part, to the use of the telegraph. The network of telegraphs in India in 1857 was used to warn British officials in the Punjab of the outbreak of trouble near Delhi, and thus to secure control of that vital area before the trouble spread there.[72] Not only was the practical use of the telegraph as a conveyor of military intelligence demonstrated, but there were broad implications in the events of 1857 as well. Britain's confidence regarding her hold on India received a shock from which she never fully recovered; both the British administration and the British military system in India were reconstructed.[73] Correspondingly, there arose an increased concern that reliable information be made available to British officials in India and in London regarding internal as well as external threats to Britain's position in the subcontinent.

As additional British troops were sent to India in the wake of the mutiny, the government was withdrawing troops from overseas garrisons in many other parts of the Empire for reasons of economy and of concern for developments on the Continent, as well as in hope of encouraging colonial self-reliance. Yet, even the self-governing Dominions continued to look to London in matters of defense. The threat to Canada from the south, which grew during the American Civil War, had to be watched closely by the British. In general, the withdrawal of troops from overseas made reliable intelligence on potential threats to the Empire all the more important. The reduction of the colonial garrisons was accelerated during the Cardwell years at the War Office, but did not bring the end of British interest in imperial affairs.

Beginning in 1869 and continuing throughout the remainder of the century, Britain acquired a new appetite for imperial adventure. This new attitude, symbolized in Disraeli's famous Crystal Palace Speech of 1872, coincided with increasing international rivalry on the Continent and in the quest for colonies overseas. One historian, a noted authority on the British Empire, has related this situation to Britain's need for better strategic intelligence.

> These conditions led British governments, for the first time since 1815, to look upon all colonies as important strategic assets and as contributors to world-wide military policies. But the problems of an expanding British Empire and its defense were inextricably related to a greater need for Britain to live by trade in an increasingly competitive world and to anticipate the moves of rivals.[74]

Virtually all of Britain's rivals were potential enemies; estimating their capabilities to wage war and their intentions was quite naturally a vital function of strategic intelligence. The challenge for Britain's strategic intelligence system was made especially difficult in the final quarter of the nineteenth century by the fact that Britain had no major allies. Every one of the world's great powers was a rival and a potential enemy of the British Empire, although some (France and Russia) stood out as the most likely enemies.

NOTES

1. Lt. Col. W.V.R. Isaac, "The History of the Development of the Directorate of Military Intelligence, the War Office, 1855-1939," p. 6. An unpublished paper prepared to mark the centenary year of military intelligence in the British army, 1955. Henceforth, it will appear as Isaac, "History of the Directorate of M.I." See also Capt. E.H.H. Collen, *Report on the Intelligence Branch, Quarter-Master-General's Department, Horse Guards*, p. 6.

2. Cardwell had served as secretary to the treasury (1845-46), president of the Board of Trade (1852-55), secretary of state for Ireland (1859-61), and secretary of state for the colonies (1864-66).

3. J.W. Fortescue saw the end of the old army with the abolition of purchase and the initiation of short service. J.W. Fortescue, *A History of the British Army*, 13, p. 560. In a chapter entitled "Cardwell and the Late Victorian Army," Correlli Barnett credits Cardwell's reforms with providing "the blue-print of the late Victorian army," although pointing out, "When Cardwell left office in 1874, his work remained unfinished in some respects, and half-baked in others." Correlli Barnett, *Britain and Her Army, 1509-1970*, pp. 309-10. See also Gen. Sir Robert Biddulph, *Lord Cardwell at the War Office*.

4. Brian Bond, "The Effect of the Cardwell Reforms in Army Organization, 1874-1904," *Journal of the Royal United Services Institution* (henceforth the title will be abbreviated by *R.U.S.I. Journal*), 105 (November 1960), p. 515. See also Bond, *The Victorian Army and the Staff College, 1854-1914*, pp. 116-17 and Albert V. Tucker, "Army and Society in England, 1870-1900," pp. 110-41.

5. W.S. Hamer, *The British Army, 1885-1905*, p. ix.

6. In 1855, Lord Panmure, the secretary of state for war, merged into one the offices of secretary at war, responsible for finance, and the secretary of state for war.

7. The problem, which was not fully solved until the early twentieth century, was essentially one of finding a way to integrate civilian power with professional military knowledge; the civilians in power required the knowledge of the soldiers. W.S. Hamer, in referring to the predicament of the secretary of state for war after the reforms of 1854-71, points out that legally, the secretary ruled supreme, "but in fact his authority was limited for the very reason that he was an amateur interfering in matters that could only be understood, and hence mastered, through highly specialized and technical knowledge." Hamer, *The British Army*, p. x.

8. Sir Robert Biddulph, *Lord Cardwell at the War Office*, pp. 17-19, 249-54.

9. The Army Enlistment Act of 1870 replaced twelve years of long service by six years of active service and six in the reserves. The practice of purchasing officers' commissions was abolished by the Regulation of the Forces Act of 1871. Finally, the Localization Act of 1873 established the "localization" of the army's recruiting system in territorial areas or districts, where line regiments were linked to militia regiments under an administrative brigade headquarters. Barnett, *Britain and Her Army, 1509-1970: A Military, Political, and Social Survey*, pp. 304-09. See also B. Bond, *The Staff College*, pp. 117-25.

10. The reorganization of 1887-88 was a step in the direction of restoring control of military affairs to the soldiers. All the principal departments of the army except finance and manufacture

were united under the authority of the commander-in-chief. Hamer, *The British Army*, pp. 128-29.

11. Capt. G.R. Frith, "The Topographical Section of the General Staff" (Chatham, 1906), pp. 4-6. This is a history of the origin and development of the topographical function within the War Office, written under the direction of Maj. Gen. J.M. Grierson, DMO. Henceforth, it will appear as Frith, "Topographical Section."

12. Frith, "Topographical Section," p. 6. See also Sir Charles M. Watson, *The Life of Major-General Sir Charles William Wilson*, pp. 74-75.

13. Lt. Col. B.A.H. Parritt, *The Intelligencers*, p. 40. See also Jock Haswell, *British Military Intelligence*, p. 17, and Isaac, "History of the Directorate of M.I.," p. 3.

14. Parritt, *The Intelligencers*, p. 40. See also Haswell, *British Military Intelligence*, pp. 17, 24-25.

15. Ibid., pp. 40-41.

16. Frith, "Topographical Section," p. 8.

17. Parritt, *The Intelligencers*, pp. 54-55. Also Haswell, *British Military Intelligence*, p. 24, and Isaac, "History of the Directorate of M.I.," p. 3.

18. Ibid., p. 42.

19. Under the capable direction of Col. Lewis Lindenthal, a former Austrian Army major general, the library assembled a large number of books dealing with military science, history, topography, and foreign armies. Many of these works, labeled "Military Depot QMG Department," are held today by the Ministry of Defence Library in London. Isaac, "History of the Directorate of M.I.," p. 8. Parritt, *The Intelligencers*, pp. 41-42.

20. Isaac, "History of the Directorate of M.I.," p. 3.

21. Between 1815 and 1854, the British Army (and, in some cases, the British-commanded army of the East India Company) fought in Nepal against the Gurkhas (1815-16), in India against the Pindaris and Mahrattas (1817-19), in southern Africa in the Kaffir Wars (1818-19, 1834-35, 1846-47, 1850-53), in the first and second Burmese Wars (1824-26 and 1852), the first Afghan War (1839-42), the first Chinese War (1840-54), the Sind (1843), the Sikh Wars (1845-49), and the New Zealand War (1845-47). Often, it won battles and campaigns against enemy forces possessing overwhelming numerical superiority.

22. The "War Department" changed its name to the "War Office" in 1857.

23. The Survey Department was a powerful institution in British India; it was responsible for topographical and revenue surveys. Since Indian revenues were directly tied to rents and the "zamindar" system of tax collection, the East India Company had a special interest in economic statistics. The scope and magnitude of the Survey Department's work was as gigantic as India itself.

24. Maj. Thomas Best Jervis in a note to Lord Aberdeen, dated 3 May 1846, published by Jervis's son William P. Jervis in *Thomas Best Jervis*, pp. 269-70. The note is also quoted in Frith, "Topographical Section," p. 9.

25. Jervis, *Thomas Best Jervis*, p. 270.

26. Frith, "Topographical Section," pp. 9-10. See also Jervis, *Thomas Best Jervis*, p. 255.

27. Jervis, *Thomas Best Jervis*, pp. 256-57. The United States Military Academy Library at West Point, N.Y. has a well-preserved copy of Thomas Jervis's "The Krima or Crimean Peninsula," reproduced from the original Russian military map. London: HMSO, 1854.

28. Jervis, *Thomas Best Jervis*, pp. 257-58. See also Frith, "Topographical Section," p. 10.

29. Maj. Thomas Best Jervis in a letter to the Duke of Newcastle, dated July 17, 1854, a portion of which is published in Jervis, *Thomas Best Jervis*, p. 276.

30. The letter to Jervis from J. Peel, dated February 2, 1855, is published in full in Jervis, *Thomas Best Jervis*, p. 282. See also pp. 259-63.

31. Henceforth, the Topographical and Statistical Department will be abbreviated by the "T&S Department."

32. In August 1856, the T&S Department was moved to a house at 4 New Street, Spring Gardens, London. Jervis, *Thomas Best Jervis*, pp. 258, 263. See also Frith, "Topographical Section," p. 11.

33. One of the books was "Despatches and Papers of the Campaign in Turkey and the Crimea,"

containing accurate colored maps of the major battles. Parritt, *The Intelligencers*, p. 69. Maps produced included "A Map of the Black and Caspian Seas," "Map of the Principal Military Communications of the Kaukasus and Contiguous Provinces," and "Map of Khiva, the Sea of Aral, and the Country between the Caspian and Herat." Jervis, *Thomas Best Jervis*, pp. 296-97. Frith, "Topographical Section," p. 13.

34. In 1856 an army lieutenant colonel, stationed in Armenia, was picked by Jervis to head a party of civil engineers, surveyors, and draftsmen, which mapped the upper Euphrates River for the first time. Jervis, *Thomas Best Jervis*, pp. 293-95.

35. Isaac, "History of the Directorate of M.I.," p. 4.

36. Bond, *The Staff College*, p. 120. Thirty-seven years earlier, Hampden Gordon had said the same thing in *The War Office*.

37. Parritt, *The Intelligencers*, pp. 69-70.

38. Haswell, *British Military Intelligence*, p. 28.

39. "Statistics" was used in the parlance of mid-nineteenth century British Army officers to refer to all information concerning the military resources of foreign powers. There is some confusion in the term, however, as sometimes it appears to have been used in a broader sense to describe all information bearing on the military capabilities of a foreign power or a colony. Therefore, elements of economic, political, and even topographical intelligence were included in "statistical" information.

40. Maj. Thomas Best Jervis in a memorandum for the Duke of Newcastle, secretary of state for war, dated March 14, 1854, reprinted in Jervis, *Thomas Best Jervis*, pp. 273-74.

41. Ibid., p. 275. See also Major Jervis's letters of 26 October 1854; 9 March 1855; 15 September 1855; and June 1856, in Jervis, *Thomas Best Jervis*, pp. 279-80, 283-84, 290-92, and 292-93.

42. Frith, "Topographical Section," p. 12. Lithography is a printing process by which a design is transferred to a flat stone surface using a special crayon or a heat-pressure system. The stone is then inked and printed. This medium was commonly employed to reproduce maps in the nineteenth century. It was also used by many famous artists of the century, whose posters were printed by lithography.

43. Both Haswell and Parritt discuss the decline of the T&S Department after 1857, but insist on the continuity between the Department of 1855-57 and the Intelligence Branch beginning in 1873. Isaac admits that "more attention was given to maps than to statistics" in the 1857-70 period, but fails to convey the full extent of the Department's impotence outside of topography. Haswell, *British Military Intelligence*, pp. 31-32. Parritt, *The Intelligencers*, pp. 89-94. Isaac, "History of the Directorate of M.I.," p. 4.

44. The committee had four members: the assistant undersecretary of state, the secretary for military correspondence, the accountant general, and the director general of military education. Their main concern appears to have been a desire to save money. They lacked technical cartographic knowledge and seemingly had little appreciation of the need for foreign intelligence collection. Frith, "Topographical Section," p. 13. Parritt, *The Intelligencers*, p. 89.

45. Frith, "Topographical Section," pp. 13-15.

46. Ibid., p. 14. Isaac, "History of the Directorate of M.I.," p. 4. Parritt, *The Intelligencers*, p. 91.

47. Sir George Aston, *Secret Service*, pp. 1-2.

48. Isaac, "History of the Directorate of M.I.," p. 4. Parritt, *The Intelligencers*, p. 93.

49. Aston, *Secret Service*, p. 2.

50. Watson, *The Life of Major-General Sir Charles William Wilson*, pp. 78-80. See also Collen, *Report*, p. 4.

51. Adrian Preston, "The Eastern Question in British Strategic Policy During the Franco-Prussian War," p. 3.

52. Ibid., pp. 4-5, 11-12.

53. Ibid., p. 27.

54. Ibid., p. 5.

55. Ibid., p. 1. See also Adrian Preston, "The Role of the Indian Army in Indo-British Political and Strategic Relations, 1745-1947," *Journal of the United Service Institute of India*, October-December, 1970.

56. Adrian Preston says that "imperial defence" meant not the voluntary military cooperation of

the self-governing dominions, but the physical defense of continental India, the marshalling and launching of its resources against the Russian heartland, and the systematic acquisition and development of such war anchorages and military bases as were strategically integral to it. Ibid., p. 3. For a different view of "imperial defence," see Richard Preston, *Canada and "Imperial Defense."*

57. Dallas D. Irvine, "The Origin of Capital Staffs," p. 165.

58. Walter Goerlitz, *History of the German General Staff, 1657-1945*, pp. 21, 31, 53.

59. Bond, *Staff College*, p. 34.

60. In the 1879 issue of the *Journal of the R.U.S.I.*, for example, there are eight articles on foreign military and naval developments, including one on the German navy and one on military railroad transport in France.

61. Robert H. Scales, Jr., "Artillery in Small Wars: The Evolution of British Artillery Doctrine, 1860-1914," doctoral dissertation (Duke University, 1976), p. 14.

62. Jay Luvaas, *The Military Legacy of the Civil War*. British observers were granted a surprisingly high degree of access by both Union and Confederate armies.

63. With the outbreak of the Franco-Prussian War in 1870, the War Office, following the practice used previously in the Austro-Italian and Austro-Prussian Wars as well as the American Civil War, dispatched extra attachés and technical military missions to the Continent to report on developments in gunnery, fortification, surgery, intelligence systems, staff organization, and mobilization procedures. Preston, "The Eastern Question in British Strategic Policy," p. 8.

64. Vagts, *The Military Attaché*, pp. 28-29.

65. Ibid., pp. 3, 9, 18, and 24.

66. Ibid., pp. 27-28.

67. At Paris, Berlin, Turin, Vienna, St. Petersburg, and Frankfurt (until 1866), not to mention two naval attachés in Paris and Washington. Ibid., p. 29.

68. For a general discussion of how the Foreign Office was organized and how it functioned in the mid-nineteenth century, see chapter 1, "The Old Foreign Office," in Zara Steiner's *The Foreign Office and Foreign Policy, 1898-1914*, pp. 1-10. See also the comments by Adrian Preston on the impact of Foreign Office control of military attachés on the quality of military reporting, in "The Eastern Question in British Strategic Policy," p. 23.

69. Watson, *Wilson*, pp. 78-81. See also Isaac, "History of the Directorate of M.I.," p. 5.

70. David L. Woods, *A History of Tactical Communication Technique*, pp. 107-08.

71. Ibid., p. 118.

72. Gordon, *The Moment of Power*, pp. 16-17.

73. Barnett, *Britain and Her Army, 1509-1970*, p. 292.

74. Richard A. Preston, *Canada and "Imperial Defense,"* pp. 83-84.

Chapter III

Charles Wilson and the Birth of an Intelligence Department at the War Office, 1870-1873

The manner in which I am trying to work out my scheme is, in the first place, to get the officers of the Department to prepare a thoroughly accurate account of the armies of the different countries as they exist at present. . . .

Capt. Charles W. Wilson
From a letter to a friend, 1871

One of the most dramatic and controversial episodes in the annals of the nineteenth-century British Empire began in March 1884, when the forces of Muhammad Ahmad, a Moslem leader who called himself the Mahdi, cut off and besieged the colorful, eccentric Maj. Gen. Charles "Chinese" Gordon and his command at Khartoum in the Sudan. Gordon, a former governor general of the Sudan (1877-79), was under orders to evacuate the Egyptian garrison from Khartoum but had taken it upon himself to attempt to crush the Mahdi. His chances for success against Muhammad Ahmad were severely reduced by the vulnerability of a line of communications from Egypt along the Nile more than one thousand miles long and by the unreliability of his poorly trained Egyptian troops. The Egyptians were terrified by the prospect of death at the hands of the Mahdi's fanatical dervishes.[1] Despite his difficult predicament at Khartoum, Charles Gordon might have managed to escape in March or April by using some Nile steamers at his disposal, but he refused to leave, and by the end of May the situation was indeed hopeless. In September, after months of debate in England about the solution to Gordon's predicament, the government of Prime Minister William Gladstone ordered Lieutenant General Lord Wolseley to organize and lead a relief expedition.

In assembling his staff for the campaign up the Nile into the Sudan, General Wolseley selected Col. Sir Charles William Wilson, Royal Engineers, as chief of his intelligence department. Given Wilson's earlier tours of duty in Cairo and the Sinai and his considerable experience in military intelligence and topography, Wolseley's choice seemed a sound one. Unfortunately, in numerous accounts that have appeared through the years about the Nile Campaign of 1884-85, Charles Wilson's prominent place has had nothing to do with his role as Wolseley's intelligence officer. Rather, he is remembered for his alleged failure as a commander during what many have seen as the most critical phase of the entire campaign. It is sad that Wilson has suffered such ignominy, not only because the blame for Gordon's death belongs elsewhere, but also because his actions during a few days in January 1885 have been allowed to obscure a lifetime of unique and valuable service to the army and to the Empire. The memory of Maj. Gen. Sir Charles William Wilson deserves a far better fate.

General Wolseley's relief expedition began moving up the Nile into the Sudan from its base at Wadi Halfa in October 1884. The logistical problems facing Wolseley and his staff were enormous and, although the situation inside Khartoum grew desperate for Gordon and his men in November, the relief force was still hundreds of miles from the besieged city. To save time in his effort to reach Gordon, Wolseley decided to send a portion of his forces overland across the desert from a staging point on the Nile at Korti. On 30 December the "Desert Column" under Sir Herbert Stewart set off in a southeasterly direction from Korti across open desert towards an objective on the Nile only one hundred miles from Khartoum. With General Stewart on this dangerous trek was Col. Charles Wilson, whose personal mission was to deliver a letter to Gordon from Wolseley.

The perilous nature of Stewart's march from Korti was fully appreciated by Wolseley. When Col. Frederick Burnaby, General Herbert's second in command, was killed during an attack on the Desert Column by ten thousand dervishes at Abu Klea on 17 January 1885, General Wolseley was consumed with anxiety about Stewart's position. His worst fears were confirmed when Stewart was mortally wounded in the course of a second attack by the dervishes only seven miles short of his objective on the Nile. Suddenly Charles Wilson found himself in command. Led by Colonel Wilson, the badly mauled British forces managed to stave off yet another enemy assault and reach the Nile. Here, rather than pushing on immediately up the river to Khartoum, Wilson paused for four days to take care of his wounded, rest his camels, and conduct reconnaissance. After loading two steamers with troops, he started up the Nile on 24 January. When Wilson and his small force arrived at Khartoum four days later, the city had fallen to the Mahdi only forty-eight hours earlier. Worst of all, Gordon had been killed.

The public furor generated in England by the failure to rescue Gordon contributed to the fall of the Gladstone government in 1885. The search for a scapegoat is a natural consequence to such embarrassing episodes, and in

1885 the primary candidates were Gladstone, Wolseley, and Wilson. It was easy to place the blame on Charles Wilson because, despite all the earlier blunders made by others, he was the one man who might actually have reached General Gordon in time to save his life. Overlooked by Wilson's critics were earlier and much longer delays during the 317 days that Gordon held out at Khartoum, delays caused primarily by political squabbling and indecision in London. As his detractors saw it, Charles Wilson had dallied needlessly while the gallant hero perished at the hands of the dervishes. Wilson was not without his defenders, particularly among his fellow officers, but he was haunted for the rest of his life by critics who portrayed him as the Englishman most directly to blame for the untimely death of the soldier many regarded as a national hero, "Chinese" Gordon. Paradoxically, the individual who, more than any other, was responsible for the creation of a permanent intelligence department at the War Office has been remembered, instead, for his alleged failure in the Sudan.[2]

Charles Wilson was never given another field command, Nevertheless, the remaining twenty years of his life were spent neither in self-pity nor in idleness. Promotions, honors, and positions of great responsibility came his way. Little more than a year after Gordon's death, Sir Charles assumed the directorship of the Ordnance Survey, a prestigious post which he retained until appointed director general of military education in 1892. Wilson received honorary degrees in law (1886, Edinburgh University) and in engineering (1893, Dublin University). During his six-year tenure as director general of military education, he was promoted to the rank of major general. In the final years of his life, Charles Wilson renewed his lifelong interest in the Middle East. Between 1899 and his death in 1905 he twice returned to Palestine on behalf of the Palestine Exploration Fund, an organization he had helped to found in 1865.[3]

Interesting though the post-1885 portion of Wilson's life may have been, the crucial role which he played in the birth of the Intelligence Branch at the War Office occurred at an earlier stage of a long and productive career. Charles William Wilson was born at Liverpool on 14 March 1836, the second son of Edward and Frances Wilson. The Wilson family had its roots in West Yorkshire and had acquired considerable interests in the colony of Virginia prior to the American Revolutionary War. Charles's uncle, Thomas Bellerby Wilson, lived in the United States and was for many years the mainstay of the Academy of Natural Sciences in Philadelphia. According to his friend and biographer, Col. Sir Charles M. Watson, Charles William Wilson set his heart on a career in the army at an early age, much to the dismay of his father, Edward. Indeed, Watson suggests that Edward Wilson's failure to lend full support to his son's efforts to gain admission to the Royal Military Academy at Woolwich may have denied Charles any chance of admittance. Young Wilson was disappointed in his hopes to attend either Woolwich or Addiscombe, the East India Company's college for artillery and engineer officers. Instead, after attending Cheltenham College for two years and Bonn University for one, he won an army officer's commission the hard way. In 1855, at the age of nineteen, Charles took a special open competitive examination for army commissions and placed second out of the forty-five entrants. Only the two men who scored the highest, Charles and one other, were offered commissions in the Royal Engineers. Young Wilson was delighted at the opportunity and accepted his commission without hesitation.[4]

The first two years of Charles Wilson's military career were routine: a basic course for engineer lieutenants at Chatham followed by two brief tours with Royal Engineer units in England. The aspiring "sapper" officer did not go unnoticed by his superiors in the army for long. Early in 1858, Lieutenant Wilson was selected as secretary for the North American Boundary Commission, an unusual but important overseas assignment. For the next four years Charles Wilson and his colleagues were engaged in the formidable task of precisely establishing the boundary between British North America and the United States from the Great Lakes west to the Pacific. Their mission was prompted in part by British fears of northward expansion by Americans. The urgency of the Boundary Commission's work was intensified in 1858 by the discovery of gold on the Fraser River near the Pacific coast, which led to the creation of a new colony (British Columbia) late that same year. There was tension also in the prairie region, where American settlers were spilling across the border from the upper Middle West, and some talked openly of annexation by the United States. The outbreak of the Civil War in 1861 turned American energies southward at a fortunate moment and allowed the Dominion of Canada to come into existence.[5]

Charles Wilson's performance on the North American Boundary Commission not only helped him establish his credentials within the Royal Engineers and the army, but also attracted favorable attention from the Foreign Office.[6] Along with other members of the commission, Wilson returned to England in 1862. After a brief interlude of fortification work along the Thames, he requested a transfer to the Ordnance Survey and volunteered for the job of surveying Jerusalem. In the succeeding five years, Captain Wilson further enhanced his excellent reputation in survey work during a series of assignments—Jerusalem and Palestine (1864-66), Scotland (1866-68), and the Sinai Peninsula (1868-69)—which twice took him to the Middle East. The young officer's technical competence, combined with his ability to operate effectively in politically sensitive areas, made him an attractive candidate for future employment with the Foreign Office.[7] In 1869, however, it was not the Foreign Office but the Topographical and Statistical Department of the War Office which sought Wilson's services.

In January 1869, while on surveying duty in the Sinai Peninsula, Captain Wilson received a letter from the director of the T&S Department, Col. Sir Henry James, asking him if he wanted to be recommended for the job of executive officer of the department. James's offer came as a surprise, since Wilson had expected to return to Scotland for another field assignment with the Ordnance Survey. He lost no time in accepting the director's proposal and Colonel James had little difficulty in arranging the appointment. Wilson returned to England in May 1869 to assume his new post.[8]

Colonel James, as described in the preceding chapter, was a "Survey man," and, although the consolidation of 1857 had ostensibly brought the older and more established Ordnance Survey under the wings of the fledgling T&S Department, James appears never to have accepted the new arrangement. Throughout his thirteen years as director of the T&S Department, Henry James had worn a second (and to him a more important) hat—as director general of the Ordnance Survey. Indicative of James's priorities was the fact he continued to live and work in Southampton, the headquarters of the Ordnance Survey, rather than in London, home of the T&S Department. He kept his executive officer in London to run the T&S Department, treating it, in effect, as a subordinate branch of the Ordnance Survey.[9] It is hardly surprising that Charles Wilson found the T&S Department in an advanced state of decay when he arrived from the Sinai in 1869.

The addition of a bright and energetic new executive officer to the staff of the T&S Department in the spring of 1869 did not result in an immediate revival of that moribund organization. Captain Wilson was appalled at the state of affairs he discovered, but he was in no position to openly criticize or to directly challenge the powerful and well-entrenched Sir Henry James. Wisely, Wilson bided his time, learned all he could about the organization, and made mental notes about what ought to be done. His patience was rewarded the following year when the Ordnance Survey was separated from the T&S Department and transferred from the War Office to the Office of Works. While James continued to serve as director general of the survey, moving with it to the Office of Works in early 1870, Charles Wilson, now only thirty-four years of age, became director of the T&S Department. His new job did not carry with it an automatic promotion, so Wilson was still a captain when he assumed the directorship on 1 April 1870.[10] Despite his lowly rank, Captain Wilson realized that a golden opportunity was at hand to translate his ideas into action. By virtue of education, intelligence, energy, and experience, Charles Wilson was exceptionally well prepared for the task.

Individual qualifications of the new director aside, Wilson's chances of making something of the T&S Department were enhanced immeasurably by the strong support and encouragement he received from the secretary of state for war. No sooner had Captain Wilson settled into the directorship than Edward Cardwell asked him to report on the condition of the T&S Department. Wilson's response, a candid and highly critical memorandum, prompted the reform-minded Cardwell to appoint a committee under Lord Northbrook, the under secretary for war. The Northbrook Committee was charged with recommending to Edward Cardwell "the best means of turning the Topographical Department to the greatest account."[11]

Captain Wilson was selected to serve as the committee's secretary, and in this capacity he drafted the report of its findings. Apparently Lord Northbrook and the other committee members were most receptive to Wilson's proposals concerning what ought to be done about the T&S Department. When the Northbrook Committee's report was published in January 1871, it was little more than a restatement of the memorandum Wilson had prepared for Cardwell some eight months earlier, during his first few weeks as director.[12] Cardwell's decision to implement the recommendations contained in the report gave Charles Wilson the final stamp of approval he needed to transform the T&S Department.

In retrospect, it seems fitting that the Northbrook Committee's report on the Topographical and Statistical Department was published during the very month Paris fell to the Germans. While it is most unlikely that Lord Northbrook released the report at this time merely because the Franco-Prussian War was in its last stages, the two events were not entirely unrelated. Edward Cardwell's success in bringing about a major reorganization within the War Office in 1870-71 was prompted in part by the rise of German military power on the Continent between 1864 and 1871. Though the revitalization of the T&S Department, outlined by the Northbrook Committee's report in January 1871 and implemented by Charles Wilson during the months that followed, was a relatively minor part of the Cardwell legacy at the War Office, it, too, must be viewed against the backdrop of the German wars of unification, especially the Franco-Prussian War of 1870-71.

The capitulation of Paris to the Germans was the climax of a series of shattering defeats suffered by the French Army since the outbreak of war in July 1870. It was apparent to even the most casual observer of the conflict that the Prussian Great General Staff played a vital role in Germany's victory and that the absence of a capital staff was a fatal weakness for the French. Also evident was the inadequacy of French military intelligence on both the tactical and strategic levels.[13] There was one notable and well-documented exception on the strategic side—the accurate and farsighted reporting of the French military attaché in Berlin. Colonel Baron Stoffel, who served in Berlin from 1866 until the war began, repeatedly warned Napoleon III and his government about Prussian preparations for war and her increasing military superiority,[14] but his reports went largely unheeded. Consequently, the French high command seriously underestimated the strength of Prussia and misread her intentions. In the course of the war the French army's tactical intelligence system often appeared inept, all the more so when contrasted with that of the Germans. The manifest weaknesses of French intelligence were not lost on Charles Wilson. Even at the end of the Franco-Prussian War, a credible strategic intelligence effort was nonexistent within the British War Office. Captain Wilson left no doubt about the situation when he wrote to a friend at the time:

> There is not at present in the possession of (our) Government a trust-worthy account of any foreign army, and I am almost ashamed to say that had any complications arisen in France last year, and had we been asked for information, we should have had to translate a German work on the French army as giving a better account of it than we could prepare ourselves.[15]

The events of the Franco-Prussian War, combined with the presence of the reform-minded Edward Cardwell at the War Office, provided Charles Wilson with ideal conditions for the transformation of the T&S Department.

Charles Wilson's plan for change within the T&S Department first emerged three months prior to the French declaration of war on Prussia, when he was asked by Cardwell to assess the state of his small organization. The prompt response by the newly appointed director of the T&S Department to the secretary of state for war's query led, as already mentioned, to the formation of the Northbrook Committee. Captain Wilson's memorandum of 30 April 1870 ranks as one of the most significant documents in the history of British military intelligence. Only two pages long, this extraordinary memorandum was concise yet comprehensive; it addressed the present condition of the Department as Cardwell had requested and went on to prescribe the major changes Wilson felt were necessary.[16]

According to Charles Wilson, the overall condition of the T&S Department in early 1870 was poor. The work of the topographical section was hampered by a chronic shortage of funds. The library and map collections were "deficient"; maps produced or collected by other departments of the War Office had not been obtained or even catalogued. And, despite guidance to the contrary which had been furnished some thirteen years earlier by the secretary for war (Lord Panmure), close coordination with topographical agencies of the self-governing colonies had not been achieved. The situation was even worse on the statistical side of the Department. The amount of reliable and up-to-date information available on foreign armies was pitifully small and "there was no information about the colonies."[17]

Captain Wilson's analysis of the statistical work of the T&S Department, although written over a century ago, dealt with what still are generally regarded as the three major functions of intelligence work at the strategic and tactical levels, alike: collection, processing/analysis, and dissemination/reporting. In its broadest sense, collection includes the planning of intelligence collection operations, the tasking of collectors or collection systems, the actual collection of information, and the transmission of information from the source or sources to a staff or central agency whose function is to produce intelligence. During the processing phase, raw information received by a staff element is recorded, filed or catalogued, collated, and analyzed, with the objectives of producing reports and estimates and building a reservoir of data which can be used at any time. Finally, the dissemination phase involves the reporting or transmission of finished intelligence (and in some cases undigested information judged to be of immediate value) to those who need it, the decision makers, most importantly. Charles Wilson's memorandum of April 1870, as well as information derived from other sources describing the T&S Department at the time, show that on the eve of the Franco-Prussian War the British War Office's strategic intelligence effort was deficient in all three functions.

Not surprisingly, Wilson addressed the problem of collection most directly. Obviously, a successful collection program is a necessary foundation for any worthwhile intelligence system; without the regular gathering of information from reliable sources there can be no processing or dissemination. Charles Wilson was acutely aware of this when he informed Cardwell in his memorandum that neither the T&S Department nor the War Office as a whole possessed an established system or plan for the regular collection of foreign military intelligence. Foreign newspapers, military journals, and official publications were not being screened. In fact, they were not even being acquired by the Department. British military attachés, potentially lucrative sources of military intelligence, were on station in a number of foreign capitals including Paris and Berlin, but they lacked direct channels of communication with the T&S Department. As Wilson put it, "the present method of obtaining information from the military attachés is very bad." Reports filed by the attachés routinely arrived at the Foreign Office on Downing Street but seldom found their way to the Spring Gardens headquarters of the T&S Department. Equally crippling was the restriction which prohibited officers of the Department from corresponding directly with military attachés, even semiofficially.[18]

The T&S Department might have compensated to some degree for its lack of control over and communication with British military attachés by sending its own officers abroad as observers, or by sponsoring such trips by officers or civilians not assigned to the Department. Indeed, the War Office had dispatched officers to America and to the Continent as observers during the wars of the 1860s. No war was under way when Wilson's report on the T&S Department was written in the spring of 1870, but when the Franco-Prussian War began in July, extra attachés and technical military missions were quickly sent to the Continent by the War Office to report on various aspects of the conflict. To what degree, if any, the T&S Department was able to influence, direct, or benefit from the work of British military observers during the Franco-Prussian War is not altogether clear, but it appears to have been minimal.

Had it been able to send even one of its own officers, the Department's wartime collection program would have been enhanced. Unfortunately, the staff of the T&S Department was too small to spare an officer for such duty. Even if officers had been available from the Department, the financial constraints within which it operated would have prohibited such a gambit unless they had been willing to go on leave and travel at their own expense. In Wilson's view, the failure of the Department to encourage or sponsor regular visits to the Continent in peacetime was at least as damaging as its inactivity during war between European powers.[19] It is significant that nowhere in the memorandum did Captain Wilson advocate or even mention covert collection or secret service. In 1870, most if not all of the information on foreign armies required by the War Office could be gathered from open sources. Whatever covert intelligence operations were needed were left to the Secret Intelligence Service (SIS) and the Foreign Office.

The defects in the T&S Department's ability to process information and produce intelligence were at least as serious as those in its collection system, though Charles Wilson was not as direct in identifying flaws in this area. One may infer the flaws from his recommendations for change in the internal structure of the Department and from what is known of its organization and strengths in April 1870. The statistical function had for many years remained in the shadow of the topographical function. Of the twenty men who worked in the T&S Department (two officers, one military clerk, thirteen civilian draftsmen, and four civilian "labourers"), not one was occupied full-time with the work of processing intelligence.[20] In fact, most were involved entirely in topographical and administrative matters.

The task of filing, collating, and analyzing the statistical information received fell to the two officers. One of these (Captain Wilson) was the director and therefore busy much of the time in running the Department. The other, Lieutenant Evelyn Baring, came closer than any other individual in the Department to being a full-time intelligence analyst. Baring was an intelligent and industrious young officer who had a working knowledge of three foreign languages. The magnitude of his responsibilities, however, which included the processing of military intelligence from all overseas areas of interest, was sufficient to have overwhelmed any man, even the future British agent and consul general in Egypt.[21]

Captain Wilson also recognized that the end products of the Department, both topographical and statistical, would be of little or no value to the War Office and the army if they were not disseminated regularly. He pointed to the existing problems in this area by recommending to Cardwell that products of the Department

> should be made useful not only to the Secretary of State but to the whole Army by publishing quarterly a small sheet containing a list of all maps and books added to the Library during the quarter, and translation of interesting articles on military matters in foreign periodicals. . . . Secondly, a series of pamphlets, descriptive of foreign armies, similar to those prepared by the Prussian Topographical Department, should be prepared and sold to officers of the Army for a small fixed sum.[22]

The Department's lack of clear-cut procedures for publicizing and distributing its products in early 1870 was related, no doubt, to the fact that it had so little to offer in the way of finished intelligence.

Of all the recommendations Charles Wilson made to Edward Cardwell in his memorandum, none were more fundamental than those concerning the organization of the Department. In his reorganization scheme Wilson aimed at a more even balance between the topographical and statistical functions and the improvement of the Department's ability to process military intelligence. The Topographical Section would collect and produce maps; its collection should consist of:

    a. The best map extant of Great Britain and colonies and all foreign countries.
    b. The best plans of foreign fortresses.
    c. Maps and plans illustrative of campaigns, battles, and sieges.
    d. Photographs of the colonies and foreign countries.

The Statistical Section was to be divided into three divisions, each under an officer responsible for the collection and processing of military information concerning particular foreign countries.

    Section A. Austria, Russia, Sweden, Norway, Turkey, Greece, Asia.
    Section B. Prussia, Germany, Italy, Switzerland, Spain, Denmark.
    Section C. France, Great Britain, Belgium, the Netherlands, America.

In addition to the Topographical and Statistical Sections, the Department should maintain "a good military library."[23]

Wilson's remaining proposals dealt primarily with collection and related budgetary considerations. He wanted a small amount of money (£250) set aside in the annual Army Estimates for the purchase of books, foreign newspapers, and foreign journals. Officers assigned to the Department were to attend the annual autumn maneuvers of European armies and "should be encouraged to travel." Additional funds (£200 per year) were required to support foreign travel, but reimbursement would be made only "on condition that the officer worked and made a useful report." Copies of all reports sent by Britain's military attachés to the Foreign Office, "whether confidential or otherwise," would be furnished to the T&S Department. Officers of the Department were to be allowed to correspond with the attachés "in a semi-official manner." All military attachés would be encouraged to provide the Department with critical analyses of the armies of their host countries and to keep it abreast of new books, maps, and official material of military significance. Military attachés would "as far as possible be selected from officers who have passed through either the Topographical Department or Staff College, or who belong to the Artillery or Engineers."[24]

Though Edward Cardwell received Charles Wilson's memorandum in May, it was not until 13 October 1870 that he appointed the committee, headed by Lord Northbrook, to examine the issues raised by the new director of the T&S Department. Europe had been shaken during the intervening five months by the opening rounds of the Franco-Prussian War and the shocking rout of the French Army (and the capture of Napoleon III) at Sedan on 1 September. No doubt the secretary of state for war was preoccupied with more urgent matters during this period, particularly beginning in July. In any case, it seems reasonable to assume that French reverses, together with the War Office's embarrassing lack of information on the armies of both France and Germany, reminded Cardwell of Wilson's paper and convinced him that radical reform of the T&S Department could be delayed no longer. The priority he accorded this reform beginning in October is indicated by the speed with which he approved the report of the Northbrook Committee, only two days after it was published on 24 January 1871.

The secretary for war's acceptance of the Northbrook Committee's report meant that Charles Wilson's recommendations had survived virtually intact as the basis for the restructuring of the T&S Department. Several additional ideas were incorporated by the Northbrook Committee. To assist the Topographical Section in its collection efforts, naval officers would be asked to send the Department information about foreign ports. Valuable foreign maps might be acquired through the "exchange of maps with foreign governments." The director of the T&S Department would also be authorized to purchase maps; for this purpose £250 per year should be allowed. Henceforth, the Statistical Section was to concentrate on foreign armies. A separate statistical branch of the War Office would be set up to maintain information on the British Army. In the future, officers assigned to the Statistical Section would be required to know at least two foreign languages. Military attachés were "to be more under the War Office" and as Wilson had recommended, all their reports would be sent to the Department. Whenever possible, they should be selected from among officers who had served in the T&S Department.[25]

Once the report of the Northbrook Committee had been endorsed by Cardwell, Captain Wilson lost no time in beginning the reorganization that his report had recommended. There was no doubt in his mind of what the purpose of the T&S Department ought to be.

> This object is to collect in peace time such information relating to foreign armies that, on the outbreak of war with any country, we should be able at once to send to press, and publish for the use of officers of our army, a pamphlet containing the fullest and most recent details concerning the hostile army: its composition, organisation, tactics, arms, artillery, dress, equipment, etc., as well as of the roads, railways, mountain passes, etc., falling within the probable area of the operations. The information thus collected would also, I think, be extremely valuable during any discussions on army reform and organisation, in Parliament and elsewhere, in time of peace.[26]

To attain this objective, Wilson felt that it was essential for officers of the Department to prepare "a thoroughly accurate account" of each foreign army, "and then, through the reports of military attachés and others, to keep careful notes of all changes which may be introduced into them."[27]

In June 1871 Sir Edward Lugard, the permanent under-secretary for war, provided the T&S Department with a written charter very much along the lines of Wilson's philosophy. The duties of its officers were

> to collect and classify all possible information relating to the strength, organization, etc., of foreign armies; to keep themselves acquainted with the progress made by foreign countries in military art and science, and to preserve the information in such a form that it can be readily consulted, and made available for any purpose for which it may be required.[28]

At long last, the raison d'être of the Topographical and Statistical Department had been clarified and announced officially by the War Office. This was but one of several signs that the Department was on a radically different course than it had been little more than one year earlier. Its ability to collect and produce maps and other topographical intelligence had not only remained the same, but it had been improved. New life had been injected into the dying statistical function. The three subsections of the Statistical Section were functioning; each was headed by an officer who was responsible for keeping track of military affairs in specified countries.[29] Indeed, except for the fact that it was still situated at 4 New Street in Spring Gardens, the T&S Department in the summer of 1871 bore little resemblance to its predecessor of April 1870.

After approximately one year's experience with the restructured T&S Department, Charles Wilson was pleased but not entirely satisfied. In 1872 he sent a new report to Cardwell, recommending that the Department be enlarged and "that an officer of high rank and position" be placed at its head.[30] He seemed to be saying that it was time that the prestige of the organization be increased. The growing influence of the Prussian General Staff was reflected in Captain Wilson's comment that England was the only European nation "which did not possess a scheme of national defence." His suggestion that sections for "home and colonial defence, railways and telegraphs, and military history" be added to the Department clearly followed the Prussian model.[31]

This time, Cardwell did not refer Wilson's report to a committee for consideration. Instead, after praising the performance of the T&S Department and its director, "that most excellent officer, Captain Wilson," he informed Parliament in February 1873 of his intention to establish an intelligence department in the near future. The T&S Department, Cardwell told the Committee on Army Estimates in the House of Commons on 24 February, would form the nucleus of the new organization, and a general officer would be selected to head it.[32]

The secretary for war carried through with his plan in little more than a month, and on 1 April 1873 the Intelligence Branch of the War Office came into existence. Maj. Gen. Sir Patrick MacDougall was named the first chief of the Intelligence Branch; his official title was deputy adjutant general for intelligence. Actually, MacDougall would often receive instructions directly from the commander-in-chief, but administratively, the Intelligence Branch was placed under the adjutant general's department. Cardwell's appointment of Sir Patrick MacDougall to the new post was an excellent choice. MacDougall had also been the first commandant of the Staff College at Camberley and was one of the army's leading reformers in the post-Crimean War years. His contribution to British military intelligence was an important one and will receive more attention in the next chapter.

Charles Wilson, promoted to major in May 1873, stayed on in the Intelligence Branch as General MacDougall's deputy for three more years. The presence of Major Wilson insured continuity in the functioning of War Office Intelligence and a smooth transition from T&S Department to Intelligence Branch. Indeed, in both internal organization and assigned responsibilities, the Intelligence Branch of 1873 was remarkably similar to the T&S Department of 1871-73. The functions of the Branch included those of its predecessor. However, in addition to the collection of topographical and statistical information, it was charged with

> the application of such information, in respect to the measures considered and determined on during peace, which should be adopted in war, so that no delay might arise from uncertainty and hesitation.[33]

The Intelligence Branch was to concern itself with more than collecting and producing military intelligence.

Sir Patrick MacDougall and his successors interpreted the "application of such information" to mean the involvement of their organization in strategic planning for the defense of Great Britain and her Empire. Thus, from the moment of its official birth in 1873, the Intelligence Branch was more than strictly an intelligence staff. It is possible to see it from this stage on as the embryo of the British General Staff, which was established in 1904, as well as the beginning of a modern military or national intelligence organization.[34] In any case, in tracing the historical development of the general staff system in the British Army, one must come to terms with the Intelligence Branch of the late nineteenth century. This is not, however, the primary purpose of this book. Therefore, although recognizing the nearly continuous presence of a planning or operational element in the Intelligence Branch (1873-85) and the Intelligence Department (1886-1904), the principal focus throughout those chapters dealing with the pre-1904 years will be on the development of the intelligence function of the Intelligence Branch/ Department.

Until at least 1886, the planning/operational element of the Branch's work was secondary in importance and at times almost insignificant compared to its intelligence role. Nevertheless, the addition of this new mission in 1873, along with an increased emphasis on the collection and production of military intelligence, necessitated some adjustments in both the manpower and the internal organization of the Intelligence Branch. Major Wilson had little difficulty in persuading General MacDougall that the Branch needed additional officers. MacDougall also decided to form a "Home and Colonial Section" to assist him in strategical planning. When the Intelligence Branch was formed in April 1873, the number of military and civilian personnel assigned rose to twenty-seven, as compared to twelve in the T&S Department of 1872-73. Significantly, officer strength increased from five to eight, and one of the newly authorized officers was appointed to head the Home and Colonial Section. Charles Wilson, as second ranking officer in the branch, was designated an assistant adjutant general (AAG), while the five section chiefs were rated deputy assistant adjutant generals (DAAGs).[35]

The administrative subordination of the Intelligence Branch to the Adjutant General's Department lasted only until July of the following year, when it was transferred to the Quartermaster General's Department. This switch in the summer of 1874 was not especially surprising, in retrospect. The question of whether intelligence belonged to the adjutant general (AG) or the quartermaster general (QMG) was an old one in the British Army. In the early eighteenth century, when the Duke of Marlborough led the English Army to victories at Blenheim (1704), Oudenarde (1708), and Malplaquet (1709), the AG's responsibilities included the supervision of outposts and security, thereby involving him in both operations and intelligence. The QMG, a staff officer traditionally associated with supply and logistics, was also responsible for selecting and laying out the camp; in the latter capacity he habitually conducted reconnaissance. Marlborough's quartermaster general, William Cadogan, performed invaluable service in directing the tactical intelligence effort for his commander, including the recruiting of guides.[36]

In the Duke of Wellington's army in the peninsula (1809-14) a century later, both AG and QMG continued to have intelligence functions. The task of reconnaissance, particularly topographical reconnaissance, belonged to the QMG; the AG had control over prisoners of war, always a valuable source of intelligence. Traditionally the AG had been the more important of the two officers, but Wellington favored the QMG, and as time went on he gave the latter most of the operations and intelligence functions. "As a result the AG's office became very much a matter of routine."[37] When the Corps of Guides was formed in 1809 to provide intelligence for British columns moving into strange territory, it was placed under the QMG's Department. By the end of the Peninsular War, there was no doubt that the QMG, Sir George Murray, was Wellington's principal intelligence staff officer. In the Waterloo Campaign of 1815, an Intelligence Department was created for the first time to support a British army in the field, and the officer selected by Wellington to head it was an assistant quartermaster general.[38] It should also be recalled that the Depot of Military Knowledge in London had been established in 1803 as a branch of the QMG's Department. The Depot remained under the QMG throughout the remainder of the Napoleonic Wars and survived until the Crimean War as the Topographical Department of the quartermaster general.

Precisely why Cardwell placed the Intelligence Branch under the adjutant general, rather than under the quartermaster general, in 1873 is a matter of conjecture. It probably was due in part to the resurgence of the AG. By the 1870s the AG had become "the unofficial deputy of the Commander-in-Chief, and his functions most closely approximated those of a chief of staff."[39] If the head of War Office intelligence, who was also charged with developing plans for the defense of the British Empire, was not going to be accorded a status equal to that of the AG or QMG, at least he would be placed only one level below the commander-in-chief's right-hand man. The return of the Intelligence Branch to the QMG in 1874 was consistent with the practice of the British Army during the Napoleonic Wars and the entire first half of the nineteenth century. Although this shift was welcomed by the QMG, it has been described as "rather of a retrograde nature" for the Branch.[40] Just as the QMG's control of intelligence operations in the field and in London during the struggle against Napoleon I had increased his power at the expense of the AG, on Wellington's staff in the field, the AG's nominal ownership of the Branch in the 1870s contributed to a revival of his prestige within the War Office.

Of far more significance than whether the Intelligence Branch was administratively subordinated to the AG or QMG was the fact that in April 1873 a permanent military intelligence organization had been established at the War Office in London. In the three years following Captain Wilson's appointment as director of the T&S Department in April 1870, Edward Cardwell and other senior War Office officials had been convinced of the need for an intelligence department. Charles Wilson was instrumental in defining this requirement, the functions of the new organization, and its internal structure. There is little doubt that his extraordinary success in injecting new life into the T&S Department in the aftermath of the Franco-Prussian War and in winning the full confidence of the secretary of state for war was a classic case of the right individual being in the right place at the right time. It should not be forgotten, however, that other conditions were present which made the realization of Wilson's plans possible, or at least far more likely. Of these, the most vital was the growth of a climate of reform in the War Office beginning in 1868. Charles Wilson had received powerful support from the man who did much to establish this new atmosphere, Edward Cardwell. Once Sir Henry James and the Ordnance Survey were removed from the T&S Department in 1870, there was little to obstruct Wilson's path. The Franco-Prussian War and the example of the Prussian Great General Staff also played a major role in the establishment of a revived T&S Department and eventually of the Intelligence Branch. To his credit, Capt. Charles William Wilson's memorandum of 30 April 1870 had called attention to the need for change before the war began.

NOTES

1. The Mahdi's forces were the same Arab army which had already annihilated some 10,000 Egyptians under Hicks Pasha at Kashgil in November 1883 and 3,500 Egyptians and black Sudanese at El Teb in February 1884.

2. Typical among contemporary accounts of the Nile Expedition of 1884-85 were Alex Mac-Donald's *Too Late for Gordon and Khartoum* (London: John Murray, 1887) and A.B. Wylde's *'83 to '87 in the Sudan*, 2 (London: Remington & Co., 1888). A sympathetic view of Col. Charles Wilson's role in the campaign is presented in chapters 14, 15, and 16 of Sir Charles M. Watson's *The Life of Major-General Sir Charles William Wilson*. Wilson tells his own story without apologies in *From Korti to Khartoum* (London: William Blackwood & Sons, 1886). Lord Wolseley felt at the time that Gladstone alone was to blame. See Adrian Preston, *In Relief of Gordon*. The continuing fascination with the life and death of "Chinese" Gordon is reflected by Charles G. Trench's *The Road to Khartoum: A Life of General Charles Gordon* (New York, 1978).

3. In 1872, Wilson was elected a member of the Council of the Royal Geographical Society and in 1874, a Fellow of the Royal Society. He also served as Member of Council of the Biblical Archaeological Society. Col. R.H. Vetch, "Wilson, Sir Charles William," *Dictionary of National Biography, Twentieth Century, 1901-1911*, (henceforth the title will be abbreviated by *D.N.B.*) pp. 687-89. See also Watson, *Wilson*, pp. 84-85.

4. Watson, *Wilson*, pp. 1-9.

5. Ibid., chapter 2, "The North American Boundary Commission," pp. 13-40.

6. Ibid., p. v.

7. Later in his career Charles Wilson was appointed by the Foreign Office to several important and politically sensitive missions: British representative on the Servian Boundary Commission (1878), Military consul general in Anatolia (1879-82), and special assistant to Sir Edward Malet, the consul general in Egypt (1882-83). Watson, *Wilson*, p. iv; Vetch, "Wilson," *D.N.B.*, p. 668.

8. Watson, *Wilson*, p. 73.

9. Parritt, *The Intelligencers*, pp. 91-94. See also Watson, *Wilson*, p. 77, and Isaac, "History of the Directorate of M.I.," p. 4.

10. Collen, *Report on the Intelligence Branch, Quarter-Master-General's Department, Horse Guards* (London, 1878), p. 4. Henceforth this will be referred to as Collen, *Report*. See also Watson, *Wilson*, pp. 77-78.

11. The Northbrook Committee (or the Committee on the Topographical Department) was imposing in its composition. It included not only Lord Northbrook (Thomas George Baring), soon to become the governor general of India and later first lord of the Admiralty, but also Gen. Sir Richard Airey, adjutant general, and Sir F. Chapman, inspector general of fortifications. Collen, *Report*, p. 5.

12. Parritt, *The Intelligencers*, p. 98.

13. Michael Howard, *The Franco-Prussian War*, pp. 44-47, 70, 73, 79, 85-86. On the strategic level, "the French nation and army as a whole was slow to appreciate the full implications of the threat which Moltke's preparations held for them ..." (p. 44). When the war began and the French and German armies were preparing for the opening battles, French commanders had no

maps except of Germany (p. 70), and tactical intelligence about the dispositions and strength of the German army "was very incomplete, as was only to be expected in view of the total absence of any organization for the collection of information" (p. 79). For news about the enemy, French troops near Saarbrücken in early August 1870 "were dependent upon civilian information and latrine rumour" (p. 86).

14. Stoffel's reports from Berlin were exceptional; when published in 1871 "they greatly contributed to the creditability and prestige of the military attaché." Vagts, *The Military Attaché, pp. 133-35. See also Lieutenant Colonel Baron Stoffel, Rapports militaires écrits de Berlin, 1866-1870*, 3d ed. (Paris: Garnier Frères, 1871), and Michael Howard, *The Franco-Prussian War,* pp. 44-45.

15. The letter is quoted in Watson's biography of Charles Wilson. The author identifies it only as "a letter which he wrote to a friend" soon after Cardwell's authority had been granted in January 1871 for the reorganization of the T&S Department. Watson, *Wilson,* pp. 79-81.

16. Recommendations contained in Charles Wilson's memorandum on the condition of the T&S Department are printed verbatim in Parritt, *The Intelligencers,* pp. 97-98. See also Collen, *Report,* p. 4; Isaac, "History of the Directorate of M.I.," p. 6; and Frith, "The Topographical Section," p. 17.

17. Charles W. Wilson, "Memorandum on the Topographical Department, the Library, Army Statistics, &c," War Office, London, 30 April 1870.

18. Ibid.

19. Ibid.

20. Ibid.; also Collen, *Report,* p. 4.

21. Evelyn Baring left the T&S Department in 1872 for India, where he served as private secretary to Lord Northbrook, the new viceroy (and Baring's cousin). From 1883, when he was appointed British agent and consul general, until 1907, Baring was virtually the ruler of Egypt. He was created the first Earl of Cromer in 1901.

22. Wilson, "Memorandum on the Topographical Department," 30 April 1870.

23. Ibid.

24. Ibid.

25. Collen, *Report,* p. 5; Isaac, "History of the Directorate of M.I.," p. 5.

26. Capt. Charles W. Wilson, letter written to "a friend" in early 1871 and reprinted in part in Watson, *Wilson,* pp. 79-81.

27. Ibid.

28. Collen, *Report,* p. 5.

29. Actually, the total number of personnel working at the T&S Department declined in the wake of the Northbrook Committee's report. Whereas twenty men were assigned to the Department in April 1870, by late 1872 there were only twelve (five officers, one military clerk and six civilians). Civilian strength had been cut by thirteen. The addition of three officers, however, enabled Wilson, the director, to put officers (deputy assistant quartermaster generals) in charge of the three statistical subsections and still have one available to work full-time on topographical matters. Isaac, "History of the Directorate of M.I.," p. 5.

30. Collen, *Report,* p. 6.

31. Ibid.

32. Ibid.; Parritt, *The Intelligencers,* pp. 99-100.

33. Collen, *Report,* p. 6.

34. W.S. Hamer has chosen to ignore the strategic planning responsibility of the early Intelligence Branch: "The Intelligence Department was simply a depository of facts for those who cared to have them, but as for any concern for drawing up plans of operations or for imperial defence in a wider perspective there was none." *The British Army,* p. 59. In contrast, Brian Bond viewed the T&S Department and the Intelligence Branch beginning in 1873 as steps toward a future general staff. *The Victorian Army and the Staff College, 1854-1914,* pp. 120-21.

35. Isaac, "History of the Directorate of M.I.," p. 6.

36. Parritt, *The Intelligencers,* pp. 17-18.

37. Michael Glover, *Wellington's Army in the Peninsula 1808-1814,* pp. 136-37.

38. Ibid., pp. 138-41; Parritt, *The Intelligencers*, pp. 44-53. See also S.G.P. Ward, *Wellington's Headquarters*, pp. 108-13, 119-21.

39. Bond, *Staff College*, p. 120.

40. Watson, *Wilson*, p. 83.

Chapter IV

Under the Shadow of a Bear: The Rise and Fall of the Intelligence Branch, 1873-1885

We of the Game are beyond protection. If we die, we die. Our names are blotted from the book. . . . When every one is dead the Great Game is finished. Not before. . . . Here were the emissaries of the dread Power of the North, . . . suddenly smitten helpless.

Rudyard Kipling,
Kim, 1901

During the 1870s, under Maj. Gen. Sir Patrick MacDougall and his able deputies, Maj. Charles Wilson (1873-76) and Lt. Col. Robert Home (1876-79), the Intelligence Branch rose from relative obscurity to a position of real importance within the War Office. To be sure, even when MacDougall departed for a new assignment in Canada in 1878, it was a long way from becoming a Great General Staff like the one in Berlin, but it was the only military staff element in London which had both defense and intelligence planning responsibilities. Though some will challenge the claim by Brian Parritt that the Intelligence Branch in this era "suddenly emerged as the most important department within the War Office,"[1] the mounting prestige of the Branch during General MacDougall's five years at the helm cannot be denied.

The secretary of state for war's decision to appoint a general officer to head the Intelligence Branch in 1873 was certain to draw attention to the new organization in army circles. Edward Cardwell's choice of Patrick Leonard MacDougall to fill the new post, however, assured the Branch of more than a fleeting moment of publicity. Sir Patrick was at the time one of the most respected and influential major generals in the British Army. The professional career of this quiet, industrious Scotsman had not been spectacular in terms of battlefield heroics and wartime field commands. Instead, he had made his mark as an administrator and a military intellectual.

Major General MacDougall had already completed thirty-seven years of military service in 1873 when, at age fifty-three, he was named deputy adjutant general for intelligence. As one of the earliest contributors among a group of British military writers labeled "a new army school" by Field Marshal Lord Wolseley, MacDougall played a vital role in bringing about an intellectual awakening in the post-Crimean War army. As Jay Luvaas has written, "Contemporaries recognized MacDougall as one of the most influential of the new school but history, unfortunately, has somehow allowed him to slip quietly out of sight."[2] His first important work, *The Theory of War* (London, 1856), was widely read by army officers in Britain and on the Continent and remained the basic text in the British Army for a decade. Besides serving as the first head of the Intelligence Branch, Patrick MacDougall had also been the first commandant of the Staff College at Camberley (1857-61). Before the end of the American Civil War he produced a remarkable book, *Modern Warfare as Influenced by Modern Artillery* (London, 1864), which illuminated many of the lessons of that war, most notably the advantage given the defense by breech-loaders and rifled artillery.[3] In the aftermath of the Franco-Prussian War during the early 1870s, MacDougall joined Wolseley in warning the British officer corps against importing the Prussian military system and tactics. His major contribution to the Cardwell reforms, the plan for the Localization Act of 1873, established the basis of the army's recruiting system in territorial areas or districts. General MacDougall's experience as adjutant general of the Canadian Militia (1865-69) was reflected by the heart of the Localization Act, wherein line regiments were linked with militia regiments to insure a ready reserve for the regular army. When Cardwell appointed Sir Patrick the head of the new Intelligence Branch in 1873, it was in part a reward for his work on the localization plan.[4]

For Charles Wilson—the individual most responsible for the creation of a permanent military intelligence organization at the War Office—the arrival of a prominent general officer to direct it was, in one sense, the culmination of four years of effort which had begun with his assignment to the Topographical and Statistical Department in 1869. Nevertheless, Wilson had understandably mixed emotions about having to give up the directorship of the T&S Department, a unique and powerful post for an army captain and one which he had thoroughly enjoyed. Any misgivings Wilson had were short-lived, however. An unselfish and dedicated man, he quickly realized that Major General MacDougall would be able to accomplish a great deal for War Office Intelligence by virtue of his seniority, reputation, and ability. For his part, Sir Patrick retained Wilson for three more years as his deputy and, far from pushing him into the background, made good use of his talents and experience.

MacDougall's professional stature and his ability to get along with men as philosophically distant as Lord Wolseley and the Duke of Cambridge gave the new organization instant prestige and enabled him to move ahead more rapidly than would have been possible for most of his contemporaries. Sir Patrick's retention of Charles Wilson as his right-hand man was a major step toward the achievement of his initial goal: to assemble a first-rate staff at the Intelligence Branch. To insure the assignment of quality officers to key positions at the Branch, MacDougall insisted from the first that only Staff College graduates be appointed to permanent posts. He was also determined to increase the number of officers working at the Branch by having young officers (captains or subalterns) attached temporarily to each of the sections. The first two "attached officers," Maj. Charles B. Brackenbury and Capt. H.M. Hozier, were assigned to the Branch for temporary duty in August 1873. By the end of 1875 this practice was well established and ten such officers were augmenting the permanent staff.[5] The hand of Sir Patrick MacDougall was also apparent in the move of the Intelligence Branch, less than one year after its birth, to a new location. In January 1874, the deputy adjutant general (DAG) for intelligence and his entire staff vacated their old offices in Spring Gardens[6] and moved to the more spacious accommodations of Adair House in Saint James Square. This new home for the Branch "had the advantage of being in close proximity to the office of the Commander-in-Chief and Head-quarter Staff" at the Horse Guards and, compared to the old site in Spring Gardens, was also much nearer the War Office on Pall Mall.[7]

The physical relocation of the Intelligence Branch was more than a symbolic gesture. Under the leadership of Sir Patrick MacDougall, the young-est branch of the War Office experienced remarkable growth in the first five years of its existence. By the time Sir Patrick left Adair House in the spring of 1878 and returned to Canada as commander-in-chief of the forces in British North America, the Intelligence Branch of the Quartermaster General's Department was firmly established as an integral, essential part of the War Office. MacDougall's successor, Maj. Gen. Sir Archibald Alison, was not as well suited for the demanding post he assumed on 1 May 1878. In the long run, the change at the top resulted in a decline in both the productivity and efficiency of the Branch, but this was not evident until the latter half of Alison's tenure (1882-85), when he remained continuously away from Lon-don. For several years after MacDougall's departure the fine staff that had been assembled and the lofty reputation earned by the Branch over the preceding five years enabled Alison and his subordinates to carry on their work in much the same fashion as it had been accomplished under Sir Patrick.

Although the individual contributions of MacDougall to the early devel-opment of the Intelligence Branch were extremely important, he had a good deal of help from Charles Wilson, Robert Home, and many others. Then, too, there were many events beyond the control of MacDougall (and Alison) which affected the development of War Office Intelligence between 1873 and the end of 1885. Just as the transformation of the T&S Department in the 1870-73 period was related to various military and diplomatic events, as well as to certain developments within the British Empire, so an analysis of the Intelligence Branch over the thirteen years that followed would be incom-plete without some reference to the major problems of British foreign and colonial affairs.

Great Britain did not fight a war against another European power between the Crimean War and 1914, but her soldiers saw frequent action in campaigns, expeditions, and small wars throughout the second half of the nineteenth century. The period 1873-85 was an unusually busy one for the British Army and the British-led armies of India and Egypt.[8] Although the campaigns in Egypt and the Sudan in the early 1880s had a direct impact on the Intelligence Branch, the war whose repercussions were felt most keenly not only at the Branch, but by the entire nation as well, was one in which Britain was not a belligerent.

The Russo-Turkish War of 1877-78, culminating in a Turkish defeat and the Treaty of San Stefano (which humiliated the Turks), focused Europe's attention on the "Eastern Question" and very nearly brought Britain to war with Russia. The weakness of Turkey and the impending collapse of the Ottoman Empire loomed more ominous than ever in the aftermath of Russia's decisive victory. It was not only the threat of Russia's gaining control of the Black Sea Straits which worried British policy makers, but also the new potential for Russian interference with Britain's lines of communication to India through Asiatic Turkey and Persia.

The British response to this perceived Russian threat included the formation of a defensive alliance with Turkey[9] and the launching of a vigorous diplomatic campaign on her behalf, which helped bring about the revision of the Treaty of San Stefano at the Congress of Berlin in July 1878. Further, in an effort to bolster Turkey's hold on her remaining Balkan territories, Britain collaborated closely in 1878-79 with the Austro-Hungarian Empire, Russia's arch rival in the Balkans.[10] Simultaneously, military and diplomatic steps were taken by London to strengthen Turkey-in-Asia against the possibility of Russian encroachment.[11] Lastly, Prime Minister Benjamin Disraeli and Foreign Secretary Robert Salisbury decided reform of the native goverment in Egypt offered the best chance for forestalling the partition of the Ottoman Empire in North Africa. The increasing interest Britain took in Egypt and the Suez Canal in the late 1870s, initially in cooperation with France, led to unilateral British military intervention in 1882.[12]

It was not only in the Middle East that British and Russian interests clashed in the 1873-85 period. Of great concern to the War Office and the government of India was the steady expansion of the Russian Empire in Central Asia toward Persia and Afghanistan. The notion of an Anglo-Russian collision in the rugged terrain of Afghanistan was not a new one in the 1870s. Since the early nineteenth century it had been apparent that the two empires might one day meet in this strategic area. As Russia slowly advanced upon Central Asia from the north, Britain approached from India. Russian and British agents intrigued and counterintrigued against one another in Persia and the Caucasus during the 1830s. In 1838 a British officer of the Bombay Horse Artillery, disguised as a horse trader, entered Afghanistan as a spy. When he informed the Indian government that a Persian army, accompanied by Russian advisers, was preparing to besiege the town of Herat in western Afghanistan, the governor general responded by invading the country with Anglo-Indian and Sikh armies. The Afghans were no more persuaded by the

British in 1838 that they were invading the country in order to save Afghanistan from the Persians and Russians than are their descendents today by a
remarkably similar rationale offered by Moscow to defend the massive Russian military intervention which began in 1979 and continues four years later.
The result was the First Afghan War (1839-42), culminating in the slaughter
of the main Anglo-Indian army in January 1842 at the hands of the Afghans
as it was withdrawing from Kabul toward the Indian frontier.[13]

The terrible defeat suffered in Afghanistan in 1842 made a lasting
impression upon the British, but did not calm the fears of the Indian government about the Russian threat. Apprehension concerning the safety of India
was revived by the Crimean War (1854-56). Despite Russia's defeat in that
conflict, her advance into Central Asia continued at a seemingly more rapid
pace following the Peace of Paris (March 1856). In a series of mountain
campaigns between 1857 and 1864, the Russians gained complete control of
the Caucasus. To the east of the Caspian Sea, they moved ever closer to
Afghanistan, annexing Tashkent and Bukhara by 1855, capturing Samarkand
in 1868, and subduing the Uzbek khanate of Khiva in 1873. When the Afghan
ruler, Sher Ali, received a Russian mission to Kabul in July 1878, there was
alarm in Calcutta and London. The viceroy of India, Lord Lytton, tried to send
a mission of his own to Sher Ali. The Afghan rejection of Lytton's mission in
October set the stage for an attack into Afghanistan by the Indian Army. This
time the British did not underestimate their enemy. The decisive defeat of the
Afghans in the Second Afghan War (1878-80) was capped in spectacular
fashion by Maj. Gen. Frederick S. Roberts's famous march from Kabul to
Kandahar. Victory over the Afghans, however, did nothing to remove the
Russian menace to India.[14]

The defeat of the Afghans outside Kandahar on 1 September 1880
completed the conquest of Afghanistan and made Frederick Sleigh Roberts a
popular hero in England. Before the Second Afghan War Roberts had been
virtually unknown outside of India. In the Indian Army, however, he had
earned a reputation as an outstanding officer in the Quartermaster General's
Department. Roberts's meteoric rise in the QMG's Department began with
his service in the Abyssinian Campaign of 1868 and climaxed in 1875 when
he was named quartermaster general of the Indian Army.[15] As QMG from
1875 until the eve of the Second Afghan War in 1878, Roberts's staff
responsibilities to the commander-in-chief of the Indian Army included both
operational planning and intelligence.[16]

At about the time Roberts finished his three years as quartermaster
general, an Intelligence Branch was added to his department. The existence of
such an organization within Indian Army headquarters after 1878 was of
incalculable value to the Branch in London. The Indian Intelligence Branch
could pull together and report on vast quantities of information acquired not
only by the Indian Army units throughout the subcontinent, but also by other
branches of the Indian government, sources to which the Intelligence Branch
in London had at best only indirect access.[17] Although primarily responsible
to the commander-in-chief in India and the government of India, the Intelligence Branch of the QMG's Department in India was able to provide valuable

strategic intelligence about India and India's neighbors to its counterpart in London. The story of its creation, therefore, is an important part of the larger story of the Intelligence Branch at the War Office. It also leads our investigation to the source of the most comprehensive, fascinating contemporary account of the Intelligence Branch in London in the 1870s.

The problem that overshadowed all others during the three years that Roberts was the QMG in India was, of course, the Russian advance toward Afghanistan. In 1875 Roberts prepared a paper for Lord Napier, the commander-in-chief in India, in which he discussed "arrangements that would be necessary" if Russia continued her expansion south of the Oxus River.[18] As Roberts saw it, the British had to find some way to discourage the Russians, and, at the same time, to prepare to oppose them with military force if they actually moved into Afghanistan. In attempting to formulate realistic plans, General Roberts and the government of India were frustrated by what he described as "the impossibility of obtaining accurate information of what was going on in and beyond Afghanistan."[19] In 1875, just as in the 1980s, thorough and meaningful military planning required reliable intelligence.

Until 1878 the Quartermaster General's Department in India had been responsible for collecting and producing military intelligence but had no Intelligence Branch to assist it. Officers of the QMG's Department were asked from time to time to do intelligence work, but in 1876, according to Frederick Roberts,

> During a long interval of comparative tranquility, this most important portion of the work of the Department was more or less neglected, until eventually it was lost sight of altogether.[20]

Actually, Roberts had noticed this failing several years earlier while serving as acting QMG. In October 1874, Colonel Roberts selected two officers from among the candidates for jobs in his department and assigned them intelligence duties "compiling 'routes' within and beyond the frontier."[21] He also established a "valuable reference library at the Headquarters Office" and claimed in the fall of 1876, "Of late years, much has been done to improve matters."[22]

Despite General Roberts's interest in intelligence and the steps he took to increase the intelligence production of the QMG's Department, there was still no Intelligence Branch in India in early 1876, more than two years after his appointment as the quartermaster general. The difficulty of obtaining reliable information regarding Russian strength, intentions, and activities in Central Asia during 1875 and 1876 had indicated the need for a better system of gathering and processing military intelligence. The Political Service, India's diplomatic service, was primarily interested in political intelligence. But it was also a valuable source of military information, both in the "native states" of India and in areas ranging from Arabia and Persia in the west to Malaya and the Dutch East Indies in the east. Like the Foreign Office in Whitehall, however, the Foreign Department of India could not be relied upon to collate, analyze, and report on the military intelligence which flowed to it from agents of the Political Service. Understandably, therefore, Roberts

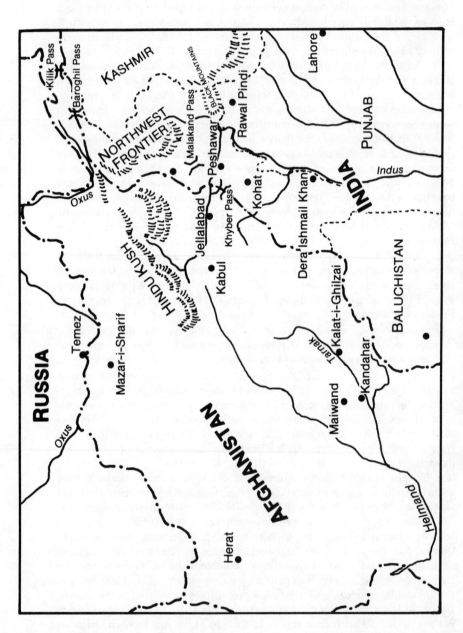

The Northwest Frontier, 1870–1880

was receptive to a thoughtful proposal which crossed his desk in the summer of 1876 for improving the military intelligence system in India.

Capt. Edwin H.H. Collen,[23] newly appointed as assistant military secretary to the government of India, submitted a memorandum in June 1876, recommending the formation of an Intelligence Branch in the Quartermaster General's Department after the model of the one in London. In twelve pages, Collen explained why India needed an Intelligence Branch and proceeded to discuss his proposals for its organization, its internal division of labor, its relations with other departments of the Indian government and to the Intelligence Branch at the War Office, and its estimated cost.[24] Sir Frederick Haines, the new commander-in-chief in India, generally agreed with Collen's ideas, but left their implementation to his quartermaster general. Roberts's response to Collen's memorandum revealed his concurrence with Collen about the need for an Intelligence Branch.[25] Both Roberts and Haines wanted more information about the Intelligence Branch in London, however, so Captain Collen was allowed to take an extended leave to London to study the Branch and make a detailed report on it.

For an entire year, Collen was attached to the Intelligence Branch in the War Office. In order to document the potential benefits of an Intelligence Branch to India and to provide a model for authorities in the Indian Army to emulate, Collen assembled a lengthy report (113 pages, excluding appendices) in which he described the history, organization, and functioning of the Intelligence Branch. Captain Collen completed his year in the Branch and his report in October 1878. At the outset of the report, he summed up his findings in three conclusions:

> (1) [A] great benefit . . . will be conferred in India by the permanent establishment of an Intelligence Department on the basis of that established at home, adapted to Indian requirements
>
> (2) A line should, as far as practicable, be drawn between the work of each department concerning Eastern Countries.
>
> (3) The two departments should work together for the common good and in the closest intercourse attainable.[26]

The establishment of the Indian Intelligence Branch in 1878 owed a great deal to Edwin Collen's initiative and determination. Both his memorandum of June 1876 and the report of 1878 were instrumental in the decisions which led to the creation of a new branch of the QMG's Department in India. *The Report on the Intelligence Branch, Quarter-Master-General's Department, Horse Guards* by Capt. E.H.H. Collen is, from the historian's point of view, however, more than a justification and blueprint for an Intelligence Branch in India. It offers a detailed and invaluable inside view of the Intelligence Branch at the War Office during the late 1870s.

The text of Captain Collen's report of October 1878 is divided into two parts. The shorter, part 2, consists of memoranda which address relations between the proposed Indian Intelligence Branch and the Intelligence Branch in London.[27] The past and present of the Intelligence Branch at the War Office are discussed in part 1, which includes an introductory memorandum and nine chapters. Only the first chapter, "History of the Intelligence

Department," is devoted to the past. Of the remaining eight chapters, the first is a short but important chapter entitled "Organization;" the other seven discuss the work of each section of the Intelligence Branch. In the second half of the historical chapter, Collen traces the steady expansion of the Branch during the five years from its establishment in 1873 to 1878. Then, he presents a clear picture of the structure of the Branch in 1878 in his chapter on organization.

Throughout its first two years, the Intelligence Branch had five sections. The Topographical Section, a carry-over from the T&S Department, was under the direct supervision of Maj. Charles Wilson. As General MacDougall's deputy, Wilson was also charged with overseeing the other four sections of the Branch: the three foreign sections (Sections A, C, and D), formerly subsections of the Statistical Section; and a new addition, the Home and Colonial Section (Section B). A fourth foreign section (Section E) was added in April 1875, in accord with a proposal advanced by Wilson for the enlargement of the Branch. In the fall of 1877, after Wilson's departure, the Topographical Section was redesignated Section F, and a new section, the Central Section, was organized to provide administrative support for the six lettered sections.[28]

The expansion of the Intelligence Branch by the addition of two sections was more than matched by an increase in the size of the staff during this period. The total number of men (military and civilian) working at the Branch rose from twenty-seven to forty-one between April 1873 and August 1878. Most of this increase was due to General MacDougall's success at having officers attached to the sections for short stints, as previously mentioned. While only one permanent officer was added, which raised the number of officers on long tours at Adair House from seven to eight, there were twelve attached officers by August 1878.[29] Prior to 1876, the typical attached officer was a recent Staff College graduate who served three to six months of temporary duty before going off to a field assignment. So indispensable did these additional officers become, however, that in March 1876 the commander-in-chief (the Duke of Cambridge) approved MacDougall's recommendation that they be attached for a minimum of one year.[30]

Six of the eight permanent officers of the Intelligence Branch in 1878 were classified as deputy assistant quartermaster generals (DAQMGs). These six men, who ranged in rank from captain to lieutenant colonel, were the heads of Sections A through F. Above them in the hierarchy were the other two permanent officers: the official head of the Branch, the deputy quartermaster general (DQMG), Intelligence Branch, and the officer who actually supervised the six sections on a daily basis, the assistant quartermaster general (AQMG), Intelligence Branch. Below the DAQMGs, in every section save Section F, were from one to three attached officers. Sections A through F had one noncommissioned officer apiece; the Central Section had five, including two sergeants major. All ten civilians of the Intelligence Branch worked in Section F (Topographical): two in the library, five in the map room and drawing office, and three in the lithography room.[31]

As the overall head of the Intelligence Branch and its only general officer, the DQMG exerted a powerful influence on the organization. Ultimately, of course, he bore final responsibility for its performance and for the reliability of the reports which it produced on a wide range of subjects. As Collen pointed out, however, "The Deputy Quartermaster-General has no executive duties." His major function was not to manage the routine work of the seven sections but to provide advice to the commander-in-chief of the British Army "on all strategical questions, and on subjects connected with the defence of the Empire, and those generally dealt within the Intelligence Branch." He was expected "to take the personal and immediate direction . . . of work connected with the home and colonial defence."[32] If he watched the work of any section closely, it was more than likely Section B, whose function was to collect and record "information about the British colonies, their strength for offence and defence, and their military positions generally. . . ."[33] Although it was always prudent for the DQMG to stay in touch with the four foreign sections and Section F (topographic matters, library, etc.), they were normally the province of the assistant quartermaster general (AQMG).

As the DQMG's deputy, the AQMG was, in effect, the executive officer of the Branch; he was also head of Central Section, the nerve center of the Intelligence Branch.[34] The AQMG was charged with the "general supervision of Sections A to F, and the direction of work." Significantly, his duties included "communication by minutes with other branches of the War Office, and correspondence with outside departments." A report produced by one of the sections which was needed outside the Branch had to receive his approval before going to the DQMG for final review, signature, and dispatch. When the Branch was directed by higher authority to furnish information about a subject which involved more than one of its sections, the AQMG gathered the pertinent information from the concerned sections and put the report together, sometimes with the assistance of the attached officers of the Central Section.[35]

The time-consuming involvement of the head of the Intelligence Branch in the performance of his principal duties as advisor to the commander-in-chief for strategic planning and the defense of the British Empire left the direction of the foreign intelligence work of the Branch essentially in the hands of the AQMG. The DAQMGs who ran the foreign sections looked to the AQMG for guidance and approval. Furthermore, Captain Collen described the AQMG as

> the medium through which information is collected by, or received from, officers and others travelling in foreign countries. Officers sent from the Intelligence Branch to report on foreign countries are instructed by him . . . as to the points about which it is desired to procure information.[36]

Probably the most critical function of the AQMG in the area of intelligence collection was to screen all incoming documents, except newspapers, books, and maps; and to determine which ones contained information of value to particular sections of the Branch. Besides reports from officers and private citizens traveling abroad, there was a continual flow of material from a variety of other sources—military and naval attachés, foreign governments, other departments of the British government, and other branches of the War Office.

The AQMG enjoyed a unique vantage point inside the Intelligence Branch by virtue of his role in monitoring all incoming and outgoing official correspondence. This gave him considerable power in the organization and direct control over two of the three phases of the intelligence cycle—collection and dissemination/reporting. The four foreign sections[37] were also involved in these two phases, but they received only that information which was judged by the AQMG to be of value to them. The reports and other documents they produced left the Branch only after having passed inspection by the AQMG. Similarly, the questions they wished to ask other departments or individuals (military attachés, for example) could be cut off, modified, or expanded by the Branch's second in command.

The task of processing was performed almost entirely within the four foreign sections. It was here that the DAQMGs and their assistants recorded, collated, and evaluated or analyzed intelligence from all sources in order to produce reports and to maintain up-to-date files about the armed forces and military capabilities of foreign countries. In this important middle phase of the Branch's foreign intelligence effort, the Central Section (and its head, the AQMG) played an indirect and relatively unimportant role compared to Sections A, C, D, and E. The individuals with the most knowledge about foreign armies were the chiefs of the foreign sections. For example, if a query reached the AQMG about some aspect of the German Army, he would normally pass it on to the chief of Section C. How did the foreign sections actually work? Collen's report permits us to answer this question in part.

If judged by a comparison of assigned geographical responsibilities of the foreign sections in 1878, Section A had the lightest workload. While each of the other three sections had at least eight geographical areas (countries or continents) to oversee, Section A had only France and her colonies and Belgium. This was partly a reflection of the centuries of enmity between Britain and France, their cooperation in the Crimean War and more recently in Egypt notwithstanding. It was also due to the considerable respect most British officers still had for the French Army, despite its tarnished reputation following the defeat of 1870-71. Since the steam engine had "bridged the Channel" and sparked the invasion scares of the 1840s to 1860s, the French Army was again considered capable of planning and launching a sudden invasion, perhaps in reaction to some colonial or Mediterranean quarrel. France was, after all, both physically and culturally the closest of the great powers. Section A was also saddled with the task of "Military History and Records of British Campaigns and Expeditions."[38]

Captain Collen found, "every kind of information about the French Army and Navy is received and classified" by Section A. This information was obtained from French official sources, newspapers, periodicals, books, "the military attaché and other sources, through the Foreign Office," and "by personal visit of the Chief of the Section, or other officers, sent officially or going privately." In fact, the chief of Section A, Maj. C.J. East, had recently returned from a tour of Algeria. His report included new information on the French Army in Algeria, on the roads and railways, on the coast line and coastal towns, and even on officers' clubs. Although Collen did not say whether Major East traveled incognito in Algeria, a concern for secrecy in the Intelligence Branch is evident in his comment that in Section A "much information is obtained and recorded which cannot be made public."[39] This may have been necessary to protect secret sources or to keep the French from learning just how much the British knew about them.

In 1878 Russia, rather than France, was viewed as Britain's most dangerous and likely adversary. Russia headed the list of areas for which Section D was responsible, and Collen leaves little doubt that Russia was top priority for the section and its chief, Capt. Francis C.H. Clarke.

> The object in Section D is to collect every item of information about the Russian Army, the coast defences of Russia, railways, etc., and to place these items in an accessible shape. . . . We find in Section D information on the movements and preparations for war, general reports on the Russian Army, visits of individual officers; information about the arsenals and manufacturing establishments and the reorganization of the artillery depots; . . . cavalry; railways, with information about the rolling stock, etc., distribution of the army and garrisons, reports on works and armaments of Russian fortresses, on camps and manoeuvres, mobilization, the changes in the organization of the army, recruiting.[40]

Section D's sources of information were basically the same as those of Section A, except that it relied more heavily on the Foreign and India Offices. Considerable information was extracted from "Russian papers" translated by Captain Clarke. The reports of military attachés and other officers "furnished much information on Russia and the Russian Army generally, and on the Russo-Turkish War." Clarke himself made visits to Russia to collect information.[41]

India, Persia, Central Asia, China, and Japan were also on the list of countries assigned to Section D. Although the Indian Army was still without its own intelligence branch in the summer of 1878, Captain Collen observed that the War Office Intelligence Branch was not attempting to collect information inside India on its own. Practically all of the intelligence about India reached the War Office and the Branch via the India Office, which also furnished valuable information on Persia, China, and Russian activities in Central Asia. A great deal of what Section D learned about China and Japan came, interestingly, from translated Russian publications.[42] Dependence on foreign sources was a risky business, but limited resources, language barriers, and the inaccessibility of certain remote or hostile areas to British officers made this dependence necessary for various parts of the world. Despite the considerable efforts of Section D to collect information on Russia from British sources, the most comprehensive published work it possessed in 1878 about the Russian Army was the translation of an 1873 Austrian publication, the "Armed Strength of Russia."[43] Language barriers and the relative scarcity of normal tourist, educational, and even commercial contacts, clearly played their part in the comparative paucity of military intelligence. Britain's St. Petersburg or Moscow sources found that many Russians were equally lacking in information on Russia in Asia. In 1875-76, the American delegation, which eventually produced Emory Upton's *The Armies of Asia and Europe*, apparently got much of its information on Asiatic Russia while in India on its way to Constantinople, Sebastopol, and Moscow.

Back in 1871, Charles Wilson had argued that one of the primary purposes of the T&S Department ought to have been the production of reliable and detailed accounts of foreign armies that could be furnished to officers in the field in times of war. Unsatisfied with the progress he was able to make in this direction prior to April 1873, Wilson continued his campaign within the newly formed Intelligence Branch. To this end, he advised General MacDougall in April 1875 it was essential for officers of the Branch "to compile for publication a complete and accurate account of the strength, organization, tactics, etc., of each foreign army."[44] The task was still far from completed in 1878, but much progress had been made. In 1875 and 1876 the Intelligence Branch produced its own accounts of the armed forces of Austria, Denmark, the German Empire, Sweden, and Norway. In 1877 similar works were completed on France and the Ottoman Empire.[45] So impressed was Captain Collen by the "Armed Strength of France" that he called attention to it as a work of "great research," which "should be referred to and studied as an example of the arduous collection and elaboration of information. . . ."[46]

As important as the publications on the armed forces of France and Turkey may have been, they represented only a small portion of the work of the Intelligence Branch in 1877. Special reports were assembled by the foreign sections on various areas, ranging from the North German coast to the Euphrates River Valley.[47] Section F was busily engaged in compiling maps of Bulgaria, Roumelia, Turkish Armenia, the Trans-Caucasus, and Egypt, and in revising the catalog of the War Office Library. Operational work was continued; "the mobilization scheme was maintained, and details for putting an expeditionary army in the field" were resolved.[48] Nor were historical endeavors neglected. Capt. Francis Clarke was engaged in a continuing project to translate the official German account of the Franco-Prussian War. Of even more interest, in 1877, were "the history of the Russian advances in Asia" between 1872 and 1876, and the journal of the ongoing Russo-Turkish War, both of which were prepared in Section D.[49] In all, the Intelligence Branch, by 1878, was involved in so many and important activities that it is not surprising that it was increasingly recognized as a vital element within the War Office.

Except for the absence of a "Railway Section," the internal structure of the Intelligence Branch of the late 1870s was quite similar to that of Germany's Great General Staff. The four foreign sections and Section B (British colonies) were comparable in their functions to the "Three Sections" of the Great General Staff: the Central Section to "Central Bureau" and the "Intelligence Office;" Section F to the "Geographical Statistical Section," "Topographical Section," and "Map Room;" and a part of Section A to the "Section for Military History." This organizational similarity was of little consolation, however, to Maj. Charles B. Brackenbury. An artillery officer who served as a section chief (with the rank of DAQMG) at the Branch in 1875 and 1876,[50] Major Brackenbury delivered a lecture to the Royal United Services Institution in 1875 in which he compared the British Intelligence Branch with the capital staffs of Germany, Austria, and France. Although there were only seven permanent officers at the Intelligence Branch, there were between sixty and seventy permanent officers on the general staffs in Berlin, Vienna, and Paris.[51] Like many statistical comparisons, however, this was somewhat specious because of the detailed railway planning and other planning required by the three great continental powers.

It was not only the great disparity in the size of the staffs that worried Brackenbury. He also expressed concern about various advantages which the three continental powers had in the area of foreign intelligence. The military attachés of Germany, Austria, and France reported directly to the minister of war or the chief of the general staff. Thus, their reports were received far more quickly than in the British system, in which attaché reports went first to the Foreign Office, "and thence through many hands before they reach the Intelligence Branch." The Second Bureau of the French General Staff, responsible for reporting on foreign armies and navies, employed twenty-four permanent officers, over three times as many as did the Intelligence Branch. Yet, the French General Staff found this number to be "insufficient." The Intelligence Office of the German General Staff worked in close coordination with the "Three Sections" on matters of foreign military intelligence and received "a considerable amount of secret intelligence even during peace." In the Austro-Hungarian Empire, "all Government Departments receiving intelligence which bears on the military strength or resources of other nations" were "bound to send it at once to the Minister of War for the use of the Staff."[52]

Although he provided no figures, Major Brackenbury indicated that Germany, Austria, and France were all spending a great deal more on their general staffs and on the associated military intelligence work than Britain spent on her Intelligence Department. This seemed to Brackenbury a shortsighted policy for Britain to have in an age when the machinery of war grew ever more complex, and the means available for transmitting information obtained overseas back to the War Office were constantly improving. Then, too, Britain was responsible for the defense of a far greater amount of territory and many more people, if the entire British Empire was considered, than were Germany, Austria, or France (including her colonies). Concluding his case for the upgrading and enlargement of the Intelligence Branch, Major Brackenbury expressed the view that Parliament would not balk at providing the Army

> the trifling sum necessary to keep us informed of the position in which
> we stand and of the means necessary to keep us secure. It would be as if a
> rich man of indifferent eyesight, knowing that he would shortly be
> placed in the presence of savage animals, should grudge the money to buy
> a pair of spectacles.[53]

The Duke of Cambridge, in response, remarked on "the very able manner in which Major Brackenbury has brought this subject to our notice . . . ," but reminded the audience of how difficult it was to convince others of the need to increase the estimates so that the "General Staff of the Army" could be expanded.[54]

As small and inadequately funded as the Intelligence Branch may have seemed, its existence was of great significance in the 1870s, for it was filling voids not only in the War Office and the British Army, but also within the entire government. In one fashion or other, at least in times of war with other European powers, strategic military intelligence had been collected and disseminated at the national level in Great Britain before 1871. Until Charles Wilson's reorganization of the T&S Department and the subsequent creation of the Intelligence Branch in 1873, however, no office or agency had existed anywhere in the government to process the information received and to arrange it in a form useful to the commander-in-chief of the army, the secretary of state for war, other members of the cabinet, or army officers in the field. Outside the War Office, two departments which might have been expected to share some of the responsibility for processing strategic intelligence were the Foreign Office and the Admiralty.

The foreign secretary controlled two potentially valuable assets for the collection of military and naval intelligence overseas: the Secret Intelligence Service and the military and naval attachés. The former, in the 1870s (and throughout most of the nineteenth century), was preoccupied with Ireland and provided little information on military affairs in Europe or anywhere else.[55]

However, as a group, the attachés were a tremendously important source. Military and naval attachés' reports were first reviewed by ambassadors, and, once approved, sent by telegraph or diplomatic pouch to the Foreign Office.

The Foreign Office's organization appeared to be well suited to the task of processing incoming dispatches. Its internal structure was not unlike that of the Intelligence Branch. Four of its eight departments in the 1870s and 1880s were political departments; each of these had a geographical area of responsibility.[56] A political department was headed by a senior or principal clerk, who, in turn, was assisted by four to six junior clerks. The typical senior clerk stayed for eight to twelve years as the head of a political department and thereby developed a detailed knowledge of his area.[57] The comparisons are obvious: political departments of the Foreign Office and foreign sections of the Intelligence Branch, senior clerks and DAQMGs, junior clerks and attached officers.

Appearances, however, are often misleading. The conduct of British foreign policy in the final quarter of the nineteenth century was characterized by what one historian has called an "essential amateurishness." Nowhere was this more evident than inside the Foreign Office, where foreign secretaries and their principal assistants delegated little responsibility, and where "the ignoring of expert advice" was the norm.[58] In general, only the top officials— the permanent under secretary and the two or three assistant under secretaries—were allowed to draft important dispatches and to advise the foreign secretary on policy matters. Despite their expertise, "senior clerks were expected only to arrange papers for the under-secretaries and foreign secretary."[59] Although senior clerks heading political departments were responsible for handling routine questions and preparing the "Blue Books"[60] for Parliament, most of the work they did was of a clerical nature: paraphrasing incoming telegrams and dispatches; checking the final drafts of outgoing letters; maintaining the registers in which all dispatches were logged; and insuring communications for the Queen, prime minister, and cabinet were properly distributed. The lot of junior clerks was even less inspiring; their time was spent copying secret dispatches and telegrams, ciphering and deciphering, sorting confidential prints, and preparing dispatch bags for embassies abroad.[61] By comparison, army officers working in the foreign sections of the Intelligence Branch were more involved in intellectual (as opposed to clerical) work and had more time for substantive analysis of information from abroad.

Even if the political departments of the Foreign Office had been permitted to assume a broader range of responsibility in their respective areas, senior clerks possessed neither the military experience nor the technical competence in military and naval matters on which to base evaluations of attaché reports. Above them, top level Foreign Office officials in the policy-making positions were interested primarily in political intelligence and simply could not afford the time to systematically analyze military or naval information. Moreover, there is no reason to believe that the under secretaries were any more knowledgeable of naval and military issues than were the senior clerks.

A shortage of men with the requisite technical knowledge and practical experience for analyzing naval intelligence was not a problem at the Admiralty in the 1870s, nor was it difficult for the Royal Navy to collect vast quantities of intelligence. Besides being a vital element of British power in the nineteenth century, the Royal Navy was an important branch of the country's globe-circling strategic intelligence network, especially for naval and economic intelligence. Until 1882, however, the Admiralty had no intelligence department and consequently did very little with the information about foreign navies and foreign sea commerce which reached Whitehall. Throughout the century, the Admiralty had had a Hydrographic Department to direct the navy's ambitious and widely respected work charting the world's oceans and their shores,[62] but the Hydrographic Department was not responsible for collecting detailed coastal topographical information, much less data on foreign navies.

In May 1881 Capt. John Colomb, a retired Royal Marines officer, attempted to impress on the members of the Royal United Services Institution, "the necessity for establishing an organized and far-reaching system of naval intelligence."[63] As Colomb saw it, the Royal Navy would have two major responsibilities in the next war: to blockade the enemy's ports and to protect Britain's sea commerce. "Systematic, organized naval intelligence," then lacking, would be needed by the navy to perform either one or both missions.

Colomb noted the existence of the Intelligence Branch at the War Office and remarked with a note of sarcasm that the Admiralty was "quite content that one solitary naval Officer should be charged with watching the naval developments and preparations of the whole of Europe." He found it intolerable that the Admiralty was dependent on the War Office "for such topographical information as is necessary for naval operations on an enemy's seaboard."[64] The danger posed to Britain's sea lines of supply by commerce raiders[65] worried Colomb most of all. Overseeing British merchant shipping and foreign ships of war was essential, but it was not enough. The Naval Intelligence Department which he advocated would also find it necessary to monitor continuously the movements of all foreign merchant steamers capable of rapid conversion to auxiliary cruisers. Warned Captain Colomb,

> It is only by the most plodding methodical daily collection and digestion
> of such intelligence during peace, that we shall on the outbreak of war
> avoid surprises by the issuing from unexpected and unobserved quarters
> of cruisers bought at one place, armed and equipped at another, and
> destroying our commerce somewhere else.[66]

At the very least, the Admiralty ought to set up what Colomb called a "Commercial Intelligence Council."[67]

It was easier, of course, for an outsider like John Colomb to criticize the internal structure of the Admiralty than for an insider to change it, particularly when the insider was a mere captain among admirals and lords. But Capt. George Tryon, founder of the Admiralty's Foreign Intelligence Committee, was a naval officer of above average ability and excellent reputation, a man "with views far in advance of his contemporaries."[68] When Tryon was appointed secretary of the Admiralty in early 1882, the first lord of the admiralty was Lord Northbrook, an individual who had been intimately involved a decade before in the reorganization of the T&S Department. Northbrook's support and, to a lesser extent, the outside pressure brought to bear on the Admiralty by John Colomb's 1881 *R.U.S.I.* paper, undoubtedly were important in the fall of 1882 when Captain Tryon established the Foreign Intelligence Committee.[69] Tryon selected Capt. W.H. Hall, Royal Navy, to preside over the committee whose function was described as the collection and organization of information about foreign navies, foreign coastal defenses, and foreign maritime matters in general. In February 1887, over four years after its establishment, the Foreign Intelligence Committee was expanded to include a war planning section and renamed the Naval Intelligence Department.[70] For all but the last several years of the 1873-85 period, then, the Admiralty was no more prepared than the Foreign Office to process strategic naval and economic intelligence.[71]

The standing of the Intelligence Branch within the War Office and the entire government was magnified by the weakness of the Admiralty and the Foreign Office in the areas of military and naval intelligence. The rapid rise of the Branch in the 1870s also owed a great deal to the overall high quality of the officers who served there during these years and to the able direction of their chief, Sir Patrick MacDougall, and his energetic and far-sighted assistants, Charles Wilson and Robert Home. The acquisition and retention of talented younger officers at the Intelligence Branch during the 1870s was quite remarkable at a time when professionalism was not a quality highly valued by many British officers. It was also a tribute to Patrick MacDougall.

The practice of purchase had been abolished in 1871, only two years before the establishment of the Branch, and among the majority of officers social connections and riding ability counted for more than did serious study of the military profession. The establishment of the Staff College at Camberley in 1857 was a significant step in furthering the cause of professionalism, and as Camberley's reputation grew in the 1860s and 1870s, competition increased among officers seeking entrance to the course.[72] Nevertheless, staff duties, especially in London, were anathema to many young officers, including graduates of the Staff College.[73] Fortunately, beginning in 1873, its very first year, and continuing throughout the remainder of the century, the Intelligence Branch was able to fill its permanent positions almost exclusively with officers who had attended the Staff College.[74] A survey of Hart's Annual Army List reveals another indication of the high caliber of officers occupying permanent positions at the Branch during the 1870s and 1880s: a disproportionately high number of engineer and artillery officers were among their ranks.[75] In general, these two smaller, technically oriented arms had long attracted officers more inclined toward the serious study of their profession than had the infantry or cavalry.

Beneath the level of the deputy quartermaster general (Sir Patrick MacDougall), ability and experience were nowhere more essential at the Branch than in the post of assistant quartermaster general, since the individual who filled it was, *de facto*, the chief of foreign intelligence. General MacDougall, during his five-year tenure as director, was served by two outstanding men in the AQMG position, both Royal Engineers. Much already has been said of the first, Maj. Charles Wilson, who left the Branch in March 1876, at the end of seven years in the War Office. Wilson was replaced by an equally brilliant contemporary and fellow "sapper," Lt. Col. Robert Home. Colonel Home's experience in both the T&S Department and the Intelligence Branch went back to 1871, almost as far back as Wilson's. Indeed, the careers of the two men appear to have been taken from the same mold, at least at first glance.[76] Robert Home was still officially the AQMG of the Intelligence Branch at the time of his death in 1879.

Charles Wilson's accomplishments in the T&S Department and its successor, the Intelligence Branch, were due in no small measure to his own vision, determination, and intelligence. It should be noted that Wilson benefitted from an uninterrupted seven consecutive years in those two organizations. This was not the case with his successor, Robert Home, and herein lies a clue to the decline of the Branch after MacDougall's departure in 1878. On three different occasions between 1871 and 1879, Home was away from the War Office and the country for extended periods. His tour of Africa in 1873-74 as Lord Wolseley's commanding Royal Engineer for the Ashanti Expedition did not greatly affect the Branch. The problem was far more serious, however, when Colonel Home was sent to Turkey near the end of 1876 to report on the defense of Constantinople little more than six months after his appointment to the position of AQMG. Home's distinguished service in Turkey during the winter of 1876-77 won him a brevet colonelcy, but his absence left the Intelligence Branch without a general coordinator for foreign intelligence. In September 1877 Colonel Home was off again for eastern Europe, this time as British commissioner for the determination of boundaries in Bulgaria. The effectiveness of the Branch in London also was reduced temporarily by the fact that two experienced and able DAQMGs accompanied Home, Capts. Francis Clarke and John Ardagh. Colonel Home never returned to the Intelligence Branch; he contracted typhoid fever in Bulgaria and returned home to England where he died early in 1879 at the age of forty-one.[77]

Robert Home's prolonged absences from his duties as AQMG in London during his three years in that post had only a slight immediate impact on the efficiency of the Intelligence Branch's foreign intelligence work and no appreciable effect on its reputation for excellence. In fact, the foreign secretary, Lord Salisbury, generously praised the officers of the Branch who had rendered able assistance to the Foreign Office during 1877-78 in Turkey, the Balkans, and at the Congress of Berlin.[78] The missions of Colonel Home in both Turkey and Bulgaria were beneficial not only to the Foreign Office but also to the collection efforts of the Intelligence Branch. Home contributed very little in his capacity as AQMG, however, and his jaunts away from England seem in retrospect to have established an unfortunate precedent that proved far more damaging to the Branch in the early 1880s. The experience of Colonel Home suggested to other officers that service at the Intelligence Branch might increase their chances for rapid promotion, particularly if periodically one could secure an overseas assignment.[79]

Home's successor as AQMG, Col. C.J. East, a former DAQMG and head of Section A, seemed a logical choice for the position. No sooner had East begun to adjust to his new responsibilities, however, than off he went to Zululand in the summer of 1879 as a member of Lord Wolseley's staff. Colonel East returned to London and his duties as AQMG at the end of the Zulu War, late in 1879, and some semblance of calm prevailed for several years, but the worst was yet to come. In July 1882 Maj. Gen. Sir Archibald Alison, the deputy quartermaster general, Intelligence Branch, left England for Egypt and a field command, taking four of the six DAQMGs with him.[80]

Sir Archibald Alison had taken over from Sir Patrick MacDougall as director of the Intelligence Branch in May 1878. Besides the fact that both men were Scots and both had been commandants of the Staff College, Alison and MacDougall were about as different as two major generals in the British Army of their day possibly could have been. Sir Archibald was everything that Sir Patrick was not. MacDougall was "an administrator rather than a man of action, a thoughtful student of war who evidently preferred to work quietly in the shadows."[81] An infantryman, Alison was a dashing and well-decorated field commander who had distinguished himself as a courageous junior officer in the Crimean War, had lost his arm in the second relief of Lucknow during the Indian Mutiny, and had commanded a brigade in some of the heaviest fighting of the Ashanti War.[82] He was without question a superb combat leader but he was not, by temperament or experience, well suited for his appointment as DQMG for intelligence. Unsurprisingly, Sir Archibald Alison was not an outstanding head of the Intelligence Branch. Almost certainly, he was ill at ease in the confines of his War Office staff job and eagerly anticipated just the sort of opportunity that materialized in 1882 when Britain intervened in Egypt. Alison returned to form in Egypt, commanding the leading brigade in the storming of the enemy entrenchments at Tel-el-Kebir and eventually received the thanks of Parliament and a promotion to lieutenant general. After Wolseley's departure General Alison was commander of British forces in Egypt until May 1883. When he returned to England, Sir Archibald did not go back to the Intelligence Branch but instead was given command of the Aldershot Division.[83] The DQMG post was allowed to remain vacant for over three years, until January 1886, when Maj. Gen. Henry Brackenbury arrived.

The sudden departure of Alison in 1882 and the failure of the War Office to name a replacement until 1886 was damaging enough, but the absence of the four majors Alison took with him to Egypt had a disastrous effect on the Intelligence Branch. The responsibility for intelligence production throughout three years of trouble in Egypt and the Sudan fell on the AQMG. Colonel East handled this task as well as possible until his departure in June 1883. His replacement, Col. A.S. Cameron, was a poor choice for the critical second position, particularly with no chief to guide him and at a time when staff officers were continually leaving the War Office for active service. Cameron was a recipient of the Victoria Cross, but apparently he had little inclination for intelligence work. When four of the six DAQMGs were sent to Egypt in 1885 to form an intelligence department for the Suakin Expedition, the productivity of the Intelligence Branch in London sank to an all-time low.[84] Not even another war scare between Britain and Russia in 1885 roused the Branch from its lethargic state.

The loss of MacDougall and Home and the absence from London of many key personnel, including the DQMG, were not the only reasons for the decline of the Intelligence Branch in the early 1880s. Another serious problem for the undermanned organization was one which began to plague the Branch in the late 1870s. Somehow the notion took hold in the War Office that since the Branch had so many officers of ability and had accumulated such detailed knowledge of foreign countries and armies, it ought to be able to make an important contribution to the solution of any problems of organization or administration that arose in the British Army. Thus, between 1875 and 1879 the Branch was required to submit detailed reports on such topics as the "war establishment" of certain units, the "examination of the lines of communication system," fortifications, the "preparations for autumn and summer manoeuvres," and "Rules for the Conduct of War Games."[85] The capability of the Branch to handle such diverse duties, unrelated to foreign intelligence, brought it additional prestige and more work. In the early 1880s the Branch was barely capable of any useful foreign intelligence work. Still, the War Office expected the Branch would continue to respond to demands for information or staff work on virtually any subject, a combination which could only lead to trouble, and eventually, to a loss of influence for the Branch.

NOTES

1. Parritt, *The Intelligencers*, p. 102.

2. Luvaas, *The Education of an Army*, pp. 101-02. Luvaas devotes a chapter to MacDougall, appropriately entitled "The New School." See also Vetch, "MacDougall," *D.N.B. Supplement, 1921-22*, pp. 993-94.

3. Ibid., pp. 110-11.

4. Ibid., pp. 113, 118-21.

5. Watson, *Wilson*, p. 83; Collen, *Report*, p. 7; Luvaas, *Education of an Army*, p. 127.

6. The headquarters of the Topographical and Statistical Department had been situated at 4 New Street, Spring Gardens, since August 1856. The new Intelligence Branch remained there only nine months. Collen, *Report*, p. 7.

7. Watson, *Wilson*, pp. 82-83.

8. The years 1873-85 saw almost continuous campaigning for the British in various corners of the world. Most important were the Ashanti War (1873-74), the Second Afghan War (1878-80), the Zulu War (1878-79), the Transvaal or First South African War (1880-81), the conquest of Egypt (1882), the campaigns in the Sudan (1883-85), and the Third Burmese War (1885).

9. The Anglo-Turkish Convention of 4 June 1878 did not represent an alliance of coequal powers. Under its terms, Britain was granted the right to occupy and administer Cyprus and in return was to assist the Sultan, under certain conditions, in the defense of Turkey-in-Asia against Russia. Christopher Howard, *Britain and the Casus Belli, 1822-1902*, pp. 102-04.

10. The Austrian policy of attempting to reduce Russian influence in Bulgaria in 1878 won favor in the British Foreign Office. Lord Salisbury, the foreign secretary, intervened on behalf of Austria late in 1878 by warning Turkey that it should not encourage local opposition to the Austrian occupation of Bosnia and Herzegovina. The major success of Anglo-Austrian collaboration in 1879 was the Russian evacuation from Bulgaria. No formal alliance ever materialized, however. C.J. Lowe, *The Reluctant Imperialists*, 1: 24-25.

11. To Lord Salisbury, plans for the defense of Turkey-in-Asia were more important than attempts to shore up Turkey-in-Europe. Building up Turkey-in-Asia would do far more to protect British communications with India from Russian encroachment. Ibid., p. 31.

12. Even after Disraeli's purchase of Khedive Ismail's Suez Canal shares in 1875, there was no thought of supplanting the French in Egypt. The turning point came in 1879 when Britain, in collaboration with France, forced the abdication of Ismail in favor of his more pliable son, Tewfik. The outbreak of a nationalistic and military revolt against Tewfik led by Arabi Pasha in 1881-82 provided justification for the naval bombardment of Alexandria (July 1882) and Wolseley's defeat of Arabi Pasha at Tel-el-Kebir (September 1882). Ibid., pp. 38-51.

13. K.W.B. Middleton, *Britain and Russia*, p. 71; Byron Farwell, *Queen Victoria's Little Wars*, pp. 5-11.

14. In 1884 the Russians conquered Merv, the last independent Moslem principality of Central Asia (and in close proximity to Afghanistan). When they clashed with Afghan troops at Pendjeh in March 1885, Britain seemed about to go to war with Russia. The explosive situation was defused to some extent by an Anglo-Russian agreement in September 1885.

15. Roberts went to Abyssinia as assistant quartermaster general of the expeditionary force under Sir Robert Napier. His excellent work in the QMG's Department during an expedition on India's Northwest Frontier in 1871 made him one of the leading figures in the QMG's Department at Indian Army headquarters in Calcutta. In February 1874 Lord Napier (now commander-in-chief of the Indian Army) selected Roberts for the post of QMG. Since this was a major general's billet and Roberts was only a lieutenant colonel, he served as acting QMG until his promotion to colonel in January 1875. Roberts later served as commander-in-chief in India (1885-93). He was promoted to field marshal in 1895.

16. In the Indian Army of the nineteenth century, the quartermaster general was the staff officer responsible for intelligence, strategical plans, and movements. Maj. Gen. Sir George MacMunn, "The Quartermaster-General's Department and the Administrative Services in India from the Mutiny to the Present Time," p. 102.

17. These included the Survey Department, the Foreign Department, and local governments and civil authorities subordinate to the government of India. The Survey Department of India in 1878 had seventy-seven army officers "employed in the Trigonometrical, Topographical, and Revenue Surveys of India" and numerous "native agents" who were potentially "invaluable in the work of intelligence." The Foreign Department was the Indian equivalent of the Foreign Office; reporting to it was the Indian diplomatic service or "Political Service." The Political Service, in turn, obtained information from police reports, spies, and informers. "A mass of valuable military information regarding Native States within and beyond" India could be collected by the "Political Officers under the Foreign Department." Collen, *Report*, Appendix 1, pp. 122-24, and T.A. Heathcote, *The Indian Army*, p. 26.

18. Lord Napier's respect for the judgement of his quartermaster general was such that he sent a copy of Roberts's memorandum to Prime Minister Disraeli, who in turn gave a copy to Lord Lytton as he was about to depart England for his new post as viceroy of India. Field Marshal Lord Roberts of Kandahar, *Forty-One Years in India* 2: 86.

19. Ibid., p. 87. It was the British insistence on establishing "listening posts" inside Afghanistan at Herat, Kandahar, and Kashgar in order to obtain accurate information of developments in Central Asia that brought war in 1878. Lowe, *The Reluctant Imperialists* 1: 78-79.

20. Letter from Maj. Gen. F.S. Roberts, QMG, to the secretary to the government of India, Military Department, Simla, 30 October 1876, reproduced in appendix 1 of Collen, *Report*, pp. 126-28.

21. Collen, *Report*, pp. 1, 116. See explanatory footnotes on both pages.

22. Letter from F.S. Roberts to secretary of the government of India, Military Department, 30 October 1876. Collen, *Report*, p. 127.

23. The future lieutenant general, Sir E.H.H. Collen, was a graduate of Woolwich (1863) and the Staff College at Camberley (1873) who had recently transferred from the Royal Artillery to the Indian Army. Upon arrival in India in 1874, he served as secretary of the Indian Ordnance Commission until his appointment as assistant military secretary to the government of India in 1876. Twenty years later, Collen succeeded Sir Henry Brackenbury as military member of the Governor General's Council in India. Gabriel S. Woods, "Collen, Edwin H.H.," *D.N.B., 1901-1911*, pp. 383-84.

24. Captain Collen's memorandum "on the formation of an Intelligence Branch, Quarter-Master General's Department, India" which is dated "Simla, 17th June 1876" is included as appendix 1 of Collen, *Report*, pp. 115-26.

25. Roberts described Collen's memorandum as "singularly able," adding, "all the points are carefully discussed." The necessity for an organization such as the one Collen was proposing "has long been recognized." Furthermore, Roberts agreed with Collen that the Intelligence Branch should be for all India and not only for the Bengal presidency. (Until 1895, the commander-in-chief in India was in direct control only of the Bengal Army, although he exercised general control of the armies of the Madras and Bombay presidencies as well.) "The establishment, if divided, would be too small to be of any practical use. . . ." Letter from Roberts to the secretary to the government of India, Military Department, 30 October 1876. Collen, *Report*, p. 1.

26. Collen, *Report*, p. 1.

27. A "system to be established for communication of information" between the two is the

subject of one memorandum. The others focus on "the division of duties between Home and Indian Intelligence Departments." An agreement reached in March 1878 gave London responsibility for "Russia in Asia, Turkey in Asia, Egypt, Africa, China, Siam, and Japan," while Simla would have "Arabia, Persia, Beluchistan, Afghanistan, India, Cashmere, Nepal, Burmah, Malaya, Ceylon, Dutch Colonies, and Foreign Colonies in India." Central Asia was "to be worked at by both branches." Collen, *Report*, pp. 99-113.

28. Collen, *Report*, pp. 6-11. Section F included the drawing office, the lithographers, the map room, and the library.

29. Ibid., pp. 7, 15; Isaac, "History of the Directorate of M.I.," p. 6. The "attached officers" of 1878 are shown in a table of "Duty Distribution, 1st August 1878," which Collen included in his chapter on organization. The table also shows the seven sections of the Branch and the names, ranks, and duty positions of all of its personnel. Collen, *Report*, p. 15. See also C.M. Watson, *Wilson*, p. 83.

30. Collen, *Report*, p. 10.

31. Ibid., p. 15. As discussed in the preceding chapter, the Intelligence Branch was moved from the Adjutant General's Department to the Quartermaster General's Department in July 1874.

32. Ibid., p. 8, 14.

33. Ibid., p. 47.

34. The AQMG performed his duties with the administrative support of the Central Section. All papers (reports, memoranda, minutes, etc.) flowing into or out of the Intelligence Branch passed through the Central Section and were seen by the AQMG. The confidential or secret papers incoming to the Branch passed through the Confidential Registry of the War Office and went directly to the AQMG without passing through the Branch registry. Except for books, maps, newspapers, and charts that arrived at the Branch (and were handled by the DAQMG of Section F), the AQMG determined the distribution of all papers received from other branches of the War Office and from other departments of government (Foreign Office, Colonial Office, Admiralty, India Office, etc.). Collen, *Report*, pp. 16-17, 39.

35. Collen, *Report*, p. 16.

36. Ibid., pp. 16-17.

37. These were Sections A, C, D, and E. Countries for which each was responsible were: A—France and her colonies and Belgium; C—Germany, Holland and her colonies, Denmark, Switzerland, United States, Central American States, and South American States; D—Russia, Spain and her colonies, Portugal and her colonies, India, Persia, China, Japan, Central Asia, New Guinea, and Polynesia; E—Austria, Italy, Greece, Sweden, Norway, Ottoman Empire, Egypt, and Africa. Ibid., p. 15.

38. Ibid., p. 42. In the general staff system which gained widespread acceptance among European powers during the nineteenth century, a military history unit was a regular component. In Prussia, Karl W. von Grolman (chief of the general staff) ordered the formation of a separate Military History Section within Department II of the War Ministry in 1816. The French Dépôt de la Guerre was established in 1688 by Louis XIV's minister of war, Louvois, to collect archival materials relating to the armies of France. The dépôt survived the French Revolution and was expanded by the Legislative Assembly and the National Convention; Napoleon relied on it to supply his generals with maps and details about various theaters of operation as well as with memoirs and historical accounts of past campaigns. A statistical department was added to the dépôt in 1826. The British Depot of Military Knowledge of 1803 had a military library for the study and collection of materials about past campaigns, and the T&S Department, from its earliest days under Thomas Jervis, published accounts of the Crimean War. Goerlitz, *History of the German General Staff, 1657-1945*, p. 53. Donald D. Howard, "The Archives de la Guerre," pp. 66-72.

39. Collen, *Report*, pp. 42-43.

40. Ibid., p. 64.

41. Ibid., pp. 63-65. A check of Col. H.G. Hart's *The Annual Army List* for 1878 shows Captain Clarke had served continually in the T&S Department and the Intelligence Branch since March 1872, longer than any other DAQMG/section chief. The branch was fortunate to have such an

1. Lieutenant Colonel Thomas Best Jervis, Bombay Engineer Corps, Indian Army (1796-1857). A renowned geographer, he was the founder and first superintendent (1855-57) of the Topographical and Statistical Department of the War Office.

2. Major General Sir Charles William Wilson, Royal Engineers (1836-1905). As director of the T&S Department (1870-73), Captain Wilson was largely responsible for its revival and transformation into a permanent military intelligence organization. Also served as deputy head of the Intelligence Branch (1873-76) under Sir Patrick MacDougall.

Reproduced by kind permission of the commandant, British Army Staff College, Camberley.

3. General Sir Patrick MacDougall (1819-1894). Shown here as a lieutenant colonel during his tenure as the first commandant of the British Army's Staff College at Camberley (1857-61), MacDougall was the first head of the Intelligence Branch at the War Office (1873-78). He was one of the leading theorists and intellectuals of the mid-nineteenth century British Army.

4. General Sir Henry Brackenbury, Royal Artillery (1837-1914). A protégé of Sir Garnet Wolseley and member of the original "Ashanti Ring," he commanded the River Column in the Sudan in 1885. Brackenbury served as director of military intelligence for five years (1886-91) and was responsible for the reorganization and expansion of the War Office's Intelligence Division.

5. Colonel Robert Home, Royal Engineers (1837-1879). Deputy head of the Intelligence Branch (1876-79).

Courtesy of the Royal Artillery Institution, Woolwich, London.

6. Lieutenant General Sir Edwin H.H. Collen, Royal Artillery (1843-1911). Assistant military secretary to the government of India as a captain (1876-78.) Recommended the establishment of the Indian Intelligence Branch within the QMG's Department.

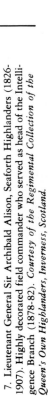

8. Colonel Lord Sydenham of Combe (George Sydenham Clarke), Royal Engineers (1848-1933). Permanent secretary of the Colonial Defence Committee (1885-92). *Courtesy of the National Portrait Gallery, London.*

7. Lieutenant General Sir Archibald Alison, Seaforth Highlanders (1826-1907). Highly decorated field commander who served as head of the Intelligence Branch (1878-82). *Courtesy of the Regimental Collection of the Queen's Own Highlanders, Inverness, Scotland.*

Courtesy of the National Army Museum, London.

9. Major General Lord Edward Gleichen, Grenadier Guards (1863-1937). While captain served twice in the Intelligence Division (1886-88 and 1894-99). Military attaché in Berlin (1903-06) and head of MO 1 at the War Office (1907-11).

Courtesy of the National Army Museum, London.

10. Lieutenant Colonel Charles à Court Repington, Rifle Brigade (1858-1925). Staff captain in Section A (French Section) of the Intelligence Division (1889-94). Military attaché at Brussels and the Hague (1898-99).

11. Brigadier General W.H.H. Waters, Royal Artillery (1855-1945). Staff captain in Section D (Russian Section) of the Intelligence Division (1891-93 and 1898-99). Military attaché at St. Petersburg (1893-98) and Berlin (1900-03).

Courtesy of the Royal Marines Museum, Southsea, Hants, England.

12. Major General Sir George G. Aston, Royal Marine Artillery (1861-1938). Intelligence staff officer in the Admiralty's Foreign Intelligence Committee and the Naval Intelligence Department (1886-89) and fleet intelligence officer for the Mediterranean Fleet (1894-95). Shown in photo as a major, ca. 1902.

13. Field Marshal Lord Wolseley (Garnet J. Wolseley) (1833-1913). An authentic national hero and one of the greatest soldiers of the late nineteenth-century British Army, Wolseley was also a tireless advocate for army reform. Adjutant general (1882-90) and later commander-in-chief of the army (1895-1901). Author of *The Soldier's Pocket-Book for Field Service* (five editions, 1869-86) in which he described the British Army's tactical intelligence system.

14. Field Marshal Lord Roberts (Frederick Sleigh Roberts), Bengal Horse Artillery (1832-1914). "Bobs" was Kipling's general, the leader of the famous march from Kabul to Kandahar and the defeat of the Afghans in 1880. During his forty-one years in India, Roberts served as quartermaster general (1875-78) and commander-in-chief (1885-93) of the Indian Army. In the final stages of his illustrious military career, he was commander-in-chief in Ireland (1895-99), South Africa (1899-1900), and of the army (1901-04).

15. Adelphi Terrace, Whitehall. Converted coach house and stables which served as the first home of the Topographical and Statistical Department of the War Office (1855-56).

Courtesy of B.T. Batsford Ltd.

16. Adair House, 20 St. James Square. The recently established Intelligence Branch was moved here from No. 4 New Street, Spring Gardens, in January 1874. It remained here until its relocation to Queen Anne's Gate in 1884.

17. Sixteen and 18 Queen Anne's Gate. Two "fine old houses" with a pleasant view of St. James Park and considerably more room than Adair House. Together, they served as the home of War Office Intelligence for seventeen years (1884-1901).

experienced intelligence officer and Russian linguist to head Section D at this critical time in Anglo-Russian relations.

42. Ibid., p. 65. Collen mentions several recent examples: "Sosnofsky's Routes" which had appeared in the 1878 *Journal of the Royal Geographical Society* and an article on the "Armed Forces of China and Japan" in an 1876 Russian journal, "Voennyi Shornik."

43. Ibid., p. 64. Enough information was available in Section D to put together a complete handbook from mainly British sources, but new information was coming in so rapidly that it would quickly have been outdated. A "concise account of the Russian Army" had been prepared "in case of emergency requiring its publication." Section D had also produced a detailed account of the Russo-Turkish War of 1877-78; this contained several chapters on the Russian Army.

44. Collen, *Report*, pp. 7-8. Major Wilson also recommended at this point that the Branch should "prepare and periodically revise an 'Ordre de Bataille' for each country" and compile "short biographies of foreign Generals."

45. The Branch also published a translated German account of the armed forces of Italy in 1875. The books on the three Scandinavian countries and Austria were authored by Capt. William S. Cooke, a DAQMG at the branch in 1875-76. The books on the German Empire and France were written by Capt. Francis C.H. Clarke and Maj. C.J. East, respectively. No author is listed for the "Armed Forces of the Ottoman Empire," but it seems likely that it was Capt. John C. Ardagh, chief of Section E in 1877. See list of "works prepared in the Intelligence Branch of the Quartermaster-General's Department, Horse Guards" on the inside back cover of Maj. Francis C.H. Clarke, *Staff Duties*. See also Collen, *Report*, p. 11-12, 15.

46. Collen, *Report*, p. 43.

47. Ibid., p. 12. Special reports were also filed on Holland, Belgium, Armenia, Trans-Caucasia, and Asia Minor.

48. Ibid., p. 11.

49. Ibid., pp. 11-12. *Der deutsch-französische Krieg, 1870-71*, 5 vols. (Berlin, 1872-81) appeared in English as *The Franco-German War 1870-1871*, translated by F.C.H. Clarke, 5 vols. (London, 1874-84).

50. Maj. Charles B. Brackenbury, Royal Artillery, was attached to the Intelligence Branch as an acting DAQMG in September 1873 and was appointed DAQMG in 1875. He was the elder brother of Henry Brackenbury, who became director of military intelligence in 1886.

51. The German Great General Staff had sixty-one permanent officers, thirty to forty additional officers, and 115 other employees (clerks, draftsmen, printers, etc.) in 1875. The Austrian General Staff employed sixty-eight permanent officers, the French General Staff sixty-nine. Maj. C.B. Brackenbury, "The Intelligence Duties of the Staff Abroad and at Home," pp. 242-67.

52. Ibid., pp. 250, 253, 257-58.

53. Ibid., pp. 242-64.

54. Ibid., pp. 266-67.

55. Deacon, *British Secret Service*, pp. 122-23.

56. After the reorganization of 1881, these areas were: Western (Europe), Eastern (Europe), American and Asiatic, and African. Before that date, the four political divisions had been: Turkish, French, German, and Spanish. Steiner, *The Foreign Office and Foreign Policy, 1898-1914*, pp. 3, 8.

57. Ibid., p. 13.

58. Lowe, *The Reluctant Imperialists: British Foreign Policy 1818-1902*, 1: 13-14. Steiner, *The Foreign Office and Foreign Policy, 1898-1914*, p. 7. See also Steiner, "The Last Years of the Old Foreign Office," p. 87.

59. Steiner, *The Foreign Office and Foreign Policy, 1898-1914*, pp. 7, 13-14.

60. A "Blue Book" was (and still is) a parliamentary publication, so named for its blue paper cover. The Foreign Office routinely prepared "Blue Books" for Parliament on major foreign policy issues of the day.

61. Steiner, *The Foreign Office and Foreign Policy, 1898-1914*, pp. 7, 13-14. In Steiner's words,

"To copy dispatches the office needed pleasant, industrious, trustworthy scribes, not brilliant scholars." See also Jones, *The Nineteenth Century Foreign Office*, pp. 65-76.

62. A summary of the accomplishments of the Hydrographic Department between 1837 and 1887 is included in Lord Brassey's chapter on the Royal Navy in Thomas Humphrey Ward, ed., *The Reign of Queen Victoria: A Survey of Fifty Years of Progress* (London: Smith, Elder, & Co., 1887), 1: 273-77. Of the 2,700 nautical charts published by the Admiralty up to 1887, 1,500 had been made from surveys made by Her Majesty's ships since 1837.

63. Capt. J.C.R. Colomb, "Naval Intelligence and Protection of Commerce in War," *R.U.S.I. Journal* (1881) 25: 555. Sir John Colomb was a naval strategist whose views eventually dominated British thinking about imperial defense in the late nineteenth century. His basic ideas on the subject first appeared in 1867 in *The Protection of our Commerce and Distribution of our Naval Forces Considered*. D.M. Schurman has written that Colomb "produced the first rational explanation of the naval place in national or even Imperial Defense thinking in the new era of iron ships and steam propulsion." D.M. Schurman, *The Education of a Navy*, p. 34.

64. Ibid., pp. 555-58, 573.

65. Commerce raiders are warships which attack an enemy's commercial shipping during wartime. Since World War I the submarine has been used most successfully as a commerce raider, but in the late nineteenth century small, fast warships—torpedo boats—were used.

66. Ibid., pp. 554, 559-62.

67. Ibid., p. 570.

68. Aston, *Secret Service*, p. 14. Like Charles Wilson, George Tryon demonstrated his talents very early in his career. At the age of twenty-nine, in 1861, Tryon was selected as the first commander of the first British seagoing ironclad fighting ship, the *Warrior*. During the Abyssinian Campaign in 1868 he distinguished himself as director of transports in Annesley Bay, impressing favorably "all the officers, naval and military, with whom he came in contact." From 1871 to 1874, Captain Tryon served as private secretary to the first lord of the admiralty and during the 1870s was given several important sea commands. After two years (1882-84) as secretary of the Admiralty, Tryon was promoted to rear admiral and appointed to command the Australian station. Sir George Tryon's career and life ended tragically in 1893 when, as a vice admiral commanding the Mediterranean station, he went down with his ship after a collison near Tripoli. John K. Laughton, "Tryon, Sir George," *D.N.B.* 19: 1199-1200.

69. Sir George Aston, who was assigned to the Foreign Intelligence Committee as a subaltern in marine artillery in 1886 and worked in the Naval Intelligence Department for several years after its establishment in 1887, credits Tryon with the creation of the Foreign Intelligence Committee. Aston, *Secret Service*, p. 14. So does Sir John Henry Briggs in his *Naval Administrations, 1827 to 1892*, p. 240. Both Lord Brassey and Donald M. Schurman feel that John Colomb also deserves some of the credit. Lord Brassey, *Brasseys Naval Annual, 1888-89*, p. 221; and Schurman, *The Education of a Navy*, p. 31.

70. Lord Brassey, *Brassey's Naval Annual, 1888-89*, p. 220. At first it was planned that an admiral would head the new bureau, but instead the experienced and respected Capt. W.H. Hall was installed as director of naval intelligence (D.N.I.). Captain Hall was the father of Reginald Hall, who became a famous D.N.I. during World War I. The establishment of the Naval Intelligence Department in 1887 owed much to Capt. Lord Charles Beresford. A lengthy confidential memorandum on the subject by Beresford, including a specific "Proposal for an Intelligence Department" was made public "through the instrumentality of a dishonest messenger at the Admiralty" and is published in full in Briggs, *Naval Administration*, pp. 229-38.

71. Even after 1882 the Foreign Intelligence Committee consisted only of Captain Hall and a few marine and navy officers, a small operation compared to the Intelligence Branch. From Aston's description, in 1886 there were two naval officers, a civilian, and one marine officer (Aston) working for Hall. "All the countries of the world were divided into two groups. . . . We had only one traveling naval attaché to obtain information from the whole of Europe." Aston, *Secret Service*, pp. 20-22.

72. See chapter 3, "Growing Pains, 1858-1870" in Bond, *The Victorian Army and the Staff College, 1854-1914*, pp. 82-115.

73. "A staff tour was still regarded by the majority of officers as a sign of weakness as it directed an officer away from his 'true vocation' i.e., serving with his regiment." Parritt, *Intelligencers*, p. 128.

74. Officers who had successfully completed the two-year course at the Staff College were awarded a "p.s.c.," indicating "passed Staff College."

75. In 1876, for example, the AQMG (Maj. Charles Wilson) was an engineer. Of the five DAQMGs listed, one was an engineer (Lt. Col. Robert Home) and two were artillerymen (Maj. C.B. Brackenbury and Capt. Francis C.H. Clarke). Thus, four of the six permanent positions were filled by "sappers" or "gunners."

76. Like Charles Wilson, Robert Home won his commission in the Royal Engineers during the Crimean War, when for a short time commissions in the artillery and engineers had been opened to public competition. After bypassing attendance at Woolwich (the military academy for engineer and artillery officers), Home put in the usual tours at Chatham and in fortification work (at Portsmouth) and served in Canada, just as Wilson did. Unlike his contemporary, Home attended the Staff College, "passing out third" in 1860. Captain Home won acclaim in the mid-1860s for a report he wrote while in Canada on the defense of the frontier against invasion. In 1870 he became secretary of the Royal Engineers Committee (a standing scientific committee). Vetch, "Home, Robert," *D.N.B.* 9: 1132-33. J. Luvaas, *Education of an Army*, pp. 94-95.

77. Vetch, "Home," pp. 1132-33; Collen, *Report*, pp. 11-12.

78. Collen, *Report*, p. 12.

79. Robert Home's promotion to brevet colonel in 1877 has already been noted. He had received his promotion to lieutenant colonel for service as Wolseley's commanding Royal Engineer in the Ashanti Campaign (1873-74). Vetch, "Home," p. 1133.

80. Parritt, *Intelligencers*, pp. 116, 151. Isaac, "History of the Directorate of M.I.," p. 7.

81. Luvaas, *Education of an Army*, p. 125.

82. Alison served in the Seaforth Highlanders in the trenches before Sebastopol in 1855-56, was mentioned in dispatches, and was promoted to brevet major. He was again mentioned in dispatches during the Indian Mutiny, returned home a brevet lieutenant colonel, and dined with Queen Victoria. At Amoafur during the Ashanti War, the officers of his staff "were struck by his self-possession, and the precision of his orders." Ernest M. Lloyd, "Alison, Sir Archibald," *D.N.B. Twentieth Century, 1901-1911*, pp. 33-34.

83. Ibid., p. 34; Parritt, *Intelligencers*, p. 151.

84. Parritt, *Intelligencers*, pp. 151-52. Isaac, "History of the Directorate of M.I.," p. 7.

85. Parritt, *Intelligencers*, p. 102.

CHAPTER V

Henry Brackenbury and the Revival of War Office Intelligence, 1886-1895

Officers about to travel, who propose to endeavor to obtain information, must acquaint themselves thoroughly with the above rules, and are to carefully observe them. They are to remember that indiscretion on their part may involve them in trouble, and may lead to their being arrested; and they are clearly to understand that the obtaining of information, no matter how valuable, will not compensate for the diplomatic difficulties that under such circumstances their conduct will have involved.

> From the DMI's "Rules to be
> Observed by Officers Travelling,
> Who are endeavoring to obtain
> Information for the Intelligence
> Division," ca. 1889

Throughout the forty-one years between the establishment of the Intelligence Branch in 1873 and the outbreak of the First World War in 1914, the low point for War Office Intelligence—in terms of efficiency, morale, and prestige—was reached toward the end of 1885. The vitality and growing influence of the Intelligence Branch, so apparent when Sir Patrick MacDougall had been at its helm in the 1870s, was little more than a fading memory only seven years after his departure for Canada. Nevertheless, Great Britain badly needed an efficient military intelligence staff in the mid-1880s. Still the world's pre-eminent imperial power, she continued to adhere to a diplomatic policy of "splendid isolation" with respect to the other great powers. There were definite advantages to Britain in going it alone, particularly since there appeared to be no direct military or naval threat to the security of the British

Isles. In Asia, Africa, and eastern Europe, however, there were serious problems with both Russia and France.

As seen from Whitehall, the most dangerous flashpoint for the British Empire in 1885 was Afghanistan and the most likely enemy, Russia. A clash between Russian and Afghan troops at Pendjeh in March revived old fears concerning Russia's intentions in Central Asia; a Russian military presence in Afghanistan would pose a definite threat to India's Northwest Frontier. So vital was Afghanistan to the security of India and so ominous was Russia's activity along the northwest border of Afghanistan in the spring of 1885 that the viceroy of India, Lord Dufferin, assured Abdur Rahman, the Amir of Afghanistan, that a Russian advance on Herat would be answered by a British declaration of war on Russia.[1] Ill feelings between Britain and Russia were exacerbated in the fall of 1885 by British opposition to Russia in the opening round of the Bulgarian crisis. Anxiety over the possibility of war with Russia was widespread throughout the British Empire in 1885. Preparations for war were most noticeable in India, where the army was increased by 11,000 British and 12,000 native troops, and regiments stationed in the Northwest Frontier area were alerted to be ready for movement into Afghanistan.[2] Continuing French hostility toward the British position in Egypt, though overshadowed by the prospect of a conflict with Russia, was a problem which could not be overlooked. For their part, the British were irritated by French attempts to make commercial inroads in Burma. Given the existing tensions with St. Petersburg and Paris, the British War Office required continuous collection and assessment of military information regarding the two powerful potential adversaries. Unfortunately, its staff then was less capable of doing such work adequately than at any time since the Franco-Prussian War.

Because of the fear of war with Russia in 1885 and the complete helplessness of many British colonies in the event of an attack by the Russian navy, the Colonial Office was deluged with appeals for help and information on defense matters from the colonies. In order to cope more expeditiously with this growing correspondence, the assistant undersecretary of state for the Colonies, H. Robert Meade, proposed in April 1885 that a small standing committee be set up with representation from the Colonial Office, the War Office, and the Admiralty. Thus, the Colonial Defence Committee, principal forerunner of the Committee of Imperial Defence, was established. This small, interdepartmental standing committee was to provide advice to the Colonial Committee of the cabinet on questions of colonial defense as well as to answer inquiries from the colonies.[3] Although it facilitated the exchange of military and naval information among the three departments, the creation of the Colonial Defence Committee could not compensate for the vacuum in the War Office's Intelligence Branch. It did provide previously lacking "continuity in the discussion of imperial defence questions,"[4] but it undertook no strategic planning and restricted its activity instead to circulating the "work of the various departments on matters like the defence of particular ports, the size and training of colonial forces and any colonial acts or ordinances dealing with defence."[5] The responsibility for the collection and evaluation of information about foreign armies remained with the Intelligence Branch of the War Office.

The Colonial Defence Committee was strengthened immeasurably during its first seven years (1885-92) by the intellect and energy of its permanent secretary, Capt. George Sydenham Clarke, Royal Engineers. Clarke (later Col. Lord Sydenham of Combe) was no stranger to intelligence work; before and during his assignment with the Colonial Defence Committee the War Office gave him a number of missions abroad to investigate and report on technical military questions.[6] When performing such missions Clarke apparently divorced himself entirely from the Colonial Defence Committee. In his capacity as permanent secretary of the committee, the only major military intelligence effort in which Captain Clarke regularly was engaged involved the gathering of data about the military resources of the colonies. He devised "elaborate forms in which all the resources of a Colony bearing directly or indirectly on defense could be entered, the forms to be corrected annually and returned for information." Additionally, Clarke provided general guidelines to the governors of colonies to assist them in planning for local defense and encouraged each to prepare a general scheme of defense to be returned annually to the Colonial Office for examination and criticism. His work, which received the approval of the committee and the secretary of state for the Colonies before dispatch to the governors, stirred high-level interest in defense in many of the colonies and produced a regular and detailed flow of military and naval information to the Colonial Defence Committee.[7] This information was of great value not only to the Colonial Office but also to the Admiralty and the War Office.

In return, what could the Colonial Defence Committee tell the anxious colonies about the armed forces of Russia, France, and the newest entrant in the race for colonies, Germany? The committee frequently turned to the Admiralty to provide answers to such questions, and with good reason. As discussed in the preceding chapter, in 1885 the Admiralty had a small but capable Foreign Intelligence Committee, which two years later was enlarged and renamed the Naval Intelligence Department. Though considerably newer, smaller, and not as well known as the Intelligence Branch of the War Office, the Foreign Intelligence Committee in 1885 was functioning far more smoothly and was, in all probability, more responsive to requests for information from the colonies.[8]

The arrival of Maj. Gen. Henry Brackenbury as the new director of the Intelligence Branch in January 1886 brought not only a remarkably rapid revival of that lethargic organization, but also the beginning of five years of growth and change comparable to Charles Wilson's reign as director of the T&S Department in the early 1870s and the early years of the Branch itself under MacDougall. A long-time protégé of Lord Wolseley and an original member of the "Ashanti Ring,"[9] Brackenbury lost no time in making his mark upon the Intelligence Branch and winning the respect of his subordinates. He was not held in high esteem by the Duke of Cambridge, the commander-in-chief of the army, no doubt because of his independent mind and his ties to the reform-minded Wolseley, then the adjutant general. At a dinner party during the first years of Brackenbury's directorship, the duke startled a young officer working at the Intelligence Branch by remarking in a somber tone, "So you are under Brackenbury? A dangerous man, my dear Gleichen, a very dangerous man!"[10] Who was this "dangerous man" who was to have such a dramatic impact on the War Office Intelligence establishment?

Henry Brackenbury was forty-eight years of age when he became head of the Intelligence Branch on New Year's Day 1886. Born in Bolingbroke, Lincolnshire, in 1837, he was the youngest son of William and Maria Brackenbury. One of his older brothers, Charles, also became a career army officer, and as a major served at the Intelligence Branch during the mid-1870s. Henry attended Eton (1850-52) and, after several years in Quebec, Canada, where he worked in a notary's office, he entered the Royal Military Academy at Woolwich in 1854. Like many of his contemporaries at both Woolwich and Sandhurst, young Brackenbury was not permitted to complete all his courses because of the critical need for subalterns in the Crimea. He received a commission in the Royal Artillery at age nineteen in April 1856, too late to see action in the Crimean War. Instead, he sailed for India in the summer of 1857 and took part in post-mutiny campaigning. Forced to return home from India in 1858 because of ill health, Brackenbury settled down to a series of routine assignments. "Brack" possessed considerable talent as a writer and it was at this stage in his career that he began to devote more and more of his spare time to writing. Besides contributing a number of articles on technical subjects to various military periodicals, he cultivated an interest in military history. After his appointment as a professor of military history at Woolwich in 1868, however, visiting European battlefields became more than an avocation. Brackenbury remained at Woolwich in this capacity until 1873, except for a brief period in 1870-71 when he went to France to supervise a British relief effort for the sick and wounded of both sides in the Franco-Prussian War.[11]

Captain Brackenbury's military career was boosted in 1873 when Lord Wolseley took him to Ashanti as his military secretary. Eager for action, Brackenbury had written to Wolseley, volunteering his services in any capacity. Wolseley provides an interesting portrait of Brackenbury during the Ashanti War (1873-74) in his memoirs:

> My military secretary was Captain Henry Brackenbury and my private secretary Lieutenant Frederick Maurice. Both were artillerymen and strangers to me at the time, but I chose them as men remarkable for their ability, and because both were thoroughly well versed in the science of their profession. The former is not only a profound reasoner with a strong will and a logical mind, but—that rare man to find in our Army—a first-rate man of business and an indefatigable worker also. Whatever he undertakes, he performs admirably and thoroughly. Had he adopted some less noble but more paying occupation in life than the Army he would have made a fortune. He spoke reasonably well, and had he made politics his career, I have no doubt that he would have risen to a very high position in that questionable trade.[12]

Beginning at the time of the Ashanti War, Lord Wolseley was Henry Brackenbury's faithful patron. Thanks in large part to Wolseley's support, "Brack" advanced from captain to brevet lieutenant colonel between 1873 and 1875. Furthermore, he accompanied the future field marshal to Cyprus (1878), Zululand (1879), the Transvaal (1879), Egypt (1882), and on the Gordon

Relief Expedition up the Nile from Egypt into the Sudan (1884-85). By the time Brackenbury assumed command of the famed River Column in the Sudan in February 1885, he was a brigadier general. Upon his return to England in August, he was promoted to major general for "distinguished service in the field."

There can be little doubt that Lord Wolseley engineered Major General Brackenbury's appointment as deputy quartermaster general and head of the Intelligence Branch in 1886.[14] In fairness, however, it should also be recognized that Henry Brackenbury was an exceptionally able officer. Although he was a keen student of military history and an excellent writer, he also had excelled as a man of action, as a professional soldier, in numerous campaigns overseas. Brackenbury's attainment of general officer rank was as much a tribute to his intellectual and soldierly abilities as it was a result of his long-time association with Wolseley.

To what degree was Henry Brackenbury qualified to assume the top military intelligence post in the British Army in 1886? In addition to his considerable talents as administrator, staff officer, and writer, he was not without experience in military intelligence. Most notably, Brackenbury had served as military attaché in Paris in 1881-82 and so played a vital role in the collection of strategic intelligence on the armed forces of France.[15] Although it is not known whether he reported back to the War Office from France in 1870-71, his duties there during the Franco-Prussian War, directing the British relief effort (on behalf of the National Society for Aid to the Sick and Wounded), gave him an unobtrusive vantage point from which to observe the armies of France and Germany. Brackenbury's travels to the Continent to visit battlefields prior to and during his tour as a professor of military history at Woolwich also gave him additional opportunities to collect information of current interest to the War Office. During the latter half of the 1870s Brackenbury traveled with Sir Patrick MacDougall to Crete and Egypt (1875-76) and developed a keen interest in the Near East. He wrote articles for *Blackwood's Magazine* and other publications between 1875 and 1879 on such topics as the strategic importance of Crete, Russia's designs on Constantinople, and the Russo-Turkish War of 1877-78.[16] Brackenbury had had little to do with India before taking over the Intelligence Branch in 1886. Outside of his participation in the suppression of the rebellion touched off by the Great Mutiny in 1857-58, his only exposure to India had been as private secretary to the viceroy (then the Earl of Lytton) for a short time in 1880. Lastly, an education at the Royal Military Academy at Woolwich had provided a solid foundation on the technical side of the military art; Brackenbury's contribution to the *Proceedings of the Royal Artillery Institution* evidence his interest in the changing technology of artillery ordnance.[17]

When Maj. Gen. (later Gen. Sir) Henry Brackenbury became head of the Intelligence Branch at the beginning of 1886, the Branch was situated at 16 and 18 Queen Anne's Gate, where it had been moved from Adair House in December 1884. It was now in "two fine old houses . . . with backs looking out on to St. James' Park" and a distant view of Buckingham Palace.[18] It was a pleasant location, but rather far removed from the environs of the War Office in Whitehall. There were certain advantages in this, although it may have contributed to the notion that the Intelligence Branch was in 1885 "a harmless but rather useless appendage to the War Office."[19] The mere presence of a brilliant, dynamic general like Henry Brackenbury, after three years of stagnation and relative inactivity at the Branch, was bound to have had a catalytic effect. Ironically, Brackenbury's first major effort as head of War Office Intelligence dealt with defense planning instead of military intelligence.

In 1885 neither the Intelligence Branch of the War Office, the Foreign Intelligence Committee of the Admiralty, the Colonial Defence Committee, nor any other branch of the British government was responsible for strategic planning for the defense of Britain and her far-flung empire. The responsibility for war planning within the War Office lay solely with the commander-in-chief, in the absence of a plans and operations staff. Had such a staff been established, in addition to the Intelligence Branch, the result would have been the *de facto* creation of a British General Staff. Despite the need that many military officers and some influential civilians saw for precisely such a staff in 1885-86, "the idea of a general staff on the German model was repugnant to many Englishmen," some of whom feared that "the military would take advantage of a planning staff to develop elaborate mobilization schemes and offensive plans that would serve ultimately to commit the civil government to a policy which it might not care to follow."[20] The lack of a planning staff, combined with increasing military dangers to the British Empire in the mid-1880s, led to the expectation that the Intelligence Branch could and should assume the additional function of strategic planning without substantial reorganization or a significant increase in funding from the Treasury.

The involvement of the Intelligence Branch in defense planning in 1886 was not an unprecedented development in the short history of that organization. The original charter of the Branch in 1873 had included the proviso that it should relate the information it was collecting in peacetime to the "measures . . . which should be adopted in war, so that no delay might arise from uncertainty or hesitation."[21] The transfer of the Branch from the adjutant general to the quartermaster general in 1874 had appeared to relieve it of the planning function, but the freedom to concentrate on purely intelligence work was short-lived. The adjutant general did not establish a separate branch of his department for strategic planning. Meanwhile, the Intelligence Branch, under the able Sir Patrick MacDougall, was saddled with more and more projects outside of foreign intelligence and once again was drawn into plans and operations. Col. Robert Home, MacDougall's deputy at the Branch, prepared a mobilization plan for the army in 1875.[22] In the late 1870s, Section B collected information about the military capabilities of the colonies in order that the head of the Intelligence Branch could advise the commander-in-chief on the defense of the Empire. As recently as 1882, Maj. Gen. Sir Archibald Alison had worked out "the organizations of the expeditionary force for Egypt, plans for the campaign, mobilization tables for the troops and concentration of troops," while head of the Branch.[23]

Henry Brackenbury was one of the strongest advocates for the estab-lishment of a British General Staff within the higher ranks of the army in the late 1880s. When he assumed his new post as deputy quartermaster general and head of the Intelligence Branch in 1886, he was appalled by the War Office's failure to have developed an up-to-date mobilization plan, a defect he regarded as a consequence of the lack of a general staff. There was little hope of any immediate steps being taken by the War Office to set up a general staff, so Brackenbury, with encouragement and support from Lord Wolseley, per-sonally undertook the demanding task of constructing a new mobilization plan. It was not illogical to Brackenbury that he should perform such work while head of the Branch because he was convinced of the need to link the intelligence product with operational needs.[24] In the absence of a general staff there was no more suitable place to attempt this than in the Intelligence Branch.

Brackenbury's initial efforts to come to grips with mobilization planning resulted in a series of reports dealing with the problems of home defense, the movement of an army corps overseas, and the condition of the army at home. One significant conclusion he reached after only three months was that "for want of the departmental services, we cannot place two complete Army Corps in the field, either for foreign service or for home defence."[25] Bracken-bury's early findings aroused considerable interest in Britain's vulnerability to an attack by an aggressive and modern European army, and he was urged by Wolseley to continue his work. In a candid summary of the international situation prepared in August 1886, General Brackenbury revealed the exist-ence of Russian plans to advance on the Northwest Frontier of India via Herat in western Afghanistan. The possibility of a Franco-Russian alliance aimed at Britain was especially frightening to the head of the Intelligence Branch at this time.[26] Near the end of 1886, a committee under Brackenbury published a three-part report containing the complete mobilization plan. Largely the work of Henry Brackenbury, the Mobilization Plan of 1886 was a realistic scheme based on careful research and "formed the basis for perma-nent arrangements that held the field for many years."[27]

A key provision of the Mobilization Plan of 1886 was that the British Army be able to field two army corps for overseas deployment. This goal, as well as other aspects of the plan, touched off a bitter debate between soldiers and civilians and led to more work for Brackenbury during 1887. Upon his request, a new post was created in the Branch in November 1887 to relieve him of direct responsibility for mobilization work. Col. John Ardagh, Brack-enbury's choice for the job, was an old hand in the Intelligence Branch who had served with Brackenbury in the Sudan. General Wolseley quickly approved Ardagh's appointment, and Brackenbury's new assistant plunged into the difficult and tedious work at hand. Even with the additional officer, however, "Brack" soon decided that the mobilization/planning function should be removed from the Branch altogether. Therefore, only three months after its creation, the Mobilization and Home Defence Section (including Colonel Ardagh) moved out of Queen Anne's Gate and into the office of the adjutant general in the main War Office buildings.[28] The Intelligence Branch was now free to concentrate on the production of military intelligence matters.

As much of a distraction as it was in 1886-87, the responsibility for mobilization planning certainly increased the importance of the Branch within the hierarchy of the War Office and probably made it easier for Brackenbury to obtain support for the expansion of military intelligence work. Well before the departure of John Ardagh and the Mobilization Section in February 1888, numerous indications of the rising fortunes of the Intelligence Branch at Queen Anne's Gate had appeared. Prying more money from the Treasury in the 1880s for any War Office endeavor, particularly for expansion, was like pulling teeth, and, to be sure, the Branch had its problems with the Treasury during Brackenbury's five years at the helm.[29] Nonetheless, General Wolseley was able to obtain a larger financial grant for the Branch at the outset of Brackenbury's directorship in 1886.[30] Henry Brackenbury appreciated the increased funding, but he was not entirely satisfied. Dismayed that officers of the Branch were forced to finance foreign travel on behalf of the War Office out of their own pockets, he sought extra funds for intelligence collection and ultimately "wheedled £600 a year out of the Treasury to pay the expenses of the officers of the Directorate to travel in the countries for which they were responsible."[31]

The transfer of the Intelligence Branch back to the adjutant general on 1 June 1887, after nearly thirteen years in the less-prestigious Quartermaster General's Department, was another step upward. General Brackenbury's title was changed at this point to director of military intelligence (DMI) and, significantly, he was now to report directly to the commander-in-chief (rather than through the adjutant general). The additional power and autonomy gained by the Branch and its director in mid-1887 helped Brackenbury solve a problem which had plagued his predecessors and had annoyed him since his arrival at Queen Anne's Gate in 1886. The DMI was unhappy with his organization's dependence upon highly transient "attached officers" who often left the Branch after serving there less than six months. In October 1887 he persuaded the War Office to reduce the number of "attached officers" assigned and to increase the permanent strength by seven staff captains. This was a crucial development, for its effect was to double the number of officers serving long tours (three to six years) at the Branch. The capstone of Henry Brackenbury's eventful first two years as head of the Branch occurred in January 1888 when he was promoted to lieutenant general. Simultaneously, the Intelligence Branch was redesignated as the Intelligence Division in recognition of its higher status within the War Office.[32]

The addition of seven staff captains to the Intelligence Branch in 1887 did not lead to major changes in the structure of the Branch/Division. The internal organization of the Intelligence Division under Brackenbury was very similar to that of the late 1870s. There were still four foreign sections (A, C, D, and E), one section oriented on colonial defense (B), and one topographic and library section (F). The geographical areas of responsibility of the foreign sections were realigned to balance the workload more equally and to group countries under the sections in a more logical fashion.[33] Section B now was responsible for the South African Republic, the Orange Free State, Cyprus, and Polynesia, as well as all British colonies and protectorates. Compared with the organization of the Branch during MacDougall's tenure (1873-78), the most striking difference was the absence of a Central Section, the once-powerful administrative section which had been run by the assistant quartermaster general (AQMG). The AQMG had functioned as a deputy to the head of the Branch until the end of 1885.[34] When Brackenbury arrived in 1886, the AQMG post remained open and the Central Section, as a separate entity, disappeared. During the brief sojourn of the Mobilization and Home Defence Section at the Branch in 1887-88, Colonel Ardagh filled this void by serving as Brackenbury's deputy, and his section also functioned as a Central Section. The departure of Ardagh and the Mobilization Section in early 1888 left the DMI without a deputy. General Brackenbury was forced to deal directly with the chiefs of the six sections and to supervise the administrative elements which formerly comprised the Central Section.[35] This resulted in more work for Brackenbury, but it also allowed him to become more intimately involved in the collection, production, and dissemination of intelligence than either Patrick MacDougall (1873-78) or Archibald Alison (1878-82) had been.

From the historian's point of view, it is unfortunate that Sir Henry Brackenbury elected to say so little about his five years as head of War Office Intelligence in his memoirs. He did concede, "[I] loved the work and believed I had found my true vocation." Rather than discussing his tour as DMI and several subsequent assignments, however, Sir Henry demurred: "My experiences during these 18 years—1886-1904—are of too recent date to be told without risk of indiscretion."[36] Indeed, there is no single document or contemporary account to describe the operation of the Intelligence Division during the period 1886-95 which can be compared with Capt. Edwin Collen's 1878 report on the Intelligence Branch for the Indian Army. Nevertheless, some of Brackenbury's subordinates in the Division had a good deal to say about its inner workings in their memoirs. Collectively, the personal accounts of officers who served under "Brack" and his successor, Maj. Gen. (later Gen.) Sir Edward F. Chapman (1891-96), constitute a most valuable reservoir of information about War Office Intelligence over the decade 1886-95. A remarkably clear picture of how the Intelligence Division functioned may be seen through the eyes of a number of alumni of Queen Anne's Gate, most notably those of Sir Charles E. Callwell, Lord Edward Gleichen, Charles à Court Repington, and Wallscourt H.H. Waters, in their memoirs.[37]

In general, sources of information and methods of collection used by the Intelligence Division under Generals Brackenbury and Chapman were similar to those employed by the Intelligence Branch under Generals MacDougall and Alison. The reports of military attachés and British officers traveling abroad continued to be the most valued sources of military intelligence. The foreign sections also culled vast quantities of information from periodicals, newspapers, books, reports, and memoranda produced by other departments of the British government, and from official publications of foreign governments.[38] Although most of the information received by the foreign sections was still obtained from open sources without resort to clandestine methods, there was an unmistakable trend toward the use of covert or semicovert methods, encouraged by Brackenbury, in connection with officers traveling abroad. The channels of communication opened with other departments of the government by Sir Henry gave the Intelligence Division access to additional information of relevance to its work, some of which had been gathered covertly.

Although other departments of the government—primarily the Admiralty, the Foreign Office, the India Office, and the Colonial Office—were exchanging information with the War Office that was of interest to the Intelligence Branch at the time of Collen's report in 1878, the flow of information was considerably expanded and expedited during Brackenbury's directorship of the Division. At the Admiralty, the establishment of the Foreign Intelligence Committee in 1882 had given the navy an extremely small, but sorely needed, staff to collect and produce naval intelligence in London and to provide guidance for naval attachés overseas. Direct communication between the Intelligence Branch and its new counterpart at the Admiralty would have profited both, but the Branch was in a state of disarray then and for the next several years. Not until the arrival of Henry Brackenbury in 1886 was substantial progress made. Unlike some of his more parochial fellow army officers, Brackenbury believed that coordination between the War Office and the Admiralty was essential, not only when an expeditionary force had to be moved to Egypt or the Gold Coast, but all the time. He insured from his earliest days at the Branch that it would conduct frequent and regular correspondence with the Foreign Intelligence Committee. When the Admiralty formed the Naval Intelligence Department in 1887, with the Foreign Intelligence Committee as its nucleus, "Brack" already had a close working relationship with Capt. William H. Hall, the first director of naval intelligence (DNI); Hall had been head of the committee since its birth.[39]

General Brackenbury's bridge-building efforts were equally fruitful with the Colonial Office, the India Office, and the Foreign Office. He was instrumental in setting up an improved interchange of information with the Colonial and India Offices. Relations with the former were further strengthened by Brackenbury's membership on the Colonial Defence Committee. To upgrade ties with the latter and open a direct channel of communication with the Indian Army, Brackenbury persuaded the Indian government to station an Indian Army officer on the staff of the Intelligence Branch. An officer of the Bengal Staff Corps joined Section D of the Branch in 1887. The DMI won an important concession from the secretary of state for war when the secretary authorized him to correspond on a semiofficial basis directly with the permanent under secretaries of the Foreign and Colonial Offices. The two under secretaries soon came to regard the DMI as "a close consultant on all issues of a military nature." As a further sign of the growing trust between the Foreign Office and the Intelligence Division, the Foreign Office began sending the DMI copies of telegrams and other messages it received from ambassadors and consular officials abroad. Previously, the Foreign Office had provided very little information to the Branch beyond passing on copies of military attaché reports.[40]

The Intelligence Division's direct channel with the Foreign Office was significant in a less obvious respect as well. The Secret Intelligence Service (SIS), England's three-hundred-year-old espionage organization, was responsible to Parliament through the Foreign Office, as it had been throughout the nineteenth century. In the late 1880s a sizable amount of money (approximately £65,000 per year) was allocated to the Foreign Office for "secret service."[41] This amount was about six times the annual budget for the War Office Intelligence Department. While most of these funds were turned over to the SIS, some secret service money was retained by the Foreign Office and used by British diplomats in attempts to buy political influence in strategic places like Persia.[42] From the available evidence, it appears that the Intelligence Division of the War Office derived very litle useful military intelligence from the efforts of the SIS between 1870 and 1899. Just as the SIS in the first half of the eighteenth century concentrated its energies close to home, keeping track of the Jacobites in England and Scotland, the SIS was preoccupied with the affairs of Ireland from 1815 to 1899.[43] Even during the Brackenbury years (1886-91), the DMI exercised no significant influence over the activities of the SIS. Although the improved communications with the Foreign Office cultivated by Henry Brackenbury still did not enable him to redirect SIS resources away from the trail of Irish terrorists, at least it helped keep the DMI out of the dark about the activities of that organization. Furthermore, there are indications that small amounts of secret service money were transferred from the Foreign Office to the Intelligence Division, beginning while Brackenbury was the DMI.[44]

The term "secret service" was loosely defined in official British circles during the 1880s and 1890s. While "secret service" activities included espionage conducted by agents of the SIS, they also encompassed efforts by ambassadors and lower ranking officials of the Diplomatic Service, political agents and envoys of the Indian government's Foreign Department, and officers of the army and navy to obtain confidential or sensitive information in foreign countries. Ambassadors and their subordinates often acquired such information from their counterparts in other embassies and from officials of host governments without resort to bribery. If money was required to loosen the tongue of a reluctant traitor, a British diplomat could use secret service funds in some instances. In the late nineteenth century, British ambassadors almost never dealt directly with paid informants; they were fully aware of the risks involved and were often reluctant to allow even lower ranking embassy officials to engage in activity which so obviously moved them into the murky world of "secret service." British military and naval attachés also stayed away from personal involvement in clandestine intelligence. Particularly in France and Russia, they were always under suspicion and were subject to surveillance by police or counterintelligence personnel.[45] "Secret service" on behalf of the War Office and the Admiralty had a far greater chance for success when conducted by officers who were in no way connected to the British embassy and who remained in the target country for weeks rather than years.

Military and naval officers, from both inside and outside the intelligence departments in Whitehall, traveled through countries of interest to their respective services. Many of these trips could in no way be construed as "secret service" operations. When Capt. Charles à Court Repington of Section A of the Intelligence Division attended the French Army's maneuvers in 1891 in response to an official invitation, for example, he had nothing to hide.[46] Similarly, Capt. James M. Grierson of Section D often visited the German General Staff in Berlin between 1889 and 1895, where he was cordially received and was regularly provided with the best available information about the Russian Army.[47] British officers attending foreign maneuvers in France, Austria, Germany, and even Russia made no effort to conceal their identities. Uniforms were worn except during travel to and from England, and officers were encouraged by the DMI to make themselves highly visible.

> Officers attending manoeuvres in all foreign countries will find it adds much to the usefulness and pleasure of their visit if they take the trouble to get themselves duly presented to as many of the Officers as possible of the army to which they are sent, especially those of high rank. Two hundred visiting cards should be taken by each officer.[48]

On the other hand, officers on "secret service" typically posed as tourists, wore civilian clothes, and avoided the authorities, especially military authorities. In the words of Edward Gleichen (in describing his own participation in a covert intelligence mission), these men were "on the spy."[49]

Practically all army officers from outside the Intelligence Division who engaged in "secret service" for the DMI were unsolicited volunteers. Indeed, the service intelligence departments and the SIS relied upon a steady flow of unpaid volunteers, both civilian and military. According to Richard Deacon, the late nineteenth century was the "golden age of the amateur and the freelance agent" for the British Secret Service.[50] These volunteer "spies" were more often than not resourceful, wealthy individuals with a yearning for travel and adventure, but motivated primarily by patriotism. Perhaps the most famous amateur spy to emerge from the ranks of the British Army during this period was Robert S.S. Baden-Powell. Baden-Powell, who later attained the rank of major general and who also founded the Boy Scouts, attended German Army maneuvers as an "uninvited guest" in order to find out about a new German machine gun. On another occasion he visited Dalmatia while posing as a butterfly collector and managed to conceal a detailed sketch of a fort in a drawing of a butterfly.[51] The Intelligence Division, its operations constrained by limited funds, was in no position to reject, without due consideration, any army officers from outside the War Office who offered their services. It was far easier for such officers to deny any connection with British Intelligence if detained in a foreign country than for a military attaché or an officer assigned to the Intelligence Division. The DMI's "Rules to be observed by Officers Travelling who are endeavouring to obtain Information for the Intelligence Division" were quite explicit:

> 1. Officers so travelling are not to consider themselves as employed by the Intelligence Division, and are, *on no account whatever*, to represent themselves to any person as being so employed, or as being engaged on any official work, or as having any official mission, unless they have received especial authority to do so from His Royal Highness, the Commander-in-Chief.

2. They must remember that the laws as regards spying are very rigorous in most countries, and they must be very careful not to place themselves in a compromising situation.

3. It may be taken, as a rule, that it is to the inspection of fortresses, defence works, magazines, arsenals, dockyards, military and naval buildings and ships of war, and to the taking away of specimens of war material by strangers, that the authorities of foreign countries especially object. On approaching fortresses, &c., Officers must never have notes or plans of any kind with them.

4. Officers travelling in foreign countries must remember that it is unsafe to send letters containing information through the post. They must never use such addresses as "Intelligence Division" or "War Office" and should send letters to the addressee by name. . . .[52]

Of course, the DMI's "Rules" were equally applicable to officers of the Intelligence Division on those occasions when they traveled "unofficially" to sensitive areas. No matter how successful army officers from outside the Division were in collecting information, Henry Brackenbury and his successor as DMI, Edward F. Chapman, insisted that officers from the foreign sections visit the countries for which they were responsible. General Brackenbury's determined campaign to get additional money for the Division was waged mainly to allow the DMI to support foreign travel more adequately; it was also an indication of the priority he attached to the need for such travel. The £600 per year yielded by the Treasury for the "DMI's Travelling Grant" was hardly a grand sum even in the 1880s, but it represented a major triumph for the DMI and was a most encouraging development for officers in the Intelligence Division. Henceforth, they could look forward to at least partial reimbursement for the expenses they incurred when traveling for the DMI, whether in or out of uniform. Their purposeful journeys to the Continent and elsewhere brought a new and significant dimension to the collection of strategic military intelligence by the British Army.

Ample testimony concerning the sort of "secret service" performed by officers from the foreign sections during the Brackenbury-Chapman decade may be found in the writings of C.E. Callwell, Edward Gleichen, and W.H.H. Waters, among others. Callwell was the staff captain and eventually the deputy assistant adjutant general (or head) of Section E (Austria-Hungary, Balkan States, Ottoman Empire, and Independent African States) from 1887 to 1892. Though sometimes risky, his extensive "unofficial" travels offered pleasant compensations.

We found in the Intelligence Department that our Chief was not particularly generous in the matter of leave of the ordinary kind; he scarcely ever went away himself. But, on the other hand, he was quite ready to let one go off to visit countries that one was concerned with officially, he indeed encouraged such trips. . . . The consequence was that in the course of four successive autumns, I was out of the country for several weeks, being fortunate in that the regions with which my section was concerned as well as those which had to be traversed on the way, offered much that was attractive from the mere tourist point of view.[53]

Relations between Britain and Austria-Hungary were very good, and Captain Callwell called upon the chief of the Austrian General Staff as well as the head of the Intelligence Department at the Ministry of War during one of his visits to Vienna. "They were all very friendly and we agreed to exchange certain items of information."[54] The Austro-Hungarian hospitality contrasted sharply with the coolness and suspiciousness of the Turkish officials encountered by Callwell. Of necessity, one had to be far more discreet when gathering intelligence for the DMI inside the Sultan's dominions. While conducting a reconnaissance of Salonika on his first trip abroad from Queen Anne's Gate, the young officer quickly learned "that the Turk had a penchant for privacy in the environs of his fortification, and that he looks upon strangers who approach these localities with a profound and not altogether unjustified suspicion." Even more caution seemed prudent one year later when Callwell visited the Turkish port of Chanak on the eastern side of the Narrows of the Dardanelles. "Wandering about the outskirts of Chanak . . ." and armed with a pair of binoculars, he was able to get a good look at the dominating Kilid Bahr heights on the far side of the Narrows, which, "with the numerous batteries that nestled at its foot," appeared to be the "Key of the Dardenelles." Before continuing on to Bulgaria via the Orient Express, Callwell enjoyed a brief stay in Constantinople.

> General Brackenbury had not wished me to go there, as he thought that our Ambassador, Sir W. White, would not like somebody from Queen Anne's Gate turning up in the place. . . . He consented (to Callwell's request to go there anyway), but with the stipulation that I was to stay there as short a time as possible, was to keep clear of the Embassy, and was not to look up our military attaché. . . .

Another important target area for Captain Callwell was the Atlantic coast of Morocco, a region "about which our information was decidedly defective."[55] In 1894 Capt. Edward Gleichen joined with Capt. George Aston of the Royal Marines (then the fleet intelligence officer for the Mediterranean Fleet) in an "intelligence trip" along the coast of French North Africa. Gleichen and Aston collected considerable information on telegraph and cable lines as well as coastal defenses in Algeria and Tunisia, but although they spent several days shooting snipe in the interior "to put the local authorities off the scent," they had some very close calls with French officials. While on a "harmless excursion" to Constantine, Algeria, the two officers were startled to read in the local newspaper that "two suspicious-looking English tourists had been seen sketching the defences of Constantine"; actually, according to Gleichen, "there were no defences there." For Captain Gleichen, the element of danger in such a venture was an added attraction.

> Those were delightful days, and I can thoroughly recommend the sport of battery and cable hunting to anyone who has a taste in that direction, for the added risk (in this case of ten thousand franc fines and five years in a fortress) gives a delicious zest to it. But you must be well prepared, not only with the requisite technical knowledge, but with knowing how to dispose of the information when you have acquired it. . . .[56]

Sometimes Intelligence Division officers were diverted from their planned travels into countries or areas for which they were not ordinarily responsible. Returning to England after observing Austrian cavalry maneuvers in Galicia in 1892, Charles Callwell received instructions from the DMI through the British Embassy in Berlin to proceed immediately on a confidential mission through Rumania into Bessarabia to verify reports of a Russian military buildup there.[57]

Of all the areas into which Generals Brackenbury and Chapman sent their officers on confidential intelligence-gathering missions, the most sensitive, and therefore the most dangerous, was imperial Russia. Xenophobia is deeply rooted in Russian history and was as much a factor in Russia's relations with other nations during the last two decades of the nineteenth century as it is today. In the 1880s and 1890s Russia spent far more on espionage and counterespionage than any other great power.[58] Capt. W.H.H. Waters was well aware of the unique problems of "secret service" work in Russia when he was chosen by General Chapman in 1891 to "discover whether any unusual movements of troops had been or were taking place on the Russo-German border. . . ."

> Russians are secretive by nature, and objected strongly to any unauthorised person endeavoring to gather military information, especially in Russian Poland. . . . It was therefore essential that my reconnaissance should be carried out with care, so as to avoid raising suspicion. Besides the uniformed Russian authorities, police, military, and other, there was also the secret police to be reckoned with, and nobody could tell when a member of it was trailing him.[59]

Several years later, Waters's reputation as a Russian expert won him the appointment as military attaché in St. Petersburg, but in 1891 he was merely an assistant to Capt. James M. Grierson, DAAG and head of Section D (Russia, India, Persia, etc.). Captain Waters wrote that his superiors at Queen Anne's Gate warned him before he left London, "if there should be any trouble with the Russian authorities, the War Office would not only disown me altogether but would likewise inflict punishment in order to show perfectly clean hands. . . ." Throughout his trip of several weeks in Russia and Russian Poland, Waters traveled as a tourist, avoided the appearance of being too curious about military activities, and wrote nothing down about what he had seen until he had reached Dresden, Germany, on his return.

> My memory happened to be a naturally good one, and it had had three years' intensive training, many years previously, at the Lyceé Impérial de Versailles, where great attention was paid to word-perfect recitations. . . . (In Russia) As soon as I saw or heard something worth noting, I repeated it to myself over and over again until it was fixed in my mind. . . . By this means there was no difficulty in remembering, in their sequence, notes about military works, troops, buildings, and all kinds of things connected with the object of my travels.[60]

W.H.H. Waters's 1891 mission to the western portion of the Russian Empire was highly successful. The detailed information which he brought back not only gave Section D and the DMI a much clearer picture of Russian troop dispositions in Poland, but it also allayed German fears about a Russian buildup there. The relationship between the Intelligence Division in London and the Great General Staff in Berlin was so close at this time that Waters allowed the "chief Intelligence officer" to read and copy his 7,000-word report in Berlin before he continued on back to England and presented it to the DMI. The head of German military intelligence thanked the young British officer for providing "most valuable information," and back at Queen Anne's Gate Waters's reception was "really very pleasantly warm," once his report had been read.[61]

As previously mentioned, Capt. George Sydenham Clarke, Royal Engineers, though not assigned to the Intelligence Division, often traveled abroad on missions for the DMI. Still the permanent secretary of the Colonial Defence Committee, Clarke went to Paris in 1889 with orders to make a careful study of "recent artillery materiel and other objects of military use, shown by the Minister of War and the great private firms." One year later Clarke and a Royal Artillery officer journeyed to Magdeburg, Germany, "to report upon a long series of trials of twenty-five natures of ordnance, some of them with novel features, made by the Cruson firm." Captain Clarke's most important trip for General Brackenbury and the War Office was also conducted in 1890. Accompanied by a Belgian engineer and with the blessing of the king of Belgium, he made a "detailed examination of the positions of Liège, Namur, and Antwerp," then under construction and "which twenty-four years later, assumed crucial importance."[62] Clarke's candid evaluation of these fortifications provided disturbing news for King Leopold II and was at the same time a prophecy of events in 1914. In his report he wrote:

> It is not the protection of Belgium against invasion which is directly sought, but the closing of a route connecting the territory of two other Powers, who, it is assumed, must sooner or later be again at war, and either of whom might conceivably select this route as offering advantages in striking at the other. . . . It is certain that the fortifications of the Meuse must be prepared to resist attack at short notice, or lose all military value. . . . Belgium unquestionably provides a striking warning against the abuse of fortification, and the widespread fallacy that forts can be substituted, in any except the most restricted sense, for men has received a fresh illustration.[63]

The failure of the French General Staff to foresee the rapidity with which the Belgium forts would fall to the Germans was a critical factor at the beginning of World War I.

Of course, the collection of military intelligence was only part of the work of the Intelligence Division. Incoming information from all sources had to be analyzed, discarded, or filed and indexed for future reference, and collated in the form of reports and memoranda. This other side of an officer's duties in any one of the foreign sections did not offer the excitement of a "confidential mission" to the Dardanelles, Algeria, or Russian Poland, but, just as in the 1870s, the analysis and production of intelligence were the normal everyday functions of most officers working at Queen Anne's Gate. Henry Brackenbury gave Capt. Charles Callwell an idea of just what was expected of an officer in one of the foreign sections when Callwell first reported for duty in 1887.

> I shan't expect you to be able to answer every question that might arise in respect to your particular work, right off the reel; I shan't even expect the information necessarily to be actually available in the department. But I shall expect you not to be helpless, but to find means of getting that information somehow within a reasonable time. If you keep your wits about you, if you look ahead, if, whenever anything crops up that you do not know all about you set yourself to find out all about it, if you keep sucking information into the place and if you see that the information you suck into the place is properly registered and so made available when required, your particular section will in course of time become a real going concern. Its archives will enable you, or whoever succeeds you, to answer any question that I or any properly authorised person may desire to ask.[64]

Although the work was interesting, for an officer fresh from regimental duty "the sedentary life proved irksome, at least during the early months and until one had become broken to it."[65] The normal duty hours in the Intelligence Division (11 a.m. until 5 p.m.) allowed officers plenty of leisure time. Actually, many officers worked for longer hours, but this did little to alter the image of the Division held by some who had never set foot there. Edward Gleichen recalled that the reputation he acquired in his battalion was that he spent his time "cutting out interesting items and pictures from 'La Vie Parisienne' and sticking them on a screen whilst my hard-worked brother officers were doing my duty!"[66]

Even in 1886-88, an enormous amount of information poured into the Intelligence Division each day. After 1888 the incoming flow increased still more as "Brack's" successful efforts to obtain travel money and improve communications with other government departments paid dividends. Although the permanent officer staff (DAAGs and staff captains) of the Division had doubled since 1885, it was still tiny compared to general staffs on the Continent. Brackenbury was a demanding DMI who had no time for incompetence or laziness. In other words, the small staff of the Intelligence Division had their hands full. By and large, under both Brackenbury and Chapman they were hard-working and productive.

Capt. Charles à Court Repington served in the "French Section" (Section A) for five years. When he arrived in 1889 he was staff captain and assistant to Maj. C.R. Simpson, DAAG. Repington attended the Staff College at Camberley in 1887-88, where he was regarded as "the most brilliant man of his year." Many years later, when his military career ended abruptly following an affair with the wife of a British diplomat in Egypt, Repington turned to journalism and gained international fame as military correspondent for *The Times* (1904-18) and the *Daily Telegraph* (1919-25). He enjoyed his work in the Intelligence Division and found it "demanding, congenial, and stimulating." He was ideally suited for duty in the French Section and in time succeeded Simpson as DAAG. "He probably knew more about the French military system and defenses than any man in England at the time." Repington decided that, in addition to handbooks on foreign armies, which were usually unclassified and received wide dissemination, the Intelligence Division ought to produce secret studies dealing with "all questions of resources, strong places, and particularly strategical matters. . . ." With his volume, *The Military Resources of France* (1895), he produced a model for similar studies of other armies and initiated a new series of publications by the Division.[67]

The nearly constant tension between Britain and Russia during the 1886-95 period gave special importance to the reports and other products of Section D. With Capt. James M. Grierson as DAAG and head and Capt. W.H.H. Waters as staff captain, the Russian Section had its own share of talent during the early 1890s. The future director of military operations (1904-06) of the British General Staff and the future military attaché in St. Petersburg (1893-98) and Berlin (1900-03) formed a small but potent team. Both knew the Russian language and were experts on the Russian military forces. As already alluded to, Grierson's friends on the Great General Staff in Berlin proved an invaluable source of information about Russia. Between 1886 and 1894 he authored a number of works on the Russian, German, and Japanese armies: *The Armed Strength of Russia* (1886), *The Armed Strength of Japan* (1886), *The Armed Strength of the German Empire* (1888), and *Handbook of the Military Forces of Russia* (1894).[68] Grierson's predecessor as head of Section D, Maj. (later Lt. Gen. Sir) James Wolfe Murray turned out several publications on Russia, including a secret report entitled, "Russia's Power to Concentrate Troops in Central Asia" (May 1888).

Another accomplished linguist in the Intelligence Division was Charles E. Callwell of Section E. Immediately prior to joining the division in 1887 he was awarded the gold medal of the Royal United Services Institution for an essay, "Small Wars"; the essay was later expanded by Callwell into a widely read book of the same title. Callwell was recalled to active duty at the outbreak of World War I and was appointed director of military operations. His published works while in Section E include *The Armed Strength of Austria-Hungary* (1891) and *Handbook of the Turkish Army* (1892). Capt. Edward Gleichen and Capt. W.E. Fairholme coauthored the *Handbook on the Armies of Bulgaria, Greece, Montenegro, Roumania and Servia* (1895). The mapping and topographical section (Section F) was busy, too, "producing its own maps and in touch with all the Geographical Societies (and their publications) in the world."[69] Maj. Leonard Darwin, later president of the Royal Geographical Society, was head of Section F during the early 1890s.

The quality of the officers assembled at Queen Anne's Gate by Henry Brackenbury was impressive, and his accomplishment in finding them and getting them assigned to the Division was a critical ingredient in the revival of War Office Intelligence during his five years as DMI.[70] Like MacDougall's reign in the 1870s, Brackenbury's act was tough to follow. Maj. Gen. Edward F. Chapman, who became DMI on 1 April 1891, was an artilleryman whose entire career had been spent in India. He had been brought home from India (where he had served as quartermaster general from 1885 to 1889) in ill health and was chosen DMI apparently because of his vast experience in the Subcontinent and because of the fear of a Russian invasion through India.[71] Chapman was "a most kind and considerate chief"[72] and, according to Edward

Gleichen, "We were all very fond of him personally." However, in many ways Chapman was like a fish out of water in his new position.

> ... [W]hy he had been pitchforked by Lord Roberts into the very difficult position of DMI at home—to deal with foreign political and other European matters of which he was necessarily entirely ignorant—we none of us could ever make out.[73]

Unfortunately for General Chapman, the major crises during his five years as DMI occurred in Europe and Africa, not in India.

Certainly the Intelligence Division missed the strong leadership of Henry Brackenbury after his departure for India in 1891. Happily, though, there was no appreciable decline in the productivity and the efficiency of the Division under Edward Chapman. What carried the Division through the 1891-95 period was the momentum established by Brackenbury. Talented officers like Callwell, Repington, Waters, Grierson and Gleichen, who had been brought in and developed by Brackenbury, also served under Chapman. The new channels for exchanging information opened up by "Brack" with the Admiralty, the Foreign Office, the Colonial Office, and the India Office continued to be used. The money he secured from the Treasury for official and "confidential" trips continued to be available, and the practice of sending officers from the Division abroad regularly was also continued. Lt. Gen. Henry Brackenbury's impact upon British military intelligence at the War Office was both positive and enduring.

NOTES

1. Lord Roberts of Kandahar, *Forty-one Years in India*, 2: 393. Herat was (and is) the most important town in western Afghanistan, a trading center only one hundred miles south of Pendjeh and about the same distance east of the border with Persia (Iran).

2. Ibid., pp. 390, 396.

3. Col. Lord Sydenham of Combe, *My Working Life*, p. 70. See also Richard A. Preston, *Canada and "Imperial Defense,"* pp. 94-95.

4. R.A. Preston, *Canada and "Imperial Defense,"* p. 95.

5. John P. Mackintosh, "The Role of the Committee of Imperial Defence before 1914," p. 491. Franklin A. Johnson, in chapter 1, "Cabinets, Committees and Conflict," of *Defence by Committee*, portrays a more active and important Colonial Defence Committee than either Mackintosh or Norman H. Gibbs in *The Origins of Imperial Defence*.

6. Sydenham, *My Working Life*, pp. 52, 95-98. Clarke's travels on behalf of War Office Intelligence are described in more detail later in this chapter.

7. Ibid., pp. 71-72.

8. Sir George Aston described the Foreign Intelligence Committee under its chief, Capt. W.H. Hall, Royal Navy. At the time of the Pendjeh scare of 1885, "questions were showered upon the Foreign Intelligence Committee of the Admiralty." *Secret Service*, pp. 14-22.

9. The "Ashanti Ring" refers to the officers General Wolseley selected to accompany him to West Africa for the Ashanti War of 1873-74. Also known as the "Wolseley Ring," the group included Redvers Buller, George Colley, Frederick Maurice, Evelyn Wood, William Butler, and Henry Brackenbury, all of whom would in the course of their careers be knighted for service to queen and country. As W.S. Hamer has written, "These were the new men of the Army, whose successes were identified with the Cardwell system." Collectively, they "represented the wind of change that was threatening established ideas and customs." *The British Army*, p. 25.

10. Maj. Gen. Lord Edward Gleichen, *A Guardsman's Memories*, pp. 140-42.

11. Alfred Cochrane, "Brackenbury, Sir Henry," *D.N.B., Twentieth Century, 1912-1921*, pp. 60-62.

12. Field Marshal Viscount Wolseley, *The Story of a Soldier's Life*, 2: 280-81.

13. Cochrane, "Brackenbury," pp. 60-62 and *Who Was Who, 1897-1916*, p. 82.

14. As adjutant general, Wolseley had a powerful voice in promotions and appointments. According to Sir Frederick Maurice and Sir George Arthur, he appointed Brackenbury head of the Intelligence Branch in 1886. *The Life of Lord Wolseley*, p. 224.

15. Gen. Sir Henry Brackenbury, *Some Memories of My Spare Time*, pp. 285-90. Brackenbury was also offered the post of military attaché in Vienna, but declined.

16. Ibid., pp. 242-49.

17. Cochrane, "Brackenbury," pp. 61-62. Near the close of his military career, Brackenbury served as president of the Ordnance Committee (1896-98) and director general of ordnance (1899-1904). Brackenbury's published books include *The Tactics of the Three Arms* (1873), *Narrative of the Ashantee War* (2 vols., 1874), and *The River Column* (1885).

18. Maj. Gen. Sir C.E. Callwell, *Stray Recollections*, 1: 304.

19. Maurice and Arthur, *The Life of Lord Wolseley*, p. 224.

20. Hamer, *The British Army*, p. 61.

21. Collen, *Report on the Intelligence Branch*, p. 6.

22. Col. R.H. Vetch, "Home, Robert," *D.N.B.* 9: 1133. See also *Memorandum of the Secretary of State Relating to the Army Estimates, 1887-88*, Cd. 4985 (1887), 50. 8-9.

23. Lt. Col. W.V.R. Isaac, "History of the Directorate of M.I.," p. 7.

24. Ibid., p. 7: Lt. Col. B.A.H. Parritt, *The Intelligencers*, pp. 152-53; and Maurice and Arthur, *The Life of Lord Wolseley*, pp. 223-24.

25. Brackenbury to the quartermaster general, 14 April 1886, W.O. 33/46. The three initial reports prepared by Henry Brackenbury were 14 April, 23 September, and 14 October 1886, "Mobilization Reports I, II, and III," No. 1, 1-4; No. 3, 1-5.

26. Deputy Quartermaster General for Intelligence, "General Sketch of the Situation Abroad and at Home from a Military Standpoint," 3 August 1886, W.O. 33/46. See John Gooch, *The Plans of War*, p. 7.

27. Hamer, *The British Army*, pp. 106-07. The committee, consisting of Brackenbury and Sir Ralph Thompson, published all three parts of the report in December 1886.

28. Isaac, "History of the Directorate of M.I.," pp. 7-8. Parritt, *The Intelligencers*, p. 153.

29. Senior officials of the Treasury apparently were suspicious of the War Office's requests for more money for the Intelligence Branch because they felt that army officers were merely trying to create unnecessary additional spaces for their fellow officers. Also, the creation of the Naval Intelligence Department (February 1887) further stiffened Treasury resistance to pleas for more money for the Branch. Gooch, *The Plans of War*, pp. 8-9.

30. Maurice and Arthur, *The Life of Lord Wolseley*, pp. 223-24.

31. Isaac, "History of the Directorate of M.I.," p. 9.

32. Ibid., p. 8. See also Parritt, *The Intelligencers*, pp. 153, 156, and Callwell, *Stray Recollections*, 1: 304.

33. Sections A-E were each staffed by a deputy assistant adjutant general (DAAG), a staff captain, and a military clerk. Geographic areas of responsibility of the foreign sections were: A—France, Belgium, Italy, Spain, Portugal, Mexico, and Central and South America; C—Germany, Netherlands, Scandinavia, Switzerland, and USA; D—Russia, India, Afghanistan, Burma, Siberia, China, Japan, Siam, Central Asia, and Persia; E—Austria-Hungary, Balkan States, Ottoman Empire, Egypt, and Independent African States. Section F's staff included a DAAG, a staff captain, a librarian, a map curator, seven draftsmen, three printers and four military clerks. Isaac, "History of the Directorate of M.I.," p. 8.

34. Actually, the AQMG was the acting head of the Branch from 1882 until the end of 1885 because of the departure of Sir Archibald Alison for Egypt in 1882.

35. To assist him in performing the functions of the Central Section, the DMI had a staff captain, two warrant officers, and a confidential clerk. Isaac, "History of the Directorate of M.I.," p. 8.

36. Brackenbury, *Some Memories of My Spare Time*, pp. 352, 354. This was Sir Henry's last published work; he died in April 1914.

37. Capt. (later Maj. Gen. Sir) Charles E. Callwell, Royal Artillery, served in the Intelligence Division from 1887 to 1892. Captain (later Major General) Lord Gleichen of the Grenadier Guards served twice in the Division: 1886-88 and 1894-99. Capt. (later Lt. Col.) Charles à Court Repington of the Rifle Brigade served in the Division from 1889 to 1894. Capt. (later Brig. Gen.) W.H.H. Waters, Royal Artillery, served twice in the Division: 1891-93 and 1898-99.

38. Callwell, *Stray Recollections*, 1: 312, 326-27; Lt. Col. Charles à Court Repington, *Vestigia*, pp. 83-84, 87; Gleichen, *A Guardsman's Memories*, pp. 142-43.

39. Isaac, "History of the Directorate of M.I.," p. 9. See also Repington, *Vestigia*, p. 88, and Parritt, *The Intelligencers*, p. 159. Brackenbury was afforded an excellent opportunity to help bring about even closer coordination between the War Office and the Admiralty when he served as a member of the Hartington Commission along with Lord Hartington, Lord Randolph Churchill, and Sir Henry Campbell-Bannerman. The Hartington Commission was appointed in

1888 to inquire into the "Civil and Professional administration of the Naval and Military departments and the relation of those departments to each other and the Treasury." An informative treatment of the work of the Hartington Commission may be found in Hamer, *The British Army*, pp. 134-47.

40. Isaac, "History of the Directorate of M.I.," p. 9. According to Edward Gleichen, Brackenbury put the Branch "into close touch with the Foreign Office . . . , the Colonial and India Offices, the Royal Geographical Society and even the Cabinet on occasion." Gleichen, *A Guardsman's Memories*, pp. 142-43. In 1891, when Maj. (later Brig. Gen.) W.H.H. Waters reported for duty, the Intelligence Division "was in constant and direct communication with the Foreign Office, which frequently consulted it on various political subjects and their bearing on the military situation." All dispatches written to the Foreign Office by ambassadors and ministers in foreign capitals "which had any bearing on politico-military matters were circulated to the Intelligence Division, so that one soon gained an excellent insight into the temperaments and abilities of England's representatives." Waters, *"Secret and Confidential,"* pp. 22-23

41. Richard Deacon, *A History of the British Secret Service*, p. 137.

42. Zara S. Steiner, *The Foreign Office and Foreign Policy, 1898-1914*, pp. 234-36.

43. Deacon, *British Secret Service*, pp. 75, 123, 146.

44. In discussing how Brackenbury encouraged foreign trips by officers of the Intelligence Division, Charles E. Callwell explained, "he had managed to arrange with the Treasury that quite a useful sum of money should be placed at his disposal annually—and no questions asked—to meet expenses incurred in such services and the Foreign Office was also sometimes ready to help. . . ." *Stray Recollections*, 1: 327. See also Waters, *"Secret and Confidential,"* p. 49.

45. Waters, *"Secret and Confidential,"* pp. 27-28. See also Alfred Vagts, *The Military Attaché*, pp. 189-90, 192, 201, 207-08, 211.

46. Repington describes making up a party of British officers each year for the French maneuvers. "I went constantly abroad, mainly to France, and visited most of the French Channel coasts, gaining an extremely good knowledge of the French military system and defences." *Vestigia*, p. 83.

47. D.S. Macdiarmid, *The Life of Lieut.-General Sir James Moncrieff Grierson*, pp. 86-87, 100-03. In a letter of 27 September 1890, Captain Grierson informed General Brackenbury that during his just completed visit to Germany he had "heard many pieces of information anent the Russian manoeuveres" from Great General Staff officers and had managed to meet the German military attaché at St. Petersburg. Grierson commented, "The Germans have extremely good information as to Russian doings in peace and plans for war, and that they get by simply putting down the roubles." See also Waters, *"Secret and Confidential,"* pp. 24-25.

48. Lt. Gen. H. Brackenbury, DMI. "Notes for the Information of Officers attending Foreign Manoeuvres."

49. See chapter 12, "On the Spy" in Gleichen, *A Guardsman's Memories*, pp. 133-39.

50. Deacon, *British Secret Service*, pp. 134-35.

51. Parritt, *The Intelligencers*, pp. 126-27. See also William Hillcourt and O.S. Baden-Powell, *Baden-Powell: The Two Lives of a Hero* (New York: Putnam, 1964).

52. Lt. Gen. H. Brackenbury, "Rules to be Observed by Officers Travelling, who are endeavoring to obtain Information for the Intelligence Division." Indications are that these rules were formulated in 1889.

53. Callwell, *Stray Recollections*, 1: 326-27.

54. Ibid., p. 344.

55. Ibid., pp. 39, 344-47.

56. Gleichen, *A Guardsman's Memories*, pp. 133-38. Gleichen's partner on his 1894 trip to French North Africa, George Aston, had been assigned to the flagship of the naval commander-in-chief in the Mediterranean in 1892. This apparently was the first time an intelligence department had been formed in a British fleet, "a system of fleet intelligence which had spread nearly all over the world by 1914." It was not surprising that the fleet was commanded by Adm. Sir George Tryon (until his death off of Tripoli in 1893), the founder of the Admiralty's Foreign Intelligence Committee a decade before. Aston, *Secret Service*, pp. 30-31.

57. Callwell, *Stray Recollections*, 1: 357-58.

58. Deacon, *A History of the Russian Secret Service*, p. 132.

59. Waters, *"Secret and Confidential,"* pp. 27-28.

60. Ibid., pp. 28-33.

61. Ibid., pp. 33, 35.

62. Sydenham, *My Working Life*, pp. 95-98.

63. Maj. G.S. Clarke, R.E., "Report on the Defences of Belgium, 1890."

64. Callwell, *Stray Recollections*, 1: 305.

65. Ibid., p. 307.

66. Gleichen, *A Guardsman's Memories*, p. 79.

67. J.E. Edmonds, "Repington, Charles à Court", *D.N.B. 1922-1930*. See also "The Voice of the Thunderer" in Luvaas, *The Education of an Army*, pp. 294-95; and Repington, *Vestigia*, pp. 89-90.

68. All of these works by Grierson may be seen at the Ministry of Defence Library in London.

69. Gleichen, *A Guardsman's Memories*, p. 143.

70. Besides those already mentioned, other officers who served at the Intelligence Division during the years 1886-95 included Maj. (later Maj. Gen.) J.C. Dalton, Maj. (later Maj. Gen. Sir) J.K. Trotter, Capt. (later Maj. Gen. Sir) Charles Barter, and Capt. (later Field Marshal Sir) Henry H. Wilson.

71. Parritt, *The Intelligencers*, pp. 161-62.

72. Repington, *Vestigia*, p. 89.

73. Gleichen, *A Guardsman's Memories*, p. 177.

Chapter VI

From the Intelligence Division to the General Staff: The South African War and War Office Intelligence, 1896-1904

> The Transvaal has, during the last two years, made military preparations on a scale which can only be intended to meet the contingency of a contest with Great Britain. . . . At the outbreak of such a war we should, at first, be in a decided numerical inferiority; moreover, we should have to face the problem of protecting a very long frontier, and should be handicapped with a certain amount of disloyalty (passive if not active) within our own borders. At least a month or six weeks must elapse before any appreciable reinforcements could arrive from England or India.
>
> From a memorandum prepared on 21 September 1898 by Maj. Edward Altham of the Intelligence Division of the War Office

British prestige was shaken to its very foundations in the autumn of 1899 by a stunning series of British Army defeats during the opening months of the South African War. Striking quickly across the borders of the Transvaal and the Orange Free State into Natal and the Cape Colony, the Boers[1] completely outmaneuvered and bottled up a large proportion of the British Army in South Africa. Officially, the war began on the afternoon of 11 October, when the Boers' ultimatum demanding the withdrawal of British troops from the frontiers expired. Three days later British forces at Mafeking and Kimberley in Cape Colony had been cut off. By 2 November the main Boer army under Gen. Piet Joubert had moved well inside northwestern

South Africa 1899

Natal and had trapped Gen. Sir George White's Natal Defence Force, the largest British force in South Africa, inside the town of Ladysmith. White's defeat at the hands of a numerically equal Boer army in the battle of Nicholson's Nek and the resultant siege of Ladysmith brought forth shock and outrage in London. Whitehall was plunged into gloom and a few snickers were heard in Berlin and Paris, but the worst was yet to come.

Confidence and optimism rose in England during November with the arrival of the main British field force, the Army Corps, and a new commander, the highly decorated Gen. Sir Redvers Buller, in South Africa. Twice the winner of the Victoria Cross in a long, illustrious military career, the sixty-year-old Buller was immensely popular among the rank and file of the British Army in South Africa. To the admiring public, he appeared to be an ideal choice to lead Britain to a rapid and decisive victory over the Boers. General Buller was given a rousing send-off when he sailed from Southampton in mid-October, and a huge crowd cheered his arrival in Cape Town at the end of the month just as Joubert was closing the ring around Ladysmith. Undaunted by the bad news which greeted his arrival, Sir Redvers decided immediately to divide the 47,000-man Army Corps and attempt the simultaneous relief of the garrisons at Kimberley and Ladysmith. He went personally to Natal to lead the effort to rescue Sir George White.

Suddenly in December 1899 came Black Week: first, the ambush and defeat of General Gatacre's force at Stormberg on 10 December; second, the Boer victory against General Methuen's frontal attack at Magersfontein on 10-11 December; third, and as a crushing climax, the decisive defeat of General Buller's 21,000 men at Colenso on 15 December. The very thought that an undisciplined army of Dutch farmers could inflict three defeats within five days upon one of the finest and best-equipped British armies ever sent overseas, an army led by an authentic Victorian hero, was an extremely difficult notion for England's soldiers, politicians, and public to accept.[2] So devastated was Sir Redvers Buller by the cumulative effect of Black Week that, in a message to Sir George White on the day after Colenso, he suggested the surrender of the besieged Ladysmith force. The severe blow to British pride, the considerable loss of life and materiel suffered during Black Week, and General Buller's own self-admitted failure led to his removal as supreme commander in South Africa and to a rising tide of criticism from inside and outside the government against the army, the War Office, and the Intelligence Division.

For the first time since the establishment of the Intelligence Branch in 1873, War Office Intelligence was subjected to the glare of public scrutiny. The experience was not a pleasant one for those serving in the Intelligence Division at the time, particularly for the director of military intelligence, Maj. Gen. Sir John Ardagh.

> There is no branch of our military organization which, during the present war, has come in for so much criticism and blame as the Intelligence Department.[3]

The nation and the government had been unprepared for war in South Africa because the Intelligence Division had failed in its duty, or so some critics proclaimed. The alleged negligence of the Division with regard to the actual military strength and capabilities of the Boers appeared inexcusable in light of the fact that the war had been brewing for several years. The Boer Republic had begun serious preparations for war after the failure of the Jameson Raid in December 1895.[4] There had been ample warning and plenty of time to collect information. Then, too, the enemy were not strangers to the British Army. Much should have been learned about them from the Transvaal Revolt of 1880-81 (also known as the First Boer War), and especially from the defeats suffered in January and February of 1881 by British regulars under Gen. Sir George Colley at Laing's Nek and Majuba Hill. Additional opportunities to observe the fighting qualities of the Boers firsthand had been afforded by native uprisings in which Briton and Boer had fought side by side. For all of these reasons it seemed that "the British War Office could not have been in the dark respecting the peculiarities of the theatre of war and of its adversaries."[5]

Nevertheless, it appeared in December 1899 that Great Britain had vastly underrated her potential enemies in the two Dutch Republics of South Africa and that this miscalculation had been a major cause of the costly defeats suffered in the opening months of the war. Within the government and the army, whose duty had it been to estimate the strength, capabilities, and intentions of possible adversaries so that proper steps might have been taken to prepare for war? Was there not an Intelligence Division in the War Office responsible for such work, and, if so, should it not receive a heavy share of the blame for failing to correctly assess the strength and the intentions of the Boers? Such questions were asked in the aftermath of Black Week and were reexamined after the war by the Royal Commission on the War in South Africa.[6] Owing to the confidentiality of the work of the Intelligence Division and of its reports, particularly regarding the military preparations of the Boers in the years prior to 1899, Sir John Ardagh, the DMI throughout this critical period, was unable to respond publicly to the criticism of his organization until October 1902, when he was called as a witness by the Royal Commission.[7]

Maj. Gen. Sir John Ardagh had succeeded Edward Chapman as director of military intelligence on 1 April 1896, three months after the abortive Jameson Raid. At the time of his return to the Intelligence Division in 1896, following six years as private secretary to the viceroy of India (1888-94) and a year as commandant of the School of Military Engineering at Chatham, Ardagh enjoyed a reputation as the "foremost politico-military officer" in the British Army as well as an authority on international law and an outstanding staff officer. He also had the advantage of close personal friendships with virtually all of the most important figures in Britain's defense establishment at that time, including Lord Lansdowne, secretary of state for war, and Lord Wolseley, the commander-in-chief of the army.[8] Lengthy experience in intelligence and diplomatic work made General Ardagh appear an ideal choice for the DMI post. Despite all the public criticism of Ardagh and his department during the South African War, he remained on as DMI until June 1901, serving a full five-year term. That Sir John was allowed to retain his position for eighteen months after the calamities of Black Week was a measure of the confidence Lord Wolseley and others continued to have in him, but it did little to ease his personal ordeal.

The intellectual capacities of John Charles Ardagh were apparent early in life. Born in 1840 at Camragh House in Stradbally, County Waterford, Ireland, he entered Trinity College, Dublin, at the age of seventeen and won honors in Hebrew and mathematics during his first year, before dropping out to apply for the Royal Military Academy at Woolwich. Young Ardagh passed first on the entrance examination to Woolwich in 1858, graduated top man in his class in April 1859, and was commissioned as a lieutenant in the Royal Engineers. John Ardagh's career pattern bears a remarkable similarity to that of another Royal Engineer who played a prominent role in the development of British military intelligence, Charles W. Wilson. Engineer assignments were interspersed with intelligence duties and special work for the Foreign Office. He spent the first fourteen years after Woolwich engaged almost solely in engineer work. It was only after completing the Staff College at Camberley at the end of 1874 that Captain Ardagh began a series of intelligence and diplomatic assignments which led ultimately to his appointment as DMI in 1896.

Ardagh served as an attached officer in the Intelligence Branch under Patrick MacDougall and Charles Wilson in 1875-76, during which time he was sent abroad to Holland on "intelligence duty." Appointed deputy assistant quartermaster general for intelligence (DAQMG) in July 1876, Ardagh was named head of Section E (Austria, Italy, Greece, Ottoman Empire, Egypt, etc.) and served in that capacity until 1881. As was typical of the DAQMGs in the Intelligence Branch of the late 1870s, John Ardagh spent little time in London. He was sent to the headquarters of the Turkish Army in Servia in August 1876. In October, he was ordered to Constantinople to report on the defenses of the city.

> In fifteen days he prepared sketch surveys of nearly 150 square miles and proved himself an expert in strategic geography. These surveys included the position of Buyuk-Chekmedje-Dere, with projects for the defence of the Dardenelles and the Bosphorus. . . . The actual works were subsequently constructed by the Turks. Ardagh also reported for the Foreign Office on the operations in Herzegovina and Montenegro, and December 1876 went to Tirnovo in Bulgaria to report on the state of the country.

Following special Foreign Office service in Italy in 1877-78, Ardagh attended the Congress of Berlin as a technical military adviser in the summer of 1878 and then was employed on a series of frontier delimitation commissions in the Balkans (1878-81). His long service in Egypt (1882-87) included a stint in early 1884 as commanding Royal Engineer and chief of the Intelligence Department under Sir Gerald Graham in the eastern Sudan. Ardagh returned from Egypt as a colonel in 1887 and served throughout most of 1888 as assistant adjutant general for mobilization, initially under the DMI, Henry Brackenbury, and, after February, directly under the adjutant general. From London Ardagh went to India in October 1888 as private secretary to Lord

Lansdowne, the new viceroy. After his tour as DMI (1896-1901) and his retirement from military service in 1902, Sir John continued to work for the Foreign Office and to remain involved in public affairs until his death in 1907.[9]

Sir John Ardagh was a quiet man, brilliant and hard-working. His young subordinates in the Intelligence Division regarded him with a mixture of respect, curiosity, and awe. A colorful description of Ardagh as DMI may be found in the memoirs of Maj. Gen. (then Capt.) Lord Edward Gleichen, who served as a deputy assistant adjutant general (DAAG) and head of Section E (Austro-Turkish) from 1897 to 1899.

> Ardagh, silent, monocled, skinny-necked (he always reminded me of a marabou stork, I fear) the writer of beautifully expressed far-seeing memoranda on the most abstruse questions, was always something of a mystery to us. He never spoke and when he sent for us to give him information on certain subjects, there was a dead silence on his part whilst we talked. I once gave him a full account of Morocco matters during the space of something like half an hour. He leant back in his chair, never interrupted once nor took a note, and at the end he slowly screwed his eyeglass in and said in a hollow, faded voice, "Thank you." Yet he had absorbed painlessly all that I had told him, and the issue was a masterpiece of writing.[10]

Capt. W.H.H. Waters, head of Section D (Russia-in-Europe and Asia) in 1898-99, found it a "real pleasure" to serve under Ardagh. He was, according to Waters, "rather silent, with plenty of dry humour, he had wonderful vision, never properly recognised."[11] Sir John's wife described him as an individual possessing "a natural dislike for talking for mere talk's sake," and, "a gift for listening sympathetically to others." These qualities, together with "a remarkable clearness of intellectual vision in unravelling a complicated situation," enabled Ardagh to gain the wholehearted confidence of the most cautious statesmen and officials, including those at the Foreign and Colonial Offices and at the Admiralty, whose cooperation was vital to the Intelligence Division.[12]

The channels of communication between War Office Intelligence and other departments of the government, opened by Patrick MacDougall in the 1870s and expanded so vigorously by Henry Brackenbury in the late 1880s, were still open when John Ardagh arrived at Queen Anne's Gate in 1896, but just barely. His predecessor, Edward Chapman (DMI, 1891-96), was not highly regarded by the Foreign Office, nor, apparently, did he enjoy good connections within the higher echelons of the War Office. Chapman's considerable experience in India and his close ties to Lord Roberts, the commander-in-chief in India, were of no avail during his term as DMI. His difficulties in the War Office stemmed not only from the fact that he was a protégé of Roberts,[13] but also because he objected to the War Office's preoccupation with the defense of the British Isles and fortification of London.[14] Chapman urged a widening of Britain's strategic horizons, an argument which was given more urgency by the growing friendship, after 1890, between republican France and tsarist Russia, especially after the signing of the Franco-Russian Military Convention in 1894.[15] Yet, as he confided to

Henry Brackenbury in 1892, Chapman was so isolated from other departments that he had found it necessary to ask an officer in the Mobilization Division to send papers to him so he could stay in touch with what was going on.[16]

As for relations with the Foreign Office, General Chapman was at a severe disadvantage when compared with Brackenbury (DMI, 1886-91) and Ardagh (DMI, 1896-1901). Both had worked for the Foreign Office prior to their appointments as DMI—Brackenbury as military attaché in Paris and Ardagh at the Congress of Berlin and on numerous other occasions as a technical advisor—and were known and respected on Downing Street. Chapman was an unknown quantity to them and an Indian Army officer to boot. Then, too, officers from the Intelligence Division traveling abroad to collect information in these years were not always welcomed by British diplomatic staffs. An officer from Queen Anne's Gate who got caught snooping about in St. Petersburg or the Dardenelles could prove a great diplomatic embarrassment. Also bothersome to the diplomats were officers who made brief visits to countries and produced sweeping but superficial reports on the military or political situation. The British ambassador in Russia, on one occasion, expressed his outrage to Chapman that an officer of the Intelligence Division had arrived unannounced and then toured the country giving instructions to various British consuls.[17]

In sharp contrast to Sir Edward Chapman, Sir John Ardagh enjoyed cordial working relationships with the Admiralty, the Colonial Office, and the Foreign Office, not to mention a strong position inside the War Office based upon his friendships with Lord Wolseley and Lord Lansdowne. Ardagh was a member of the Colonial Defence Committee, a position which facilitated the regular exchange of information with the Naval Intelligence Department and the Colonial Office. Neither the Colonial Office nor the Foreign Office hesitated to ask the DMI for his expert opinion on the military aspects of colonial or diplomatic problems. The Foreign Office relied heavily on the advice of Ardagh and his staff in international boundary disputes. In return, the Intelligence Division once again began receiving a steady flow of information from the Foreign and Colonial Offices. Queen Anne's Gate was only a few minutes' walk from the Downing Street offices of these two departments. Into Ardagh's Intelligence Division poured "the stream of reports from Ambassadors, Consuls, Governors, Agents and other officials, whose duty it is to keep the British Government in touch with events . . . in every portion of the world."[18]

Major General Ardagh's official responsibilities as DMI differed little from those of his predecessors. The Intelligence Division was still a kind of substitute for a British General Staff, but it was not a true general staff. Six years before Ardagh became DMI the War Office seemed to be on the verge of a major reorganization leading to the formation of a general staff. One of three major recommendations made by the Hartington Commission,[19] which published its reports in 1890, was the creation of a general staff headed by a chief of staff. A second recommendation called for the abolition of the position of commander-in-chief and the establishment of a War Office Council as an official source of advice to the secretary of state for war.[20]

Opposition to the recommendations of the Hartington Commission arose from conservative and liberal elements alike. Lord Wolseley, Lord Roberts, the Duke of Cambridge (commander-in-chief from 1856-95), and Queen Victoria were upset at the proposal to abolish the post of commander-in-chief. The members of the cabinet found the idea of the establishment of a chief of staff unacceptable.[21] So powerful was the opposition that the recommendations of the commission were not implemented. Though a War Office Council was established in 1890, the position of commander-in-chief was not abolished, and the council was unable to provide independent advice to the secretary for war as intended by the commission. In this atmosphere, Secretary for War Edward Stanhope felt it unwise to take any steps toward the creation of a general staff.[22]

When the venerable Duke of Cambridge finally retired in 1895, he was replaced as commander-in-chief by Lord Wolseley. One week after Wolseley's appointment was announced in August 1895, the new secretary for war, Lord Lansdowne, unveiled his reorganization scheme for the War Office. That this reorganization was made official by an order in council shows that the recommendation of the Hartington Commission in 1890 regarding the creation for a general staff along continental lines was still far from implementation. A general staff for the British Army was no more palatable to the government in 1895 than it had been in 1890. On the other hand, another recommendation of the Hartington Commission—that a standing Defence Committee of the Cabinet be set up—was at last put into effect. Unfortunately, the committee's sphere of activity was severely restricted; "it met infrequently, and accomplished little."[23] When it did meet, the DMI usually was not invited to attend.

The duties assigned to the DMI when Sir John Ardagh arrived at Queen Anne's Gate in April 1896 were prescribed by a memorandum under the order in council of 21 November 1895. The DMI

> deals with the preparation of information relative to the military defence of the Empire and the strategical consideration of all schemes of defence; the collection and distribution of information relating to the military geography, resources, and armed forces of foreign countries, and of the British colonies and possessions; the compilation of maps; and the translation of foreign documents. He conducts correspondence with other departments of the State on defence questions, and is authorized to correspond semi-officially with them on all subjects connected with his duties.[24]

The Intelligence Division and a separate "Office in Charge of Mobilization" were located within the Department of the Commander-in-Chief; their heads, the DMI and the assistant adjutant general for mobilization services, worked directly for the commander-in-chief. The Department of the Commander-in-Chief, therefore, would substitute for a general staff. But the commander-in-chief was expected to perform a wide range of duties that left insufficient time for him to function as an effective chief of staff. He was principal advisor to the secretary of state for war on all military questions and was also to exercise "general supervision" over all other military departments of the War Office—the Adjutant General's Department, the Quartermaster

General's Department, the Department of the Inspector General of Fortifications, and the Department of the Director General of Ordnance.[25]

Significantly, the DMI was responsible only for the collection, production, and dissemination of military intelligence. Neither the DMI nor any other officer of the commander-in-chief's staff was tasked specifically with the critical responsibility of assisting Lord Wolseley with the strategical distribution of the British Army and with the preparation of war plans for the most likely contingencies. The absence of a British general staff at the end of the nineteenth century put the British War Office at a distinct disadvantage and resulted in a glaring weakness in its ability to prepare for war. This defect was remedied only by the major reforms which followed the South African War.

> The preparation of schemes for military operations is a duty which, above all others, requires close study by a staff of specially qualified officers. To leave it to be sandwiched into the spare moments of an exceedingly busy individual, however high in rank, and however distinguished a soldier, was an oversight the more strange insomuch as in the Intelligence Division there already existed the nucleus of the Staff required to do the work.[26]

Yet the Intelligence Division was not asked to do such work in the 1896-99 period, and the DMI was not even included as a member of the War Office Consultative Council[27] set up by the order in council of 21 November 1895. Sir John Ardagh's statement as a witness before the Royal Commission on the War in South Africa further amplified the position of the Intelligence Division in the years before the South African War.

> I think the Intelligence Department . . . has not now and has not for many years had, the influence on the military policy of the country that it ought to have . . . my position (as DMI) was very subordinate indeed to the influence exercised by the great military officers at the War Office—the Commander-in-Chief, the Adjutant-General, the Quartermaster-General, the Inspector-General of Fortifications; they were as a rule Lieutenant-Generals or higher rank while I was a Major-General, and rank goes for a good deal in confabulations of military people.[28]

Including the DMI, eighteen officers were assigned to the Intelligence Division during the period 1896-99. The internal organization was virtually unchanged since the reign of Sir Henry Brackenbury (1886-91). There were now seven sections under the DMI rather than six; the library had been separated from Section F (formerly the topographic and library section) and a new Section L had been formed. The four foreign sections (A, C, D, and E) had the same geographical areas of responsibility as before, and Section B focused on the colonies and "imperial defence." Section B was responsible for, among other things, the collection of intelligence in South Africa.[29]

The pressures on Section B intensified after the Jameson Raid. Yet, the section was not augmented, even in the summer and fall of 1899, when war in South Africa seemed about to break out at any moment. With a staff of two officers, a deputy assistant adjutant general (DAAG) and a staff captain, and a clerk, Section B was assigned the following projects:

(1) An annual examination of schemes of home and colonial defence.

(2) The observation of military operations conducted in any part of the Empire except India.

(3) A study of the organization, numerical strength, and efficiency of the Colonial Forces of the Empire.

(4) The collation and submission to the Commander-in-Chief of Information concerning the military forces and plans of the two S. African republics.

(5) A study of boundary questions affecting British Colonies and Protectorates.

(6) The collation, preparation, and distribution of information concerning the resources and topography of all parts of the Empire except the United Kingdom and India.

(7) The consideration of strategical questions connected with submarine cables and their control in war.

Section F, the "Maps and Printing Section," also had responsibilities related to the preparation for the Boer War. With a staff of three officers and some twenty-three draftsmen, printers, and clerks, Section F was responsible for "the provision of maps required for military purposes throughout the Empire."[30] Obviously, these two sections, and particularly Section B, were understaffed for the accomplishment of their duties.

A useful description of the inner workings of the Intelligence Division in this period, and especially Section B, may be found in Sir William R. Robertson's memoirs, *From Private to Field-Marshal*. Robertson, who rose to the top of his profession during World War I when he was named chief of the Imperial General Staff, was an exceptional individual who had come up through the ranks. While a young cavalry lieutenant in India, his achievements as a linguist brought him an appointment in the Intelligence Department of the Indian Army at Simla. Robertson's notable intelligence work in India,[31] where he mainly had been concerned with the problems of the Northwest Frontier, helped him become the first "ranker" (ex-enlisted man) to gain admittance to the Staff College. Upon graduation from Camberley in December 1898, Captain Robertson was assigned to the Intelligence Division at the War Office on a three-month temporary appointment working for Capt. W.H.H. Waters in Section D (Asia and Russia-in-Europe). Robertson quickly won a permanent appointment in the Division, and at the end of his three months with Waters he was assigned to Section B as a staff captain under the immediate supervision of its chief, Maj. (later Lt. Gen.) Edward A. Altham. Upon Altham's departure for South Africa in September 1899, Robertson became chief of B Section and remained there until December 1899, when he, too, was ordered to South Africa.[32]

As Robertson explained it, his section dealt with all military questions—"their number being exceeded only by the variety of their character"—concerning any of the forty distinct and independent states of the Colonial Empire and various other dependencies, territories controlled by British companies, and protectorates under the supervision of the Foreign Office. The area which received the most attention was, of course, South Africa, where "trouble had been brewing for some two years past and was daily becoming more acute."[33] How and where did Section B obtain intelligence about the military forces and plans of the two Boer Republics and the required topographical information about various areas of South Africa?

Before the war, the great bulk of useful and important intelligence on the military strength of the Dutch Republics and the terrain of South Africa was collected from legitimate, overt sources and not through the employment of secret agents or other covert sources. Some of these sources were official publications of the Transvaal and Orange Free State governments; reports of British Army officers (in particular, the staff intelligence officers for Cape Colony and Natal) and of British civilian officials (most important was Sir W. Conyngham Greene, the British agent at Pretoria, who sent reports of purely military interest directly to the Intelligence Department); Custom House returns (which allowed B Section to form accurate estimates of the arms and ammunition being received by the Boer Republics); and information based on the observation of British civilians traveling within the Boer Republics. Topographical information was obtained from already existing maps, which were rare for the Transvaal and the Orange Free State. The mapping section had all the maps of South Africa that were known to exist. Other valuable information was obtained through communication with the Naval Intelligence Department and the Foreign and Colonial Offices. Robertson described the receipt of the raw intelligence by B Section:

> Every Saturday the Cape Mail brought us a budget of correspondence, official and private, which had to be sifted, studied, and distributed; it was known that war-like stores were gradually being accumulated both by the Transvaal and the Orange Free State and it was our duty to watch these as closely as conditions would allow. . . .

He went on to explain that he and his boss, Altham, initiated "special reconnaissances of main routes and strategical localities," not indicating whether these missions were overt or covert.[34]

Occasionally the Intelligence Division did send officers down to South Africa on "secret service" in the years 1896 through 1899. Altham himself had spent several months there in 1896. The officers wore civilian clothes and posed as travelers as they went about their assigned missions—gathering topographical intelligence and furnishing information about roads, railroads (likely avenues of advance in the event of war), bridges, and other items of potential military concern.[35] The true mission of the officers was not known by most who came in contact with them in South Africa, but their work was hardly that of the traditional spy. They traveled in civilian clothes mainly because the Colonial Office was worried lest any friction be aroused with the Boers; British officers traveling about openly collecting information would have created the risk of hostile demonstrations and a further deterioration of Boer-British relations.[36] Yet it is highly unlikely that these officers went unnoticed by the excellent Boer intelligence network in South Africa.[37]

In late June 1899, when war with the Boers seemed imminent, no less than ten officers were sent on special missions to South Africa to gather additional information and also to begin building up the field intelligence capability of the British Army in South Africa. Considering the meager funds provided the officers, they did yeoman work, but there were too few of them.

In the words of the editor of *The Times History*, in his statement before the Royal Commission in March 1903,

> The eight or ten or a dozen officers who went out did very good work, I know, but they were fewer than the men I employed myself as *Times* correspondents and I should have been ashamed to send *Times* correspondents anywhere, or even a commercial traveller, with the sum of money they were given.[38]

Indeed, the extremely small budget of the Intelligence Division (about £11,000 per year) was a serious limitation on what could be done, either by B Section or F Section (responsible for maps). When compared to the more than £90,000 per year being spent by the Transvaal Intelligence Department or the £270,000 per year being spent by the German General Staff,[39] the amount of money allowed for the Intelligence Division appears paltry indeed.

The Admiralty had little interest in the collection of intelligence about the Boer Republics since the Boers had no navy. Therefore, the Naval Intelligence Department could offer little or no information on South Africa to the army's Intelligence Division. The civilian Secret Intelligence Service (SIS), however, was financed generously, experienced, and capable of making a significant contribution to intelligence-collection activities in South Africa during the years before the war. It was still preoccupied with Ireland and also concerned about the possibility of a Chinese rising and was of little or no help to the Intelligence Division. A belated effort was made after the war had already erupted, when a famous secret agent of the SIS was sent on an espionage mission to the Netherlands to find out about Boer activities in Europe.[40] Long before this, however, officers of the Intelligence Division had realized that they alone would have to develop an effective intelligence network in South Africa.

What of the end product of the Intelligence Division? Was the division guilty of the "criminal ignorance" of which some of the public and even responsible politicians accused it in the early months of the war, when "a cloud of despondency lowered over England as the mail brought news of reverse after reverse"?[41] The formal charges made against the Intelligence Division at the outset of the Royal Commission on the War in South Africa were as follows:

(1) That it had failed to assess correctly the numerical strength of the Boers.

(2) That it was ignorant of their armament, especially their artillery.

(3) That it had failed to fathom the Boers' offensive designs on Natal.

(4) That in any case, no warnings to the above had been given to the Government.

(5) That our troops were left unfurnished with maps and were without topographical information.[42]

Given its lack of funds and its lack of power within the War Office, the Intelligence Division did its job amazingly well. It was consistently accurate in its estimates of the numerical strength of the Boer armies, the numbers and types of armaments they possessed, and the intentions of their leaders.

In the opinion of the Royal Commission on the War in South Africa,

> It was not the function of the Intelligence Division of the War Office to formulate from information it had collected an estimate of the force

> required to guard against the dangers which that information dis-
> closed . . . it becomes necessary to look to some higher authority. . . .
> Obviously, this is to be found only in the Commander-in-Chief with
> whom, as already stated, rested the duty of preparing schemes of offen-
> sive and defensive operations.[43]

Quite rightly, the Intelligence Division should not have been blamed for the failure to reinforce the British garrison in South Africa sufficiently before the commencement of hostilities. In fact, as the Royal Commission pointed out, the special reports prepared by Major Altham and Major General Ardagh over the three-year period 1896-99 and the handbook "Military Notes on the Dutch Republics of South Africa" (initially published in 1898 and revised in June 1899), all of which were provided to the commander-in-chief, "contained information which was in many respects remarkably accurate."[44]

Singled out for special praise was a memorandum prepared by Altham on 11 June 1896, in which reasons were given for abandoning the long-held assumption of the British that in the event of war the Boers would not make a determined advance into either Natal or Cape Colony during the month or six weeks required to bring sufficient British reinforcements into South Africa. It was judged not impossible that "the two Boer States may make a dash at Natal," considering their increased military strength, their political aspirations, and their desire to possess Natal and a seaport at Durban.[45] Subsequent memoranda by General Ardagh (October 1896 and 15 April 1897) and Major Altham (21 September 1898, 3 June 1899, and 8 August 1899) gave résumés of the situation at the time, stressing the growing military potential of the Boer Republics, the probability of the active military cooperation of the Orange Free State with the Transvaal in the event of war, the likelihood of war, and the decided numerical inferiority in which British troops would find themselves at the outbreak of war. It was urged repeatedly that local defense plans be prepared by commanders in Natal and Cape Colony and that other defensive preparations, including the strengthening of the garrisons, should be carried out.[46]

The warnings of the Intelligence Division did not go entirely unheeded; the total regular army garrison of 3,699 in 1895 was gradually increased to 8,500 by 1 August 1899 and then to 20,000 before the start of the war in October.

If the Boer advances into Natal and Cape Colony—foretold by the Intelligence Division—were to be countered effectively, much larger reinforcements than these would have been needed.

> It was however, the great desire of Her late Majesty's Government to
> settle the differences between Great Britain and the South African
> Republic by negotiations without involving South Africa in war. The
> Government believed that on learning of the large reinforcements from
> England, the Boers would at once break off negotiations and commence
> hostilities.[47]

That the secretary of state for war, Lord Lansdowne, and the secretary of state for the colonies, Joseph Chamberlain, were opposed to sending large numbers of troops to South Africa in the summer of 1899 can be seen clearly in the exchange of memoranda and letters between Wolseley and Lansdowne at the time, and in Chamberlain's memorandum for the cabinet of 6 September 1899. Chamberlain, who like Lansdowne had been receiving the reports of the Intelligence Division, was convinced that it was exaggerating the size of the Boer forces.[48]

Instead of exaggerating the size of the Boer forces, the Intelligence Division had come very close to estimating their numerical strength correctly. In the revised edition of "Military Notes on the Dutch Republics" prepared in June 1899, it was stated that there were 31,329 men liable for military service in the Transvaal (this figure was correct according to Boer records captured at Pretoria during the war) and 22,314 in the Orange Free State (according to captured records, the actual number was 23,305), and that the total number who would be in the field at the start of the war would be about 40,000, not counting the foreigners and Cape Colonists who would join with the Boers.[49] Apparently, the Boers themselves were not sure how many men they did have in the field on 11 October 1899 (or at any time during the war), but, in the judgement of the authoritative *Times History*, the actual number was between 37,000 and 40,000 and by December "when they stood at their highest, about 45,000."[50] Even more accurate were the estimates in "Military Notes" of Boer armaments. The two republics were believed to have a total of 107 guns in their artillery units (the actual number was 99). Similarly, the estimates of the number of rifles and the amount of rifle ammunition in the inventories of the two Boer Republics were close to the mark.[51]

The inadequacy of the maps provided to field commanders in South Africa in the early stages of the war contributed in several instances to British defeats, most notably the defeat of General Methuen's force at the Modder River on 28 November 1899, when he and his staff were completely mistaken about the course of the river. This problem was cited by Field Marshal Lord Roberts as one of the seven major defects in the preparation for the conflict.[52] Nevertheless, as the Royal Commission learned in its examination of this subject, the Intelligence Division was not capable of producing its own maps and was entirely dependent on what could be obtained from the various countries for which it was responsible. Except for "inaccurate compilations from rough farm surveys," no maps of the Transvaal and the Orange Free State were in existence, but, "with the limited means at its disposal, the Intelligence Division did everything it could to map the parts of the country deemed to be of most importance," and it had obtained all the maps already in existence which might have been of use. The Royal Commission was informed that £17,000 would have been required for mapping alone, if the Intelligence Division had been authorized to perform the necessary surveys.[53]

Although the Intelligence Division did an excellent job in correctly determining enemy intentions, numerical strength, and armaments, as well as in providing as much useful topographical information and maps as it could obtain with limited resources, it did fail in one very important respect not mentioned in the Royal Commission's *Report*. It neglected to explain that, in comparing relative strength of Boer and British forces available in South Africa, one British soldier did not equal one Boer. The true strength of the Boers could not be gauged merely by knowing how many men, guns, and rifles they had, which is what the reports and estimates of the Intelligence Division implied. Quite unlike the British Army, which required large numbers of men for logistical support and protection of lines of communication, "forty thousand Boers meant practically forty thousand rifles available for the firing line."[54] Boer strength was increased still further by their mobility (every man was mounted and, in the South African terrain, "one mounted man was worth three on the ground"), their individual initiative, their excellent use of rifle fire and cover, their powerful motivations—intense hatred of the British and love of their own country—and their development of infantry tactics particularly suited to the terrain of South Africa; all of which served to minimize their own casualties and to maximize those of their enemy.

Thus, the actual disparity in the capabilities of the opposing forces in October 1899 was even greater than that portrayed by the Intelligence Division. That it failed to perceive this, or at least to stress this aspect of its estimate, is understandable. In any case, this underestimation was not an important factor in British unpreparedness for the South African War, compared to the inadequate communication between the producers of intelligence and the top-echelon decision makers of the government.

The responsibility of the Intelligence Division for the disasters of December 1899 aside, Black Week led to acrimonious infighting within the government and to a major reorganization of the War Office less than one year after Sir Redvers Buller was defeated at Colenso. A bitter dispute between high-ranking army officers and politicians erupted following Black Week. The commander-in-chief of the army, Lord Wolseley, claimed that civilian interference in the administration of the army had been the major cause of the defeats. Lord Salisbury, the prime minister, and Lord Lansdowne, the secretary of state for war, defended the government's policy. Additional troops had not been dispatched to South Africa, they maintained, because such a move might have destroyed or fatally disrupted the sensitive negotiations that the government was carrying on with the Boer leaders in the hopes of averting war.[55] At the height of this civil-military controversy, the government dissolved Parliament and called for a general election in the fall of 1900. Following a Conservative victory, Lord Salisbury continued on as prime minister and Lord Lansdowne was succeeded as secretary of state for war by St. John Brodrick. Lansdowne moved to the Foreign Office.

Lord Wolseley, at the request of Queen Victoria, prepared a memorandum in November 1900 stating his concept of what might be done to improve the higher administration of the army. In his memorandum he proposed that, if control of the army could not be returned to the commander-in-chief, the office should be abolished. Although disagreeing with the recommendations made by Lord Wolseley, the government recognized the necessity to investigate the whole organization of the War Office, and a committee of inquiry was appointed in mid-December 1900. The report of the Dawkins Committee, issued in May 1901, was a clear victory for the Wolseley side of the dispute, and the government was forced to accept some alteration in the existing organization of the War Office. Broad concessions were granted to the professional soldiers at the expense of the politicians by a War Office memorandum of 12 October 1901 and an order in council of 4 November.[56]

The reorganization of late 1901, brought about by the memorandum and order in council, had several effects upon the Intelligence Division. The Mobilization Division was again amalgamated with the Intelligence Division, and the new organization was upgraded in status to a department. Its head, a lieutenant general, was called the director general of mobilization and military intelligence (DGMI).[57] Unlike the DMI, the DGMI was a member of the War Office Council and regularly attended the meetings of the Defence Committee of the cabinet; his status thereby was considerably enhanced.[58] Although Great Britain still did not have a general staff, the 1901 expansion of the Intelligence Department represented a definite step in that direction. The director general of mobilization and military intelligence was responsible for

> the preparation and maintenance of detailed plans for the military defence of the Empire and for the organization and mobilization of the regular and auxiliary forces, the preparation and maintenance of schemes of offensive operations, and the collection and distribution of information relating to the military geography, resources and armed forces of foreign countries and of the British colonies and possessions.[59]

The newly appointed director general, Lt. Gen. Sir William Nicholson, soon abolished the existing eight sections of the Intelligence Department[60] and consolidated their functions under three subdivisions, each to be headed by a colonel: the Strategical Subdivision, the Foreign and Indian Subdivision, and the Special Duties Subdivision.[61] Of the three, the Foreign and Indian Subdivision was obviously the heart of War Office Intelligence.

Again, Sir William Robertson's recollections provide a valuable inside view of the War Office intelligence system. Major Robertson returned to his old post in B Section (imperial defence) of the Intelligence Department in November 1900, after serving for a year in the Field Intelligence Department in South Africa. In late 1901, when the Intelligence Department was reorganized, Robertson was chosen by Sir William Nicholson to head the Foreign and Indian Subdivision. The appointment, which meant that he would become one of the youngest colonels in the army, surprised Robertson and dismayed some senior officers, who were quite naturally envious. Since the outbreak of war in 1899, the Intelligence Division/Department had been manned mainly by reserve officers; practically all of the regular officers had requested assignment to South Africa, and Sir John Ardagh had been unwilling or unable to keep them from going. Robertson, upon taking over as head of the Foreign and Indian Subdivision, found that,

> chiefly owing to an inadequate staff, imperfect organization and the lack of clear direction, there was not, with one exception, which shall be nameless, a single up-to-date statement giving a comprehensive and considered estimate of the military resources of any foreign country. . . . The few officers employed in it had worked hard and done their best, but the system and circumstances were all against them.[62]

War Office intelligence had slipped far below the high standards of the 1896-99 period.

The most urgent problem, in Robertson's view, was the need to obtain more complete information about the military forces and resources of foreign countries. A second problem was to obtain guidance from the government about the countries with which Great Britain would most likely go to war. Given such guidance, or at least a better idea of what the government's policy was, the Department could have given higher priority to the most important problems. Time being wasted on unimportant tasks might have been saved. Robertson himself was left to distinguish where the main threats to the British Empire lay and to decide where to concentrate the intelligence effort.[63]

Nonetheless, progress was made toward the acquisition of better military intelligence abroad. The key, Robertson and Sir William Nicholson agreed, was to obtain more funds for intelligence work and to develop a better method of selecting officers for military attaché duty. Additional money was allocated, "thanks to the ready cooperation of the Foreign Office." The money enabled Robertson to send his subordinates on visits to the countries with which they were dealing more frequently, "so that they might acquire a personal knowledge of them and not be entirely dependent, as some of them were, upon what they read or were told." Attention was given to the appointment of better qualified military attachés,[64] but proficient officers were not always provided. Unfortunately, the most important posts, more often than not, still went to officers selected because of their personal wealth, the attractiveness of their wives, or because they had the right connections in the Foreign Office.[65]

The Berlin post was a notable exception to the usual practices in the selection of British military attachés, even well before the Nicholson-Robertson efforts at reform. The presence of Col. (later Lt. Gen. Sir) James Grierson in the German capital from 1896-1900 assured the Intelligence Department and the Foreign Office of thorough and expert reporting. The future director of military operations of the British General Staff (1904-06) and corps commander (1914) was at the time probably the most knowledgeable officer in the British Army concerning Germany and her army. An artilleryman and an 1877 graduate of Woolwich, Grierson had been involved in intelligence work of various sorts almost continuously throughout his career: reporting on the Austrian Army in the occupation of Bosnia and Herzegovina (1879) and on the Russian Army on maneuvers in Poland (1880); serving in the Quartermaster General Departments in India (1881, 1887-88) and Egypt (1882, 1885); and in the Intelligence Division in London (1886, 1889-95). During his long tour with the Intelligence Division, Grierson made frequent trips to Berlin, where he was warmly received by Kaiser Wilhelm II and officers of the German General Staff. Until he began his tour as military attaché in Berlin in 1896, Grierson had been a warm admirer of the Germans. During the four years there, however, he gradually began to distrust the Germans and to detect a change in the previously friendly attitude of the Kaiser and his army toward Britain.[66]

At the War Office, Col. William Robertson reached a similar conclusion in 1902.

> I had not been a year in my new post (head of the Foreign and Indian Sub-Division), however, before I became convinced, and stated so officially, that instead of regarding Germany as a suitable ally, we ought to look upon her as our most formidable rival. . . .

Of course, Robertson and his subordinates could not afford to concentrate their efforts solely on imperial Germany. Lord Roberts had succeeded Lord Wolseley as commander-in-chief in November 1900, and not surprisingly his main interest was still India and the Russian threat to the British position there.[67] There was new interest in Japan at the War Office, spurred by the signing of an Anglo-Japanese military alliance in 1902 and shared concern over the Russian threat in the Far East. Late in 1903 the first four British Army officers were sent to Japan to study the language and the army. In the Near East, the weakness of the Ottoman Empire was still a major worry and occupied much of Robertson's time.[68] To improve the foreign intelligence production effort, Colonel Robertson assembled a new team at Winchester House;[69] by January 1903 all but one of the heads of his subsections had been changed.

As Robertson and his fellow officers were struggling to upgrade the collection and production of foreign intelligence overseas and in London, the long war in South Africa ended and, in October 1902, the Royal Commission on the War in South Africa began to take evidence from the first of 114 witnesses. Because the Intelligence Department's prewar work was viewed so favorably and because the 1901 reorganization of the War Office had specified that the director general of mobilization and military intelligence would be included on the Defence Committee and the War Office Council, the majority of the members of the Royal Commission saw no need for fundamental reform in the existing War Office organization or in the functioning of the Mobilization and Intelligence Department. To give the War Office Council and its work greater importance, the report of the Royal Commission (July 1903) did recommend that it be established on a permanent basis. It also recommended that, in the future, the commander-in-chief should be more fully informed of the cabinet's policy and its decisions.[70] A note of dissent was evident in Lord Esher's appendix to the report, in which he expressed the view that radical reorganization of the War Office was needed, including the abolition of the position of commander-in-chief and a structuring of the War Office along the lines of the Admiralty, so that the secretary of state for war's policy would carry "the weight which attaches to the views of the First Lord of the Admiralty." In any case, neither the report of the Royal Commission nor Lord Esher's appendix made a significant impact on British military intelligence at the War Office level.[71]

Several months before the Royal Commission's report was published, however, a less publicized report appeared, which directly affected the Intelligence Department. A committee under the Earl of Hardwicke had been appointed by Secretary of State for War St. John Brodrick in August 1901, to review the "Permanent Establishment of the Mobilization and Intelligence Department." The initial objective of the Hardwicke Committee had been to evaluate Sir William Nicholson's claim that more money and men were needed within the Department; the report, published in March 1903, recommended the officer strength of the Department be increased from twenty to twenty-nine.[72]

Lord Hardwicke's committee also delved into other areas, including the problem of whether or not intelligence officers should be specially trained, the proposition that officers assigned to the Intelligence Department should have equal chances of promotion and tours of active service with officers in other staff appointments, and, perhaps most significantly, the question of whether or not the DGMI should have executive power to put his recommendations into effect. While the committee agreed that Intelligence Department officers should have equal opportunity for professional advancement with other staff officers, no real agreement was reached on the necessity of special training for intelligence officers. The greatest amount of controversy was generated over the degree of authority that should be accorded to the "head of intelligence." Despite a strong protest by Sir William Nicholson, who felt that the committee had overstepped its bounds when it took up this question, the Hardwicke Committee expressed its conclusion that intelligence should remain only an "advisory department."[73] The Intelligence Department was prohibited from implementing its own recommendations; only the commander-in-chief could approve the plans or recommendations of the Department or act on the intelligence that it provided him.

By far the most important War Office reforms in the post-Boer War era were instituted by the War Office (Reconstitution) Committee. As British historian Brian Bond has written, "In its celerity, boldness, and comprehensiveness, the work of the War Office (Reconstitution) Committee has no parallel in British military reform and few in any other branch of administration."[74] Lord Esher's dissenting memorandum attached to the report of the Royal Commission on the War in South Africa proved to be the seed of this new committee. Soon after publication of the Elgin report in the summer of 1903, the Balfour government broke up.[75] When Balfour formed a new cabinet in September he asked Lord Esher to become his secretary of state for war. Reluctant to sacrifice his independence through association with a political party, Esher turned down the offer.[76] Instead, another consistent critic of War Office administration, H.O. Arnold Forster, became secretary of state for war. Nevertheless, Esher persuaded the prime minister to appoint a three-man committee to investigate the structure of the War Office.

The War Office (Reconstitution) Committee was appointed in early November 1903, with Lord Esher as chairman. Also named to the committee were Adm. Sir John Fisher and Sir George Sydenham Clarke, with Maj. Gerald F. Ellison picked by Esher to be secretary.[77] Lord Esher and his colleagues worked with great dispatch. They determined at the outset, in late December, that there was no need to take formal evidence because it was unnecessary to add to the enormous volume of evidence already available in the *Minutes of Evidence* of the Royal Commission. High military and civilian officials "whose views and experience could throw light upon our investigations" would be consulted, but their comments would not be recorded as evidence.[78] In the hope that the government would act promptly on the committee's recommendations, Esher issued each of the three sections of the report as soon as it was completed. The third and final section appeared in March 1904.

In the actual writing of the report, Fisher contributed little, and Clarke wrote only those portions dealing with military finance and decentralization.[79]

> The famous report was, in its fullest aspect, the work of two men, Esher and Ellison. . . . Contemplating the great changes wrought by this small group (the Esher Committee), wrought indeed for the most part by one public-minded peer and one Lieutenant-Colonel on the Staff, the mind is tempted to regard the whole history of the Esher Commission's Report as somewhat miraculous in nature.[80]

Lord Esher wrote the first sections dealing with the Committee of Imperial Defence and the Army Board while Ellison contributed those on the general staff and the organization of the staff in the field.

The report of the Esher Committee is best known for several proposals: (1) that a permanent nucleus of the Committee of Imperial Defence be established;[81] (2) that the office of commander-in-chief be abolished and an army council be constituted to conduct the business of the War Office;[82] and (3) that a general staff be established at the War Office.[83] Only by means of a highly trained general staff, concluded the Esher Committee, "can the standard of training and of preparation of the military forces of the Crown be made to correspond with modern requirements."[84] Great emphasis was placed on the need to carry out the recommended reforms immediately, before opposition could be mounted in Parliament and in the army.

The Army Council was created on 6 February 1904 and the Commander-in-Chief's Office and the old War Office Council were abolished. In May 1904 Balfour also set up the Committee of Imperial Defence on a permanent basis and gave it a secretariat. The Esher Committee was able to bring about the replacement of virtually all the high-ranking officers in the War Office. Lt. Gen. Sir Neville Lyttleton was appointed the first chief of the general staff. Not until Richard B. Haldane had replaced Arnold Forster as secretary of state for war, however, was the general staff finally established on a permanent basis.[85]

What did the Esher Committee have to say about military intelligence and the Intelligence Department? In the broadest sense, the Esher Committee attempted to solve the problem highlighted in the report of the Royal Commission on the War in South Africa: that an undesirable gap existed between intelligence and policymaking at the highest levels of government. The proposal to strengthen the Committee of Imperial Defence as a means to insure that, "in time of emergency a definite war policy, based upon solid data, can be formulated,"[86] was directed at this problem, as were the proposals for the creation of an army council and a general staff. In other words, the concern of the Esher Committee was not so much that more or better military intelligence was needed by the War Office and the cabinet, but instead that the information produced be utilized more efficiently and brought to the attention of military and civilian decision makers who required it.

The particular section of the report which described the proposed general staff affected the Intelligence Department directly. The general staff would contain three directorates: Military Operations, Military Training, and Staff Duties. The Intelligence Department would vanish and its functions (except mobilization) were to come under control of the Military Operations Directorate.[87] The new organization came to life in February 1904. Maj. Gen. James M. Grierson was brought in to be the first director of military operations. Initially, this directorate contained four subdivisions: MO1—Imperial Defence and Strategical Distribution of the Army; MO2—Foreign Intelligence; MO3—Administration and Special Duties;[88] and MO4—Topographical Section. At first glance, the general staff seemed to impose an additional administrative level (the chief of the general staff) between the director of military operations, who was on the same level as the DGMI had been, and the secretary of state for war.[89] However, the Esher Committee provided the following guidance:

> It is essential to prevent the members of the Council from becoming immersed in detailed administration. . . . The main administrative work of the military branches will, therefore, be carried out by Directors acting under the Members of Council.[90]

Thus, the director of military operations, not the chief of the general staff, would have large administrative powers. Furthermore, the director would be the real "expert" on matters of military intelligence and strategical planning.

According to William Robertson, there was little change in the work of his Foreign Section (which was now MO2). His title was changed to assistant director;[91] MO2 was expanded from four to eight subdivisions, and the number of officers working for him increased from nine to twenty. Robertson did comment that the new organization at last had enabled the military intelligence producers to "furnish the Foreign Office and C.I.D. with considered military advice" in regard to pressing international questions.[92]

The incentives provided for general staff duty (recommended by the Esher Committee) were helpful in attracting the most talented officers to War Office intelligence jobs. Especially attractive was the provision that "continuous employment in the General Staff should be restricted to four years, and should, in all cases, qualify an officer for accelerated promotion."[93] Also of assistance to the foreign intelligence effort was the encouragement given by the Esher Committee's report to the practice of sending abroad officers filling intelligence positions in the Directorate of Operations to personally acquaint themselves with the countries for which they were responsible. Furthermore, the report suggested that officers belonging to technical branches (such as artillery, engineers, or medical corps) be attached to the directorate to act as liaison officers with the master general of the ordnance.[94] Not so farsighted was the committee's apparent endorsement of the old doctrine that intelligence officers at the War Office could, in time of war, be counted on for release and assignment to field intelligence positions.[95]

In conclusion, the shocking military defeats suffered by the British Army at the hands of the Boers in the fall of 1899 did not result from a failure of Britain's strategtic intelligence system. The Intelligence Division at the War Office, the organization responsible for producing strategic military intelligence, was understaffed and insufficiently funded, and it received no help of consequence from the Secret Intelligence Service with regard to the South African problem prior to the war. Despite these shortcomings, the Division performed its intelligence functions well, at least in South Africa. Extremely accurate information about the military capabilities and intentions of the Boer Republics was produced and disseminated by the Division from 1896 until the beginning of the South African War in 1899. The necessary concentration of limited resources on South Africa led to the deterioration of the intelligence effort in other parts of the world, the situation which so distressed William Robertson when he returned to the Division in late 1900. The logical solution to this problem, outlined by the Hardwicke Committee, was to give the Intelligence Department more officers and a larger budget. Neither the Royal Commission on the War in South Africa nor the Esher Committee found anything wrong with the strategic intelligence system. What was lacking in 1899 was a contingency planning body which could turn the intelligence produced into something useful for mobilization. The experience of the South African War brought about the realization that Great Britain could no longer afford a fundamental discontinuity between strategic intelligence and strategic planning/decision making.

NOTES

1. "Boer" means "farmer" in Dutch. The Boers, also known as Afrikaners, were descendants of seventeenth- and eighteenth-century Dutch, French Huguenot, and German settlers of South Africa. The first permanent European settlement of South Africa occurred in 1652, when a provisioning station for the Dutch East India Company was established on the Cape of Good Hope. The Cape remained a Dutch colony until 1814 when it was assigned to Great Britain by the Congress of Vienna. Rising tensions between British and Boers and the search for new farmland led to the Great Trek (1835-43) when some 12,000 Boers left the Cape. Initially many of these Boers settled in Natal, but after the British annexed Natal in 1843 most moved into the interior where, during the 1850s, the Boer republics of the Orange Free State and the Transvaal were established. The British annexation of the Transvaal resulted in the Transvaal Revolt (or First Boer War), 1880-81, and the restoration of independence for the Transvaal.

2. Boer fortunes sagged following the arrival of Lord Roberts as the new commander-in-chief in South Africa in January 1900. Kimberley, Ladysmith, and Mafeking were relieved and both the Orange Free State (24 May 1900) and the Transvaal (3 September 1900) were annexed by Britain. Formal Boer resistance ended in July 1900, and President Paul Kruger of the Transvaal fled to Dutch protection. Roberts, succeeded by his chief of staff, Herbert Kitchener, went home in December 1900 as the war appeared to have been won. Yet, Boer leaders launched a sustained guerrilla war which continued for eighteen months. They finally capitulated to the British and accepted British sovereignty under the terms of the Treaty of Vereeniging (31 May 1902). British forces, less than 25,000 at the beginning of the war, eventually totaled nearly half a million men. It is believed that the Boers never had more than 40,000 men in the field at any one time. The official history of the war was not completed until 1910: Capt. Maurice H. Grant and Maj. Gen. Sir Frederick Maurice, *History of the War in South Africa*. A wealth of material on the origins of the war and on the war itself may be found in *The Times History of the War in South Africa*, edited by L.S. Amery. The best of the recent work on the war includes Edgar Holt, *The Boer War*; Rayne Kruger, *Good-Bye Dolly Gray*; Byron Farwell, *The Great Anglo-Boer War*; and Thomas Pakenham, *The Boer War*.

3. Maj. Gen. F.S. Russell, "The Intelligence Department," p. 725.

4. The causes of the South African War (or Second Boer War) are deep-rooted and complex and cannot be addressed here. Suffice it to say that the Boers resented British incursions into their republics. The First Boer War (1880-81) had been fought in response to the British annexation of the Transvaal. Anti-British sentiment was further inflamed when the discovery of gold in the Witwatersrand (1886) brought hordes of British prospectors into the Transvaal. To protect itself from the growing number of foreigners on its soil, the Transvaal government denied the "Uitlanders" (foreigners) citizenship and taxed them heavily. The Jameson Raid was an ill-fated attempt by Dr. Leander Starr Jameson and 500 men to spark an uprising by the Uitlanders against the Transvaal government. As the Boers considered this to be nothing less than an officially sponsored British plot to seize their country, their response was to form a military alliance between the Transvaal and the Orange Free State (1896).

5. *German Official Account of the War in South Africa*, trans. by W.H.H. Waters (London, 1904), 1: 11.

6. The high cost to the British of the conflict (22,000 men dead from the British Empire forces

and £200 million) and the disturbing fact that it had taken so long (two years, eight months) for the British Army to defeat the Boers led to demands for a full investigation. Heavy pressure on the Conservative government of Arthur J. Balfour (who had succeeded his uncle, Lord Salisbury, as prime minister in July 1902) led to the appointment of the Royal Commission on the War in South Africa scarcely more than three months after the end of hostilities. The Royal Commission was appointed on 9 September 1902 to "inquire into the military preparations for the war in South Africa." Between 8 October 1902 and 10 June 1903, the commission sat fifty-five days to hear evidence from 114 witnesses, including practically everyone concerned with the higher direction of the war, military and civilian. Its chairman was the Earl of Elgin, and the commission included Lord Esher, Field Marshal Sir Henry Norman, Adm. John Hopkins, and Sir George Dashwood Taubman-Goldie. The *Report* and *Minutes of Evidence* of the commission were issued in July 1903.

7. Britain's Official Secrets Act was not passed until 1911, during a wave of fear about German spies. Nevertheless, Sir John was restrained by "the obligations of official reticence" from responding to the charge that the Intelligence Division had failed in its duty. "Never was there a finer example of loyalty to the Government and of willingness to sacrifice personal reputation to the interests of the State." Susan Countess of Malmesbury, *The Life of Major-General Sir John Ardagh*, pp. 328-30.

8. Lt. Col. Isaac, "History of the Directorate of M.I.," p. 9. Ardagh was private secretary to Lord Lansdowne during the latter's terms as viceroy of India (1888-94). Just prior to going to India he had been deputy adjutant general for mobilization, working directly for Lieutenant General Wolseley, then the adjutant general.

9. Ibid. Col. R.H. Vetch, "Ardagh, Sir John Charles," *D.N.B.*, pp. 50-53. After retirement from the army in 1902 Ardagh succeeded Lord Pauncefote on the permanent court of arbitration at the Hague and became a British government director of the Suez Canal. In 1906 he served as one of the four British government delegates at the conference held by the Swiss government for the revision of the Geneva Convention of 1864. General Ardagh's last public duty was as a delegate of the British Red Cross Society at the eighth international Red Cross conference (held in London in June 1907).

10. Lord Edward Gleichen, *A Guardsman's Memories*, pp. 176-77. As mentioned in the preceding chapter, Gleichen served twice in the Intelligence Division prior to the South African War: 1886-88 and 1894-99. He returned again to the War Office from 1907 to 1911.

11. W.H.H. Waters, *"Secret and Confidential,"* p. 243.

12. Malmesbury, *The Life of Major-General Sir John Ardagh*, pp. 283-84. Sir John Ardagh married Susan, widow of the third Earl of Malmesbury, in February 1896, shortly before taking up his duties as the DMI. It was the first and only marriage for Ardagh, aged fifty-five.

13. As mentioned in the previous chapter, Chapman was quartermaster general in India from 1885 to 1889, during the first four years of Frederick Roberts's seven years as commander-in-chief in India. Chapman had spent many years in the QMG's Department prior to 1885. He was also chief of staff of the famous Kabul-Kandahar Field Force in Afghanistan in 1880, under command of Roberts. General Roberts, who returned from India in 1893 and was made a field marshal and commander-in-chief in Ireland in 1895, had long opposed the "military reformers" at home and was therefore the great rival of the leading reformer, Field Marshal Lord Wolseley (who had preceded Roberts as commander-in-chief in Ireland and who became commander-in-chief of the army in 1895). Field Marshal Lord Roberts served as the last commander-in-chief of the army, 1902-04.

14. A major debate over defense had taken place within the British government in 1888-89, principally over what appeared to be the increasing threat of invasion of the British Isles and the way to counter it. The Royal Navy emerged as the winner of the debate, gaining in the Naval Defence Act of 1889 a large amount of money to be spent on shipbuilding. The major effect on the War Office, summed up in a famous memorandum by Secretary of State for War Edward Stanhope in 1891, was that the top priority for the British Army would be "the effective support of the civil power in all parts of the United Kingdom." Col. John K. Dunlop, *The Development of the British Army, 1899-1914*, Appendix A, p. 307. See also John Gooch, *The Plans of War*, pp. 10-12.

15. Chapman to Roberts, 4 October 1892 and 19 October 1892, W.O. 106/16.

16. Chapman to Brackenbury, 21 October 1892, W.O. 106/16.

17. Lt. Col. Parritt, *The Intelligencers*, pp. 162-63.

18. Ibid., pp. 164-65; Malmesbury, *Life of Ardagh*, pp. 280-85.

19. A commission was set up in 1888 under Lord Hartington to "Enquire into the Civil and Professional Administration of the Naval and Military Departments and the relation of those departments to each other and the Treasury." Sir Henry Brackenbury, (then DMI), Lord Randolph Churchill, and Sir Henry Campbell-Bannerman were members. The third major recommendation of the Hartington Commission was that a defense committee be set up so that the estimates of the army and navy could be considered together before they were submitted to the cabinet. See Hamer, *The British Army*, pp. 134-47.

20. *Reports of the Royal Commissioners Appointed to Enquire into the Civil and Professional Administration of the Naval and Military Department*, xxii-xxiii, xix, xxvi-xxvii.

21. Presumably, some members of the cabinet shared the view of Sir Henry Campbell-Bannerman, the sole member of the Hartington Commission who opposed the creation of a chief of staff and a general staff. Sir Henry feared that in "deposing the Pope at the War Office" (the commander-in-chief) and simultaneously creating a chief of staff, the War Office might find itself with "a new Pope." Hamer, *The British Army*, pp. 141-42, 146.

22. John Gooch, *The Plans of War*, p. 13; Hamer, *The British Army*, pp. 145-46.

23. Bond, *The Staff College*, p. 172.

24. Royal Commission on the War in South Africa, *Appendices to Evidence*, pp. 274-75.

25. Ibid., pp. 274-78.

26. Malmesbury, *Life of Ardagh*, pp. 273-74.

27. The War Office Consultative Council consisted of the secretary of war, the under secretaries (permanent and parliamentary), the financial secretary, the commander-in-chief and the heads of the other principal military departments.

28. Statement of Maj. Gen. Sir John Ardagh on 31 October 1902, Royal Commission, *Minutes of Evidence I*, Appendix A, p. 154.

29. Royal Commission, *Appendices to Evidence*, p. 46.

30. Royal Commission, *Report*, Appendix A, p. 154.

31. Lieutenant Robertson's study of native languages in India was motivated in part by the fact that the Indian government offered monetary rewards for passing examinations in these languages, which in turn helped Robertson "to keep my head, financially, above water." Before joining the Indian Intelligence Department in 1892 he had qualified in five native languages: Hindi, Urdu, Persian, Punjabi, and Pushtu. The Northwest Frontier Section of the department, in which Robertson served for five years, dealt with independent and quasi-independent territories extending some 2,000 miles from Tibet to the Arabian Sea and including Afghanistan, Kashmir, and Baluchistan. Robertson wrote the five volume *Gazetteer and Military Report on Baluchistan*, and in 1894 was sent to explore the routes leading into India from the Pamirs. Field Marshal Sir William Robertson, *From Private to Field-Marshal*, pp. 41-65.

32. Robertson, *From Private to Field-Marshal*, pp. 91, 95, 98. See also Maurice, "Robertson, Sir William Robert," *D.N.B. 1931-1940*, pp. 738-43.

33. Ibid., p. 96.

34. Royal Commission on the War in South Africa, *Report*, pp. 154-60; Statement of Lt. Col. E.A. Altham on 15 October 1902, Royal Commission, *Minutes of Evidence I*, pp. 20-24; Robertson *From Private to Field-Marshal*, p. 97.

35. Amery, *The Times History of the War in South Africa*, 2: 21. See also *German Official Account of the War in South Africa*, 1: 18.

36. Royal Commission, *Report*, p. 129.

37. The preparations of the Boers in the years prior to the South African War included not only the accumulation of large stores of weapons and other military necessities, but also a major intelligence effort targeted against the British. In the years 1896-98, the Transvaal Intelligence Department was outspending British Intelligence by more than twenty to one on secret service in South Africa. "There were few towns or villages in South Africa where there was not an agent of the Transvaal. The slightest movement of British troops was at once reported to Pretoria." Amery, *Times History*, 2: 84. See also "Military Notes of the Dutch Republics of South Africa," prepared by Section B of the Intelligence Division.

38. Statement of L.S. Amery on 24 March 1903, Royal Commission, *Minutes of Evidence II*, p. 465.

39. Amery, *Times History*, pp. 39, 84.

40. Born in Russia near Odessa in 1874, the illegitimate son of a Jewish doctor from Vienna and the wife of a colonel in the Russian army, Sigmund Rosenblum—alias Sidney Reilly—was one of the bravest and most famous spies ever to work for the British Secret Service. Sidney Reilly was first recruited to work for the SIS in Brazil in 1895, when he saved the lives of two British officers during an expedition up the Amazon River. His first official assignment for the SIS began in 1897, when he was sent to the Caucasus and Persia to determine the extent of Russian activities and Russian intentions in Persia. In 1899 he went to Holland on an SIS mission, where he passed himself off as a German and attempted to find out about Dutch aid to the Boer Republics in South Africa. Robin Bruce Lockhart, *Ace of Spies*, pp. 22-23, 26-27, 29, 32; Richard Deacon, *British Secret Service*, pp. 137, 138-40.

41. "The War Operations in South Africa," *Blackwoods Edinburgh Magazine* (January 1900): 145.

42. Malmesbury, *Life of Ardagh*, pp. 333-34.

43. Royal Commission, *Report*, p. 14.

44. Ibid., p. 148.

45. Ibid., p. 10.

46. Ibid., pp. 154-56.

47. Ibid., pp. 153-54.

48. Lord Wolseley to Lord Lansdowne, 8 June 1899, 17 August 1899, 24 August 1899; Lansdowne to Wolseley, 20 August 1899, 27 August 1899; Sir Joseph Chamberlain's memo of 6 September 1899. Great Britain, *Cabinet Papers 1880-1914*.

49. Royal Commission, *Report*, pp. 157-58. See also *German Official Account*, 1: 19.

50. Amery, *Times History*, 2: 88.

51. Royal Commission, *Report*, pp. 156-57. The "Military Notes" estimate of rifle ammunition was 33,000,000 rounds. The actual figure was 33,050,000.

52. Statement of Lord Roberts on 4 December 1902. Royal Commission, *Minutes of Evidence I*, p. 430.

53. Royal Commission, *Report*, p. 160.

54. Amery, *Times History*, 2: 89.

55. Thomas Pakenham argued that the British high commissioner for South Africa, Sir Alfred Milner, undermined these negotiations because of his belief that war with the Boers was necessary unless major reforms were made by the Transvaal government. *The Boer War*, p. 17. That Pakenham sees Milner as a villain is shown by the title of part 1 of his 700-page book, "Milner's War."

56. Hamer, *British Army*, pp. 181-90.

57. Lt. Gen. Sir William Nicholson replaced Sir John Ardagh as chief of the combined department, often referred to as "the Intelligence Department."

58. This put the DGMI on a par with the adjutant general, the quartermaster general, and the director general of ordnance.

59. Royal Commission, *Appendices to Evidence*, pp. 280-91, 292.

60. Two new sections had been added to the Intelligence Division during the first year of the South African War: Sections H (Special Duties) and L (Library). In addition to administrative work, Section H, under Maj. J.E. Edmonds, was responsible for cable censorship, surveillance of suspected spies (in conjunction with Scotland Yard), press correspondents, and inquiries regarding prisoners of war.

61. The Strategical Subdivision was responsible for the "military defence of the Empire including the preparation and maintenance of plans of offensive or defensive operations" and the "collation and distribution of information relating to the military geography, resources, and armed forces of the Empire" (other than India); the Foreign and Indian Subdivision for the "collation and distribution of information concerning the military geography, resources, and armed forces of India, Egypt and all foreign countries"; and the Special Duties Subdivision for secret service, censorship, preparation of maps, and the maintenance of libraries. Royal Commission, *Appendices to Evidence*, p. 282.

62. Robertson, *From Private to Field-Marshal*, pp. 129-30.

63. Ibid., pp. 130-33.

64. "Better qualified" meant the officers were selected on the basis of their military qualifications and for their knowledge of the language of the country to which they were assigned.

65. Robertson, *From Private to Field-Marshal*, pp. 130-32.

66. Col. James Grierson was followed as military attaché in Berlin by his former assistant in Section D (Russian) of the Intelligence Division, Col. W.H.H. Waters (1900-03). After Waters came Colonel Lord Gleichen, another veteran of Queen's Anne's Gate (1888-89, 1894-99). While DMO on the general staff (1904-06), Major General Grierson played a major role in the military conversations between Britain and France, which strengthened the Entente Cordiale and paved the way for Anglo-French military planning prior to World War I. D.S. Macdiarmid, *The Life of Lieut.-General Sir James Moncrieff Grierson*, pp. 113-17; "Grierson, Sir James Moncrieff," *D.N.B. 1912-1921*, pp. 228-30. Alfred Vagts, *The Military Attaché*, pp. 310-12.

67. Robertson, *From Private to Field-Marshal*, pp. 133-39.

68. Isaac, "Field-Marshal Sir William Robertson when head of the Foreign Military Intelligence Section, War Office," pp. 5-6.

69. The intelligence sections of the Mobilization and Military Intelligence Department moved from Queen's Anne's Gate to Winchester House, St. James Square, in 1901 in order to be near the offices of the commander-in-chief in Pall Mall. "History of the Directorate of M.I.," p. 11.

70. Royal Commission, *Report*, pp. 138, 142.

71. Ibid., pp. 144-45.

72. Actually, because of increased work levied on the department by the Defence Committee, the Treasury approved a total strength of thirty-eight officers, ten of whom would be performing "Defence Committee Work." "Report of the Committee Appointed to Review the Permanent Establishment of the Mobilization and Intelligence Division."

73. Ibid.

74. Bond, *Staff College*, p. 214.

75. The report of the Royal Commission on the War in South Africa is also known as the Elgin Report, after its chairman, the Earl of Elgin. The Balfour government did not fall because of reaction to the Elgin report, but over the old issue of free trade vs. protection.

76. Reginald Balliol Brett, second Viscount Esher, never held high government office despite his considerable ability and advantages of education and social position. He was, nevertheless, a very influential man in the highest circles of British government, with his influence reaching a peak between 1903 and 1905, when he was a confidant of King Edward VII, a close friend of Prime Minister Arthur Balfour, and he had excellent contacts with other influential members of the government and high-ranking army officers. He was first exposed to the inner workings of the War Office when he served as private secretary to Lord Hartington, secretary of state for war in the early 1880s. Hamer, *The British Army*, pp. 223-25. See also chapter 2, "The Triumph of Lord Esher," in Gooch, *The Plans of War*, pp. 32-59.

77. Adm. Sir John Fisher had recently returned from commanding the Mediterranean Command, considered the most important seagoing position in the Royal Navy. He became first sea lord several years later. Sir George Sydenham Clarke did not return to England from Australia (where he had been governor of Victoria) until Christmas, 1903. He had served as secretary to the Hartington Commission (1888-1890) and, after work on the Esher Committee, served as secretary of the Committee of Imperial Defence. Maj. (later Lt. Gen. Sir) Gerald Ellison was a bright young staff officer who had already done considerable work on staff reorganization while assisting Col. G.F.R. Henderson prepare a staff manual in 1902. Ellison served later as military secretary to Secretary of State for War Richard B. Haldane.

78. War Office, *Report of the War Office (Reconstitution) Committee*, part 1, Cd. 1932 (1904), p. 7.

79. Dunlop, *The Development of the British Army, 1899-1914*, pp. 204-05. According to Dunlop, Sir John Fisher was notable chiefly for his "cheerful and all-embracing preference for Naval methods" and for little else, as far as the committee was concerned.

80. Ibid., pp. 205, 212.

81. War Office, *Report of the War Office (Reconstitution) Committee*, part 1, pp. 4-5. The C.I.D. was created in December 1902 by the Balfour government as a follow-up to the Defence

Committee. It was set up to consider the strategical needs of the Empire. The Esher Committee proposed that the permanent nucleus would consider all questions of imperial defense and would obtain and collate information from the Admiralty, the War Office, the India Office, the Colonial Office, and other departments of state. Headed by a permanent secretary, it would be a sort of "super general staff" for the cabinet. For an examination of the C.I.D., see Nicholas d'Ombrain, *War Machinery and High Policy—Defence Administration in Peacetime Britain, 1902-1914* (London: Oxford University Press, 1973).

82. War Office, *Report of the War Office (Reconstitution) Committee*, part 1, p. 9. The proposed Army Council would have seven members: the secretary of state for war (to be the head) and two other civilian members; and four military members: the chief of the general staff, the adjutant general, the quartermaster general, and the master general of ordnance. Thus, the Army Council would parallel precisely the structure of the Board of Admiralty (as Fisher had advocated in his appendix to the report of the Royal Commission) and the secretary of state would have the same relationship with the Crown as the first lord of the admiralty. (See also part 2, pp. 5-6 and part 3, p. 4.).

83. Ibid., part 2 Cd. 1968 (1904), pp. 21-25.

84. Ibid., p. 24.

85. By the special army order of 12 September 1906.

86. War Office, *Report of the War Office (Reconstitution) Committee*, part 1, p. 4.

87. The mobilization function was to be placed under the Military Training Directorate. War Office, *Report of the War Office (Reconstitution) Committee*, part 2, pp. 23, 25.

88. "Special duties" included covert intelligence, i.e., the controlling of spies and agents. Parritt, *The Intelligencers*, p. 223.

89. By virtue of the order in council of November 1901, the DGMI had been added to the membership of the War Office Council, where he had direct access to the secretary of state (See p. 88).

90. War Office, *Report of the War Office (Reconstitution) Committee*, part 2, p. 6.

91. Formerly, Robertson and the heads of the other sections had been assistant quartermaster generals.

92. Robertson, *From Private to Field-Marshal*, pp. 137-38.

93. War Office, *Report of the War Office (Reconstitution) Committee*, part 2, p. 24.

94. War Office, *Report of the War Office (Reconstitution) Committee*, part 2, p. 23.

95. Ibid.

Chapter VII

The British Tactical Intelligence System in the Nineteenth Century

> The Staff Officer for Intelligence is the recipient of all information bearing on the force, position, and organisation of the enemy, as well as any changes in his *ordre de bataille*. All information collected by spies, and any journals, despatches, &c., captured from the enemy, are examined by him. He questions all prisoners. The department under his orders supplements by reconnaissances in the theatre of war the information gathered by the Intelligence Division of the War Office, and the maps prepared by it in time of peace.
>
> Lt. Col. J.S. Rothwell, ed., *Staff Duties: A Series of Lectures for the Use of Officers at the Staff College*, Staff College, Camberley, 1890

In the preceding five chapters, the origins and development of a permanent intelligence organization at the War Office have been examined. Although the focus thus far has remained entirely on the strategic aspect of British military intelligence, this is not to say that tactical or field intelligence[1] was unimportant to the British Army during the last three decades of the nineteenth century. To the contrary, timely and accurate information about the enemy and the area of operations was as vital to British field commanders during the numerous colonial campaigns or "small wars" of the nineteenth century as it had been to the Duke of Wellington in the Peninsular War (1808-14).[2] Whenever British armies engaged or were preparing to engage their enemies on the field of battle, tactical intelligence assumed paramount importance. An investigation of the development of Great Britain's military intelligence system must include, therefore, the examination of its tactical, as well as its strategic, aspects. The objective of this chapter is to examine the British Army's tactical intelligence system in the nineteenth century and on the eve of the South African War. In succeeding chapters, we shall see how this system fared in South Africa and the changes and growth it underwent prior to World War I.

While the need for a permanent intelligence organization in London was not accepted by the civilian and military leadership of the British Army until after the Franco-Prussian War, the need for tactical intelligence in combat had been appreciated throughout the history of the English (until 1707) and British armies. Before the sixteenth century, commanders of English armies usually were their own chiefs of intelligence. The field intelligence system consisted mainly of a spy network, cavalry reconnaissance, and personal observation. The precise date is unknown, but probably beginning in the late fifteenth or early sixteenth century, commanders of English armies in the field began to appoint scoutmasters whose duty it was "to discover the whereabouts and intentions of the enemy." The responsibilities of the scoutmaster were succinctly described by King Henry VIII in 1518.

> It is the office of the Scoutmaster when he cometh to the field, to set and appoint the scourage, he must appoint some to the high hills to view and see if they can discover anything. Also, the said Scoutmaster must appoint one other company of scouragers to search, and view every valley therabouts, that there be no enemies laid privily for the annoyance of the said camp. . . .[3]

Scoutmasters reached the zenith of their influence during the English Civil War in the mid-seventeenth century, when commanders on both sides relied on them to coordinate the intelligence-gathering activities of scouts and spies. The most famous of these was Sir Samuel Luke, scoutmaster general in the Parliamentary Army of the Earl of Essex from 1642 to 1645. The reports of Luke's agents dealt not only with the disposition and movements of the Royalist forces, but also with their logistics, morale, and "technical developments." Relatively little is known about the methods and performance of George Downing, the scoutmaster general in Oliver Cromwell's New Model Army. After the defeat of the Scots at Worcester in 1651 and the final capitulation of the Royalists in May 1652, the need for tactical military intelligence rapidly disappeared and the scoutmaster's importance began to decline as a result.[4]

The English Army continued to have a scoutmaster general until 1686, when, after the accession of King James II, the duties formerly performed by the scoutmaster, the provost marshal, and the harbinger (responsible for supplies) were combined under the newly created post of quartermaster general. For the next hundred years, the British Army had "neither an individual nor an organization primarily concerned with the collecting and collating of military intelligence. Instead, the Commander himself assumed responsibilities of Head of Intelligence."[5] John Churchill, Duke of Marlborough, whose brilliant record as commander of the English Army on the Continent (1702-11) qualified him as one of the great captains of history, was typical in this regard.

Marlborough's quartermaster general from 1701 to 1712 was a burly young Irishman named William Cadogan. A major and only twenty-six years old in 1701, Cadogan proved to be a splendid choice for QMG. Marlborough rewarded him with rapid promotion, and in 1709 he attained the rank of lieutenant general. With his "talent for minutiae," Cadogan "transformed the Duke's concepts into practicable orders and carried out a myriad ancillary duties and special missions in addition."[6] William Cadogan was especially valuable to Marlborough in his role as "chief reconnoitier." In all ten campaigns of the War of the Spanish Succession, he continually moved ahead of the main body—accompanied by a small reconnaissance party or a cavalry squadron, or even sometimes in command of the advance guard—to seek the best campsite for the next night's halt, to recruit guides, and to locate the enemy. General Cadogan's ability to make calm, reasoned assessments of the enemy's forces and intentions was prized by his commander. Unlike the scoutmaster generals, however, Marlborough's QMG did not direct the clandestine intelligence effort. The duke built up his own network of spies, informers, and agents and charged his secretary, Adam Cardonnel, with the day-to-day supervision of their work.[7] The obvious result of such a division of responsibilities was that Marlborough was, *de facto*, his own intelligence chief. Only he had continual access to all the available information. Therefore, he alone was in a position to evaluate and collate this information and to form a complete estimate of the enemy situation.

A similar division of intelligence duties between quartermaster general and private secretary was used by Prince Ferdinand of Brunswick, the commander of "his Britannic Majesty's Army in Germany" during the Seven Years' War (1756-63). The practice of a commander serving as his own intelligence officer was demonstrated even more clearly on the other side of the Atlantic during the same war. At the Battle of Quebec in 1759, Gen. James Wolfe, who commanded the British force, did not use his quartermaster general or anyone else to assist him in directing a most successful intelligence effort. Wolfe personally interrogated deserters from General Montcalm's army, dispatched scout units to gain tactical information, conducted his own reconnaissances of the French positions, read all intelligence reports, and formed his own estimate of the enemy situation. The pendulum began to swing away from this trend during the American Revolutionary War (1775-83). Major John André, the young British officer executed as a spy by the American army in 1780, was the "officer in charge of intelligence" on the staff of Gen. Henry Clinton in New York. In this capacity, André, who was also adjutant general, collected reports from scouts, interviewed deserters and prisoners, and established a spy network behind American lines. One of Major André's agents was the infamous American traitor, Gen. Benedict Arnold.[8]

During the Napoleonic Wars (1792-1815), the organization and methods of the French Army received increasing attention from other European powers, including Great Britain. In the area of military intelligence, on both the strategic and tactical levels, the British borrowed heavily from the French. As mentioned in chapter I, the Depot of Military Knowledge was established in London in 1803 as a branch of the Quartermaster General's Department. The main inspiration for the depot was the Dépôt de la Guerre in Paris.[9] Five years before the creation of the Depot of Military Knowledge, however, the British Army had begun to modify its field intelligence system along the lines of the current French system. The sobering experience gained by the British contingent of an allied force which fought a losing campaign against the French in Flanders and Holland (1793-95), and the growing threat of a French invasion of the United Kingdom after 1797, led to the formation of the Kent Corps of Guides, the first such British unit, in March 1798.

The counties of Kent and Sussex, located along the southeast coast of England and directly across the English Channel from France, were considered the most likely landing choices for a French invading force aimed at London. A corps of guides was raised in Kent (and in Sussex one year later), so, if the regular army was deployed there to oppose a French invasion, it would receive immediate assistance from a unit of men with local knowledge and scouting ability who could act as guides. The use of guides—usually local men hired to guide an army through strange terrain—was not new in the British Army, but the concept of a corps of guides was borrowed from the French Army.[10] Napoleon's Corps des Guides was formed in 1796, during the Italian Campaign. The Corps des Guides performed so well in Italy, it became a special favorite of Napoleon's and in Egypt (1798) was expanded from company to regimental size. Though originally established to conduct "special reconnaissance tasks" and to provide intelligence directly to Napoleon or his *cabinet*,[11] the corps, after 1798, became more and more an elite unit which provided personal bodyguards for Napoleon and his principal commanders. The Kent and Sussex Corps of Guides, each consisting of three officers and sixty men, were modeled after the original (1796-97) Corps des Guides in both size and mission.

Britain's two units of guides were disbanded almost immediately after the signing of the Treaty of Amiens with France in March 1802, but the idea of a corps of guides was not forgotten. When the British found themselves at war with France again, fourteen months later, all counties along the southern coast of England were urged to create corps of guides; four (Kent, Sussex, Cornwall, and Devon) responded favorably to the government's request. Following the defeat of the combined French and Spanish fleets by Adm. Horatio Nelson's fleet at Trafalgar in 1805, the threat of a French invasion of England faded rapidly, and interest in the various corps of guides in the southern counties declined as well. All but the Devon Guides soon ceased to exist.[12] Yet, the most famous British Corps of Guides of the Napoleonic Wars era was not even activated until the early campaigns of the Peninsular War.

One of the most serious problems which confronted the Duke of Wellington and his generals in Portugal and Spain during the Peninsular War was the absence of reliable maps. The only maps available when the British landed in Portugal in 1808 were the series of maps compiled by the Spaniard,

D. Tomás López. Practically worthless in Portugal but reasonably accurate for a traveler in Spain, the López maps were not based on a trigonometrical survey, and the methods used for indicating the quality of roads were of only marginal use to a general. It was soon evident to the British that "the only dependable manner of collecting (topographical) information was by constant reconnaissance, sketching, and map-making carried out by officers acting under the orders of a staff officer at Headquarters."[13] When Col. (later Maj. Gen. Sir) George Murray was appointed as Wellington's quartermaster general in 1809, one of his first actions was to initiate a systematic survey of Portugal. Sketching officers were sent out throughout central Portugal, and by the end of 1810, Wellington's headquarters had an accurate, large-scale (one-quarter inch to the mile) map of the area of interest. These same assistant QMGs later performed similar work in Spain.[14]

The dearth of good maps, along with the scarcity of British officers and men fluent in Spanish and Portuguese, were the main reasons for George Murray's decision to raise the Peninsula Corps of Guides in April 1809, at about the time he began the survey of Portugal. The Peninsula Corps of Guides was initially a small, irregular unit consisting of a sergeant, a corporal, and sixteen men who were mainly Spanish guerrillas and French Army deserters. Wellington was sufficiently impressed by the performance of the Corps of Guides, and in late May, less than two months after its formation, he directed that it be expanded and officially established as part of the army. The corps was to be commanded by an officer of the QMG's Department; its NCOs and men were to receive the pay and allowance of cavalry. Capt. George Scovell, a deputy assistant quartermaster general (DAQMG) and an old friend of Colonel Murray, was chosen as the first commander of the Peninsula Corps of Guides. Under the capable Scovell, the guides achieved an excellent reputation and continued to expand. By April 1812 the authorized strength of the unit had risen to 150 privates, and George Scovell, still the commander, had been promoted to lieutenant colonel. Like Napoleon's Corps des Guides, the Peninsula Guides gradually became more than mere guides in the traditional sense. They were used for special reconnaissance missions and as interrogators, and also in such nonintelligence roles as dispatch carriers and military police. The Peninsula Corps of Guides was the first officially established unit of the British Army whose primary mission was the gathering of intelligence.[15]

Wellington's field intelligence system during the Peninsular War consisted of far more than the topographical work of the QMG's Department and the multifaceted activities of the Corps of Guides. Cavalry patrols conducted routine reconnaissance missions each day; every morning they moved out ten or fifteen miles toward enemy lines, returning in the afternoon or evening with a report of the enemy's movements. There was also a network of observation posts manned by the cavalry (and sometimes by the infantry) to keep watch on the French from fixed positions at the edge of the main army. Beyond the observation posts and the cavalry patrols were the "observing officers" who rode deep into enemy-held territory to uncover the location and strength of the French and, if possible, their intentions.[16] The exploits of these daring and resourceful officers are nearly legendary, but their successes would not have been possible without the active and consistent support of the Portuguese and Spaniards. Indeed, the support of the local inhabitants of the peninsula was the key to the success of Wellington's intelligence system.

> Throughout the occupied parts of the Peninsula, in every town and most villages, there were 'correspondents', men who reported every movement made by the French, counting the files as battalions or detachments marched through towns and identifying the regiments. These were the bravest and most valuable of all patriotic Spaniards, who made it possible for Wellington to build up a detailed order of battle for the enemy's army and to anticipate their next move.[17]

The "correspondents" or "confidential persons" were the backbone of Wellington's secret service. Some provided their information directly to observation posts or to the far-ranging "observing officers," while others corresponded only with Wellington or one of his subordinate commanders.

One other major source of tactical intelligence for Wellington was the constant flow of captured enemy dispatches brought in by the Portuguese and Spanish guerrillas who became quite adept at waylaying French couriers. At the beginning of the Peninsular War, French couriers rode alone and the messages and letters they carried were not enciphered. Eventually, no dispatch traveled without the protection of a squadron of dragoons, and important dispatches were enciphered. The use of ciphers, especially the Great Paris Cipher,[18] caused problems for the British since there were no cipher experts at Wellington's headquarters. When asked after the war about who actually worked at deciphering enemy dispatches, the duke replied, "I tried it: everyone at Headquarters tried: and between us we made it out."[19]

The personal attempts of the Duke of Wellington to decipher French messages underscores the fact that, like Marlborough and Wolfe, he was his own director of military intelligence, at least until 1815. All reports of enemy movements, regardless of their source, were brought to Wellington. Apparently these reports were not summarized or collated before they reached him. The QMG's Department under Col. George Murray handled topographic intelligence and the Corps of Guides, but Wellington never permitted the department to take full control of secret intelligence. As the years went by, however, he took George Murray into his confidence and allowed the QMG's Department to relieve him of some of the more tedious tasks associated with the clandestine effort. George Scovell of the QMG's Department, commander of the Corps of Guides (1809-13), demonstrated a special talent for breaking codes. After 1811 all enciphered enemy correspondence which reached headquarters was sent immediately to him.[20] The most famous of the "observing officers," Maj. Colquhoun Grant, gained favorable attention from Wellington and in March 1814 was selected to command the Peninsula Corps of Guides and to serve, simultaneously, as "Head Intelligence Officer." Grant's dual appointments indicate that, during the final months of the Peninsular War, Wellington was moving toward turning over control of the field intelligence system to the Quartermaster General's Department. This process was carried one step further during the Waterloo campaign of 1815. At the beginning of the "Hundred Days," Lt. Col. Colquhoun Grant, now an assistant quartermaster general, retained his post as senior intelligence officer at headquarters and was also named head of the new Intelligence Department.[21] It can be argued that even at Waterloo, despite appearances to the contrary, the Duke of Wellington continued to be his own DMI. Nevertheless, the organization headed by Colquhoun Grant was unique in the annals of the British Army. For the first time, a British army in the field had an Intelligence Department.

Interest in field intelligence within the British Army declined sharply after the defeat of Napoleon and in the forty years from 1815 to 1854 was practically nonexistent. The army engaged in numerous small wars and campaigns, but in most cases the campaigns were launched with little knowledge of the geography and climate of the area of operations or of the strength, weapons, and tactics of the enemy. The organized intelligence effort was minimal. Most small British or British-led forces in various parts of the world did have "one or two extra officers attached to the Quartermaster-General's Department who were responsible for intelligence, but few if any could speak the language of the country in which they were operating; they were seeing the terrain for the first time and had no background knowledge of the local inhabitants."[22]

In the Indian Army of the late 1840s, there was one notable exception to the general apathy which prevailed in matters of tactical intelligence. When Col. Sir Henry Lawrence took up a new assignment in 1846 as political agent on the Northwest Frontier, he recommended the establishment of a corps of guides, whose main function would be to collect intelligence and to act as guides for troops in the field.[23] The men were to be "chosen for their fidelity and organized for mobility and their clothes should be loose, comfortable, and designed for efficiency." Colonel Lawrence felt that such a unit would be useful in helping him govern the Punjab, particularly if the men were natives of the area. The Indian Corps of Guides was formed in December 1846 with Lt. Harry Lumsden in command. The guides became the first Indian Army unit to discard the conspicuous scarlet uniform and don khakis. In their training the emphasis was on individual initiative. From the beginning, the duties that were assigned to Lumsden's corps were diverse. Sometimes they collected land revenue as well as intelligence. The guides first distinguished themselves as a fighting unit during the Second Sikh War (1848-49), and their record throughout the remainder of the century was so outstanding that one historian of the Indian Army has written,

> The Guides did not in fact become a normal part of the Commander-in-Chief's army until the end of the century; they were raised with a special role and special objects, yet they seem, looking back, to sum up the classical period of the later nineteenth century, when the Indian Army were Soldiers of the Queen.[24]

Despite the numerous combat honors won by the guides, they continued for many years to function as intelligence collectors as well. In an annual inspection report in 1852, a general commented,

> The Corps has been composed of the most varied elements; there is scarcely a wild or warlike tribe in Upper India, which is not represented

in its ranks. . . . It is calculated to be of the utmost assistance to the Quarter-Master-General's Department as intelligencers, and most especially in the escort of reconnoitring officers.[25]

The Indian Corps of Guides was one of a kind; there were no other guide units in the British and Indian Armies during the period between Waterloo and the Crimean War.

Neglect of military intelligence on both the strategic and tactical levels came back to haunt the British Army in the Crimean War (1854-56). Britain was ill-prepared for war with a major European power when she joined France in declaring war on Russia in March 1854. The lack of adequate logistical planning by Britain resulted in grossly inadequate medical services in the Crimea, as well as in shortages of transport, clothing, and ammunition. Though not as widely publicized in contemporary press accounts of the war, military intelligence failures and shortcomings were as serious as those in the logistical area. Prior to the Anglo-French landings there in September, little was known about the Crimean Peninsula by the British commander, Field Marshal Lord Raglan, and his staff, except for the information they were able to discern from the Russian military map which had been obtained so fortuitously by Maj. Thomas Jervis during a holiday trip to Belgium just before the war began (see chapter II). The defunct Depot of Military Knowledge in London, now only a dying relic of the Napoleonic Wars, was unable to provide any useful information about the Russian Army or the fortifications at Sevastopol. After the war, Lord Raglan bitterly complained, "the Crimea was as completely an unknown country to the Chiefs of the Allied armies as it had been to Jason and his Argonauts when they journeyed to the same place in search of the Golden Fleece." Since there was no British military attaché in St. Petersburg until the 1860s, the only other sources of strategic military intelligence were the British ambassador in the Russian capital and the British consuls.[26] Apparently the French were no better prepared than their ally in this regard.

When the British and French armies landed on the Crimean Peninsula in September 1854 and began their advance on Sevastopol, it was soon obvious that British tactical intelligence was in even worse shape than British strategic intelligence. The Intelligence Department formed for the Waterloo campaign by Wellington had long since been forgotten, and a corps of guides was not established in the Crimea until June 1855, over one year after the war started. Lord Raglan's first quartermaster general, Lord de Ros, was an eccentric officer who "not only lacked experience but did not seem in the least anxious to acquire it."[27] In general, British cavalry units in the Crimea were poorly trained for, and uninterested in, reconnaissance missions. Dashing about to look for the enemy was undignified. In this war, the valiant but suicidal charge of the Light Cavalry Brigade at Balaklava was more in style. Lord Raglan had no faith in clandestine intelligence methods and shared with many of his contemporaries an emotional antipathy to the use of spies. At the same time, no officer on Raglan's staff was assigned to be the head intelligence officer. Gen. Richard Airey replaced the incompetent de Ros as QMG less than one month after British troops arrived in the Crimea, but he was fully occupied trying to untangle the logistical nightmare and had little time for intelligence work. Tactical intelligence provided to the British commander during the battles of Balaklava and Inkerman in the fall of 1854 was neither accurate nor timely. By default as much as any other reason, the control of British field intelligence in the Crimean War passed into the hands of a civilian.[28]

Charles Cattley, a civilian with no previous military experience, was appointed Lord Raglan's interpreter at the outset of the war.[29] Because Cattley (who changed his name to Calvert for security reasons after his arrival in the Crimea) was fluent in Russian and had some recent knowledge of the area, and because no one else was doing the job, he gradually assumed responsibility for all intelligence duties and was appointed "Head of Intelligence" by Raglan in the spring of 1855. Mr. Cattley interrogated prisoners and deserters, developed and ran a network of Turkish spies, and eventually formed a small corps of guides to work for the QMG. In contrast to Wellington, Raglan avoided personal involvement in intelligence, and Charles Cattley, therefore, was more truly "head of intelligence" in the Crimea than was Colquhoun Grant in the closing months of the Peninsular War and at Waterloo. Before his death from cholera in July 1855, Cattley began producing periodic written estimates of Russian strength, order of battle, and morale, and the logistical situation inside Sevastopol. These reports were provided to Lord Raglan, and, after his death in June 1855, to his successor, Gen. Sir James Simpson. Some were also distributed to division commanders.[30]

Breaches of security among his own officers had irritated the Duke of Wellington in the peninsula, but the advent of the electric telegraph and the presence of newspaper correspondents on the battlefield (for the first time) greatly increased the threat of damaging information leaks during the Crimean War. The most famous of the early war correspondents was William Howard Russell of *The Times*, who chronicled the many ills of the British Army in the Crimea. Some of his dispatches constituted serious breaches of security. Detailed information about the state of Raglan's force which appeared in Russell's articles in *The Times* was telegraphed to St. Petersburg from London. Czar Nicholas I is reported to have said, "We have no need of spies. We have *The Times*." At the insistence of Lord Raglan, the secretary of state for war wrote to the editor of *The Times* in December 1854, requesting restraint in the publication of material from the Crimea. This plea had little effect, however, and the newspaper continued to print Russell's articles, as well as private letters (which were uncensored) revealing the often appalling conditions facing British soldiers in the Crimea.[31] Similar problems regarding information security within a theater of war arose in South Africa half a century later.

Even after the costly experience of the Crimea, where old lessons about field intelligence had had to be relearned and commanders had been confronted with new problems, there was no concerted effort within the British Army to transform hard-won practical knowledge into a new, official tactical intelligence doctrine. The corps of guides formed by Mr. Cattley in 1855 was disbanded at the end of the war in 1856, and no move was made to establish a permanent intelligence unit for future field duty. For a long time after the

Crimean War, the British Army's neglect of the field intelligence system in peacetime did not detract noticeably from its combat performance overseas. The tactical intelligence requirements of British forces in the many campaigns and conflicts between the Crimean and South African Wars were generally satisfied by the same system which had sufficed from 1815 to 1854.

In India, following the suppression of the Mutiny in 1857, the British continually faced formidable native foes on the Northwest Frontier and in Afghanistan and the system was somewhat more advanced. This was demonstrated not only by the establishment of the Madras Guides in 1781 and the existence of the Indian Corps of Guides beginning in 1846, but also by the constant attention given by the Quartermaster General's Department of the Indian Army to its intelligence duties throughout this period. In 1878, Capt. Edwin H.H. Collen of the Indian Army proposed that field intelligence units be trained in peacetime so as to be prepared to operate under control of intelligence departments in wartime.[32] This revolutionary idea (for the 1870s) was rejected by Collen's superiors in Calcutta, but it is not surprising that it was first suggested by a British officer in India.

The Ashanti campaign in West Africa (1873-74) and the Zulu War (1878-79) perhaps best typify the army's field intelligence system in late nineteenth-century small wars. In the Ashanti campaign, conducted against a numerically superior native force on the Gold Coast, General Wolseley's "Head of Intelligence" was a young officer named Redvers Buller. The Intelligence Branch of the QMG's Department in London was only six months old and could offer no help to Buller and Wolseley. Therefore, Buller, a charter member of the "Ashanti Ring," who also served as Wolseley's intelligence officer in Egypt in 1882, had to build an intelligence organization from scratch as quickly as possible. Between his arrival in October 1873 and the climactic final battles with the Ashantis in early 1874, the energetic Buller recruited native interpreters and spies and formed a 250-man Corps of Scouts to move ahead of the main force. Wolseley considered the support rendered by this ad hoc organization so essential to the success of the campaign that he obtained a brevet majority for Redvers Buller.[33]

In the Zulu War, the annihilation of Lord Chelmsford's center column of 4,100 men at Isandlhwana on 22 January 1879 was due more to Chelmsford's disregard for the available intelligence than to a failure of the intelligence system or to the lack of a formal intelligence organization. Chelmsford had no intelligence officer on his staff when he invaded Zululand, but thanks to the information collected by civilian border agents who had employed spies and informants inside Zululand long before the invasion, the British had detailed knowledge of the Zulus' organization and tactics. In his highly acclaimed *The Washing of the Spears*, Donald R. Morris observes, "no expeditionary force had ever started a native war so well informed about its enemy." A pamphlet describing the complete Zulu order of battle and their tactics had been published with Chelmsford's support in November 1878 and distributed to every British company commander.[34] Knowledge of enemy tactics and organization was of no avail at Isandhlwana, however, because Chelmsford incorrectly interpreted or ignored information from captured Zulus and his own reconnaissance parties about the location of the main Zulu unit moving to attack his column. When Chelmsford marched into Zululand for a second time at the end of March, he took two civilian intelligence officers with him and deployed scouts from the Natal Volunteer Guides in the lead of his force. One of the two civilians, William Drummond, was designated "Head of Intelligence." The other, John Dunn, raised a unit of native scouts, recruited spies, and served as an interpreter. In Zululand, as in the Crimea twenty-five years earlier, the appointment of an officer to be head of intelligence was not mandatory. Understandably, some commanders continued to prefer British civilians who knew the local language and country.[35] In both the Ashanti campaign and the Zulu War, there was no military intelligence staff or unit in existence before the campaign began.

In fact, the British Army in this period had a regulation which permitted commanders in the field to establish field intelligence departments only after war was actually declared, or when hostilities involving British forces appeared imminent in an overseas theater. This regulation was still in existence at the beginning of the South African War in 1899.[36] Although it was thirteen years old at the time, the fifth edition of General Wolseley's *The Soldier's Pocket-Book for Field Service* (1886) presented an accurate picture of the army's tactical intelligence system on the eve of the second Anglo-Boer war.[37] Lord Wolseley, fully aware of the restrictions on setting up a field intelligence organization, stressed the role of War Office Intelligence prior to the start of a conflict.

> From the moment war is declared until peace is made, it is of utmost importance that we should know what the enemy is doing. . . . Until the troops are actually in the field, such information must be gleaned by our Intelligence Department in London, and by our Foreign Office people. . . . The means of starting an intelligence department should, if possible, be taken with you from England, or sent on before you. . . . When war is impending with any country, a number of officers should be sent to travel through it and collect information.[38]

Once war had begun, the heart of the system was the Field Intelligence Department. All intelligence officers in the field and those who worked for them (guides, scouts, interpreters, etc.) belonged to it. Of course, the tactical intelligence system encompassed more than just the Field Intelligence Department. Informants and spies reporting from behind enemy lines worked for the Department but were not part of it. As always, individual soldiers and cavalry (or mounted infantry) units performing security or reconnaissance missions were vital contributors to the system.

> Once in the field a knowledge of the enemy's doings must be obtained by the commander in the best way he can. . . . The general commanding an army appoints an officer as the chief of his intelligence department, working of course under the chief of the staff and the utmost care must be taken in the selection. . . . As in some countries proper officers cannot be found for this purpose who can speak the language, English civilians taken from the consular service may be given this work to do, and be attached to the army professedly as interpreters.

General Wolseley further described the qualifications needed by the chief of the Field Intelligence Department. The individual selected should have a generally calm and distrustful disposition. He should be intimately acquainted with the manners and customs of the people of the country. The organisation of the enemy's army should be engraven on his mind and the names of all officers commanding corps, divisions, &c., &c., should be in his possession.[39]

The Soldier's Pocket-Book for Field Service of 1886 provided detailed instructions for the field commander and his staff, and not only told how to choose an intelligence officer and how to set up a field intelligence organization, but also explained how the entire system should operate. All three phases of intelligence work were addressed: collection, processing-analysis, and dissemination-reporting. Collection received more thorough treatment than the others; each of the various sources used in the collection of tactical intelligence was discussed. Reconnaissance, which was divided by Lord Wolseley into four classes, was considered "the most reliable method of obtaining information as to the enemy's movements." The "3rd Class of Reconnaissance" was performed by a staff officer accompanied by a small cavalry detachment.[40] While this was often the most efficient means of collecting information about the enemy, it was also extremely dangerous. In Wolseley's words,

> There are no occasions in life when officers have such opportunities for displaying coolness and intrepid bravery, joined to extreme caution, as when sent out with a troop of cavalry to reconnoitre.[41]

Scouting missions, which were discussed as a specialized form of the "3rd Class of Reconnaissance," typically would be carried out by an officer and two dragoons, who attempted to slip through the enemy's outposts, collect information, and return without being observed. The necessary qualifications, for scouting in particular and the "3rd Class of Reconnaissance" in general, were simple.

> Next to courage, daring, physical strength, good horsemanship, good eyesight, and quick intelligence, an aptitude for finding one's way over a country is the qualification most necessary for all ranks employed upon this duty.

Scouting was a means recommended as superior to sending out entire cavalry troops or squadrons to collect reliable information, because the use of men and horses was "greatly economized."[42]

Other sources of tactical intelligence listed in *The Soldier's Pocket-Book* included balloon observation; interrogation of prisoners and deserters, spies, local inhabitants; and intercepted enemy telegrams and dispatches. Commanders were advised under which conditions a particular source could be most effectively used. Captured prisoners were not to be questioned near the point of capture, but were to be led directly to headquarters for interrogation by intelligence officers. The management of spies was certain to be difficult because so few were likely to be trustworthy, but the intelligence officer was expected to be able to provide suitable monetary rewards for the occasional dependable spy. As for local inhabitants, it was far easier to organize an effective field intelligence department if the local civilians were friendly, "as the Spaniards were during the Peninsular War."[43] The new dimension in communications intelligence afforded by the widespread use of the electric telegraph was appreciated by Wolseley.

> In all the wars of this and future ages, the electric telegraph will be greatly used. It must be remembered, that a telegraph operator can, with a small pocket instrument, tap the wires anywhere, and learn the messages passing along them. A few such men living concealed within the enemy's territory could obtain more news than dozens of ordinary spies.[44]

Col. George A. Furse, in his book *Information in War*, adds three different sources of information to Lord Wolseley's list: military police, newspaper reports, and documents found on prisoners or among the effects of the enemy's dead.[45]

Wolseley's instructions were brief but quite specific on the analysis and dissemination of the information collected. Each morning the intelligence officer was expected to prepare a written report of the enemy situation for his commander. This report would be based on all the available sources and would include "all suspicious circumstances observed by the outposts." The whole object of the system was to insure that all information about the enemy, "whether gleaned from individual officers out amusing themselves, or from the outposts, or from any other source, should be placed at the disposal of the man to whom the Commander looks for the information."[46] This individual was, of course, the head of the Field Intelligence Department or the "Head of Intelligence." His duties included not only the management of the intelligence collection effort, the conduct of personal reconnaissances, and the administration of the Field Intelligence Department, but also the collation and analysis of undigested information arriving at headquarters and the production of intelligence for the commander. In a large operation, the senior intelligence officer on the staff of the commanding general normally would have a number of officers working for him within the Field Intelligence Department, while in a small campaign involving relatively few British troops (the Ashanti Campaign in 1873-74, for example), the department might consist of one officer and the various native guides and scouts that he was able to recruit.

When the 1886 edition of *The Soldier's Pocket-Book for Field Service* was published, the senior intelligence officer and all officers of the Field Intelligence Department belonged to the Quartermaster General's Department, just as they had in Wellington's time and throughout the nineteenth century, except for the brief period (April 1873 to July 1874) when Edward Cardwell had placed the new Intelligence Branch in London under the adjutant general. In June 1887, however, War Office Intelligence moved for a second time, from the QMG to the AG, and there it stayed until 1901.[47] The rearrangements in London were mirrored in the field. Thus, at the start of the South African War in 1899 all intelligence officers in the field were assigned to the Adjutant General's Department. In practice, they reported directly to their commander or to their superiors in the field intelligence department.[48]

The need to disseminate the intelligence product assembled at headquarters for the commanding general down to subordinate commanders and to the troops was not viewed in the same light as it is today. Security was the overriding concern, no doubt with the Crimean experience in mind.

> It is much better that the enemy's movements should not be known to the army generally: if they are, they will be canvassed by a host of newspaper correspondents, and in the end the enemy will learn that his doings are known, which will make him more watchful; whereas it is a great matter to lull him into the pleasing notion that we are a stupid people, without wit or energy enough to find out what he is doing or intending to do. . . .[49]

The view expressed in *The Soldier's Pocket-Book* was that commanding generals should tell their subordinates only that information about the enemy which they really needed to know.

The means of communication available in the field for the transmission of intelligence were many. The electric telegraph, when it was available, tremendously enhanced the capability for rapid reporting and dissemination.[50] The telegraph, however, was only infrequently of use to scouts on reconnaissance or to spies behind enemy lines. In fact, it was generally true that in the days before the wireless radio, those in a position to collect the most valuable intelligence were least likely to be able to communicate their observation quickly back to headquarters.[51] The use of signal flags or the heliograph for relaying messages was sometimes possible, but often the reports of scouts or reconnaissance patrols did not reach headquarters until the scout or patrol had returned from his mission or at least had traveled back far enough from enemy territory to arrive at a telegraph station or heliograph.[52] When they could be used, the telegraph and heliograph made military communications much more effective than they had been in earlier times, but they also made interception by the enemy more likely than in the days when all important dispatches were hand-carried.[53] Colonel Furse, in his discussion of this subject in 1895, added such exotic means of communication as carrier pigeons, "the electric light from the arc lamp thrown on to the sky," and underground cables for telegraphic or telephonic communication.[54] No means of communication available in 1899 was entirely secure, but certainly the dispatch delivered by courier was the most secure in combat. Indeed, it remains so today.

The British Army's field intelligence doctrine of the 1890s, as described in *The Soldier's Pocket-Book for Field Service* of 1886 and amplified by Colonel Furse and others, clearly bore the imprint of the intelligence system which evolved within the Duke of Wellington's armies in the Peninsular War and in the Waterloo campaign at the beginning of the century. The role of the "Head of Intelligence" had been expanded somewhat and more precisely defined since 1815, and technological innovations of the post-Napoleonic era (especially the electric telegraph) had been taken into account. Some lessons of the Crimean War had been incorporated as well, along with the diverse experience gained by the army in small wars in every corner of the world. Yet, on the whole, the tactical intelligence system of 1899 was strikingly similar to that of 1815. This system had served the army rather well in most Victorian military campaigns. As we shall see, this was not the case when it was put to the test in the final conflict of Queen Victoria's reign, the South African War of 1899 to 1902.

NOTES

1. The term "field intelligence" was used in the report of the Royal Commission on the War in South Africa as well as in official British army manuals of the period. "Field intelligence" was the information about the enemy forces and the local geography required by the commander in the field to accomplish his mission. "Tactical intelligence" and "combat intelligence" are the terms used most frequently today. Henceforth, "field intelligence" and "tactical intelligence" will be used interchangeably.

2. Col. Charles E. Callwell's classic, *Small Wars: Their Principles and Practice*, includes a chapter on field intelligence. Callwell, who served in the Intelligence Department from 1887 to 1892, retired from active service in 1909 only to be recalled in August 1914 and appointed director of military operations and intelligence at the War Office. As a captain attending the Staff College in 1885-86, he had written an essay entitled "Small Wars" for which he received the gold medal of the Royal United Services Institution. This essay was expanded into a book which was adopted as an official textbook for the British Army in 1896. *Small Wars*, revised in 1899 and 1906, won acclaim for its author in Britain and abroad.

3. Lieutenant Colonel Parritt, *The Intelligencers*, pp. 1-2.

4. Ibid., pp. 2-6. See also Jack Haswell, *British Military Intelligence*, p. 16.

5. Ibid., pp. 7-13.

6. David Chandler, *Marlborough as Military Commander*, p. 70. See also Parritt, *The Intelligencers*, pp. 17-18.

7. Chandler, *Marlborough*, p. 78. Ironically, the Duke of Marlborough was dismissed by Queen Anne in 1712 because of charges made in the House of Commons that he had misappropriated public funds. He was able to refute these charges totally by showing "the money had been spent on his superb intelligence service." Correlli Barnett, *The First Churchill*, pp. 262, 267. See also Parritt, *The Intelligencers*, pp. 18-21.

8. Parritt, *The Intelligencers*, pp. 22-32.

9. The Dépôt de la Guerre had been established in 1688 by Louis XIV's minister of war, Louvois, as a ministerial archive. After the French Revolution began, the Legislative Assembly expanded the Dépôt's functions to include the analysis of military memoirs, the collection of maps and reconnaissance reports, and the formulation of recommendations on sites for defensive positions, bridges, and canals. Napoleon relied on the Dépôt to provide his generals with maps and details about various theaters of operation. Donald D. Howard, "The Archives de la Guerre," pp. 66-67.

10. Parritt, *The Intelligencers*, pp. 33-37, 44. The Kent and Sussex Corps of Guides formed in 1788-89 were not units of the British regular army. They appeared as volunteer infantry in the 1800 edition of the Militia, Yeomanry, and Volunteers List. The four guides units formed in 1803 by southern English counties, including Kent and Sussex, were also local volunteer units not intended for service outside their counties. In British India, there was a small Madras Corps of Guides as far back as 1781. See Capt. E.H.H. Collen, *Report on the Intelligence Branch*, p. 118.

11. At Imperial Headquarters, Napoleon's personal staff, the *maison*, was a staff within a staff. Its military department, the *cabinet*, included intelligence and topographic sections. All intelligence (from espionage and reconnaissance) went directly to the *cabinet*. Gunther E. Rothenberg, *The Art of Warfare in the Age of Napoleon*, pp. 209-10.

12. Parritt, *The Intelligencers*, pp. 37-40, 42-43. Additional material on these early corps of guides may be found at the Public Records Office in London under WO 4/171, WO 6/138, and WO 40/10.

13. S.G.P. Ward, *Wellington's Headquarters*, pp. 103-08. Ward's chapter 4, "The Collection and Transmission of Intelligence" offers a detailed, well-documented description of Wellington's intelligence system. See also Michael Glover, *Wellington's Army in the Peninsula*, p. 133.

14. Glover, *Wellington's Army in the Peninsula*, pp. 138-39. "Each of these officers received his instructions from Murray, whose interest in his surroundings and people and strong historical sense fitted him for holding as he did the sole responsibility for the collection of such information for his commander." Ward, *Wellington's Headquarters*, p. 109.

15. Parritt, *The Intelligencers*, pp. 44-47. Although officially established by Wellington, the Peninsula Corps of Guides was not a regular British Army unit. When Wellington's army finally left Portugal in the spring of 1813, the Corps of Guides consisted of two troops, each having a captain, six other officers, a sergeant major, sixteen NCOs and seventy-five troopers. Glover, *Wellington's Army in the Peninsula*, p. 134.

16. Ward, *Wellington's Headquarters*, pp. 113-17; Glover, *Wellington's Army in the Peninsula*, p. 139.

17. Glover, *Wellington's Army in the Peninsula*, p. 139.

18. The Great Paris Cipher consisted of a long list of arbitrary numbers, each referring to a place, a person, or a military term. There were also numbers for individual letters, numerals, and common syllables. Fortunately, the French usually left some word in the clear which gave a clue to the rest of the dispatch. Glover, *Wellington's Army in the Peninsula*, pp. 140-41.

19. Ward, *Wellington's Headquarters*, p. 120.

20. By the autumn of 1812, it was rare for Scovell to leave a single word untranslated. Glover, *Wellington's Army in the Peninsula*, p. 141.

21. Maj. Colquhoun Grant was captured in 1812 while on a long-range reconnaissance mission. At the time of Grant's capture, Wellington said sadly, "He was worth a brigade to me." The intrepid Grant managed to get messages through to Wellington while still a prisoner. Later, he escaped and went to Paris, disguised as an American; from there he sent Wellington news of Napoleon's march into Russia. Four months after his capture in April 1812, Grant was back in the peninsula doing intelligence work for Wellington. Parritt, *The Intelligencers*, pp. 48-51; Ward, *Wellington's Headquarters*, pp. 120-21.

22. Haswell, *British Military Intelligence*, p. 25; Parritt, *The Intelligencers*, p. 57.

23. The idea of a corps of guides was not new in the Indian Army. There had been a Madras Corps of Guides as early as 1781, whose purpose had been to make military maps and to provide intelligence. They were reduced in numbers in 1791, however, and their mission thereafter was primarily surveying. The Madras Corps of Guides accompanied Col. Arthur Wellesley (the future Duke of Wellington) in the campaign against the Mahrattas in 1799. Philip Mason, *A Matter of Honour*, pp. 328-29. See also Col. C.J. Younghusband, *The Story of the Guides*.

24. Mason, *A Matter of Honour*, pp. 328-29.

25. Indian Army Annual Inspection Report, 1852, quoted in Parritt, *The Intelligencers*, pp. 60-61.

26. Christopher Hibbert, *The Destruction of Lord Raglan*, pp. 32-33; Parritt, *The Intelligencers*, pp. 62-63, 71.

27. Ibid., p. 15.

28. Ibid., p. 33; Parritt, *The Intelligencers*, pp. 72-77.

29. Born at St. Petersburg of English parents, Charles Cattley spoke fluent Russian, French, and Italian. When Britain entered the Crimean War in March 1854, he was British vice consul at Kertch on the northeastern tip of the Crimean Peninsula. The Russians did not order Cattley out of Kertch until May, and at that time he wrote a report on the situation in the Crimea, including a fairly accurate estimate of Russian strength in Sevastopol, which came to Raglan's attention about one month prior to the allied troop landings in September.

30. Parritt, *The Intelligencers*, pp. 77-81.

31. Ibid., pp. 83-86. See also Philip Knightley, *The First Casualty; From the Crimea to Viet Nam*, pp. 3-17. In one article, published in *The Times* on 23 October 1854, Russell revealed the number

of pieces of British artillery that had been moved to the front, the exact dispositions and names of two regiments, and the fact that round shot was in short supply.

32. Collen, *Report*, pp. 117-19. In 1878 there was also a guides unit in the Bombay QMG's Department, but the Bombay and Madras Corps of Guides were primarily civilian in character.

33. Parritt, *The Intelligencers*, pp. 112-16.

34. Donald R. Morris, *The Washing of the Spears*, pp. 328-29.

35. Lord Wolseley always selected military officers to be "Head of Intelligence." Capt. (later Maj. Gen. Sir) John F. Maurice was Wolseley's intelligence officer when Wolseley succeeded Chelmsford in South Africa in July 1879. Parritt, *The Intelligencers*, pp. 117-23.

36. Statement of Lt. Col. E.A. Altham on 15 October 1902, Royal Commission on the War in South Africa, *Minutes of Evidence I*, p. 28.

37. The 1886 *Pocket-Book* was the most recent edition in 1899 and represented official British Army doctrine. Wolseley had written the original edition of *The Soldier's Pocket-Book* (1869) while working for Col. Patrick MacDougall in Canada. The third and fourth editions were published in 1874 and 1882, respectively. A wealth of additional information on the tactical intelligence system in 1899 is available in Maj. Charles E. Callwell, *Small Wars*, and Col. George A. Furse, *Information in War*.

38. Ibid., p. 90.

39. Ibid., p. 91.

40. Ibid., p. 208. The other three classes of reconnaissance were, first—reconnaissance in force; second—reconnaissance made by a detachment of all arms, of sufficient strength to protect themselves and secure their retreat; third—reconnaissance made continually by individual officers from the outposts.

41. Ibid., p. 210.

42. Ibid., pp. 218-19.

43. Ibid., pp. 91-93. In Charles Callwell's view, this favorable condition was not likely to be present in most "small wars." See chapter 4, "Difficulties under which the Regular Forces Labor as Regards Intelligence," in *Small Wars*.

44. Ibid., p. 93.

45. Furse, *Information in War*, pp. 27-28.

46. Wolseley, *The Soldier's Pocket-Book for Field Service* (1886), 5th ed., pp. 93-94.

47. In June 1901, Lt. Gen. Sir William Nicholson replaced Maj. Gen. Sir John Ardagh as head of War Office Intelligence and was given the title director general of mobilization and military intelligence (DGMI). Nicholson's department was now equal in status to those of the AG and QMG, but his subordinates were listed officially as AQMGs and DAQMGs in the War Office List of 1903.

48. The "Head of Intelligence" normally would be rated as an assistant adjutant general (intelligence), and his subordinates in the Field Intelligence Department and those officers assigned as intelligence staff officers at lower level headquarters were usually deputy assistant adjutant generals for intelligence. These were abbreviated as AAG (I) and DAAG (I), respectively.

49. Wolseley, *The Soldier's Pocket-Book for Field Service*, 5th ed., pp. 92, 102.

50. "Dissemination" here means the transmission of processed or raw intelligence from higher headquarters to lower headquarters that might benefit from it. "Reporting," on the other hand, indicates intelligence being passed from lower to higher headquarters.

51. The Italian physicist and inventor Guglielmo Marconi successfully demonstrated a wireless telegraph (radio) in 1895, but radios were not used in the South African War and were not used in the field on a large scale in time of war until World War I.

52. Statement of L.S. Amery, Royal Commission, *Minutes of Evidence II*, p. 466. One serious drawback of the heliograph was that it needed bright sunlight; cloudy or inclement weather rendered it useless.

53. The vulnerability of the telegraph to intercept by the enemy led to the development of new codes and ciphers for use in the field as well as for diplomatic communications. The field cipher was actually born in the American Civil War, when telegraphs were used extensively by both the North and South. In the words of David Kahn, "The telegraph created modern cryptography." *The Codebreakers*, pp. 190-91, 298-99.

54. Furse, *Information in War*, p. 293.

Chapter VIII

British Tactical Intelligence in the South African War, 1899-1902

> The acquisition of information is so surrounded with impediments, is affected by such a variety of circumstances, that there is little prospect of an officer becoming a thoroughly useful intelligence officer in the field unless he takes up the subject as a specialty.
>
> Col. George A. Furse,
> *Information in War*, 1895

The makings of the British Army's Field Intelligence Department in South Africa were already on hand when the Boers began their invasion of Natal and the Cape Colony in October 1899. Just as recommended in *The Soldier's Pocket-Book*, officers were sent to South Africa to collect information beginning in June 1899, approximately four months before Britain declared war on the Boer Republics in response to the invasion. Since 1896, the Intelligence Division in London had been sending officers down from time to time on "secret service." Also, intelligence officers had been designated on the staffs of the British commanders in Natal and Cape Colony. However, the decision to send ten "special officers" to South Africa in the summer of 1899 was based on the belief that war with the Boers was imminent.[1] As was discussed in the preceding chapter, these officers collected a great deal of information about the Boers and the topography of South Africa, which was useful not only to the Intelligence Department in London, but also to the Field Intelligence Department which eventually was formed. Here the line blurs between strategic and tactical intelligence; the "special officers" of 1899 contributed to both, though more significantly to the latter.

The "special officers" who arrived in South Africa in June 1899 received little assistance from the intelligence staff officers in Natal and Cape Colony, because those two individuals had become so overwhelmed with administrative duties that they could no longer afford time for intelligence work. The foundation of the Field Intelligence Department in South Africa may be credited primarily to the ten "special officers." Two of the officers, Maj. David Henderson and Lt. Col. Archibald Murray, were chosen because of their previous experience in South Africa. They were assigned to Cape Colony and Natal, respectively, to "get together people who would be useful, local colonists and so on, as scouts and guides" and, in general, to lay the groundwork for the establishment of field intelligence departments in the two colonies. The other "special officers" included Colonel Baden-Powell and Maj. Edward Altham, who still held the appointment of deputy assistant adjutant general at the Intelligence Department in London. Baden-Powell went to Mafeking in northern Cape Colony, while Altham joined Murray in Natal.[2]

The productive efforts of the "special officers" notwithstanding, there were several problems with the special assignment which were highlighted by the Royal Commission on the War in South Africa. Ten officers were too few, given the enormity of the potential theater of war,[3] and not enough money was provided to them. They were also hampered by the restrictions which prohibited the establishment of a field intelligence department until after the declaration of war and which made it illegal for them to develop their own sources of information. In other words, they could not recruit spies, informants, or even guides. The "special officers" had to collect intelligence on their own, while masquerading as tourists. Some of the officers, like Baden-Powell and Altham, had had previous intelligence assignments, but many had not. There was no formal schooling program in the army for training intelligence officers (or for practically any specialty except artillery and engineers) and no separate career pattern which would allow an officer to serve only on intelligence assignments without damaging his chances for promotion.[4] Many were graduates of the Staff College at Camberley, where they had received courses in such intelligence-related subjects as "Topography," "Reconnaissances," "Staff Duties," and "Foreign Languages."[5] The fact is, however, that these officers were not military intelligence specialists as we know them today. They were infantry, cavalry, artillery, or engineer officers serving tours in intelligence and fully expecting to return to normal troop or staff assignments in their own branches. Finally, the need to send Major Altham and others from the Intelligence Department in London to South Africa badly crippled Sir John Ardagh's already understaffed organization. The notion, prevalent in 1899, that Queen Anne's Gate could serve in wartime as a pool of available and experienced officers who would go overseas to set up and run a field intelligence department was quickly outmoded by the South African experience. Even in the first few months of that lengthy conflict, the demand for trained and experienced intelligence officers in the field completely outstripped the capacity of the Department to supply them.[6]

Although shortcomings in the existing tactical intelligence system were apparent to some prior to October 1899, only when the war began did the need for change clearly become evident. In all fairness, some of the alleged intelligence failures which occurred in the earliest battles of the war were more the results of commanders' mistakes and their general attitude toward intelligence than of the inadequacy of the system itself. In the broadest context, however, their shared attitude was part of "the system."

At the beginning of the second Anglo-Boer War in the autumn of 1899, the major British force in South Africa was in Natal, under the command of Lt. Gen. Sir George White. A sixty-four-year-old Irishman, White had spent his entire career in India, where he had served with distinction in campaigns in Afghanistan, Baluchistan, and Burma (where he won the Victoria Cross), and had succeeded Lord Roberts as commander-in-chief in India (1893-98). Sir George's two senior staff officers, Col. Ian Hamilton and Col. Henry Rawlinson, were brought from India as well. Of the three, only Ian Hamilton had served previously in South Africa and had combat experience against the Boers. General White selected Lt. Col. Archibald Murray as his "Head of Intelligence," a logical choice since Murray had been in Natal for several months before Sir George's arrival. Other than the information he had been able to gather on his own about the terrain of Natal and the plans of the Boers, Murray's main contribution prior to the outbreak of hostilities had been to prepare quietly for the activation of a locally recruited unit, which would become the backbone of the field intelligence department in Natal. The Natal Corps of Guides, officially established in October 1899, was an all-volunteer unit composed of "about 45 white men and 50 natives. The white men were British subjects selected from Natal, the Orange Free State, and the Transvaal for their special acquaintance with the different districts, knowledge of the Dutch and Kaffir languages, and experiences of veldt life, including riding and shooting."[7]

The Natal Corps of Guides and Rimington's guides in Cape Colony were in the tradition of the Peninsular Corps of Guides; they were units of scouts more than units of guides. The old distinction between scouts and guides had faded since the eighteenth century, but there was still a requirement for traditional guide work, especially in South Africa, where much of the country was unmapped or poorly mapped.[8] The men who actually functioned as guides for the army in South Africa were local men, often black men, hired and controlled by intelligence officers. They were part of the Field Intelligence Department for as long as the army remained in the particular area where the guides knew the terrain and could be of service.

Archibald Murray's work in Natal paid dividends. The value of the Natal Corps of Guides as an intelligence unit was evident in the first battles between the British and the Boers. Only days before the Boer attack on the British force at Dundee in northwestern Natal, Sir George White sent Lieutenant Colonel Murray from his headquarters at Ladysmith to join the staff of Major General Penn Symons at Dundee. With timely and accurate information flowing to him from the Natal Corps of Guides, Murray was able to inform Penn Symons of every movement of the approaching Boer forces. In Murray's words, "We had full information."[9] As the Boer army crossed the borders from the Transvaal and the Orange Free State into Natal, reconnaissance by cavalry units and reports reaching Dundee from farmers and native blacks supplemented the information provided by the guides.

Unfortunately for the British, Penn Symons had a mental block. He totally discounted the possibility that the Boers would dare attack an entire brigade of the British Army. So confident was he, he did not even bother to post pickets on the dominating hills east and northwest of Dundee. Boer spies within the town kept the Boer commanders apprised of this lapse, and the Boers took full advantage of it. By occupying the high ground in force during the night of 19-20 October, they were able to place the Dundee garrison in a virtually untenable position. The British fought back stubbornly and managed to drive the Boers off one of the hills, but Penn Symons was mortally wounded, and the British suffered over 500 casualties altogether. Two days later, unable to dislodge the Boers from the hill containing Dundee's water supply, the British withdrew. The defeat suffered by Penn Symons's 4,000 men at Dundee was in no sense caused by a lack of information about the enemy. This is clear not only from Murray's testimony before the Royal Commission after the war, but also from the writing of Maj. Gen. Sir Frederick Maurice in the British official history of the war. Maurice remarked of Gen. Penn Symons,

> His information continued to be full and accurate. Erasmus' advance, Meyer's concentration at the Doornberg, Kock's circuitous passage over the Biggarsberg, were all known to him. On October 19th he received detailed warning that an attack was to be made on him that very night by Erasmus from the north, Meyer from the east, and Viljoen from the west.[10]

The real problems at Dundee were Penn Symons's contempt for the Boer fighting capabilities and his own self-confidence and stubbornness.

The fledgling Natal field intelligence department had done surprisingly well while facing its first test. Unfortunately, within two weeks Murray and the rest of his staff were trapped in Ladysmith when the Boers brought the remainder of Sir George White's force under siege there, following the battle at Nicholson's Nek. Consequently, when Gen. Sir Redvers Buller arrived in South Africa as commander-in-chief at the end of October 1899 and went immediately to Natal to take personal charge of the Ladysmith relief effort, he had to organize a new field intelligence department.

On a smaller scale, but equally effective in the early days of the war, was the intelligence department of Col. (later Maj. Gen.) Robert S.S. Baden-Powell at Mafeking in the "Far North Cape." Before numerically superior Boer forces under Gen. Piet Cronje had surrounded and besieged Baden-Powell's 1,200 colonial irregulars, "B.P." had initiated clandestine operations east across the border into the Transvaal.[11] To oversee these spy missions, Baden-Powell relied upon several intelligence officers. His agents in the Transvaal had subagents "about the country who were very well informed as to what was going on, so that we could tell exactly the number coming against us, and everything and what their intentions were."[12] Baden-Powell and his determined little garrison survived over seven months of siege; the relief of

Mafeking in mid-May 1900 was followed by a joyful celebration in England, and Baden-Powell was honored as a national hero. Good intelligence played an important role in his success.

While the field intelligence system, such as it was, functioned rather well at Dundee and Mafeking, the three defeats suffered by the British during Black Week in December 1899 were due in large measure to a lack of adequate information about the terrain and the enemy. More at fault than the field intelligence system, however, were the generals commanding British forces at each of the three engagements—Sir William Gatacre at Stormberg, Lord Methuen at Magersfontein, and Sir Redvers Buller at Colenso—who demonstrated a lack of appreciation for adequate intelligence and an unwarranted optimism concerning the capabilities of their own troops.

Gatacre not only failed to order a reconnaissance of the route to be followed by his 3,000 men in an all-night march to planned attack positions near Stormberg, but he also neglected to take his intelligence officer along on the operations. This officer, a captain, was "well acquainted with the ground in the vicinity of Stormberg." The guides who actually led Gatacre's column on that fateful night of 9-10 December 1899 were unfamiliar with the area and were unsupervised by any officer. Unfortunately, they lost their way and took a wrong route, which was much longer than the one intended. The result was that the troops, who had been up since 4 a.m. on 9 December, arrived exhausted in the vicinity of Stormberg just after dawn on 10 December. Furthermore, when the light of morning began to appear, Gatacre did not send out flank and advance guards, even though his force was moving along a road surrounded by hills. So unaware of Boer dispositions was Gatacre, he spent what little energy was left in his command on a futile assault against a small but well-concealed Boer unit which suddenly opened fire from atop a rugged hill as he approached Stormberg. Had he known the actual enemy situation, he could have moved beyond the hill and seized his objective, Stormberg. The Boers on the hill, however, easily repulsed the feeble British effort to displace them, and Gatacre, losing control of his men, led a disorganized withdrawal from the area.[13]

The Highland Brigade, widely considered to be the finest fighting brigade in the British Army, led Lord Methuen's attack against Magersfontein Hill, in what the British hoped would be the last battle of the drive to relieve the besieged garrison at Kimberley. Advancing through pouring rain in the early morning hours of 11 December, the Highland Brigade, commanded by one of the most admired men in Scotland, Maj. Gen. A.J. ("Andy") Wauchope, had an officer from Methuen's intelligence staff as guide. Major Benson (DAAG [I]) had conducted a personal reconnaissance of the general area of Magersfontein and had selected the route to be taken by the Highland Brigade. Neither Benson's reconnaissance, the daily cavalry patrols, nor any other means of intelligence collection at Methuen's disposal had discovered the fact the Boers were not in force on Magersfontein Hill, as it had appeared during the days before the attack. Instead, using unconventional tactics similar to those they had so successfully implemented at the battle of Modder River on 28 November, the bulk of the Boer riflemen were positioned in camouflaged trenches at the foot of Magersfontein, where they planned to gain surprise and where their rifle fire would be the most devastating against the expected British infantry assault. Subsequently, the Highland Brigade unknowingly moved toward Magersfontein and, drawing near to the hill, began to deploy into fighting formation from the tightly packed column of the march. Just at this moment, Boer riflemen unleashed a furious and sustained fire, killing General Wauchope and a number of his men and throwing the Highland Brigade into considerable confusion. Eventually, the brigade fell back with heavy losses. Since the success of Lord Methuen's entire battle plan depended on the Highland Brigade overrunning key Boer positions, the decision was made to retire, and the Boers celebrated their second victory of Black Week.[14]

The defeat at Colenso on 15 December 1899, while not as costly in terms of men killed or captured as were the defeats at Magersfontein or Stormberg, was the most crushing blow to British pride. The commander of the 21,000 British troops there was the highly regarded Gen. Sir Redvers Buller. Reverting to an old precedent set in the Crimean War, Buller had selected a civilian, a Natal farmer named T.K. Murray, to be head of intelligence. The newly formed intelligence staff produced a reasonably accurate estimate of the Boer strength at Colenso[15] on 13 December, two days before the battle. An incomplete reconnaissance of the Boer positions, however, left Buller ignorant of the precise locations of the Boer units in the Colenso area.

Certainly, to determine the enemy dispositions under such circumstances was a difficult and dangerous task. Buller's force was encamped south of the Tugela River in full view of the Boers (the British tents could be seen and counted easily by the Boers), whereas the Boer commandos[16] on the north bank in the vicinity of Colenso were well entrenched and nearly impossible to detect unless a scout or scouting party actually crossed the Tugela and approached the trenches.[17] The terrain along the south bank of the Tugela opposite Colenso was relatively flat and open and thus could be approached by scouts or officers conducting reconnaissance only at night, unless they wished to subject themselves to the fire of Boer sharpshooters. For reasons never fully revealed, a night reconnaissance of the Colenso area was not conducted.[18]

Sir Redvers Buller began his abortive attempt to cross the Tugela at Colenso early on the morning of 15 December. Buller had subjected the Colenso area to an artillery bombardment and it seemed probable to him that, since no activity had been reported on the north bank where the Boers were generally believed to be, they had withdrawn. His hopes rose higher still on 15 December when, as the advance parties of British infantry reached the south bank of the river, there was still no movement or response from the enemy.[19] The Boers merely had allowed the British to walk into their trap, and when they suddenly opened fire Buller's army was badly mauled and driven back. Sir Frederick Maurice wrote of the humiliating defeat at Colenso, "Imperfect knowledge of the topographical conditions of the problem and of the dispositions of the enemy, combined with misapprehension of orders, sufficed to wreck it at the outset."[20]

Following Black Week, General Buller was relieved from command of British forces in South Africa, and one of Britain's most distinguished soldiers, Field Marshal Lord Roberts, then the commander-in-chief in Ireland, was named to replace him. The son of an Irish general and a veteran of forty-one years of service in India, the sixty-seven-year-old Frederick Sleigh Roberts was the most beloved of late-Victorian British military heroes. He had won the Victoria Cross for conspicuous gallantry during the Indian Mutiny as a twenty-six-year-old lieutenant, and later made his mark in the Indian Army as a superb staff officer in the QMG's Department (see chapter IV). Diminutive in physical stature (approximately five-foot-two), the white-haired Roberts was loved by his men in India, who had nicknamed him "Bobs." He was best known to the British public for his role in the victorious Second Afghan War (1878-80), especially for leading the epic march from Kabul to Kandahar. By an ironic twist of fate, on the very Sunday in December 1899 when Lord Roberts met with Prime Minister Robert Salisbury at 10 Downing Street to accept the offer of supreme command in South Africa, a telegram arrived from Natal with the news that his only son, Lt. Frederick Roberts, had died of wounds suffered several days earlier at Colenso.[21] The loss of Freddie was a terrible blow to the old general, but did not deter him from continuing his preparations for the voyage to South Africa.

Lord Roberts arrived at Cape Town aboard the *Dunnottar Castle* on 10 January 1900, accompanied by Major General Lord Kitchener,[22] his chief of staff, and Col. George F.R. Henderson, chief of intelligence. Dismayed but undaunted by Buller's defeat at Spion Kop on 24 January, Roberts and his staff lost no time in assembling a large force on the Modder River with the objective of relieving Kimberley and sweeping north through the Orange Free State and the Transvaal to crush the Boers. Roberts began his drive in early February 1900 and in eight months succeeded in most of what he set out to accomplish, including the occupation of Bloemfontein, capital of the Orange Free State, and Pretoria, capital of the Transvaal, and the defeat of the Boers on most occasions when they chose to stand and fight.

During this final portion of the conventional phase[23] of the Boer War, a combination of factors resulted in improved tactical intelligence on the Imperial forces' side. As he had demonstrated earlier in his career while QMG in India, Lord Roberts genuinely believed in the necessity for good intelligence and for well-qualified and experienced intelligence officers on his staff.[24] Had he been able to pick from all the colonels in the British Army at that time, it is doubtful that Lord Roberts could have selected a better officer than Col. George Francis Robert Henderson to be his chief of intelligence. Unfortunately, Colonel Henderson[25] served as chief of intelligence only until mid-March 1900, when he had to be evacuated from South Africa because of a sudden serious illness. His contributions to the field intelligence system were considerable, nonetheless.

Born in St. Helier, Jersey, in 1854, George F.R. Henderson was the eldest son of a prominent English educator.[26] After attending Leeds grammar school, George won a history scholarship to St. John's College, Oxford, in 1873. He attended St. John's for three years and then entered the Royal Military College at Sandhurst. Upon graduating from Sandhurst, he was commissioned a second lieutenant in the York and Lancaster Regiment in May 1878. George served with his regiment in a number of overseas assignments. In the late 1880s he became widely known in Britain after publishing articles and books dealing with the history of the American Civil War. Largely as a result of his growing fame as a writer, he was appointed as an instructor at Sandhurst in 1890 and as a professor at the Staff College two years later. It was during his lengthy tour at the Staff College that G.F.R. Henderson reached the pinnacle of his career as a military writer and educator. As professor of military arts and history at Camberley from December 1892 until the winter of 1899-1900, when he left for South Africa, Henderson exercised considerable influence upon the younger generation of British Army officers.[27] The publication of *Stonewall Jackson and the American Civil War* (London, 1898) placed him in the first rank of military historians of his day.

As chief of intelligence in South Africa, Colonel Henderson enjoyed the full confidence of Lord Roberts. With active encouragement by the commander-in-chief, he began to reorganize and expand the Field Intelligence Department "as soon as he arrived in South Africa."[28]

> When Roberts arrived, even the free spending of money to secure some of the information that ought to have been available long before had not been thought of. This at least could be set right, and Henderson succeeded, immediately on landing, in persuading Roberts to entrust him with sums of money and the means of collecting a staff which had been denied to his less fortunate predecessors.[29]

Henderson insisted on including headquarters intelligence staff officers at all levels, all intelligence-collection units, and those officers working independently in the field in the revitalized Field Intelligence Department. One of his first accomplishments was to assemble, "from such sources as were available," maps of the Orange Free State and the Transvaal. These maps, one of which had been prepared by the Transvaal revenue authorities and printed in Austria, were far from perfect, but they were enormously preferable to no maps at all, and, as Roberts later wrote, "When the advance into the Transvaal began, these maps were of the utmost service."[30] Colonel Henderson was an outstanding chief of intelligence during the few months he was in South Africa. Then, too, his influence extended beyond the realm of intelligence. In the field in South Africa,

> 'his boys' of the Staff College came to him at all hours, eager to discuss those actual problems of war which they had so often studied in theory, glad of the chance given them of referring their doubts and difficulties to the instructor the influence of whose teaching they still felt.[31]

Colonel Henderson, with some help from Lord Roberts, engineered the transfer of one of his brightest former students, Capt. William R. Robertson, from the Intelligence Department in London to South Africa to be one of his assistants. Sir John Ardagh's loss was George Henderson's gain. Robertson, who reached Cape Town only ten days after Roberts and Henderson, had been head of Section B (responsible for the colonies, including South Africa) and therefore was intimately familiar with the military capabilities of the Boers and with the events to date in South Africa. When Captain Robertson arrived at Roberts's headquarters on 20 January, the staff was engaged in final preparations for the relief of Kimberley and the advance into the Orange Free State. At about this time, Henderson was charged with creating an elaborate deception plan to keep the Boers in doubt about the planned route of advance. Not even Robertson and Henderson's other assistants on the intelligence staff at headquarters knew of the actual plan.

> Henderson, always an ardent advocate for mystifying and misleading the enemy, was especially active, and revelled in the deceits he practiced. He sent out fictitious telegrams to commanders in clear, and then on one excuse or another countermanded them in cipher; circulated false orders implying a concentration of troops at Colesberg . . . ; gave 'confidential' tips to people eager for news whom he knew would at once divulge them . . . on the whole it is probable that no military plan was ever kept better concealed from friend or foe.[32]

Meanwhile, Robertson and his colleagues were fully occupied with keeping close track of Boer movements, particularly those of Transvaal Gen. Piet Cronje near Magersfontein. One of their collection techniques was to infiltrate several Dutch-speaking men into Cronje's commandos, "with a promise of substantial pecuniary reward if they brought us the information we required." Cronje began to pull out when he learned that Roberts had bypassed him and had relieved the Kimberley garrison. The initial confusion at headquarters about Cronje's activities and the direction in which he was moving was cleared up by one of the infiltrators, who managed to return to British lines with information.[33]

Lord Roberts and his chief of intelligence were very much aware of the tactical intelligence lessons to be learned in the defeats suffered prior to their arrival in South Africa, and they attempted, during the period of reorganization and preparation in early 1900, to rectify some of the more pressing problems. Official British Army doctrine did not provide for an intelligence officer for the staff of any unit smaller than a division, but under the new arrangement, an intelligence officer was "told off to every column, no matter what the size of the column might be." In practice, this did not mean that an intelligence officer would be present with every unit operating independently, no matter how small, but it did mean that brigades and even half-brigades would have their own intelligence officers.[34]

The mere assignment of an intelligence officer to a commanding general's staff, however, did not oblige the general to employ the officer for purely intelligence duties. An example is the case of Sir George Aston, who was sent from Lord Roberts's headquarters intelligence staff at Bloemfontein down to a division to be the intelligence officer.

> There I found that the new intelligence officer was looked upon as sort of handy man, expected to undertake odd jobs of every description. . . . Intelligence officers did so much of other peoples' work that they had little time for their own. . . . [These odd jobs were] all in addition to the responsible work of locating the enemy, providing maps, guides, and

interpreters and all the usual matters which come within the scope of the present-day intelligence officer.[35]

The fact that Aston and other intelligence officers with divisions and brigades were required to perform some duties unrelated to intelligence no doubt reduced their effectiveness in their primary jobs, but at the same time their very presence made a recurrence of Stormberg far more unlikely.

A second intelligence lesson painfully learned at Magersfontein and Colenso was that traditional methods of reconnaissance, especially cavalry reconnaissance, were ineffective and totally unsuited to the new conditions of warfare.[36] G.F.R. Henderson long before had gained his own appreciation of the difficulties of reconnaissance on the modern battlefield, primarily from his study of the American Civil War. Consequently, as chief of intelligence, he placed great emphasis on the necessity for excellent scouting techniques. In his view, "cavalry of the existing type is of very little value except to keep touch with the enemy's scouts."[37] Specially trained mounted infantry (M.I., as they were called in South Africa) or, better yet, a few brave and skillful scouts were most effective for reconnaissance against the Boers. Even before Henderson's arrival in South Africa, this problem had been recognized, and the corps of guides formed in Natal and Cape Colony in October 1899 provided men at least partially trained as scouts to British commanders during the early battles of the war.

In faraway Scotland, soon after Black Week, Major Lord Lovat began recruiting a special unit of scouts. The approximately 240 men, chosen by Lovat from hundreds of volunteers, were mostly Highland stalkers whose years of experience in tracking wild game in the rugged wilds of Scotland had put them on a par with Boer scouts. "Lovat's Scouts" arrived in time to lend intelligence support to Roberts's advance from Bloemfontein to Pretoria. While putting his unit together in Scotland, Lovat had proposed that it should be split up upon arrival in South Africa so that a few of his men could serve with each infantry brigade and artillery unit, but the War Office in London insisted that Lovat keep his men together. If Lovat's advice had been followed, his scouts probably would have been far more helpful to Lord Roberts and his army; as it was, they were attached to the Highland Brigade where they served admirably as the brigade's advance guard.[38]

Due to the general improvement in scouting and to the greater interest in tactical intelligence shown by the commander-in-chief, Lord Roberts was provided with reasonably accurate information on which to base his tactical decisions during the march from the Modder River all the way to Pretoria, which was occupied on 5 June 1900.[39] Unlike his predecessor Sir Redvers Buller, who on occasion ignored reports of the enemy strength prepared by his field intelligence department and then made his own, Lord Roberts relied heavily on the estimates of his intelligence department from the very first.[40] With the aid of accurate information about the enemy and Henderson's clever deception plan, the Boer line of communications was blocked by Roberts's main forces while Maj. Gen. John D.P. French led a cavalry force to the relief of Kimberley on 15 February 1900. In late February, Roberts trapped Cronje at Paardeberg, forcing the Boer general to surrender with 4,000 men, and then advanced on to Bloemfontein on 13 March. After Bloemfontein the capability of the intelligence system was challenged still further, for the enemy was "neither to be placed nor numbered for more than a few hours at a time, so swift were his movements, so variable his combinations, and so favorable the country to the tactics in which he excelled." Yet, in the march north from Bloemfontein to Kroonstad, Johannesburg, and Pretoria, "the main Boer forces were maneuvered, often almost bloodlessly, out of one position after another."[41] It is fair to say that this rather remarkable feat could not have been accomplished without the improvements that had been made in the intelligence system.

Lt. Col. C.V. Hume took over as "Director of Military Intelligence (South Africa)" following the departure of Col. George Henderson in the spring of 1900. Hume continued the good work started by Henderson, and, in July 1900, produced a paper describing the progress of the Field Intelligence Department. The document formally set out for the first time the requirement for intelligence officers to be deployed with independent columns and for the coordination of all intelligence officers from a central headquarters. New ideas advanced by Hume included a call for military counterintelligence units and the recommendations that all intelligence officers have their own small, specialized staffs (to include interpreters and scouts) and that they have executive control of intelligence-collection units. He further recommended that censorship and the reading of private mail come under the control of the Field Intelligence Department.[42] The new phase of the war which began in the fall of 1900 gave Hume's suggestions, which initially received little attention, new life.

The summer of 1900, between the fall of Pretoria in June and the flight of President Kruger and annexation of the Transvaal in September, was a period of transition from conventional to guerrilla war for the Boers. As Lord Roberts gathered his strength at Pretoria and prepared to push east to Komati Poort on the border with Portuguese East Africa (Mozambique) in early July, Boer commandos under Gen. Koos De La Rey slipped completely undetected around Pretoria into the western Transvaal. Striking unexpectedly at three British outposts, De La Rey forced Roberts to delay his offensive in the east for nearly a month. In the meantime, in the Orange Free State, Gen. Christiaan De Wet led 2,600 men out of the Brandwater Basin on the night of 15 July and successfully eluded a large British force that pursued him. These events of July 1900 foreshadowed the hit-and-run tactics that became the standard Boer strategy during the remainder of the war.

The improvements in the British tactical intelligence system during the conventional phase of the war were not sufficient to cope with the problems posed by the Boers' switch to guerrilla war. In characterizing this part of the war, Capt. Maurice Grant provides some insight about the difficulties of Roberts's (and, beginning in December 1900, Kitchener's)[43] field intelligence department:

> . . . in their expiring struggle they reverted to weapons that were peculiarly their own and precisely those in which their opponents were least practiced. Casting off the trammels of formal warfare, they compelled

> the British Army to conform and agitated the whole vast theatre of war
> with an infinite complexity of movement which never for a moment
> desisted, nor for more than a moment was marked by any distinguishable
> trend.[44]

The lack of "any distinguishable trend" is a serious and often crippling
problem for an intelligence organization. No matter how good its means of
collection, the organization requires some knowledge of patterns of enemy
action in order to analyze the information collected correctly and, ultimately,
to determine enemy intentions.

Lt. Col. William R. Robertson was more specific in describing the
situation facing Lord Roberts's intelligence department:

> The system of guerilla warfare adopted by the Boers . . . made Intelli-
> gence duties much more difficult than before. The enemy's plan now was
> to act aggressively against different points on our line of communication,
> and to pick up elsewhere any helpless or unwary detachment which
> promised to be an easy prey, and as the bodies he employed were widely
> dispersed, moved swiftly, were subject to variable combinations, and
> were favored by the nature of the country, it was impossible to place or
> number them for more than a few hours at a time.

Robertson further relates that some information was derived through the
seizure of mail bags containing correspondence between Boers, but it was
usually outdated for tactical purposes by the time it fell into British hands. For
the most part, intelligence staff officers and their commanders relied on the
work of scouts who "would track the commandos from place to place, and
sometimes lie out watching them for several days and nights in succession,
bringing or sending back most valuable intelligence."[45] Major Lovat was
ordered by Lord Kitchener to return to Great Britain and to raise another unit
of scouts in the Scottish Highlands, so highly were the services of the
Highland stalkers valued.[46] Even when the scouts were able to collect vital
information, the problems of communications sometimes negated their success. Not only did the scouts have to range further and more quickly to keep
up with the various independent Boer units, but British columns also ranged
far from their own headquarters, compounding the problem. "Intercommuni-
cation between the different British columns was bad. . . . At headquarters
we were usually able to trace De Wet's movements. The difficulty was to
inform the columns within useful time."[47]

Kitchener's director of military intelligence throughout most of the
difficult counterguerrilla phase of the South African War was Lt. Col. David
Henderson, who served in that capacity from February 1901 until the end of
the fighting in May 1902. Born in Glasgow in 1862, David Henderson was the
youngest son of a shipbuilder. He was educated at the University of Glasgow
and entered the army in 1883 after attending Sandhurst. After joining the
Argyll and Sutherland Highlanders Regiment, he served in South Africa,
Ceylon, and China. Prior to the Second Boer War, David Henderson was not
as well known as George Henderson. Within the army, however, he had
already earned a reputation as an extremely bright and hard-working professional.[48] Though Col. George Henderson died soon after the end of the war,

David Henderson was destined for general officer rank and a long and distinguished career.

David Henderson contributed greatly to the development of the tactical intelligence system in South Africa while serving as DMI under Lord Kitchener. He established precise requirements for intelligence officers at different levels, provided them with a format for daily and weekly reports to insure uniformity, and prescribed times when reports were to reach higher headquarters. He insisted that intelligence be passed down to subordinate units, not just up to the next higher headquarters. Henderson's headquarters was in Pretoria, and South Africa was divided into four intelligence districts: Cape Colony, Orange River Colony, Transvaal, and Western District. An intelligence officer was responsible for each district, and he, in turn, divided his district into subdistricts, each of which had its own intelligence officer. Information was continuously exchanged among subdistrict officers and intelligence officers with independent columns. District officers were expected to send telegrams to the DMI each day, "giving an epitome of the Intelligence Reports of the District." In addition, every Sunday evening they were to furnish by telegraph a weekly summary, "giving their view of the general situation, numbers of the enemy, and any other information they may think necessary. This should be followed by a manuscript report, giving a full statement of the Intelligence for the week." Any information about the enemy which was of immediate importance "should be at once sent by telegraph to the DMI." District officers also provided monthly Boer casualty reports to Colonel Henderson and were responsible for the issue of ciphers for the encoding of telegrams.[49]

Cooperation between military intelligence and military police is vital in almost all counterguerilla campaigns and this was true of the last two years of the South African War. David Henderson understood this, but he was also concerned lest his subordinates in the Field Intelligence Department be misused by provost marshals or local commanders. His priorities were clear:

> The first duty of every Intelligence Officer is to obtain for the General, or other Officer on whose Staff he is serving, as full and accurate information as possible of the strength, position, movements, and intentions of the enemy. . . . Every assistance should be given to the Provost Marshal in carrying out the instructions as to clearing the country, but he [the intelligence officer] should remember his chief duties are with regard to the enemy, and that the herding of cattle is *not* an Intelligence duty.[50]

Other responsibilities of the Field Intelligence Department outlined by Henderson were the hiring and supervision of agents, scouts, interpreters, and guides; the distribution of maps and ciphers; censorship (presumably of either or both the press and the private mail); "departmental accounts;" routine correspondence dealing with prisoners of war, "property of burghers," and the staff of the F.I.D.; the collection of information about "routes and topography, stores of arms or ammunition, and Boer leaders;" and the collection of material "for the History of the War."[51] Instructions for "secret service expenditures" were quite specific. Only the four district intelligence officers were authorized to spend secret service money without obtaining prior approval from the DMI. In cases of extreme urgency, however, other intelligence officers could use money for clandestine operations so long as they had received written concurrence from their commanders. Distinctions were made between expenditures for the "White Sections" and "Native Sections"; payments to the former had to be documented by separate vouchers, while those to the latter required only "the strength of the Intelligence Officer's signature to the statement."[52]

British dependence upon the telegraph for rapid communications throughout South Africa and its vulnerability to intercept were recognized by the Boers from the beginning of the war. In the early phase of the war, the Boers frequently tapped the telegraph wires and intercepted sensitive messages being passed in the clear (without encipherment).[53] In order to tighten their own security, the British began to encode practically all telegrams dealing with operations and intelligence. Under David Henderson, they even attempted to reverse the dominance of the Boers in the area of communications intelligence. Small parties of men were sent out into the veldt to intercept Boer heliograph messages. Telegraphic censorship was imposed by the British on telegrams sent outside South Africa throughout the war, but the censorship stations at Cape Town, Durban, and Aden were not under the control of the Field Intelligence Department; information derived from this sort of censorship was almost entirely strategic, not tactical, intelligence. During the first months of the war, for example, "a very considerable amount of information was gained by means of telegrams passing through Aden regarding the source of the enemy's food supplies. . . ."[54] In May 1901, the intercept and decoding of an encrypted telegram from a Boer general to Transvaal President Kruger (in Holland at the time) provided Kitchener with timely and highly valuable information on prospects for peace negotiations. In the field, communications intelligence never played the crucial role in the South African War that it did in World War I.

Despite the notable successes of David Henderson and others in improving the field intelligence system, the British were never able to equal the Boers in timeliness and quality of tactical intelligence. With the exception of scattered actions in Natal and Cape Colony, most of the guerrilla war was fought within the territory of the two former Boer republics. This gave the Boers every advantage in their own intelligence effort, simply because the civilian population was overwhelmingly pro-Boer and the British forces could not make a move without the nearest Boer commando being informed instantly.[55] Kitchener's awareness of the role played by civilians was a major reason for his decision in December 1900 to intern all Boer women and children in refugee camps (later called concentration camps). In a less direct sense, it was also an important factor in the development of his famous blockhouse system.[56] The Boers' strength in the field declined steadily during the last year and a half of the war, but fierce resistance continued because of the quality of a few leaders such as Gen. Christiaan De Wet and General Botha. To catch these leaders became Kitchener's primary objective. Hence, lines of fortified blockhouses were constructed across hundreds of miles of the

Transvaal, into which the British attempted to "drive" them. Many columns of the Imperial Army now operated independently, and each was accompanied by an intelligence officer. With his own extraordinary intelligence system, however, Christiaan De Wet was able to slip through the blockhouse lines.[57]

During the latter stages of the war, growing numbers of Boers gave up the fight, many returning to their farms and some going to work as scouts or spies for the British. Naturally, these men were despised by the Boers still in the field, but the "hands-uppers" were a definite boon to the Field Intelligence Department. Another extremely important supplement to British scouting and espionage operations was the use of nonwhite natives. This was true throughout both the conventional and guerrilla phases, but the British were increasingly reliant on the natives in the counterguerrilla campaigns.[58] Boer leaders knew this and were at times able to use it to their own purposes, as Gen. Ben Viljoen did in the eastern Transvaal in the spring of 1901. "Viljoen then gave out to the natives—the best intelligence department of his adversaries—that he was bound for Pietersburg."[59] The ruse worked and Viljoen escaped his pursuers.

An excellent account of the use of natives by the British for scouting and espionage purposes during the last six months of the war is contained in Maj. Gen. J.F.C. Fuller's *The Last of the Gentlemen's Wars*. Fuller, a subaltern at the time, was placed in command of seventy native scouts organized into two groups, in December 1901. His immediate superior, Captain Cox, DAAG (I), told him that his duty would be to keep track of the enemy within an area of roughly four thousand square miles. Fuller's scouts were a mixture of Kaffirs, Basutos, and half-caste Hottentots, who had for the most part been servants and field hands on Boer farms before the war. Fuller and his scouts were fairly successful in their endeavors, but he concluded that he would have done far better if he had had only five Kaffir scouts and thirty mounted infantry.[60]

The number of people working for the Field Intelligence Department in South Africa grew dramatically during the guerrilla phase of the war, mostly because so many independent units required their own intelligence officers. Near the end of the war, the Department included 132 officers, 2,321 white civilian subordinates, and a large number of natives (estimated to be in the thousands).[61] Very few of the officers had any prior experience in intelligence work. A former officer in the Field Intelligence Department in South Africa wrote acidly shortly after the war,

> On what principle an Intelligence Officer to a column was appointed I have yet to learn. . . . frequently the I.O. was ignorant of the district and the ways of the people, and moreover, unable to understand native languages. And usually he was casual, supremely self-confident, and wedded to week-old telegrams. "You must be mistaken" was his favorite comment on a scout's report, unless it tallied with his own theories.[62]

The tactical intelligence system of the British Army, by the end of the South African War in May 1902, had undergone significant change. Prior to 1899, the system which had evolved within the Duke of Wellington's armies in the peninsula and at Waterloo had, with various modifications, proven satisfactory in most small colonial wars. But the South African War, which ultimately involved over 500,000 British and imperial troops, and in which the British Army met hostile mounted riflemen; smokeless, long-range rifle fire; and long-range artillery, was not a small colonial war. Although some weaknesses in the existing tactical intelligence system were apparent before the system was put to the test in South Africa, only when the fighting began in the fall of 1899 did the need for change become obvious to those leading the army in South Africa and to officers in the Field Intelligence Department. The army implemented significant changes when shocking defeats and unnecessary loss of life were traced to a faulty intelligence system, among other causes. The British Army in South Africa was fortunate to have had two officers of the caliber of George and David Henderson to develop and implement a new tactical intelligence doctrine on the battlefield.

The conventional phase of the war demonstrated the need for intelligence officers on the staffs of units below division level and also the inadequacies of standard techniques of reconnaissance. It also revealed a lack of appreciation for intelligence on the part of high-ranking officers who should have known better. Lord Roberts brought a more enlightened attitude concerning field intelligence to South Africa when he arrived after Black Week. More attention was given to the Field Intelligence Department, and it rapidly grew in strength and importance. Changes were made in reconnaissance methods, decent maps were obtained and reproduced, and other modifications were implemented by George Henderson and his successor, C.V. Hume. The result was a much improved system which worked reasonably well until the Boers began to shift their strategy to the conduct of a protracted guerrilla war.

With the advent of guerrilla war, additional modifications were necessary, and the Field Intelligence Department was reorganized and expanded still more. The control of intelligence operations, however, was centralized to a considerable degree under the strong and capable leadership of David Henderson. Despite the many innovations and constant improvements which characterized David Henderson's tenure as DMI in South Africa, the natural advantages of the Boers as guerrillas fighting in their own land with the support of the civilian population were virtually impossible to overcome. Their intelligence system was so effective that they were able to outmaneuver British troops in some situations, even when the Field Intelligence Department had accurate intelligence of their strength and disposition.

The considerable increase in the number of officers assigned to the Field Intelligence Department in the closing stages of the war, which was necessitated by Kitchener's strategy, placed an unbearable strain on the army's ability to assign qualified, experienced intelligence officers to the Department, an ability that was questionable even at the outset of the war. Criticisms that were made after the war about the lack of trained, experienced intelligence officers available for duty in South Africa during the war reflected the need for professional intelligence officers in the British Army, or at least for staff officers in the field in wartime who were intelligence specialists.

NOTES

1. Royal Commission on the War in South Africa, *Report*, p. 160.

2. Royal Commission on the War in South Africa, *Report*, p. 160.

3. From Cape Town on the southwest coast of Cape Colony to Pietersburg in the northern Transvaal, for example, is a distance of nearly 1,000 miles "as the crow flies."

4. Statement of Lt. Gen. William G. Nicholson, Royal Commission, *Minutes of Evidence I*, p. 379.

5. Bond, *Staff College*, p. 140.

6. Statement of Lt. Col. E.A. Altham, Royal Commission, *Minutes of Evidence I*, pp. 22-23. See also statement of Lt. Col. Archibald Murray, *Minutes of Evidence II*, pp. 327-28. The devastating effect of this program on the Intelligence Department in the fall of 1899 is described by Sir William Robertson in *From Private to Field-Marshal*, pp. 95-103. The turnover in Robertson's Section B alone was so great that, between September 1899 and January 1900, no fewer than five different officers served as his assistant. Then, he, too, left for South Africa.

7. In Cape Colony, Maj. Mike Rimington, also one of the ten "special officers," formed a similar unit which came to be known as Rimington's Guides. Only those white men who spoke fluent Afrikaans were recruited. Royal Commission, *Report*, p. 160. See also the statement of Brig. Gen. Michael F. Rimington, 5 February 1903, Royal Commission, *Minutes of Evidence II*, p. 26.

8. Originally, guides had been men able to find their way in a strange country and to speak the local language and who were used for guiding regular troops through an unmapped or hostile country. Scouts were men specially skilled in "scouting," gathering intelligence about the enemy by walking or riding a horse into the enemy area, observing enemy activity and dispositions without being seen, if possible, and reporting back to headquarters. Scouts, in the traditional sense, are still very much a part of armies in the 1980s. Today, some fly in helicopters, while others ride in Jeeps or armored reconnaissance vehicles.

9. Statement of Lt. Col. Archibald Murray, Royal Commission, *Minutes of Evidence II*, p. 327.

10. Maj. Gen. Sir Frederick Maurice, *History of the War in South Africa*, 1: 127.

11. As mentioned in chapter V, the founder of the Boy Scouts had a real passion for scouting, and intelligence work in general. See Richard Deacon, *A History of the British Secret Service*, p. 148; and Parritt, *The Intelligencers*, pp. 126-27. See also William Hillcourt and O.S. Baden-Powell, *Baden-Powell*.

12. Statement of Maj. Gen. R.S.S. Baden-Powell, Royal Commission, *Minutes of Evidence II*, pp. 427-28.

13. Maurice, *History of the War*, 1: 302-03.

14. Maurice, *History of the War*, 1: 317-19.

15. Approximately six thousand to seven thousand men under Gen. Louis Botha. See Maurice, *History of the War*, 1: 317-19.

16. The commando was the basic military unit of the Boers; normally it was made up of burghers from a particular town or district and ranged in size from several hundred to over one thousand men.

17. A balloon was available for observation missions, but the "pestilent contrivance" could rise no more than three hundred feet and therefore was highly vulnerable to Boer rifles. Conse-

quently, it stayed well south of the Tugela, where it was totally ineffective for reconnaissance. See Major General Callwell, *Stray Recollections*, pp. 84-85.

18. According to L.S. Amery, who was present at Colenso as a correspondent for *The Times*, "it would have been perfectly easy" for scouts "to wade or swim across the Tugela at night," but Buller and other generals were unwilling to allow junior officers to run the risks to get the information needed. Statement of L.S. Amery, Royal Commission, *Minutes of Evidence II*, p. 466.

19. Maurice, *History of the War*, 1: 336-37.

20. Maurice, *History of the War*, 1: 374-75.

21. Lieutenant Roberts was mortally wounded in a gallant attempt to recover twelve field guns of the Royal Artillery which had been abandoned on the south bank of the Tugela River. He received the Victoria Cross posthumously.

22. Lord Kitchener of Khartoum (Horatio Herbert Kitchener) had been sirdar (commander-in-chief) of the Egyptian Army since 1892 and had recently completed the conquest of the Sudan, a campaign climaxed by the great victory at Omdurman (1898). Only forty-nine when he became Roberts's chief of staff, Kitchener had spent his entire career in the Middle East. For several years during the 1880s he worked in the intelligence department of the Egyptian Army (1882-85). His fluency in Arabic and knowledge of Arab culture enabled him to make deep reconnaissances into the Egyptian and Sudanese deserts, disguised as an Arab, to collect intelligence and to organize pro-British Arab irregular units. In 1899, Kitchener was Britain's youngest and most dynamic general, an officer of great natural ability and burning ambition. His reputation with Wolseley and many other senior officers was that of an *enfant terrible*. See Philip Magnus, *Kitchener*, pp. 30-46, and Sir George Arthur, *Life of Lord Kitchener*, 1: 47-93.

23. Actually, some guerrilla operations were initiated by the Boers in the western Transvaal after Roberts had moved east of Pretoria in his drive to Delagoa Bay from Komati Poort on the Transvaal-Portuguese East Africa border, but all-out guerrilla operations began only after the flight of President Kruger across the border and the escape of two thousand Boers under Botha and Viljoen from Roberts in September 1900.

24. Statement of Field Marshal Lord Roberts, Royal Commission, *Minutes of Evidence II*, p. 69.

25. By coincidence, two officers named Henderson played key roles in the development of British field intelligence during and immediately after the South African War. Maj. David Henderson, already introduced as one of the "special officers," later in the war became director of military intelligence in South Africa. David and George F.R. Henderson were not related.

26. William George Henderson, the father of George Henderson, became dean of Carlisle in 1884.

27. Jay Luvaas writes, "Henderson must have been an unusual teacher, and there is abundant evidence that he was an effective one. By 'the charm of his personality and the inspiration of his teaching,' he exercised an influence that was 'almost unique' in the history of the Staff College." *The Education of an Army*, p. 242. See also Bond, *Staff College*, pp. 155-56.

28. Statement of Lt. Col. William R. Robertson, Royal Commission, *Minutes of Evidence II*, p. 29.

29. L.S. Amery, *Times History*, 3: 355.

30. Field Marshal Roberts, "Memoir" (a biographical tribute to G.F.R. Henderson, written in April 1905) in Col. G.F.R. Henderson, *The Science of War*, pp. xxxv-vi. Henderson's last book and perhaps his most important, *The Science of War*, was a collection of essays and lectures he had written while at Camberley, which was published in 1905, two years after his death in Egypt.

31. Ibid., pp. xxxvi-vii. See also Amery, *Times History*, 3: 355.

32. Robertson, *From Private to Field-Marshal*, pp. 106-07.

33. Ibid., pp. 103-11.

34. Statement of Lieutenant Colonel Robertson, Royal Commission, *Minutes of Evidence II*, p. 29.

35. Sir George Aston, *Secret Service*, pp. 8-9.

36. A "tactical revolution" had been caused by the development of the breech-loading rifle and smokeless ammunition. Rifles (the Boers used the Mauser) had a greater range, accuracy, and rate of fire; and riflemen, firing from trenches or using the terrain as cover, were practically invisible because of smokeless ammunition.

37. Col. G.F.R. Henderson's preface to Count Adalbert W. Sternberg's *My Experience of the Boer War*, pp. xxii, xxxii.

38. Statement of Major the Lord Lovat, Royal Commission, *Minutes of Evidence II*, pp. 474-75.

39. Statement of Robertson, Royal Commission, *Minutes of Evidence II*, p. 29.

40. Maurice, *History of the War*, 2: 88-89, 146, 188-89, 230-31, 410.

41. Capt. Maurice H. Grant, *History of the War in South Africa*, 3: 41.

42. Parritt, *The Intelligencers*, pp. 186-90.

43. Lord Kitchener succeeded Lord Roberts as commander-in-chief of Imperial forces in South Africa in December 1900 and remained in that position until the end of the war in May 1902.

44. Grant, *History of the War in South Africa*, 3: 422.

45. Robertson, *From Private to Field-Marshal*, pp. 120-21.

46. Statement of Major Lovat, Royal Commission, *Minutes of Evidence II*, p. 474.

47. Robertson, *From Private to Field-Marshal*, p. 125.

48. H.A. Jones, "Henderson, Sir David," *D.N.B., 1912-1921*, pp. 249-50.

49. Lt. Col. David Henderson, Director of Military Intelligence, "Intelligence Organisation and Administration (South Africa), Revised Instructions," pp. 2-3, 6-9.

50. Ibid., pp. 1, 10.

51. Ibid., pp. 5-6.

52. Ibid., pp. 18-19.

53. Christiaan R. De Wet, *Three Years War*, p. 122. See also Philip Pienaar, *With Steyn and De Wet*, pp. 87-109.

54. Until November 1901, when a new cable route between South Africa and Australia was completed, only two telegraphic cables linked South Africa with the outside world: the one from Cape Town went up the west coast of Africa, and the other went from Durban, Natal—via Delagoa Bay, Mozambique—up the east coast of Africa, through Aden, the Red Sea, and the Mediterranean to Gibraltar. War Office, "Telegraphic Censorship during the South African War, 1899-1902," pp. 1-8.

55. Maurice, *History of the War*, 2: 16. See also Deneys Reitz, *Commando*, and De Wet, *Three Years War*, p. 284.

56. Amery, *The Times History*, 5: 269.

57. Grant, *History of the War*, 4: 514, 515, and De Wet, *Three Years War*, pp. 260-66.

58. Basutoland, conveniently located between Natal, Cape Colony, and the Orange Free State, and on the whole pro-British (the natives hated the Boers), was the Switzerland of the war as a center of espionage operations. See Amery, *The Times History*, 2: 139.

59. Grant, *History of the War*, 4: 145.

60. Maj. Gen. J.F.C. Fuller, *The Last of the Gentleman's Wars*, pp. 149-51, 266. See also Callwell, *Stray Recollections*, 2: 147-48.

61. Royal Commission, *Report*, p. 160.

62. R. Murray White, "Scouting," p. 474.

Chapter IX

David Henderson and the
Tactical Intelligence System, 1902-1914

> In order to attain success in his work, it is necessary that an Intelligence officer should have the confidence and support of his General, of his brother staff officers, of the heads of departments, and of the officers holding responsible commands in the force. . . . The spectacle of an Intelligence man entering camp in the early morning on a tired horse tends to raise the Intelligence Corps in the esteem of the army, and there will always be occasions when the display of a little personal gallantry, or the cheerful endurance of exceptional fatigue or discomfort, on the part of Intelligence officers or men, will have a good effect in inspiring that confidence which is required.
>
> Lt. Col. David Henderson
> *Field Intelligence, Its Principles
> and Practices*, 1904

The size and complexity of the British Army's tactical intelligence organization in South Africa during the final stages of the South African War gave it a false aura of permanency. In fact, Lt. Col. David Henderson's Field Intelligence Department of 1901-02 proved no more able to survive the wave of cutbacks and deactivations which followed the Treaty of Vereeniging (31 May 1902) than were its predecessors during the similar postwar periods of Waterloo, the Crimean War, and countless small wars of the Victorian era. The existence of a large, expensive Field Intelligence Department employing thousands of civilians in South Africa seemed an unnecessary luxury once Briton and Boer were no longer at each other's throats.

The smoothly running organization which supported Lord Kitchener's forces in the spring of 1902 had evolved over a period of nearly three years, through a gradual process of expansion and refinement. In a matter of days and weeks, during the summer of 1902, this same organization was dismantled with lightning speed. Units of guides and scouts were disbanded or shipped home. South African civilians who had worked for the Department for several years returned to their farms or villages. Most intelligence officers serving on brigade and division staffs left South Africa with their units within weeks of the cease-fire. There were exceptions, but few of these officers were ever again assigned intelligence duties in the field. In other words, there was a real danger in 1902 that a great deal of the tactical intelligence experience which had been gained by the British Army in South Africa would be irretrievably lost, as former intelligence officers and men scattered to the four winds.

Some remnants of the Field Intelligence Department endured beyond 1902 in South Africa. On a greatly reduced scale, the British Army continued to conduct covert intelligence operations, aimed mainly at keeping track of unrepentant Boers and any ties they might have had to potential British enemies on the Continent. South Africa was also an excellent base for secret service missions targeted against German Southwest Africa, an area of growing concern to British intelligence.[1] These clandestine intelligence activities appear to have been financed and directed primarily from London. In any case, their principal objective was to gather strategic, not tactical, intelligence. The continuation of British covert intelligence operations in South Africa and the presence of intelligence officers on the staffs of the British Army's headquarters in Cape Colony and Natal after May 1902 were only reminders of the once mighty Field Intelligence Department.

The rapid demise of the Field Intelligence Department in South Africa following the Treaty of Vereeniging demonstrated that, even at the beginning of the twentieth century, the traditional British Army doctrine concerning tactical intelligence organizations still prevailed, except in the special case of India. Field intelligence departments were formed only in wartime or when hostilities were believed to be imminent. A few intelligence officers were required overseas in peacetime with British troops, but for the most part they were assigned to large headquarters, and their everyday duties were more akin to those of intelligence officers in the Directorate of Military Operations in London than to those of field intelligence officers.[2]

The principal exception to the practice of feast or famine for field intelligence organizations in the pre-1914 British experience was the Indian Army. The Indian Army was unique in many respects, superior to the British Army in some ways, backward and primitive in others. The perception that it lagged behind the British War Office in the area of strategic intelligence production had led to the Indian government's decision to send Capt. Edwin Collen to London in 1878 so that he might learn about the Intelligence Branch and be able to assist Indian Army authorities to establish an intelligence department in their own Quartermaster General's Department. There is no evidence that the Indian Army made a similar effort to find out about the field intelligence methods of the British Army. To a large extent the reverse was true; many British officers acquired tactical intelligence expertise, or at least some practical knowledge of the subject, while serving in India. Throughout the latter half of the nineteenth century, the Indian Army necessarily maintained an effective tactical intelligence system. To be sure, there were times when resources allocated to field intelligence were cut back rather severely, but they could never be totally eliminated as they sometimes were in the British Army. In India, particularly on the Northwest Frontier, British or British-led native troops were almost always involved in active campaigning of one sort or another, and even when they were not, the potential for conflict was a strong incentive for the retention of a tactical intelligence capability. It also lent a certain urgency to the need for a continuous interchange of information between the intelligence branch at Simla and intelligence officers in the field.

Tactical intelligence in the Indian Army was the beneficiary of a second major difference between the Indian and British armies. The relationship between the intelligence branch of the Quartermaster General's Department in India and intelligence staff officers in the field with Indian Army units was generally much closer than that which existed between the War Office intelligence organization in London and field intelligence personnel with British Army units in other overseas areas. This was due, in part, to a blurring of the line between tactical and strategic intelligence in India. Though its overall orientation was more strategic than tactical and it was responsible for collecting and producing intelligence about distant regions of Asia ranging from French Indochina and Siam to Tibet and Persia,[3] the Indian Army's intelligence branch regularly produced intelligence of immediate value to field commanders. Compared to the Foreign Intelligence Section in London, a substantially larger proportion of Simla's products were prepared specifically for use during field operations. In 1902, for example, the intelligence branch at Simla had compiled,

> ready for issue at a moment's notice, in the event of operations across the Afghan frontier, no less than 23 military books, with a total of nearly 4,500 octavo pages; and four other books are in the course of preparation.[4]

Conversely, officers performing field intelligence duties in and on the fringes of India often collected information of strategic import for the branch at Simla.[5] Certainly this was true in the case of the "nucleus Intelligence Corps at Peshawar," a small field intelligence unit established in the Northwest Frontier region in 1904 with peacetime responsibility for central and northern Afghanistan, Kashmir, and Russian Turkestan. Its ability to provide tactical intelligence in support of military operations was also evident.

> At the time of the frontier expeditions of 1908, in particular, the information supplied by it was precise, early, and valuable, and was superior to information received from any other source: a fact which was acknowledged by both the civil and military authorities on the spot.[6]

A further contribution to the harmony between Simla and the Indian Army's field intelligence organization was the practice of transferring officers back and forth between Simla and tactical intelligence assignments. In this way, the Indian Army developed intelligence specialists like William Robertson, an exceptional linguist who was fluent in five native languages of India when he was chosen for an assignment to the Intelligence Branch in 1892. Then, too, the prevailing philosophy in the Indian Army was that an officer was far better prepared for duty in the Simla Intelligence Branch if he had served a prior tour as a tactical intelligence officer. No less an authority than Lord Roberts expressed precisely this view before the Royal Commission on the War in South Africa early in 1903:

> I think you would find that a man would do much better in the Intelligence Department if he had practical experience or had been trained under the Quartermaster-General in the field.[7]

How relevant was the Indian Army's modus operandi in the field of tactical intelligence for the British Army as a whole? Had the South African War convinced senior British officers of the need to set up a special training program to produce field intelligence officers and to maintain at least a skeletal field intelligence organization in peacetime? The fate of the Field Intelligence Department in South Africa at the end of the war was no doubt discouraging to some advocates of the Indian Army's system, but it did not represent the final answer to the questions posed above. As will be shown in this chapter, the Indian Army and the South African War were not the only important factors which influenced the development, between 1902 and 1914, of the British Army's field intelligence system.

Both the Royal Commission on the War in South Africa and the Hardwicke Committee[8] grappled with the topic of field intelligence. A number of the witnesses who appeared before the Royal Commission were critical of the British army's pre-South African War tactical intelligence system and were not convinced that all of its weaknesses had been satisfactorily remedied in South Africa. The commission's report, which completely exonerated the Intelligence Division in London from any blame for the British defeats of 1899, was not so kind in its treatment of field intelligence. There was no denying the fact that the failure to properly reconnoiter enemy positions and the South African terrain had cost the British Army dearly during Black Week and the entire opening phase of the war. This was the sort of problem, however, which British commanders and their intelligence officers had been able to recognize and solve in the field long before the end of the war, as discussed in the preceding chapter.

A more enduring problem, one whose effects grew increasingly apparent as the British poured hundreds of thousands of troops into South Africa and as the war dragged on onto its second and third years, was the lack of trained field intelligence officers in the British Army. As one former field intelligence officer put it,

> I think we suffered during the war from the want of trained men in the Intelligence Department not only to collect but to collate and get the information down into a useable form. I think highly trained officers are wanted for that.[9]

The importance of good field intelligence work in South Africa called into question the old idea "any junior officer" could be assigned to a tactical intelligence position. While it could be argued that many of the young officers who were thrown into such jobs during the war eventually became quite good at their work, the army's nearly total reliance on a program of on-the-job training in combat was bound to result in serious problems. What was needed, as a former infantry brigade commander told the Royal Commission, was "a trained man who knows exactly what to do when he starts."[10]

Unfortunately, even at the end of the South African War, there was still no consensus about how trained field intelligence officers should be produced. In Lt. Col. Archibald Murray's words,

> The best method of training a sufficient number of officers for this particular branch of a staff officer's duty, is not as yet very clearly laid down.[11]

Some trained men could be reassigned from the Indian Army, but this would not provide the quantity needed for a large conflict. As several witnesses reminded the Royal Commission, shipping virtually the entire staff of the War Office's Intelligence Division out to the theater of war was not the answer, either. There were not enough men to go around, the effect on the London operation was devastating, and most importantly, an officer's experience at Queen Anne's Gate did not adequately prepare him for all aspects of field intelligence work. Attendance at the Staff College, it was thought, was helpful in preparing officers for intelligence staff positions in the field, but Camberley was charged with turning out all-around staff officers, not intelligence specialists. The South African experience showed that the man who was most likely to achieve immediate success as a field intelligence officer was the relatively rare individual who had attended the Staff College and who had also served a tour in the Intelligence Division or in South Africa. Because there were so few of these men and because the demand for officers to fill intelligence billets grew continually, one witness described a situation where, eventually, "anybody was made [an] Intelligence Officer, there were not enough of them, and they were hopelessly overworked."[12] The Royal Commission on the War in South Africa appeared concerned about the question of how the British Army ought to train officers for tactical intelligence duty in future wars, but neither it nor the Hardwicke Committee[13] reached any conclusions on the matter.

Compared with the Royal Commission, the Hardwicke Committee showed little interest in the tactical intelligence system. In accord with its charter, its investigation centered entirely upon the War Office's intelligence and mobilization branches, which were then unified under the director general of mobilization and military intelligence (DGMI). Field intelligence was discussed only in the context of whether or not the Intelligence Division was the best training ground for field intelligence officers. Lt. Gen. Sir William Nicholson, the DGMI, believed that it was. When questioned by the committee on this point, he replied matter-of-factly that one of the peacetime functions of the Division was to "train Officers for intelligence work in the field."[14] The views of other senior officers diverged widely, however. As far as Lt. Gen. Sir Ian Hamilton could recall, none of the many intelligence officers

Courtesy of the National Army Museum, London.

18. Major General Sir John Charles Ardagh, Royal Engineers (1840-1907). In the view of some, Ardagh was considered "the foremost politico-military officer" of his day in the British Army. Following a series of important intelligence and diplomatic assignments, he served as private secretary to the viceroy of India (1888-94) and as commandant of the School of Military Engineering at Chatham. Sir John was director of military intelligence for five years (1896-1901).

19. Field Marshal Sir William Robert Robertson (1860-1933). A remarkable individual who rose from the ranks, Robertson was selected as chief of the Imperial General Staff (1915-18) during World War I and afterwards served as commander-in-chief of the Home Forces (1918-19) and of the British Army of Occupation on the Rhine (1919-20). Earlier in his career, he had extensive experience in intelligence work during assignments in the Indian Intelligence Department (1892-97), the Field Intelligence Department in South Africa (1899-1900), and War Office Intelligence (1898-99 and 1900-07).

Courtesy of the Imperial War Museum, London.

20. Lieutenant General Sir David Henderson, Argyll and Sutherland Highlanders (1862-1921). One of the founding fathers of British military aviation in the pre-World War I era, Henderson was the first director-general of military aeronautics (1913-14) and commanded the Royal Flying Corps in France during the first three years of World War I. He was also DMI in South Africa (1900-02) and was instrumental in the modernization of the British Army's tactical intelligence system between 1902 and 1914.

21. Lieutenant General Sir James Moncrieff Grierson, Royal Artillery (1859-1914). Grierson directed War Office Intelligence and helped to initiate joint Anglo-French military planning while serving as the first director of military operations at the War Office (1904-06). He demonstrated a special aptitude for intelligence work throughout his career and before gaining his appointment as military attaché in Berlin (1896-1900), he had served in both the Indian (1881-02) and War Office (1886, 1889-95) Intelligence Departments.

22. General Sir Edward Francis Chapman, Royal Artillery (1840-1926). Decorated veteran of the Indian Army and quartermaster general in India under Lord Roberts (1885-89). Director of military intelligence at the War Office (1891-96).

23. Lieutenant General Sir Edward Altham, Royal Scots (1856-1943). One of the British Army's most able intelligence officers around the turn of the century. Served continuously in important intelligence staff positions at the War Office and in South Africa for seven years beginning in 1897. Later the quartermaster general in India (1917-19).

Reproduced by kind permission of the commandant, British Army Staff College, Camberley.

24. Colonel George Francis Robert Henderson, York and Lancaster Regiment (1854-1903). One of the greatest teachers and historians of the late nineteenth-century British Army. Professor of military arts and history at the Staff College, Camberley (1892-99). DMI in South Africa under Lord Roberts (1899-1900).

26. Major General Sir James Keith Trotter, Royal Artillery (1849-1940). Served five years in War Office Intelligence (1890-95) as staff captain and DAAG. Deputy director of mobilization and military intelligence (1903-04).

25. Major General Lord Baden-Powell (Robert S.S. Baden-Powell) (1857-1941). Hero of the Boer siege of Mafeking (1899-1900) and world famous as founder of the Boy Scouts (1907). Possessed a special talent for reconnaissance and "secret service."

27. Brigadier General Sir Edward Edmonds, Royal Engineers (1861-1956). Engineer officer and military historian. One of the most brilliant officers of his generation. Edmonds served in various positions within War Office Intelligence between 1899 and 1910, twice as head of the Special Duties Section (1899-1901 and 1906-10).

Courtesy of the National Portrait Gallery, London.

28. Field Marshal Sir William Gustavus Nicholson, Royal Engineers (1845-1918). Protégé of Lord Roberts and a veteran of long service in India (1871-99). Director-general of mobilization and military intelligence at the War Office (1901-04). Senior British military attaché with the Japanese Army during the Russo-Japanese War (1904-05). Chief of the Imperial General Staff (1908-12).

Courtesy of the Regimental Collection of the Queen's Own Highlanders, Inverness, Scotland.

29. Lieutenant General Sir John Spencer Ewart, Cameron Highlanders (1861-1930). Well-decorated soldier from a distinguished military family. Veteran of Tel-el-Kebir (1882), the Nile expedition (1884-85), the Sudan Frontier (1885-86), Omdurman (1898), and the South African War. DMO at the War Office (1906-10) and GOC of the Scottish Command (1914-18).

From a painting by Oswald Birley. Courtesy of the British Library, London.

30. Field Marshal Sir Henry Hughes Wilson, Rifle Brigade (1864-1922). Wilson was best known before World War I as the commandant of the Staff College (1907-10) and DMO at the War Office (1910-14). Earlier in his career he had served for three years in War Office Intelligence (1894-97). During the final year of World War I, he was selected by Lloyd George to succeed Sir William Robertson as chief of the Imperial General Staff (1918-22).

Courtesy of the National Army Museum, London.

31. Major General Sir Charles Edward Callwell, Royal Artillery (1859-1928). An accomplished linguist and a prolific writer throughout his military career, Callwell served for five years (1887-92) in Section E of the Intelligence Division and for three years (1904-07) as head of MO 1 (Strategical Section). During World War I, he was director of military operations and intelligence at the War Office (1914-16).

Courtesy of the National Portrait Gallery, London.

32. Lieutenant General Sir George Mark Watson Macdonogh, Royal Engineers (1865-1942). Head of MO 5 (Special Duties) for four years immediately before World War I (1910-14). Macdonogh was DMI at the War Office for two years (1916-18) during the war itself. Adjutant general to the forces (1918-22).

Originally published in a supplement to "Architect and Building News," 6 July 1934.

33. Winchester House, 21 St. James Square. The newly formed Mobilization and Military Intelligence Department moved here from Queen Anne's Gate in November 1901. War Office Intelligence remained at this location for exactly five years.

Courtesy of the National Army Museum, London.

34. War Office Building, Whitehall. The Directorate of Military Operations moved from Winchester House on St. James Square to the "new War Office" in November 1906. War Office Intelligence did not relocate again before the beginning of World War I.

who had served under him in South Africa, all of whom had done well, had had any previous training in the Intelligence Division.

> From his point of view, . . . they were simply Officers whom he had picked up on the veldt. Intelligence work in the field was a different class of work from that performed in the Intelligence Division at Head-quarters, and witness thought that the best training for the former was the local knowledge and experience acquired by actually having lived on the spot.[15]

On the other hand, Gen. Sir John French's staff had included "one excellent Intelligence Officer who had been trained in the Division. This officer had an advantage over the rest in knowing from the beginning how to set to work." French agreed with Ian Hamilton that "Office and Field Intelligence work were very different," but "other things being equal," he preferred "as his Intelligence Officer a man who had served in the Division."[16]

Some witnesses before the Hardwicke Committee thought the logical solution to the question of how to train officers for field intelligence duty was for the British Army to adopt the general staff system. Gen. Sir Henry Brackenbury, the director general of ordnance and a strong advocate for the establishment of the British General Staff since his tour as DMI in the late 1880s, was one of these. In December 1902 he advised the Hardwicke Committee that officers assigned to the Intelligence Division should be sent overseas "as Intelligence Officers on all expeditions." It was desirable that the army's most talented young officers seek duty in the Division (or on the General Staff, once established), but they were unlikely to do so unless "there were reasonable opportunities for going on active service" in wartime.[17] Lt. Col. Edward Altham, a highly regarded officer who had served both in the Intelligence Division and as a field intelligence officer in South Africa, told the Royal Commission that "it would be a great advantage in future to have a permanent nucleus in time of war."[18]

Altham's proposal was echoed in recommendations advanced by the War Office (Reconstitution) Committee in early 1904. In the section of its report entitled "The Organization of Staff Duties in the Field," the Esher Committee outlined its concept of staff organization and functions under the new general staff system which it advocated for the army. The duties of the three principal staff officers in the field would correspond to those of three of the four military members of the army council at the War Office: the chief of the General Staff, the adjutant general, and the quartermaster general.[19] The General Staff officer in the field would be responsible for operations and intelligence, just as the chief of the General Staff at the War Office was. Furthermore, the staff officer in the field in wartime would have been trained for his particular duties in peacetime, regardless of his branch. In other words, General Staff officers would be capable of handling either operations or intelligence responsibilities. The senior General Staff officer, whenever more than one was assigned to a staff, would be designated chief of the General Staff under the general officer commanding (GOC). Though there would no longer be a chief of staff, "the nature of his duties will necessarily confer a dominant position to the Chief of the General Staff in the field."[20]

The General Staff branch of the GOC's staff in large units, certainly at division level and above, would include intelligence officers. However, in addition to operations and intelligence, the General Staff in the field was also to be charged with

> selection of lines of communication, and advice as to their garrisons, framing orders regarding moves of men and material, selection and protection of camps and bivouacs, organization higher than the unit, telegraphs and signalling, and censorship.[21]

Due to the myriad of other functions for which the General Staff branch in the field was to be responsible, the danger remained that tactical intelligence might not be given the necessary attention, especially in peacetime. Would a General Staff officer who had never served in the Intelligence Division (or in the Directorate of Military Operations proposed by the Esher Committee) receive sufficient preparation for a field intelligence job in war? The War Office (Reconstitution) Committee failed to answer this question. In the final analysis, it did not come much closer than the Royal Commission or the Hardwicke Committee did to answering the question of how to train officers for wartime field intelligence duty.

The apparent indecisiveness of the British Army in the first several years after the South African War, with regard to the training of field intelligence officers, was related to Britain's diplomatic position vis-à-vis the Continent. Even if a decision had been made in 1903 or 1904 to set up a course for field intelligence officers, the designers of the course would have been faced with some difficult choices about its content and objectives. With respect to the great powers of Europe, the official British position remained one of isolation until the Entente Cordiale of April 1904. Anti-German feeling was on the rise in the War Office, but the Anglo-French staff talks were several years away. The mission of the British Army was still thought to be the defense of the United Kingdom and the protection of the British Empire. The army did not know who its next enemy would be. Thus, it would have been pointless to train officers for field intelligence work in a particular part of the world (except in India) or for a major war on the Continent. All the army could have done was to prepare them generally for intelligence work in the field and to teach them the techniques of scouting, reconnaissance, and the recruitment of spies-informers.[22]

For the French and German armies at this time, the need for tactical intelligence training did not present such a difficult problem. They knew against whom and where they would fight the next war. French intelligence officers, for example, could concentrate on learning German, familiarizing themselves with the very terrain over which the fighting would most likely take place, and acquiring as much knowledge as possible about the German Army. Also, an officer involved in intelligence work on the General Staff in Paris or Berlin was more likely to be effective immediately as an intelligence staff officer in the field in the event of a Franco-German war than was his British counterpart, who was sent from London to a similar assignment in a colonial war in a remote and little known area of the Empire. The heavy dependence of the French and German armies on the capacity and location of their railways (and those in Belgium) made the intelligence officer's most important task, that of estimating enemy intentions, relatively easy once he possessed detailed knowledge of the railway system and the strength and disposition of the enemy forces. It was perhaps the realization of their particular problem that made British officers unsure of exactly what to do about peacetime field intelligence training.

One of the most significant contributions to the British Army's field intelligence system during the years immediately after the Second Boer War was a manual published by the new General Staff in April 1904, shortly after the release of the final portion of the Esher Committee's report. The author of *Field Intelligence, Its Principles and Practices* was Lt. Col. David Henderson, the third and last director of military intelligence during the South African War. At the end of the war, David Henderson was generally recognized as the British Army's leading authority on tactical intelligence. Interestingly, this thoughtful and far-sighted officer was to play a pioneer role in another vital facet of the army's development before and during World War I.

When the American inventor Wilbur Wright startled Europe with his record-breaking flights in a power-driven airplane in 1908, David Henderson became interested in the use of the airplane in war. It was more than a coincidence that the army's leading expert on field intelligence, a man who believed "reconnaissance is the method of most vital importance,"[23] became one of the founding fathers of British military aviation. The virtually unlimited potential of the airplane as a vehicle for battlefield reconnaissance was a fascinating prospect for Henderson. In 1911, at the age of forty-nine, he learned to fly. Soon thereafter he served on a technical subcommittee of the Committee of Imperial Defence; the subcommittee's mission was to develop a detailed plan for the creation of a British "Flying Corps." The subcommittee's report, which bore "the mark of his wide and practical experience," recommended the formation of an aviation branch of the army. Thus, David Henderson was instrumental in the establishment of the Royal Flying Corps (R.F.C.) in April 1912. As director general of military training (1912-13) and as the first director general of military aeronautics (1913-14), Brigadier General Henderson oversaw the expansion of the R.F.C. and its preparations for World War I. In August 1914 he took the R.F.C. to France, where it quickly proved to be an invaluable source of battlefield intelligence deep behind enemy lines during the initial engagements of the British Expeditionary Force. Except for a brief interlude in the fall of 1914, Henderson remained in command of the R.F.C. in France until October 1917, when he was knighted and promoted to lieutenant general. Near the end of the World War I, Sir David developed the plans for the amalgamation of the Royal Flying Corps and the Royal Naval Air Service into the Royal Air Force.[24]

Lt. Gen. Sir Neville Lyttelton, the first chief of the General Staff, wrote in the preface to David Henderson's *Field Intelligence, Its Principles and Practices*,

> This work is based on the practical experience of the Field Intelligence Department during the late South African War (1899-1902) and is approved as the textbook for the study of that important branch of the duties of the General Staff in the field.[25]

Whether Lyttelton or anyone else asked Henderson to produce a manual for field intelligence officers or whether he did so on his own is unknown, but Henderson, who returned from South Africa in the fall of 1902, was the ideal man for the job. Thanks to David Henderson, most of the tactical intelligence lessons of the recent conflict were preserved. While he did not prescribe a course for training field intelligence personnel, at least he provided the army with an up-to-date guide to the duties of a field intelligence officer that could be of use to the uninitiated.

Field Intelligence was a concise, well organized field manual consisting of eight short chapters. Three chapters dealt with methods of collection; the other five covered personnel and organization, the interpretation of battle-field information, the provision and handling of guides, the preparation and dissemination of reports, and counterintelligence.[26] Even today, when the methods of tactical intelligence have become increasingly technical and highly sophisticated, both on the ground and in the air, Henderson's little book is worthwhile reading for tactical intelligence officers. Methods may have changed, but the basic principles are still valid. Henderson's description of the qualifications of a successful field intelligence officer in 1904 provides a superb guide for his modern counterpart.

> The successful Intelligence officer must be cool, courageous, and adroit, patient and imperturbable, discreet and trustworthy. He must understand the handling of troops and have a knowledge of the art of war. He must be able to win the confidence of his General, and to inspire confidence in his subordinates. He must have resolution to continue unceasingly his search for information, even in the most disheartening circumstances and after repeated failures. He must have endurance to submit silently to criticism, much of which may be based on ignorance or jealousy. And he must be able to deal with men, to approach his source of information with tact and skill, whether such source be a patriotic gentleman or an abandoned traitor.[27]

Another example of the timelessness of some of the advice offered in *Field Intelligence* may be found in the author's caution to would-be tactical intelligence officers to avoid the "assumption of superior knowledge. . . . Every item of information offered, officially or privately, should be gratefully acknowledged. Even if the news be of the stalest, it should be accepted as if it were of urgent importance."[28]

The three chapters of *Field Intelligence* devoted to the collection of information were clearly written, but sparse in detail. This is particularly true of the chapter on reconnaissance, a subject about which David Henderson knew a great deal.[29] "Any failing in reconnaissance," warned Colonel Henderson, "is almost necessarily fatal." He drew a line between the reconnaissance duties of the cavalry and those of individual intelligence officers.

> Intelligence officers should, at all times, and as a matter of routine, employ themselves and their own men in reconnaissance. Whether operating with advanced cavalry, an advanced or rear guard, or a detached force, the officers and men of the Intelligence should be constantly with, and beyond, the furthest line of covering troops.[30]

As a spur to the new intelligence officer, Henderson suggested, "it should be a point of honour throughout the Intelligence branch that, of all the information collected by reconnaissance, the most important and accurate should be that acquired by their own endeavors." There is a special section on the difficulty and crucial importance of reconnaissance at night.

> The art of moving by night with silence and certainty is one that can be learned only by practice. . . . Intelligence officers should make every effort to perfect themselves and their men in night movements. . . . The trouble and possible hardship will be well repaid, even from a selfish point of view, for the scout who is skilled in night work has an assurance of safety which is entirely wanting in him who is dependent on daylight.[31]

With an eye to the future, Henderson observed that although most reconnaissances were still being performed on horseback and on foot, "the bicycle and the motor car are likely to be used freely in the future." The intelligence officer or scout conducting reconnaissance ought to use the best available means of transportation to perform his mission. "He will be judged by results, not by methods."[32]

In the chapter on collection through "Examination of Persons and Documents," sensible advice is offered to the intelligence officer on the questioning of prisoners, deserters, and local inhabitants, and on the handling of documents. No stone could be left unturned in the constant search for clues to the activities and intentions of the enemy. "The Intelligence officer who is tireless, watchful, and adroit in examining prisoners, and deserters, in questioning inhabitants, in poring over uninteresting letters or deciphering unintelligible scraps of waste paper, will surely find his reward." Though it would not be possible for an intelligence officer personally to conduct interrogations of all prisoners, he "should lose no opportunity of doing so." The proper techniques of interrogation were emphasized.

> Skill in eliciting information grows rapidly with practice. . . . Sympathy with inhabitants, camaraderie with prisoners, affected suspicion of deserters, are often successful. Gentleness will sometimes melt reserve, harshness may break it down. . . . A bottle of brandy is a powerful weapon against a physically exhausted man. A method frequently found effective in important cases is to bring an unwilling witness first before an officer who will question him harshly and threaten him, and then hand him over to the care of a sympathetic underling.[33]

Special care was required in the questioning of women, an area which Henderson described as "a very difficult matter." Regardless of whether a woman was a suspected enemy spy or a local informant, "a countess or a rag picker, she must be treated with respect." When interrogating a woman, "the man is always at a disadvantage." A woman who initially was reluctant to provide information was unlikely to begin providing information because of fear for her personal safety, "but anxiety for others will often lead to truthful admissions." The most challenging test of an interrogator's skill arose in the questioning of a hostile local civilian or prisoner of war. The only safe refuge of an unwilling subject was absolute silence; "if a man can be made to talk, he should be made to tell. Any endeavour to prevaricate or mislead" was to be countered with punishment or the threat of punishment. As a part of the discussion on the handling of documents, several paragraphs are devoted to the censorship of letters and telegrams. Information extracted from censorship would be of "great value" to the commander of a force operating "in the midst of a hostile or semi-hostile population. . . ."[34] As much as any chapter in *Field Intelligence*, this particular chapter reflects the recent South African experience and David Henderson's practical approach to the duties of a tactical intelligence officer.

For the inexperienced intelligence officer in a theater of war, Colonel Henderson's third chapter on the acquisition of information, "Secret Service," was extremely important. Assuming he was a Staff College graduate, the officer would be well versed in the methods of individual and unit reconnaissance. Prior combat experience in command and staff positions, along with a reasonable amount of common sense, might suffice, in many situations, as a guide to the "examination of persons and documents." Only when he was actually placed in an intelligence position, however, would the officer begin to learn about the sensitive and demanding nature of secret service in war.

> An Intelligence officer who desires to gain information of value by means of secret service should first look to his own qualifications. Discretion is absolutely essential, and this is best ensured by absolute blank silence on the subject of secret service, save to those few whose enlightenment is necessary. . . . An Intelligence officer should divulge also to one chosen person, preferably an officer of his own branch, full details of his secret service work, . . . in order that there may be no break in case of mishap to himself. No other person should have any knowledge of the secret service organization; it should not even be known for certain whether such an organization exists or not.[35]

To be successful, a secret service operation must ascertain the reliability of its agents and "guard against the possibility of an untrustworthy agent giving valuable information to the enemy. . . . A high moral character is not, unfortunately, one of the necessary qualifications of a successful secret service agent." It was equally important for the intelligence officer to gain and carefully preserve the confidence of his agents. "Good agents will not serve a careless employer." Colonel Henderson gave special attention to the problems of communicating with agents.

> An officer engaged on secret service will find his stiffest problem in the arrangement of communication with his agents. Dangers, difficulties, and obstacles crop up at every turn. . . . Certainty of speedy communication is of extreme importance; the agent is of no use until he has reported. And yet, communication of any kind is seldom easy.[36]

Officers embarking on secret service ventures for the first time were cautioned to be prepared for "a very large proportion of failures in their enterprises. . . . Nevertheless, the occasional information derived from this source is, as a rule, so valuable that an Intelligence officer should never allow the most depressing succession of failures to discourage his efforts." The expenditure of money for secret service was to be reported "to the superior by whose authority the service is being carried out," but nowhere in *Field Intelligence* are there detailed instructions on the field intelligence officer's management of secret service funds.

The analytical and reporting functions of the tactical intelligence officer are discussed in two chapters entitled "The Value of Incomplete Information" and "Classification and Distribution of Information—Maps and Intelligence Reports." Once again, Henderson's guidance for the pre-World War I British intelligence officer is as valid today as it was then.

> It is impossible to go on eliciting and comparing scraps of information without habitually endeavouring to penetrate their bearing on, and their proportionate importance in, the general problem. Each isolated item of information is automatically considered as a possible link in a chain of circumstantial evidence which may finally recommend, or even morally prove, a certain theory. It is the duty of Intelligence officers to keep the problem always before them; to marshal the corroborative or contradictory facts; . . . to clear away the mist caused by rumour or by the enemy's artfulness. They should always be ready to lay before their superiors a clear exposition of the facts which may be accepted as bases for speculation. . . . And they should be prepared to give, if required, a personal opinion on the enemy's situation, either political, strategic, or tactical, and its bearing on the campaign.[38]

Information regarding the enemy in war would never be complete, according to Henderson, but the well-prepared and diligent intelligence officer would, in many situations, be able to fathom the intentions of the enemy based on the "slender indications" available. An efficient system of classifying and recording incoming information was essential for the analysis and production of tactical intelligence. Such a system would facilitate the preparation of verbal and written reports for commanders. Henderson suggested certain subjects were "better and more conveniently dealt with if special extracts from all reports which deal with them are made and collected," but, quite appropriately, he left the selection of the subjects to be recorded separately to the discretion of the intelligence officer.[39]

Colonel Henderson emphasized the field intelligence officer's duty to insure the timely dissemination of his often perishable product.

> Next to the acquisition of information, its distribution to those who may be able to utilise it, is the most important duty of the Intelligence branch. . . . With care and method, accurate distribution may be reduced to a certainty. Nevertheless, it will always happen that unless special measures are taken and definite arrangements are made, a very large proportion of available information will disappear or be delayed in transit.[40]

In general, there were two channels of reporting with which the intelligence officer would have to concern himself. The more important channel went directly to commanders; its information was the sort which might influence their tactical decisions. "It is understood that all important information is first communicated to the immediate commander of the recipient," but the commanders of higher, adjacent, and subordinate units might also have needed this information. The intelligence officer's job was to decide to which commanders a particular piece of information should be sent "at once," and to which it should be forwarded "at the first convenient opportunity." The second, less important channel involved communications between intelligence officers. The officers were authorized to correspond directly with each other, and "all supplementary information" was to be exchanged in this manner. Intelligence officers of the major subordinate commands in a theater of operations were expected to provide reports at regular intervals to the director of military intelligence (DMI) in the theater. As David Henderson had done in South Africa, the DMI would determine which types of reports would be required, how often they would be sent, and "whether by telegraph, letters, or verbal report." The DMI's decisions in this regard were to be based upon "the circumstances of the campaign."[41]

The final chapter of *Field Intelligence*, "Frustration of the Enemy's Endeavours to Gain Information," deals with the proper procedures for tactical counterintelligence, a function currently termed "operations security" (abbreviated OPSEC) by the U.S. Army. The primary responsibility for preventing enemy scouts and cavalry units from overtly collecting information about major British Army units in the field rested with the cavalry screen and the outposts. The intelligence officer was expected to take a direct interest in the enemy's attempts to infiltrate "disguised observers" through the line of outposts.

> The granting of passes through the outpost line and the authorisation to admit persons unprovided with credentials is entirely a matter to be dealt with by the General Staff. Intelligence officers will be held responsible if it should be proved that the enemy's espionage has been successful. . . . The blocking of communication is the first, simple, obvious precaution against espionage, and an Intelligence officer who cannot get it enforced had better resign at once.[42]

The best protection against spies inside an army was "the alertness of all ranks to note any suspicious action or question." An intelligence officer might encourage such vigilance, but he must be careful to avoid promoting "spy fever, a most pernicious affection of the nerves which sometimes attacks all ranks, and may paralyse an army." In addition to the individual efforts of the intelligence officer and the general watchfulness of the army, it was also helpful to employ a few selected men of the provost marshal's police, the Intelligence Corps, and the Army Service Corps, each of whom would have "special opportunities of watching and judging those who might be employed by the enemy."[43]

Although David Henderson did not advocate the maintenance of permanent tactical intelligence organizations in the British Army, he did recommend, "all persons, except staff officers and secret service agents, permanently engaged on Intelligence duties in a campaign, should be formed into an Intelligence Corps." The composition of the Intelligence Corps would vary, depending on the nature of the enemy and the theater of war. In a typical small war, the corps would consist mainly of native guides, interpreters, and scouts, "and only a few European superiors would be required." In "civilised warfare" against a European enemy,

> the case is quite different; interpreters, and possible guides, would be for the most part educated men, and in many cases it would be necessary to put them on the footing of officers. To fulfil the conditions of the modern customs of war, it is also necessary that, in civilised warfare,

> Intelligence subordinates should be properly commissioned or enlisted
> soldiers, and should wear uniforms, otherwise they may, if captured, be
> dealt with as unlicensed partisans.[44]

The proposed Intelligence Corps would be commanded by an officer "attached to Headquarters, and taking his instructions from the Director of Military Intelligence on the Headquarters Staff." The corps was to be capable of carrying out all normal intelligence duties, but certain specialists— "telegraph operators to tap or use the enemy's wires, signallers to accompany special reconnaissances or to intercept the enemy's communications"— would be borrowed as needed and were not envisioned by Henderson to be permanent members of the corps.[45]

Unquestionably, the publication of Henderson's *Field Intelligence, Its Principles and Practices* by the British General Staff in the spring of 1904 was an extremely important event in the pre-World War I development of the British Army's tactical intelligence system. The various editions of Lord Wolseley's *The Soldier's Pocket-Book for Field Service* had provided field intelligence officers of the last three decades of the nineteenth century with a brief, officially sanctioned guide to their duties, but tactical intelligence was only one of a multitude of subjects covered. A far more detailed description of the field intelligence system had been offered by Col. George Furse in his *Information in War*. Furse's book was not published under War Office auspices, however, nor are there any indications that he obtained even semiofficial support from the director of military intelligence at Queen Anne's Gate.[46] David Henderson's *Field Intelligence* appears to have been the first official British Army manual intended solely as a guide for field intelligence officers throughout the army. Compared to *The Soldier's Pocket-Book* and *Information in War*, it had the additional advantage of incorporating the experiences of the South African War.

Lt. Col. David Henderson did not rest on his laurels after the publication of *Field Intelligence*. Although the author of the document is not identified, Henderson's hand is evident in a second 1904 publication of the General Staff on the subject of tactical intelligence: "Regulations for Intelligence Duties in the Field." These regulations were published by the War Office in August 1904, only three months after the appearance of *Field Intelligence*. In the preface, the chief of the General Staff wrote,

> The following regulations for the performance of the Intelligence duties
> of the General Staff accompanying an Army in the Field are published
> for the guidance of General Officers and all concerned.[47]

Practically all of the subjects in *Field Intelligence* were addressed in the regulations. In most cases, however, fewer details were included in the regulations, which were oriented toward the administration and organization of the tactical intelligence system, rather the administration and organization of the tactical intelligence system, rather than toward the collection, analysis, and dissemination of intelligence. Certain questions left unanswered in *Field Intelligence* received attention in "Regulations for Intelligence Duties in the Field." For example, nearly half of the twenty-eight pages of regulations in the document were devoted to a detailed explanation of the procedures for obtaining and administering special funds for intelligence operations, including secret service. Regulations numbers 6 and 7 prescribed "the minimum establishment of the General Staff required for field intelligence" duties at various levels of command (above army corps, army corps, division, brigade, detached column, etc.) in wartime.[48]

It may be assumed that the author(s) of the 1904 field intelligence regulations placed great emphasis on the control and administration of intelligence funds as a direct result of the recent South African experience. No precise figures on the annual budgets of the Field Intelligence Department during the South African War are available, but a conservative estimate of the costs of secret service and other intelligence collection activities conducted by an organization which employed thousands of civilians must be measured in hundreds of thousands, and perhaps millions, of pounds sterling. As the DMI in South Africa during the final sixteen months of the war, David Henderson had been in the best position to monitor the overall field intelligence budget. Henderson and a few other officers who were aware of the actual amount of money spent by the Field Intelligence Department probably realized that the cost of intelligence activities, especially secret service, in the event of British participation in a future war on the Continent, would far surpass that of any prior conflict, even the cost of Wellington's intelligence service in the peninsula. The lethality of the smokeless, long-range Mauser rifles used by the Boers had rendered traditional methods of scouting practically obsolete and, at best, very costly in terms of casualties. In turn, this elevated the importance of wartime secret service and pushed the Field Intelligence Department's budget sharply upward. As pointed out in the preceding chapter, many of the best British spies in South Africa were African natives. Though most of them were paid far less than white civilian employees of the Field Intelligence Department, the value of "educated" native spies was so great that, "as an inducement, they eventually received higher pay than a major in the British Army." It is not difficult to understand why field intelligence was so expensive for the British Army in South Africa, and furthermore, why at least one experienced intelligence officer advised the Hardwicke Committee in late 1902 that regulations ought to be drawn up to govern the conduct of secret service.[49]

Despite what may have appeared to some senior officers as the excessive red tape required in the handling of special funds (and the irritation which they may have felt at being told by the War Office that a certain minimum number of General Staff officers at every level of command down to brigade would function as intelligence officers), the "Regulations for Intelligence Duties in the Field" of 1904 allowed the commander-in-chief of an army in the field (and his DMI) a good deal of flexibility in establishing and operating a tactical intelligence organization.

> As soon as the army takes the field, the General Officer Commanding-in-Chief will have entire control of the whole of field intelligence, and he may arrange or alter the composition or distribution of the personnel employed on intelligence duties, both officers and men, in such manner as from local or other conditions he may consider advisable to ensure the efficient and economical performance of the intelligence services. . . . He will authorise and control all expenditure on intelligence and secret service.[50]

The senior intelligence officer of the General Staff in the theater of war, the DMI, was responsible to the commander-in-chief for "the efficiency of the whole of the intelligence services of the army," the secret service, the accountability of all intelligence funds, and for other general staff duties assigned him by the commander-in-chief. The intelligence duties of the General Staff in the field, as outlined in the regulations, were generally those discussed by Henderson in *Field Intelligence*. They included

> information regarding the enemy; frustration of the enemy's efforts to gain information; the conduct of reconnaissances other than reconnaissances in force; information regarding the country and its resources; provision of guides and interpreters; provision, revision, and distribution of maps; flags of truce and correspondence with the enemy; political work with reference to the civil population; care of captured documents; ciphers, censorship, other than that of the Press; intelligence diaries.[51]

Needless to say, the lone General Staff officer authorized to perform the intelligence duties of an infantry division in wartime was a very busy man!

David Henderson's recommendation in *Field Intelligence* concerning the formation of an Intelligence Corps for an army in the field was fully incorporated into the General Staff regulations of 1904. As directed in regulation number 5,

> To enable the General Staff to deal with the large and varied staff of subordinates required for Field Intelligence work, with the accounts, which are of a somewhat technical nature, and with secret service, all officers (other than officers of the General Staff) and subordinates employed on intelligence duties in the field will be grouped in a separate organisation, under the control of the D.M.I. of the force.[52]

The Intelligence Corps would not include secret agents, but it would provide an administrative headquarters for all interpreters, guides, scouts, and other specialists who would contribute to the field intelligence effort. The members of the corps, excluding the regular officers assigned to it, were to be paid from intelligence funds. In the event of war with another European power, all civilians serving in the Intelligence Corps would be temporarily commissioned or enlisted and would wear uniforms. What sort of training they would receive was not mentioned.[53]

Although the concept of an Intelligence Corps was accepted in principle through its incorporation in the field intelligence regulations of 1904, little was done by the General Staff to prepare for its wartime implementation. Throughout this period, Col. David Henderson repeatedly urged the War Office to conduct preliminary planning for the creation of an Intelligence Corps to support the British Expeditionary Force. Finally, in 1912, with the threat of a European war looming on the horizon, the Directorate of Military Operations responded. Col. George M.W. Macdonogh, head of the Special Duties Section (MO 5),[54] began to compile a list of linguists and others possessing skills likely to be of value in intelligence work on the Continent. These men, all of whom were civilians, would be asked to join the Intelligence Corps if and when Britain went to war. Included on Macdonogh's list were university lecturers, masters of public schools, businessmen, artists, musicians, and professional adventurers of all kinds. On 5 August 1914, within hours of Great Britain's declaration of war on Germany, the War Office sent them telegrams to report to Southampton, and, practically overnight, the Intelligence Corps sprang to life. One week later, two officers from India (Maj. T.G. Torrie, Lucknow Cavalry Brigade, and Capt. J.A. Dunnington-Jefferson) sailed from Southampton with an advance contingent of the Intelligence Corps. The issue of equipment to members of the corps was completed at Le Havre, France, and they were given some instruction in reconnaissance and demolitions before being ordered to the front on 19 August. Once at the front, most were further assigned to be specialists in interrogation, cipher, reconnaissance, liaison, photography, and order of battle. By the end of August, the strength of the Intelligence Corps had reached fifty members and it was still growing.[55]

The activation of the Intelligence Corps in August 1914 and its immediate deployment to France with the B.E.F. would not have been possible without George Macdonogh's work in earmarking qualified personnel in advance, but it ought not be forgotten that Macdonogh and the General Staff originally were prodded into action by David Henderson. Moreover, the existence of the Intelligence Corps in 1914 is attributable directly to Henderson's earlier accomplishment of winning General Staff approval for an official field intelligence doctrine in 1904. Both *Field Intelligence* and "Regulations for Intelligence Duties in the Field" were still in effect when Britain went to war in 1914; no comparable manuals or regulations had been written to replace them and furnish General Staff officers with an updated guide to the performance of their tactical intelligence duties. Several significant changes were implemented in the British Army's field intelligence system during the decade prior to 1914, most notably in the areas of reconnaissance and communications, but they did not alter the basic structure of the system outlined by David Henderson in 1904. Lt. Col. James E. Edmonds, at the outset of a "confidential" lecture to an audience of British officers in January 1908, remarked, "There is not very much literature on the subject of intelligence work in war. . . . There are, however, two official British books." Edmonds identified these as *Field Intelligence* and "Regulations for Intelligence Duties in the Field."[56] Had his lecture been delivered in the summer of 1914, Edmonds's statement would have been equally true. There were still only "two official British books" which dealt comprehensively with the field intelligence system.

The instructions provided to field intelligence officers in Wolseley's *The Soldier's Pocket-Book for Field Service* had been intended primarily for use during the expeditions and small wars in which the British Army participated throughout the latter half of the nineteenth century. Two years after the end of the South African War, when David Henderson wrote *Field Intelligence*, British officers were still concerned with the prospects of having to fight colonial wars in Asia and Africa against non-Europeans. Due to their recent South African experience and to growing Anglo-German friction, however, they were beginning to turn their attention to the tactical problems of waging a war on the Continent. The "two official British books" of 1904 on the subject of field intelligence generally were well balanced with respect to colonial warfare and "civilised warfare," accurately reflecting a period of doctrinal transition and uncertainty about the army's raison d'être. Following the beginning of the Anglo-French staff talks in 1905-06, the British General Staff increasingly focused on the problems of preparing the British Army for a European war. By 1907-08, General Staff officers interested in the field intelligence system and in training officers for field intelligence duties for the next war were concentrating their efforts almost exclusively on the probability of fighting an enemy "whose leading, staff methods, initiative, and strategy" would be on a par with Britain's for the first time since Waterloo.[57]

As already mentioned, the head of MO 5, Col. James Edmonds, presented a lecture in January 1908 dealing with tactical intelligence. The theme of Edmonds's talk, entitled "Intelligence in European Warfare," was the contrast between the duties of a field intelligence officer in a small war and those of his counterpart in a war on the Continent. Colonel Edmonds offered no new principles of field intelligence to supplement or replace those of David Henderson, nor did he identify any new methods of collection. Rather, he attempted to impress upon prospective tactical intelligence officers the idea that European warfare would require "far greater vigilance, far closer watching of the enemy, and far greater secrecy . . . than [war] against the foes we have been accustomed to meet." Also, once Britain entered a war against Germany, for example, intelligence officers in the field would find that it was too late to collect topographical information in the theater of war as well as certain basic information about the German Army.

> In European warfare, it may be assumed that we shall be provided with good maps, with some handbooks describing the organization, tactics, uniforms and characteristics of our enemy and others minutely describing the theatre of war, especially its fortresses, its railways, roads, bridges, telegraph system etc. . . .

In most colonial wars, there had been sufficient time to collect such information at the beginning of a campaign in order to supplement the data about the enemy and the area of operations provided by the Intelligence Branch in London. In a future European conflict, warned Edmonds, British field intelligence officers must be able to concentrate on the "main work of the Intelligence Department" from the outset: "to obtain information as to the location and movements of the enemy's forces. . . ."[58]

Not surprisingly, Colonel Edmonds's lecture included a number of references to tactical intelligence methods employed by both sides in the Russo-Japanese War (1904-05). Although he had not been among the British officers sent out by the General Staff to observe the war, he certainly was familiar with the three volumes of *The Russo-Japanese War: British Officers' Reports*, assembled within the Directorate of Military Operations prior to July 1907. The reports of British officers from both sides of the conflict revealed that a superior tactical intelligence system had been a significant factor in the victories of the Japanese Army in battle after battle. Just as the British had against the Boers in 1899, the Russians and Japanese discovered the inadequacies of traditional methods of reconnaissance in the opening engagements of the war. The Japanese, however, adapted quickly to the new conditions of the battlefield; the Russians did not. Furthermore, as Col. W.H.H. Waters reported, the Russian General Staff had been poorly informed about the quality and strength of the Japanese Army before the war broke out. A gross underestimation of Japanese capabilities before the hostilities was compounded by the Russian Army's failure "to reconnoitre frequently and intelligently" on the field of battle.[59]

Secret service had also played a vital role in the collection of tactical intelligence during this conflcit in the Far East. Colonel Edmonds observed that this was one area in which the Russians enjoyed some success, but the Japanese had more than offset the activities of Russian agents with their own efficient secret service, which on occasion "employed Chinese jugglers and conjurers, who were great favorites with the Russian soldiery, to collect information." Edmonds argued that the Russo-Japanese War had reconfirmed the need for clandestine intelligence operations in the field as a means of obtaining tactical information, particularly with the aim to determine the strength and location of the enemy's reserves.[60] Like David Henderson, Edmonds stressed the importance of tactical counterintelligence.

> Preventing the enemy from obtaining information is, in European warfare, almost as of great importance as securing information for one's own side; with civilian inhabitants, foreign military attachés and newspaper correspondents about, it will be impossible to obtain complete concealment, but measures must be taken to secure that they see as little as possible and hear nothing, and that all communications leaving the area of operations are censored.

Edmonds noted that the Japanese had shown a keen awareness of this problem and had adhered to "an excellent rule" which forbade officers from even speaking to attachés and newspaper correspondents. An officer designated by the director of intelligence escorted them and insured that they saw only what the Japanese wanted them to see.[61]

Besides Colonel Edmonds, several other senior intelligence officers from the General Staff's Directorate of Military Operations were invited to present lectures on tactical intelligence at Camberley and other places in the United Kingdom during 1907 and 1908. In March Col. Edward Gleichen, head of MO 2 (the European section), gave a talk, "Intelligence Duties in the Field," to a group of prospective field intelligence officers. Gleichen, who had been a field intelligence officer in South Africa (1899-1900) and the Sudan (1901-03), did not take issue with the general principles of tactical intelligence set down by David Henderson in 1904. He pointed out, however, that intelligence is not an exact science; "the beauty of intelligence work is that there are no rules." Though not as narrowly limited to European warfare as Edmonds had been in his lecture, Colonel Gleichen did highlight the differences in the nature of field intelligence duties in small wars versus those in war on the Continent. In the latter instance, the duties of the intelligence officer

> will be a good deal more exhausting, mentally. In the first place, there will be a good many more people to deal with, and calls on his time and interviews will be incessant—especially if the war is being carried on in a friendly country. The information sought for will have to be more detailed, and distributed probably over a larger area. More agents will be

> necessary, the spies selected will have to be more carefully instructed; more means of communication will probably be available; and more documents and offices of all sorts will have to be searched, . . . the billet of Intelligence Officer in a campaign in a thickly populated and civilized country can hardly be described as a "soft job."

Gleichen voiced special concern about the possibility that a field intelligence officer might be tasked with various General Staff duties relating to "the arrangements of his own troops," thereby detracting from the performance of his primary duty, the collection of information about the enemy. Intelligence officers were to guard against this, although there would be occasions when they should assist other members of the staff.[62]

Lectures on field intelligence to students at the Staff College and elsewhere, by experienced intelligence officers like James Edmonds and Edward Gleichen,[63] sparked a continuing interest in the subject within the British Army during the pre-World War I years. They also added a valuable dimension to the training of staff officers for future tactical intelligence duties. The Russo-Japanese War provided an interesting backdrop to Edmonds's lecture on field intelligence in European warfare. In a more general sense, the collective writings of both the participants in and the observers of that conflict also spurred thoughtful officers to consider the problems of tactical intelligence on the battlefields of the future.

Still another important stimulus to the study of current tactical intelligence practices among European armies and their implications for the British Army were the annual reports on foreign maneuvers compiled by the General Staff. The reports of 1908-13 contained sections or paragraphs on the latest developments in European armies in areas of particular interest to field intelligence officers, such as reconnaissance, aeronautics, tactical counterintelligence, and communications. Naturally, German and Austro-Hungarian maneuvers were accorded close scrutiny in these areas, but so were those of Britain's entente partners, France and Russia.[64]

More than anything else, the growing realization among the British officer corps, especially after 1906, that the British Army would probably fight its next war on the Continent was responsible for the unprecedented degree of interest in field intelligence displayed by many officers. One of the most interesting manifestations of this trend occurred in the spring of 1907, when a course was established by the British Army's Eastern Command to train officers for field intelligence duties in wartime. Eight carefully selected officers from units of the Eastern Command attended the four week "Intelligence and Reconnaissance Course" at Dover in April. During the two weeks just prior to the start of the course, they were given time off to prepare for it by conducting "certain reconnaissance work" and studying "various books on intelligence, notably the 'Regulations for Intelligence Duties in the Field' and David Henderson's *Field Intelligence*." The course itself emphasized "practical work and consisted of reconnaissances, memory sketches, reports, night work, intelligence schemes, and lectures" by Cols. William Robertson and James Edmonds, among others. The "intelligence schemes" developed for the course were intended to teach officers how to elicit information from various types of people, how to sift and collate reports, how to write a précis, and how to keep intelligence diaries and registers. They proved to be valuable exercises.[65]

The number of officers trained was very small, but the mere fact that a field intelligence course had been established by a major command of the British Army in peacetime was enormously significant in the evolution of the army's tactical intelligence system before World War I. Only three years earlier, not even David Henderson had recommended that a course for officers to prepare them solely for intelligence duties in the field be instituted.

The Eastern Command's "Intelligence and Reconnaissance Course" was conducted annually after the first course in 1907. Still only one month long, the course had undergone considerable revision by the time it was offered for the second time in April 1908. Criteria for the selection of officers to attend the course were more firmly established. The eight officers chosen were "on the Staff College list, . . . were good at reconnaissance work, and . . . in the opinion of their Commanding Officers, were likely to show special aptitude for . . . intelligence duties in war." Instead of spending two weeks in preparation for the course, the officers selected were required to spend two months studying the prescribed books and the conduct of reconnaissances as directed by the General Staff of the Eastern Command. They were tested on this preparatory material to ensure they were "sufficiently grounded (in the fundamentals) to be able to reap full advantage from the instruction given." The course itself, as in 1907, was "entirely practical" and was enriched by lectures given by General Staff officers who were "specialists in their subjects, and in almost all cases have had practical experience of intelligence work in war."[66]

The young lieutenants and captains who attended the "Intelligence and Reconnaissance Course" in 1908 had been thoroughly exposed to the ideas of David Henderson. *Field Intelligence* continued to be the basic textbook for the course, and Brigadier General Henderson, at the time assigned to the office of the inspector general of the forces, appeared as a guest lecturer. Henderson's latest work, *The Art of Reconnaissance* (London, 1907), had also been added to the suggested reading list. James Edmonds, also a visiting lecturer during the 1908 course, praised *The Art of Reconnaissance* as "a useful book recently published . . . in which the immense importance of good information is brought out, hints as to its acquirement by scouts and patrols are given and its transmission when obtained is practically dealt with."[67] David Henderson's timely new contribution to the field of tactical intelligence incorporated the lessons of the Russo-Japanese and South African Wars. The first edition includes chapters on "Independent Reconnaissance," "The Scout," "The Patrol," "The Reconnaissance of Ground," and "The Transmission of Information."[68]

David Henderson's objective in writing *The Art of Reconnaissance* was, in his own words,

> to present a view of the subject of reconnaissance as a whole, in the hope of assisting those whose duty or ambition it may be to prepare themselves to undertake the pursuit of information in war.

He offered a mild apology to his peers for "perhaps overstepping the debatable ground which lies between the provinces of reconnaissance and cavalry tactics." Such trespassing seemed necessary, however, at a time when the ability of horse cavalry to conduct mounted reconnaissance in the next European war was highly questionable.[69] While Henderson's book was up-to-date when published in July 1907, the techniques of reconnaissance (and communications) were changing so rapidly that he felt compelled to make some revisions barely one year later.

The chapter headings of the second edition of *The Art of Reconnaissance*, which was published in October 1908, are the same as those of the first. When the third (and final) edition appeared in May 1914, however, a ninth, significant chapter had been added: "Aerial Reconnaissance." Brigadier General Henderson was, of course, extremely interested in aviation and had been appointed director general of military aeronautics the previous year. In the preface to the third edition, he comments,

> A book on reconnaissance, in which the possibilities of aerial scouting are not considered, must be classed as obsolete, and yet, in this new field, experience is so limited, and progress is so rapid, that any dogmatic pronouncement on military aeronautics would, at this stage, have no permanence and little value. I have therefore in this new edition done no more than add a chapter on aerial reconnaissance. . . .[70]

Like their French and German contemporaries, most British officers during the final years before World War I believed reconnaissance would be the primary mission of military aircraft (balloons and airships/dirigibles, as well as airplanes) in the coming war. The possible utilization of airships and airplanes to attack the enemy was recognized to a degree, but was accorded a low priority among potential missions for British aircraft. A memorandum produced within the British War Office in 1912 recommended the establishment of a military flying school on the Salisbury Plain on the grounds,

> the efficiency of the aeroplane for purposes of military reconnaissance has been proved both in foreign manoeuvres and in actual warfare in Tripoli and without doubt, aeroplanes have now become an important adjunct to the equipment of an army in the field.[71]

In order of priority, the missions for airplanes in support of ground forces were to be the following: "(a) Reconnaissance, (b) Prevention of enemy reconnaissance, (c) Inter-communication, (d) Observation of artillery fire, and (e) Infliction of damage upon enemy." The requirement to maintain the already existing Airship Company, consisting of two airships and assorted support equipment, for long-range reconnaissance missions was also expressed in this memorandum.[72]

The utility of airships for tactical and strategic reconnaissance on land and at sea was explored by *Times* military correspondent Charles à Court Repington in a 1910 article in *Blackwood's*. Repington took into account technological advances in methods of communications. The adaptation of "wireless telegraphy" (radio) for use on board airships had enhanced dramatically their ability to transmit intelligence to the ground almost instantly and over great distances. Consequently,

> . . . there cannot be much doubt that in favoring weather the best watch
> in the air will secure the advantage of prompt and accurate information
> of the movements of fleets and flotillas at sea and of masses on land.

Thanks to their speed and height above the ground, airships would be able to escape destruction by artillery when used in support of ground forces.[73]

Aerial reconnaissance, whether from dirigibles or airplanes, was primarily visual reconnaissance until the beginning of World War I. Aerial photography had been used in warfare as early as the American Civil War, when photos of Conferederate positions at Richmond were taken from a Union balloon in 1862. Balloons were used, to a limited degree, during the Franco-Prussian War (1870-71), and a balloon unit was formed in the British Army in 1884. During the 1880s and 1890s, a number of experiments were conducted by British and Belgian officers, inventors, and daredevils with the aim of improving aerial photography taken from balloons and kites. Fascinated with the potential value of aerial photos to military intelligence, Col. Robert S.S. Baden-Powell confirmed the potential of kites as camera platforms in 1897, when he produced good photographs taken from a kite at a height of over four hundred feet. Four balloon sections of the Royal Engineers took part in the South African War, but were not employed extensively for photographic missions. Just after the South African War (1903-06), the German engineer, Alfred Maul, conducted a series of experiments with rocket photography and was able to obtain photos from altitudes of up to 2,600 feet. In 1904, the War Office Committee on Military Ballooning urged "special and early experiments be made in connection with a dirigible balloon, man-lifting kites, and photographic equipment for the balloon sections."[74]

The first photographs taken from an airplane were probably taken from a plane piloted by Wilbur Wright in the vicinity of Rome in 1909, but the quality of the pictures was poor. The French gained the lead in this field at the end of 1909 when "the first effective stills" were taken from an airplane. The first recorded use of an airplane in war occurred in the Italo-Turkish War (1911-12) in October 1911, when Captain Piazza of the Italian Army flew a visual reconnaissance mission over Turkish units near Tripoli in North Africa. The same pilot was also the first to take photographs from an airplane in combat; on 24 and 25 February 1912 he successfully photographed Turkish positions from his monoplane. Another Italian officer took motion pictures of the enemy from an airship in April of the same year. The French Army continued to experiment with aerial photography, and at the outset of World War I it had photo reconnaissance units equipped with cameras capable of taking clear pictures from airplanes flying at three thousand feet. Britain's Royal Flying Corps lagged behind the French in this area until the fighting began. After observing the excellent results obtained by their allies and after conducting a special study of the organization, equipment, and methods of French photographic reconnaissance units during the fall of 1914, the R.F.C. formed an experimental photographic section in early 1915. Four men, headed by Lieutenant Moore-Brabazon, designed a new camera, which turned out to be the best aerial camera in existence anywhere at the time, in less than two months. Techniques continued to be improved, and, by mid-1915, the

British were mounting cameras on the bodies of airplanes (rather than having observers hold the instruments themselves). With the enthusiastic endorsement of R.F.C. commanding general, Maj. Gen. David Henderson, the British had formed their own photo reconnaissance units.[75]

The development of balloons, kites, airships, and airplanes as vehicles for aerial reconnaissance, and the simultaneous improvement of aerial photographic capabilities, added a new, highly significant dimension to tactical intelligence on the eve of World War I and in the first year of the war. The entire field of imagery intelligence (IMINT), which today is a highly sophisticated and vital facet of both the tactical and strategic intelligence systems of the armed forces of all the world's leading powers, began to emerge as a practical tool of war in the pre-World War I era. David Henderson and the British Army made important contributions in those pioneering days of aerial reconnaissance.

During the pre-1914 decade the increasing use of the radio for tactical communications by all European armies opened up an entirely new area of communications intelligence (COMINT). The British Army experimented with "wireless" during the South African War, but since the Boers had little or no wireless equipment of their own, the potential for exploiting the intercept of wireless transmissions was not fully realized by either side. Thus, Britons and Boers concentrated on the intercept of telegraph and heliograph messages and on the improvement of ciphers for use in the field. Between the end of the South African War and 1914, the British Army, and especially the cavalry, sought to improve its own ability to communicate via radio, but little thought was given to preparing for the intercept of enemy radio messages for intelligence purposes in combat. The British army's *Field Service Regulations* of 1909 failed to mention radio intercept as a means of intelligence collection, as did the 1914 edition of David Henderson's *The Art of Reconnaissance*. The 1909 *Field Service Regulations* was reprinted with amendments in 1914, and the tactical value of aerial reconnaisance was emphasized for the first time in an official General Staff document intended for use in the field, but radio intercept (and communications intelligence in general) was largely ignored.[76] By 1912 the British Army had wagon-mounted wireless transmitters in service, which were intended for use by cavalry units. By the end of 1914, however, they "were being employed almost exclusively to intercept enemy communications, a task which was carried out with appreciable success."[77]

The British and French had greater opportunity to intercept German radio communications on the Western Front than did the Germans theirs, at least during the first two years of World War I. This was due to the fact that the war was fought primarily on French soil, where the French were able to use their own wire-cable network for tactical communications. Thus, French and British radios were freed for intercept work, which proved a lucrative source of intelligence, since the Germans did have to rely far more on their wireless equipment for communications. Initially, the telephone lines connecting the trenches with one another and with higher headquarters were considered secure, but both sides learned to eavesdrop on each other's phone lines. This was accomplished by soldiers who crawled across no man's land

and actually tapped the enemy's lines, by wireless receivers fitted with repeater coils (capable of picking up telephone conversations at one hundred yards), and by low resistance telephone receivers implanted in the ground, where they were effective in intercepting phone conversations of the enemy as far away as one thousand yards.[78]

The British Army's tactical intelligence system was not without its problems in August 1914. Despite the modest effort to train officers for field intelligence duties which began five years after the end of the South African War, the number of officers who received such training between 1907 and 1914 was far too small for the requirements of a major European war. The Indian Army remained the most fertile ground for the development of tactical intelligence specialists and the best place for an officer to acquire practical experience in field intelligence. In peacetime there were no British Army counterparts to Indian Army units like the Intelligence Corps at Peshawar or the Indian Corps of Guides.

When Great Britain declared war on Germany on 4 August 1914, the Intelligence Corps was quickly activated through the notification of the civilians on Colonel Macdonogh's list, but no officer had been selected in advance to command the new unit. A qualified officer had to be found immediately, and in the hour of need the British General Staff turned to a major in the Indian Army who happened to be home on leave and thus readily available. The fledgling Intelligence Corps which Major Torrie took to France in August 1914 was, at first, no more than an untrained, disoriented group of civilians who had no idea of what their duties would be or even of what uniforms they were supposed to wear. The British Army had more intelligence-related equipment and technology than trained intelligence personnel when the Great War began, but it lagged behind its French ally in aerial camera technology, and only after the opening round of the war did British officers begin to comprehend the enormous potential of communications intelligence in the age of wireless.

On the other hand, the tactical intelligence lessons of the South African War had not been lost, thanks to the efforts of David Henderson. Furthermore, beginning in 1904, the British Army had an official field intelligence manual to guide the new intelligence officers, and a set of regulations which provided necessary ground rules for the increasingly complex and costly business of running a wartime field intelligence department and which included the administration of secret service funds. After 1906, some of the army's more thoughtful intelligence officers (David Henderson, James Edmonds, Edward Gleichen, William Robertson, and others) turned their attention to the problems of tactical intelligence in a war on the Continent. The British Army kept pace with, and at times moved into the forefront of, aerial reconnaissance developments. The establishment of the Royal Flying Corps in April 1912, and the preparation for war it received in the two years that followed, gave the army an invaluable intelligence collection asset which proved its worth beginning in August 1914. The far-sighted David Henderson deserves a great deal of credit for helping to bring about the birth of the R.F.C. He was also instrumental, behind the scenes, in 1912 in persuading the

General Staff to begin planning for an Intelligence Corps to accompany the British Expeditionary Force to France. While the Intelligence Corps of August 1914 was poorly prepared to go directly to a theater of war and perform its mission in combat, the fact that the head of MO 5 had assembled a list of men for duty in the corps prior to the outbreak of war and the speed with which the corps was formed and moved to France were significant accomplishments. In any case, the function of the corps, at least initially, was to provide the B.E.F. with a pool of linguists and other intelligence specialists who could then be detailed to the General Staffs of divisions, corps, or general headquarters. In this respect, the Intelligence Corps was successful even before the end of August 1914.

NOTES

1. Capt. Edmund Ironside of the Royal Field Artillery, later a field marshal and chief of the Imperial General Staff, was an undercover British agent in German Southwest Africa for two years (1908-10), posing as a pro-German Boer and working as an oxen driver for the German Army. Lt. Col. B.A.H. Parritt, *The Intelligencers*, pp. 223-24.

2. Between 1902 and 1914, overseas posts for British military intelligence officers (in addition to military attachés) included South Africa, Egypt, Cyprus, Teheran, and the Persian Gulf.

3. In 1900, the Intelligence Branch of the Quartermaster General's Department in India was subdivided into four sections, each manned by a deputy assistant quartermaster general (DAQMG), a staff captain, and clerks. Section responsibilities were as follows: "Section F—Afghanistan, Baluchistan, Kashmir, Gilgit, Chitral, Northwest Frontier, and Waziristan; Section W—Russia in Asia, Persia, China on the Russian Frontier, Province of Bagdad, and Turkey-in-Asia (jointly with the Intelligence Division of the War Office); Section E—Nepal, Tibet, Sikkim, Bhutan, French Indochina, Borneo, Dutch East Indies, Philippines, Japan, Korea, China, Arabia, Somaliland, and Abyssinia; and Section T—Native States in India. Correspondence, Library, Maps, and Topographical Section." War Office, Intelligence Division, "War Office Systems of Foreign Countries and India," London, pp. 100-101.

4. Statement of Lt. Col. W.R. Robertson, 28 November 1902, "Minutes of Evidence," *Report of the Committee Appointed to Examine the Permanent Establishment of the Mobilisation and Intelligence Division*, p. 37.

5. In a secret Indian Army memorandum of 1911, a proposal for the expansion of the permanent field intelligence establishment in India was justified by the following statement: "It has long been recognized that it is unsound for the Army to depend on the Foreign Department (the Indian government's Foreign Office) for its trans-frontier intelligence, as the information thus afforded is mainly political, and the agents employed are not sufficiently well informed on military matters to be able to collect information which would be of much use to the Army." Appendix 16, "Expansion of existing nucleus of an Intelligence Corps," *Memorandum on the duties and requirements of the Army in India at the present time with special reference to the proposed reduction of Military Expenditure in India*, p. 115.

6. Ibid. The annual budget of the Intelligence Corps at Peshawar was 20,000 rupees in 1909-10.

7. Statement of Field Marshal Lord Roberts, 10 February 1903, Royal Commission of the War in South Africa, *Minutes of Evidence II*, p. 69.

8. The Hardwicke Committee was a committee headed by the Earl of Hardwicke, appointed by the secretary of state for war in August 1901 to review the "Permanent Establishment of the Mobilization and Intelligence Department."

9. Statement of Lt. Col. Archibald Murray, 11 March 1903, Royal Commission on the War in South Africa, *Minutes of Evidence II*, p. 327.

10. Statement of Maj. Gen. Sir Charles E. Knox, 11 March 1903, Royal Commission on the War in South Africa, *Minutes of Evidence II*, p. 323.

11. Royal Commission on the War in South Africa, *Report*, p. 130.

12. Statement of L.S. Amery, 24 March 1903, Royal Commission on the War in South Africa, *Minutes of Evidence II*, pp. 465-66. See also statements of Lt. Col. Edward Altham, 15 October

1902, *Minutes of Evidence I*, pp. 22, 28, and Lt. Col. Archibald Murray, 11 March 1903, *Minutes of Evidence II*, pp. 327-28.

13. The report of the Hardwicke Committee was published in March 1903; the report of the Royal Commission on the War in South Africa was published about four months later in July 1903.

14. Evidence of Lt. Gen. Sir William Nicholson, 5 November 1902, "Minutes of Evidence," Report of the Hardwicke Committee, (March 1903), p. 21.

15. Evidence of Lt. Gen. Sir Ian Hamilton, 8 December 1902, "Minutes of Evidence," Report of the Hardwicke Committee, p. 47.

16. Evidence of Gen. Sir John French, 23 December 1902, "Minutes of Evidence," Report of the Hardwicke Committee, p. 56.

17. Evidence of Gen. Sir Henry Brackenbury, 3 December 1902, "Minutes of Evidence," Report of the Hardwicke Committee, pp. 42-44.

18. Statement of Lt. Col. Edward Altham, 15 October 1902, Royal Commission on the War in South Africa, *Minutes of Evidence I*, p. 23.

19. War Office, *Report of the War Office (Reconstitution) Committee*, section 9, pt. 3, pp. 25-26, 28. The only military member of the Army Council who would not have a counterpart in the field was the master general of ordnance.

20. Ibid.

21. Ibid., p. 28.

22. For a discussion of Britain's changing diplomatic position in the post-Boer War period, see chapter X.

23. Lt. Col. David Henderson, *Field Intelligence, Its Principles and Practices*, p. 8.

24. H.A. Jones, "Henderson, Sir David," pp. 249-50. See also Sir Walter Raleigh and H.A. Jones, *The War in the Air*, Vol. 1. In January 1918, Sir David Henderson became vice-president of the newly formed Air Council. After tours as area commandant in France (August-October 1918) and military counsellor at the British embassy in Paris (1918-19), he became director of the League of Red Cross Societies in Geneva, where he died in August 1921.

25. Henderson, *Field Intelligence*, "Preface," dated 29 April 1904.

26. The chapter titles are "(1) Personnel and Organization, (2) Reconnaissance, (3) Examination of Persons and Documents, (4) Secret Service, (5) The Value of Incomplete Information, (6) Classification and Distribution of Information, Maps and Intelligence Reports, (7) The Guiding of Troops, and (8) Frustration of the Enemy's Endeavors to Gain Information."

27. Henderson, *Field Intelligence*, p. 1.

28. Ibid., pp. 3-4.

29. Chapter 2, "Reconnaissance," is only six pages long. Henderson and his superiors probably thought more detail was unnecessary because reconnaissance was a subject about which much had been said and written by British officers over the previous decade—Col. George A. Furse's *Information in War*, Col. Charles E. Callwell's *Small Wars, Their Principles and Practice* (1899), and the lectures and writings of Col. G.F.R. Henderson from 1891-1903, some of which were later published in *The Science of War*, all contain considerable material on reconnaissance and it was also given reasonable attention in the instruction presented at the Staff College at Camberley. If David Henderson felt chapter 2 was inadequate, he more than made up for it three years later with *The Art of Reconnaissance*.

30. David Henderson, *Field Intelligence*, pp. 8-10.

31. Ibid., pp. 10, 12.

32. Ibid., p. 13.

33. Ibid., pp. 14-15.

34. Ibid., pp. 15-16, 20.

35. Ibid., p. 21.

36. Ibid., pp. 21-22, 24-25.

37. Ibid., pp. 21, 26.

38. Ibid., p. 28.

39. Ibid., pp. 28-31.

40. Ibid., pp. 30-31.

41. Ibid., pp. 31-32, 36-37.

42. Ibid., pp. 45-46.

43. Ibid., p. 47.

44. Ibid., p. 6.

45. Ibid., p. 7.

46. The preface by Lt. Gen. Neville G. Lyttelton to the third edition of Callwell's *Small Wars, Their Principles and Practice* is a good example of semiofficial support from the War Office, in this case from the chief of the general staff. While recommending the book to officers as a "valuable contribution" on the subject, Lyttelton cautions that it should not be regarded as "an expression of official opinion on the subjects of which it treats."

47. Lyttelton, preface (dated 3 August 1904) to "Regulations for Intelligence Duties in the Field," War Office, General Staff.

48. War Office, General Staff, "Regulations for Intelligence Duties in the Field," pp. 6-9, 17-28. For a force exceeding the strength of an army corps, the DMI would be a brigadier general or colonel of the General Staff, assisted by a lieutenant colonel and two majors or captains of the General Staff, as well as by two attached officers. An infantry division was authorized at least a major or a captain of the General Staff.

49. Evidence of Col. James K. Trotter, 12 November 1902, "Minutes of Evidence," Report of the Hardwicke Committee, p. 23; Parritt, *The Intelligencers*, pp. 203-04. Wellington, Frederick the Great, Napoleon, the Germans in 1870, and the Russians and Japanese in 1904-05 all spent vast sums of money on wartime secret service. In 1870, it is estimated the German secret service, headed by William Stieber, had placed at least ten thousand spies in France ahead of the German Army. Lecture notes of Gen. Sir Walter Kirke, n.d. (circa 1925), Kirke Papers, Intelligence Corps Museum, Ashford, Kent. Peacetime expenditure on secret service by Britain (Foreign Office, War Office, and Admiralty) remained at a fairly constant level between the South African War and 1914. Between 1906-07 and 1912-13, the figure was £50,000 annually. According to an official British government appraisal prepared in 1912, the comparable figures for secret service budgets of other major powers were as follows: Austria-Hungary—£62,500 (1910, 1911); France—£40,000 (1909, 1910, 1911); Germany—£80,400 (1909, 1910, 1911); Russia—£380,000 (1910), £335,000 (1912). "Annual Expenditure on Secret Service by the Governments of Austria-Hungary, France, Germany, Great Britain, Italy, and Russia According to their Respective Published Budgets," Parliamentary Papers, 1912-13 (Cd. 6144, April 1912).

50. War Office, General Staff, "Regulations for Intelligence Duties in the Field," regulation number 3, p. 5.

51. Ibid., regulation number 4, pp. 5-6.

52. Ibid., p.6.

53. Ibid., regulations numbers 16, 17, p. 11.

54. Col. George M.W. Macdonogh, Royal Engineers, succeeded Col. James Edmonds as head of MO 5 in 1910 and continued in that position until August 1914. He then served as head of the intelligence section within the General Staff at general headquarters (GHQ) of the B.E.F. from August 1914 until early 1916 and was promoted to brigadier general in November 1914. Following promotion to major general, Macdonogh was appointed director of military intelligence on the General Staff at the War Office, a position in which he served with distinction until 1918. Lt. Gen. Sir George Macdonogh was adjutant general to the forces from 1918 to 1922. "Macdonogh, Lieut-General Sir George Mark Watson," *Who Was Who, 1941-1950*, p. 723.

55. Maj. D.S. Hawker, "Working Notes for a History of the Intelligence Corps." See also Parritt, *The Intelligencers*, p. 231. Maj. T.G. Torrie, the first commandant of the Intelligence Corps, was brigade major of the Lucknow Cavalry Brigade at the time of his appointment. His successor as commandant was Capt. (later Field Marshal Lord) A.P. Wavell of the Black Watch. Initially, the members of the corps wore rank and file khaki uniforms with second lieutenant badges of rank, general service buttons, and the Royal Coat of Arms cap badge. Within a few months, they were officially graded as staff lieutenants, 2d class.

56. Edmonds Papers, 4/1, Lt. Col. J.E. Edmonds, "Intelligence in European Warfare," pp. 1-2. Liddell Hart Centre for Military Archives, Kings College, London. Also mentioned by Edmonds are Callwell's *Small Wars*, Furse's *Information in War*, and Henderson's *The Art of Reconnaissance*.

57. Ibid., p. 8. An earlier version of this same lecture, entitled "Intelligence in European Warfare, with Illustrations from the Russo-Japanese War," had been presented by Colonel Edmonds in April 1907 to an "Intelligence and Reconnaissance Course" for officers at Dover.

58. Ibid., pp. 3-8.

59. General Staff, War Office, *The Russo-Japanese War, Reports from British Officers Attached to the Russian Forces in the Field*, 3: 155-57.

60. Edmonds, "Intelligence in European Warfare," pp. 10-12.

61. Ibid., p. 24.

62. Edmonds Papers, 7/3, Count Gleichen, "Intelligence Duties in the Field," pp. 1-4, 8.

63. During the Eastern Command's Intelligence and Reconnaissance Course, conducted at Dover in April 1907, the visiting lecturers and their topics included: Maj. G.K. Cockerill of MO 5, "Acquisition of Intelligence," "Organization of Secret Service," and "Cyphers and Cyphering"; Col. (later Field Marshal) George F. Milne, formerly of MO 2, "On intelligence duties and on the organisation of the Intelligence Department in the South African War"; Col. William R. Robertson, formerly assistant director of military operations and head of MO 2, "Intelligence in peace, work junior officers are likely to be called upon to carry out"; Maj. J.K. Tod, head of the Indian Section MO 3, "Intelligence in Indian Warfare"; and Col. James Edmonds, "Intelligence in European Warfare, with Illustrations from the Russo-Japanese War." Among the lecturers for the same course one year later were Brig. Gens. David Henderson and William Robertson. General Staff, Eastern Command, "Report on the Eastern Command Intelligence and Reconnaissance Course, 1907," pp. 4-7.

64. In the 1908 *Report on Foreign Manoeuvers*, for example, the chapter on the German Army's maneuvers discusses techniques used by scouts and "reconnoitring officers," balloon reconnaissance, and methods of communication used, to include field telegraphs, telephones, and "wireless telegraphy." A section of the chapter on Germany in the 1910 *Report* is devoted to "Dirigible Balloons." Wireless messages were transmitted to ground stations from the dirigibles, but these messages "were read and understood by the hostile stations, as well as by their own." The 1911 *Report* includes a special section on "Aeronautics" in which the French Army was recognized as the leader in military aviation among the European powers.

65. General Staff, Eastern Command, "Report on the Eastern Command Intelligence and Reconnaisance Course, 1907" pp. 3-9. This report includes a complete syllabus of the course.

66. General Staff, Eastern Command, "Report of the Eastern Command Intelligence and Reconnaissance Course, April, 1908," pp. 3-4, 9-10. The syllabus shows that the course director adhered closely to David Henderson's *Field Intelligence* in organizing the material to be presented.

67. Edmonds, "Intelligence in European Warfare," p. 2.

68. Other chapter titles are "Principles and Methods," "Protection and Security," and "Contact Reconnaissance." Henderson, *The Art of Reconnaissance*.

69. Ibid., p. v.

70. Ibid., p. iii.

71. War Office, "Memorandum on Military and Naval Aviation," Cd. 6067 (1912), pp. 2, 5.

72. Ibid., p. 8. For a thorough, well-documented treatment of the pre-World War I British airship program, see Robin Higham, *The British Rigid Airship, 1908-1931*.

73. Col. Charles à Court Repington, "The Airship Menace," p. 6. During World War I Germany's zeppelins flew at altitudes up to 16,000 feet, but even at that height eventually they became terribly vulnerable to airplanes firing incendiary ammunition and antiaircraft guns on the ground.

74. War Office, *Final Report of the Committee on Military Ballooning*, p. 25.

75. W.O. II G. Downton, Intelligence Corps, "Notes and pictures on the History of Photographic Interpretation," n.d., Intelligence Corps Museum, A176; John W.R. Taylor and David Mondey, *Spies in the Sky* (New York: Charles Scribner's Sons, 1972), pp. 19-25. See also Raleigh and Jones, *The War in the Air*, Vol. 1.

76. War Office, General Staff, *Field Service Regulations, 1909*. The paragraph on the duties of the General Staff in the 1914 edition does list cyphers and censorship (of telegraphs, telephones, and cables), but no mention is made of intelligence collection from these sources. On the other

hand, an entire section of the *F.S.R.* discusses the proper use of airplanes and airships for reconnaissance.

77. Wing Comdr. M.T. Thurbon, "The Origins of Electronic Warfare," pp. 57-61. See also Maj. Gen. R.F.H. Nalder, *Royal Corps of Signals* (Royal Signals Institution, 1958). In October 1914, British wireless intercept was "reinforced by the arrival of the first wireless 'compass' station from France. This set was designed to give the accurate direction of any enemy station whose working it intercepted. . . . If two or more bearings could be obtained on any enemy station, within reasonable distance, the position of the latter could be accurately plotted." "The Signal Service in France, 1914-1919," (Institution of the Royal Engineers, 1921), Kirke Papers, A58, Intelligence Corps Museum, Ashford, Kent. Radio direction-finding techniques have improved greatly over the past seventy years and remain an excellent tool of intelligence collection today. The most impressive system now employed by NATO in Western Europe is the American "GUARD RAIL V," an airborne radio direction-finding system possessing an instantaneous "downlink" capability for the transmission of intelligence to ground stations.

78. Ibid., p. 57; David Kahn, *The Codebreakers*, pp. 313-14.

Chapter X

Preparation for a European War: British Strategic Military Intelligence, 1904-1914

> All things considered, however, the balance of opinion seems now to be in favour of a simultaneous left wheel of the (German) armies to the north of, and pivoted on, Metz, their right flank possibly reaching as far as Aix-la-Chapelle, with the main action in the direction of the Trovée de la Meuse. . . .
>
> British General Staff
> *Special Military Resources*
> *of the German Empire*, 1912

The South African War and a rapidly changing world scene stimulated more change within the War Office and the British Army during the final one and a half decades before World War I than during any comparable period between 1870 and 1914. The changes brought about in the field and in London during the conventional and counterguerrilla campaigns of 1899-1902 and those brought about by the various committees and commissions established by the government in the aftermath of the war, touched upon practically every aspect of the means by which the army prepared for and fought wars. Although the military capabilities of the Boer Republics were hardly comparable with those of Germany or of any other great power of the day, and though there were many unique features of the theater of war, the experience gained by the British Army in South Africa was of crucial importance in improving its readiness for war on the Continent. Such experience is never cheap. The cost of military triumph over a tough, stubborn, and unorthodox foe was unexpectedly high. Today, the price of Britain's victory in South Africa seems almost insignificant when measured against the immense expenditure of human lives and national wealth which characterized the conflict that erupted in the summer of 1914.[1] When compared with the countless small wars waged by Britain between 1856 and 1899, however, the South African War seemed costly indeed.

Long before the end of the second Anglo-Boer War in May 1902, it was apparent to Britain and her European rivals that Britain would lose more than men and materiel. The greatest cost of the South African War, at least when viewed from Berlin, St. Petersburg, and Paris, was a perceptible loss of British international prestige. The world's preeminent colonial power had found it necessary to deploy nearly half a million troops from throughout the Empire to South Africa. It had taken thirty-two months of fighting to defeat the Boers and to force their grudging acceptance of British sovereignty. The vulnerability of the British Isles to an invasion from the Continent during the latter stages of the war, not to mention the weakness of the British position in India, was obvious to all. The requirements of the South African War had drained Britain of virtually every regular and reserve army unit, and the burden of defending the United Kingdom against potential invaders rested almost entirely upon the navy. Had the Russians chosen this moment to move against Afghanistan and the Northwest Frontier of India, no reinforcements would have been available from England. The effect of the South African War upon the international position of Britain at the turn of the century was not unlike the effect of the Vietnam War upon the worldwide perception of American military power during the last decade. The fact that the British ultimately prevailed over the Boers made little difference in this respect.

The South African War contributed to a general weakening of Britain's military and diplomatic position, but her supremacy as a colonial and naval power had faced mounting challenges since the mid-1880s. Chancellor Otto von Bismarck's decision in 1884 to launch Germany on a vigorous quest for the acquisition of overseas colonies, together with the ambitious naval construction program designed by Adm. Alfred von Tirpitz and approved by the Reichstag in 1898 seemingly had placed Germany on a collision course with the British Empire. More importantly, German naval policy was designed deliberately to exploit, for colonial purposes, the strategic deadlock between Britain and her two traditional nineteenth-century rivals, France and Russia, which had concluded a military alliance in 1894. The accompanying German effort to organize a pro-Boer league of great powers had further exacerbated Anglo-German relations. The diplomatic isolation with regard to continental entanglements maintained throughout most of the nineteenth century by Britain now appeared to place her in a position of increasing jeopardy. By the late 1890s there were enormous pressures on the government and the Foreign Office to fundamentally alter the direction of British foreign policy.

For many Englishmen at the time, it was extremely difficult to perceive Germany as a potential enemy. Despite unmistakable indications of Berlin's growing coldness towards London, particularly after 1898, a number of influential men in the British government continued to believe that it was Russia that presented the greatest threat to the Empire.[2] Russian imperialism was now perceived as a menace to British interests, not only in the Near East and India, but in the Far East as well. The Foreign Office had not been particularly concerned about Russian activities in the Far East until the crisis precipitated by the Russian occupation of Port Arthur in December 1897. The principal objective of Britain's China policy, beginning in 1898, was to check the consolidation of Russia's control over Manchuria and to prevent her southward expansion.[3]

At times halfheartedly over the next three years, Britain sought an alliance with Germany in order to oppose Russia more effectively in the Far East. The notion that British and German objectives in China were practically identical, as proclaimed by Arthur Balfour and Joseph Chamberlain, turned out to be no more than wishful thinking. The first year of the South African War served to heighten still further the apprehensions in London about the dangers of isolation. A renewed effort to reach an accord with Berlin was mounted at the end of 1900 and during the first six months of 1901 by the new foreign secretary, Lord Lansdowne.[4] When this failed, pro-German sentiment inside the Foreign Office and the cabinet declined rapidly, and relations with France began to improve. Within War Office Intelligence and the Foreign Office, there was a growing conviction that Germany, not Russia, was Britain's most formidable and dangerous rival.[5] The problem of countering the Russian threat to the "Open Door" policy in China remained nonetheless.

Lansdowne was determined to improve Britain's position in the Far East and was willing to negotiate with any power, including Russia, which might enable him to attain his goal. After the breakdown of the Anglo-German talks, he tried several times to negotiate with the Russians in 1901. Lansdowne turned to the Japanese after failing to conclude an agreement with either Germany or Russia. The solution which the foreign secretary finally found for Britain's Chinese predicament had not even been seriously considered by his predecessor, Lord Salisbury. The Anglo-Japanese alliance was the first decisive break with the policy of "splendid isolation," and it was not an easy task for Lansdowne to convince the cabinet, headed by Salisbury, to support such a radical departure from the past.[6] The agreement between Britain and Japan, signed on 30 January 1902, was a defensive naval alliance which did not end Britain's diplomatic isolation from the European continent. It did, however, increase the pressure on Britain and France to improve relations with one another and thereby to avoid being drawn into war against each other by their allies.[7]

Like the British Foreign Office, the Quai d'Orsay entered a period of uncertainty and transition after 1898. The twin humiliations of the Dreyfus affair and the Fashoda crisis had brought France's international prestige to its lowest point since the defeat of 1870. The architect of the new course in French foreign policy, Théophile Delcassé, became foreign minister in June 1898, shortly before the Anglo-French confrontation at Fashoda. Delcassé's strong desire to strengthen France's international position during his tenure

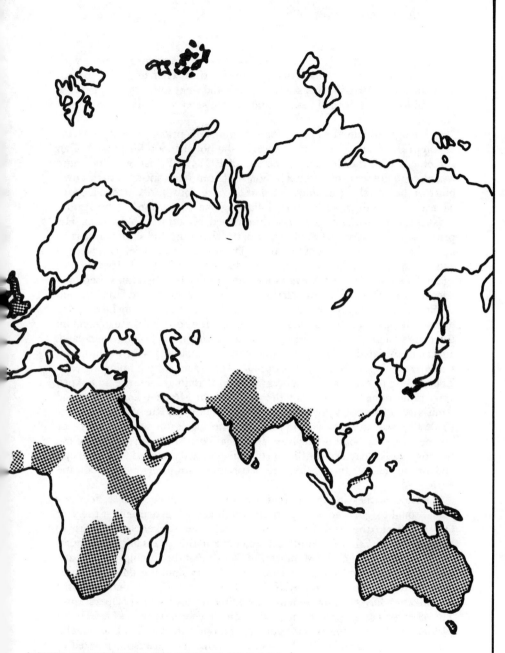

THE BRITISH EMPIRE IN 1914

at the Quai d'Orsay (1898-1905) and his interest in a rapprochement with London were evident from his first months in office, when he made repeated overtures to the British ambassador in Paris and went so far as to suggest the desirability of "a cordial understanding between England, France, and Russia."[8]

Though initially the French foreign minister's priority was the revitalization of the Franco-Russian alliance, he did not abandon his pursuit of an agreement with the British. By the end of 1901 the British were far more receptive to French diplomacy. The South African War continued to tie down much of the British Army, and, for a number of reasons, anti-German feelings were on the rise. In early 1902, following the conclusion of the Anglo-Japanese naval alliance, Delcassé intensified his efforts in London. His principal instrument was Paul Cambon, the charming and skillful ambassador of France at the Court of St. James. The main French objectives were to gain a "free hand" in Morocco and to avoid a future conflict with Britain. Once again, Delcassé did not achieve immediate results, but the atmosphere was encouraging. The improving relationship between France and Great Britain was given another boost in the spring of 1903 by the visit of King Edward VII to Paris. In July Lansdowne and Delcassé met at the Foreign Office in London; their discussion of colonial issues such as Morocco, Egypt, Newfoundland, and Siam initiated a process of diplomatic negotiations which culminated with the signing of the Entente Cordiale in the spring of the following year. The settling of colonial differences between Britain and France on 8 April 1904 came none too soon. On the day Foreign Minister Lansdowne and Ambassador Cambon signed the accords in London, the Russo-Japanese War (1904-05) was already two months old. The successful surprise attack by Japanese torpedo boats on the Russian fleet at Port Arthur on 8 February and the ensuing Far Eastern conflict further heightened the need for friendship and for the maintenance of channels of communication between London and Paris.

Besides witnessing the beginning of the Russo-Japanese War, February 1904 brought significant change to the Intelligence Department at the War Office. Within the War Office, several steps were taken that month to implement the Esher Committee's recommendation to establish a General Staff (see chapter V). The Mobilization Division of the Intelligence Department was transferred to the Directorate of Military Training, one of the three directorates of the General Staff. The Intelligence Department, less the Mobilization Division, was renamed the Directorate of Military Operations.[9] This change was effected rather rudely on 11 February, when Lt. Gen. Sir William Nicholson, the director general of mobilization and military intelligence, was replaced abruptly by Maj. Gen. James M. Grierson, selected by Esher as the first director of military operations (DMO). Col. (later Field Marshal Sir) Henry Wilson, who was in Nicholson's office discussing the chaotic atmosphere at the War Office when Grierson suddenly appeared, described the occasion in his diary.

> The Triumvirate (Lord Esher, Admiral Sir John Fisher, and Sir George S. Clarke) are carrying on like madmen. This morning I was in Nick's room

> talking over things with him . . . , when in walked Jimmy Grierson and
> said Esher had ordered him up from Salisbury to take over Nick's office.
> Nick himself had not been informed, nor had he been told to hand
> over. . . . This is most scandalous work.[10]

Apparently Esher was convinced that only if he and his colleagues moved swiftly and without warning to replace the senior military officers at the War Office was there any chance for rapid implementation of their controversial recommendations.

The major areas of responsibility assigned to the DMO in the General Staff organization designed by the Esher Committee—strategic planning and military intelligence—were no different from those handled by Sir William Nicholson's Intelligence Department, except for the absence of the mobilization function. More was expected of the DMO, however, in the development of strategic plans for the defense of Britain and the Empire. The internal organization of the Directorate was almost identical to that of its predecessor, although the number of personnel assigned rose from seventy-seven to ninety-four during the first eight months of its existence. In this same period, officer strength was increased from thirty-one to forty-three. A fourth section was added to the three carried over from the Intelligence Department by transferring the topographic subsection from the Special Duties Section. Thus, the four sections of the Directorate of Military Operations in 1904 were as follows: MO 1—Strategical Section; MO 2—Foreign Intelligence Section; MO 3—Administration and Special Duties; and MO 4—Topographical Section.[11]

Commensurate with its heavier responsibilities, the Strategical Section was enlarged; it now had four, rather than two, subsections and was manned by seventeen personnel, including ten officers.[12] Due to the loss of the mapmaking function, MO 3 became the smallest of the four sections, responsible for only "special duties" and the General Staff Library. "Special duties" included censorship, counterintelligence, and, apparently, covert intelligence operations.[13] During the first months of the South African War, the Special Duties Section (then Section H) first appeared in the Intelligence Department. Section H, headed by Maj. James E. Edmonds from 1899 to 1901, provided administrative support to the DMI and the entire Department and was also responsible for "cable censorship, surveillance of suspected persons in conjunction with Scotland Yard, press correspondents, enquiries regarding prisoners of war," and "violations of [the] Geneva Convention."[14] The Special Duties Section of 1904 was nearly identical in both size and function to Edmonds's Section H, except for the addition of the library. The new Topographic Section (MO 4) was charged with the collection of topographical information, the compilation and storage of maps, the issue of maps for war, and the selection of officers for topographical work. As in the days of the old T&S Department (1855-73), many of the people working in the Topographical Section were civilians.[15]

MO 2, the Foreign Intelligence Section, experienced the largest increases in officers and total personnel during the period immediately after the formation of the Directorate of Military Operations.[16] Increasing specialization within the various War Office intelligence organizations, with regard to the collection, analysis, and production of military intelligence, is a continual trend in the story of British military intelligence since 1870. This is well documented in the steady growth of foreign intelligence section(s), from the Statistical Section (one officer) of 1870, through the four foreign sections of the 1880s and 1890s (eight officers) and the six subsections of the Foreign and Indian Section of late 1903 (fourteen officers), down to the eight subsections and twenty-one officers of MO 2 in 1904. The addition of two new subsections in 1904 was a reflection of the War Office's renewed interest in the United States and the Far East.[17] The British now rated the United States a great power. As a consequence, Canada seemed less defensible than in the nineteenth century, and the threat posed by the world's newest great power was all the more dangerous.

Col. William R. Robertson, head of the Foreign and Indian Section of the Intelligence Department from late 1901 until the establishment of the Directorate of Military Operations in early 1904, continued to perform the same duties as assistant director of military operations (ADMO), MO 2, until January 1907. The able, hard-working Robertson won rapid promotions while working his way into the upper echelons of War Office Intelligence under Sir John Ardagh and Sir William Nicholson. Less than one year after his return from duty with the Field Intelligence Department in South Africa, Robertson's selection as head of the Foreign Section over a number of officers with more seniority in the Intelligence Department won him a brevet lieutenant colonelcy and the guarantee of promotion to colonel in three years. In his own words, Robertson went from being "one of the oldest lieutenants in the army" to being "one of the youngest colonels" between 1895 and 1903. Colonel Robertson got along very well with Sir William Nicholson, and in his memoirs expressed sympathy for the way the DGMI was removed by the Esher Committee in 1904. Fortunately, he was equally comfortable with the new DMO, an individual he described as "my old friend Grierson."[18] "Jimmy" Grierson and "Wully" Robertson shared the conviction that Germany was Britain's main enemy.[19] In any case, Robertson's reputation within the War Office and the Foreign Office was such that by the time Grierson arrived at Winchester House in 1904 it would have been difficult for any incoming DMO to remove him or to ignore his advice.

Grierson and Robertson were not the only top officials of the new Directorate of Military Operations with prior experience in War Office intelligence. The head of the Strategical Section (MO 1) was none other than Col. Edward A. Altham, who had served a three-year tour in the Department (1897-99) prior to the South African War and, as chief of the Colonial Section, had been Robertson's superior in 1899. Altham returned from South Africa to the Department in late 1900 and, like Robertson, had been picked by General Nicholson to head one of the three sections following the reorganization of 1901. Considering Altham's previous duties in the Department, he was an excellent choice for the Strategical Section (also frequently called the Imperial Section). When Colonel Altham left the General Staff in the fall of 1904, his replacement as ADMO, MO 1, was another veteran (1887-92) of the Intelligence Department, Col. Charles E. Callwell. Robertson's successor as ADMO, MO 2, Col. Edward Gleichen, had served two earlier tours in the Department (1886-88 and 1894-99) and was military attaché in Berlin (1903-06). At the head of the Special Duties Section and MO 3 during this period was Col. James K. Trotter, whose first tour in War Office Intelligence lasted five years (1890-95). The reservoir of experience among these officers, not to mention the personal ties they had developed with one another, gave General Grierson and the Directorate of Military Operations a well-prepared, uniquely qualified group of individuals in key positions during a critical period of diplomatic realignment and strategic planning.

The interrelationship of strategic intelligence, military planning, and diplomacy within the British government in the pre-World War I era is illustrated by the role of the Directorate of Military Operations in the transformation of the Entente Cordiale from a colonial agreement of 1904 into what was practically an Anglo-French military alliance against Germany by early 1913. From the first days of the Directorate in 1904, General Grierson and Colonel Robertson were convinced that the likelihood of an Anglo-German war was so great "that the only policy consistent with the interests of the Empire was an active alliance with France and Belgium. . . ."[20] The First Moroccan Crisis, touched off by the landing of Kaiser Wilhelm II at Tangier on 31 March 1905, provided the first severe challenge to the Entente. Contrary to the expectations of the German Foreign Office, the British offered strong support to French Foreign Minister Delcassé in the face of the German provocations and, instead of falling apart, the Entente was strengthened. Adm. Sir John Fisher, the first sea lord and one of the "triumvirs," contributed to the war scare during the first Moroccan Crisis by talking openly of a preventive war against Germany.[21] Meanwhile, the possibility that the crisis might erupt into a full-scale Franco-German or European war reaffirmed Grierson's notion that the Directorate ought to conduct a thorough examination of German military capabilities against France on the Continent, including the invasion of Belgium, and to develop strategic options for the employment of the British Army in the event of such a war. Actually, the DMO had ordered his staff to begin just such a study in January 1905; by the time the Kaiser made his famous ride through the streets of Tangier, the concluding phase of this project, the "strategic war game" of April and May 1905, was about to get under way.[22]

Sometime in the latter half of 1904, General Grierson, assisted by Colonels Robertson and Callwell, had initiated a series of studies aimed at developing strategies that Britain might adopt in case of war with Russia, France, or Germany. The most ambitious and realistic of these endeavors was launched at the beginning of 1905, when the DMO directed MO 1 and MO 2 to prepare a war game which would begin with a German attack on France. It was assumed that a portion of the German Army would violate Belgian neutrality in order to outflank French fortifications and Britain would be drawn into the conflict by its treaty obligation to aid Belgium.[23] The primary purpose of the war game was to "elucidate the problems with which Britain might as a consequence be faced."[24] Colonel Robertson acted as the German commander when the game was played during April and May. The campaign plan he worked out was similar in many ways to the Schlieffen Plan developed in 1905 by the chief of the German General Staff. Once the German Army moved into Belgium with eight corps (473,050 men) to break the stalemate which had developed along the Franco-German frontier, the small Belgian Army (100,000 men) was doomed without prompt British reinforcement, or so the war game indicated. The main conclusion derived by General Grierson and his associates from this exercise was that the intervention of a relatively small British force against German lines of communications in Belgium might turn the tide of a Franco-German war. If the Belgians could hold on by themselves initially, "an Anglo-Belgian force would be able to apply effective pressure on the German communications system after the tenth day of British mobilization." The DMO's "strategic war game" of April and May 1905 constituted "the first thorough British evaluation of the problems of continental warfare" during the pre-World War I period.[25]

Grierson and Robertson continued their study of the problems raised in the war game. In the summer of 1905 they visited together "portions of the Franco-Belgian frontier on which much of the fighting in 1914 took place."[26] The knowledge they gained from their deliberations and travels during the first half of 1905 proved to be useful in August. Prime Minister Arthur Balfour asked the DMO for an assessment of Belgium's ability, if supported by Britain, to cope with a violation of her borders by either Germany or France and for an analysis of the advantages either country might derive from the invasion of Belgium. Prompted by the secretary of the Committee of Imperial Defence (C.I.D.), Sir George S. Clarke, Balfour also wanted to know how quickly two British Army corps could be landed in Belgium. The DMO's response, completed in September, reflected the thinking of Grierson and Robertson and the results of the war game. German violation of Belgian neutrality was considered extremely likely; twenty-three days were needed to transport two corps to Belgium.[27]

As planning for the employment of the British Army on the Continent progressed within the General Staff throughout 1905, discussions with the French General Staff became increasingly desirable to General Grierson and others. The DMO realized that the detailed plans and arrangements necessary for successful British intervention on the Continent could not be finalized without direct coordination with the French, as well as with the Belgians. At the same time, and for reasons of its own, the French high command was seeking more information about the British Army, particularly its potential as a French ally on the Continent against the Germans. The alleged defection of a senior German officer, calling himself the "Vengeur," had given the Second Bureau (intelligence) of the French General Staff "a fairly accurate impression of Count von Schlieffen's current thinking" in early 1904. The revelations of the "Vengeur" provoked a long and acrimonious debate among France's military leaders about whether or not the current French war plan, Plan XV, should be revised to counter the flanking maneuver through southern Belgium by nine German corps foretold by the mysterious defector.[28]

Though skeptical of the new information, Generalissimo Henri Brugère, the officer designated to become the wartime commander-in-chief of
the French Army, directed a secret reconnaissance of the German border
during the winter of 1904-05. The results convinced him an attack through
Belgium was a definite possibility, and in 1905 he modified Plan XV accordingly, although he still believed the main German effort would occur in
Alsace-Lorraine. In addition to indications the Germans were planning to
move through Belgium, there were several other significant developments in
1905 which made the idea of British military cooperation more attractive to
French military leaders. The weakness of the Russian Army in the wake of its
defeat at the hands of the Japanese and the French military attaché's surprisingly positive assessment of the British Army, especially its excellent performance in the summer maneuvers of 1903, caused Brugère and others to
look across the Channel with rising interest. Unflinching British support for
France during the First Moroccan Crisis fueled widespread speculation in
France about the likelihood of an Anglo-French alliance. In November 1905
Generalissimo Brugère asked Lt. Col. Victor Huguet, the French military
attaché in London, for a private estimate of the capabilities of the British
Army to mobilize and move a sizable force to the Continent. The information
Huguet was able to assemble for the generalissimo was not obtained from the
most authoritative sources. Consequently, he overstated British capabilities
slightly, but this only served to whet Brugère's appetite for cross-Channel
staff talks. Even as Huguet was working on his special report for Brugère,
Gen. Jean Brun, the French chief of staff, initiated his own study of the
possible contributions of the British Army against the Germans on the
Continent.[29] In the military sphere, at least, the stage was set for the Anglo-
French military conversations of 1905-06.

The question of whether it was the British or the French who initiated
the military and naval conversations which began in December 1905 has
never been answered in full. Certainly, the general staffs of both powers
wanted the conversations, and, given the prolonged tensions between France
and Germany which subsided only after the Algeciras Conference of early
1906, they were practically inevitable. This is not to say that the general staffs
were solely responsible for the "unofficial" conversations which occurred
between 20 December 1905 and 15 January 1906 or for the "official" staff
talks authorized thereafter by the British Foreign Office.[30] As important as
were the roles played by French Ambassador Cambon, Sir George Clarke of
the C.I.D., Charles à Court Repington, and others, the crucial first meetings
were those between Colonel Huguet and Major General Grierson on 20-21
December. These conversations between the French military attaché and the
director of military operations constituted the only direct exchanges of
information between military personnel of the two countries during the
period of "unofficial" conversations. Sir George Clarke opened a second
"unofficial" channel through Huguet to the French General Staff in early
January, using Charles Repington as the intermediary. Like Grierson,
Repington was an old hand in War Office intelligence circles. The promising
army career of *The Times*'s military correspondent had ended abruptly three

years earlier, but Repington's previous assignments in military intelligence, as well as his particular expertise on the armies of France and Belgium, gave him strong qualifications for Clarke's delicate mission.[31]

Once the Anglo-French military conversations were officially sanctioned by the British Foreign Office in mid-January 1906, the active participation of Sir George Clarke and the Committee of Imperial Defence faded quickly. The logistical planning which now dominated the conversations did not concern the C.I.D. directly. From this point, the DMO had full responsibility for the conduct of joint military planning with the French (and Belgian) General Staffs. Grierson and Huguet held their first "official" meeting on 16 January, and they continued to meet frequently until the beginning of May. Two days later, the British military attaché in Brussels, acting under orders from Grierson, initiated Anglo-Belgian staff talks with the chief of the Belgian General Staff. Discussions with the Belgians were not conclusive and were never resumed after the spring of 1906. Those with the French, however, produced agreement on a number of details regarding the movement of British troops to the Continent, including the use of French, rather than Belgian, ports. These early Anglo-French agreements proved crucial because Antwerp—as port, fortress, and rail center—was rejected as an area of concentration for the British Expeditionary Force. Therefore, the B.E.F. in 1914 was positioned on the left wing of the French Army rather than in the rear of the German Army. General Grierson traveled to the Continent several times between January and May to inspect the ports offered by the French and the areas of northern France and Belgium to which British troops would likely be committed in the event of war with Germany.[32]

Over the four years between May 1906 and the arrival of Brigadier General Wilson as DMO in August 1910, the staff talks with the French continued sporadically and with little result. This was due in part to the departure of Grierson and his replacement by Maj. Gen. John Spencer Ewart in August 1906; the new DMO apparently did not get along with Huguet. The energies of Ewart, and indeed of the entire General Staff, were directed during these years to the organization and training of the British Expeditionary Force, without which the strategic planning of Grierson and Wilson would have been meaningless when the Germans marched into Belgium in 1914.[33]

Henry Wilson took over the Directorate of Military Operations following a tour as commandant of the Staff College at Camberley (1907-10). He brought to his new duties the conviction Europe would soon be at war, and the British must join with the French against the Germans. The future field marshal and chief of the Imperial General Staff was an ardent advocate of British Army participation on the Continent. Building on the important work of his predecessors, Grierson and Ewart, and taking advantage of his own excellent contacts within the French high command, Wilson soon rejuvenated the dormant Anglo-French military conversations. At the same time, he pressed his subordinates, particularly Colonel Gleichen (head of MO 2-Foreign Intelligence Section), for more information about the German Army and for a fresh analysis of German war plans. The DMO also conducted personal reconnaissances of the Franco-Belgium area assigned to the British Expeditionary Force by the French General Staff, with special emphasis on the rail nets and the frontiers with Germany.[34] Henry Wilson was the DMO from the summer of 1910 until the beginning of World War I. Largely as the result of his energy and determination, by early 1913 there existed detailed and workable plans for the rapid movement of the B.E.F. to France. These plans, which had been thoroughly coordinated with the French General Staff, were further refined by Wilson and his staff prior to August 1914.[35]

The Entente Cordiale of 1904 was gradually transformed by the military conversations of 1905-13 into something closely resembling a military alliance. The military and diplomatic implications of these conversations were enormous. Without them, it is doubtful the British Army would have been able to make any significant contribution to the Allied war effort on the Continent in the critical opening months of World War I. The emergence of a continental school of military strategy within the Intelligence Department and its successor, the Directorate of Military Operations, between the end of the South African War and the spring of 1905, was an essential factor in British preparedness for and willingness to engage in staff talks with the French. Moreover, the three officers most closely associated with the creation and continued development of the continental school within the British General Staff in this era—William Robertson, James Grierson, and Henry Wilson—shared a similar perception of the threat posed to France and Europe by the German Army and of the German intention to invade Belgium as an integral part of their plan to defeat France. Although after 1904 only Robertson was involved primarily in intelligence, as opposed to operations, all three had had previous assignments in military intelligence. Generals Grierson and Wilson demonstrated, throughout their respective tours as DMO, a full appreciation of the need for good intelligence as a prerequisite for strategic planning. Both men took a strong personal interest in the collection as well as the production of strategic military intelligence by the Directorate they headed.

The growth of a continental school inside the Directorate of Military Operations prior to 1906 was welcomed by several key officials at the Foreign Office,[36] but it met with a less than enthusiastic response from the naval imperialists of the Admiralty and the Committee of Imperial Defence. From its birth in 1902[37] until the beginning of the military (and naval) conversations with France in 1905-06, the C.I.D. was dominated by the senior service and the supporters of the "blue water" school, which included Prime Minister Arthur Balfour. The strategic view of the "blue water" school was that the army was no longer needed for home defense since the Royal Navy alone was fully capable of defeating any attempted invasions of the British Isles. The army's most important mission would continue to be the defense of India against the Russians. In a broader sense, the army would concern itself mainly with the threat posed by the Dual Alliance to the overseas Empire.

By the time the Directorate of Military Operations began to give serious consideration to plans to intervene against the German Army on the Continent in 1905, the Russian Empire's recent defeat in the Far East had weakened the navy's argument that British troops could not be withdrawn from India. Rather than supporting the DMO's war plan to move British divisions to France or Belgium, however, the Admiralty countered with a plan to conduct amphibious operations on the north coast of Germany. Adm. Sir John Fisher, the First Sea Lord and a member of the C.I.D., encountered stiff opposition from the DMO and Sir George Clarke, secretary of the C.I.D., during the final stage of the "unofficial" conversations in January 1906. Angered at the rejection of his ill-conceived plan for a Baltic operation, Fisher adamantly refused to agree to provide transports to ferry troops across the Channel. This led to a bitter clash between Fisher and Clarke, long a reliable ally of the Royal Navy, and to the withdrawal of the first sea lord and the director of naval intelligence from the C.I.D. "After this time, Fisher virtually boycotted the C.I.D. in protest of Clarke's intrusions into what the Admiral regarded as his special province."[38]

The Admiralty's sudden abdication of its powerful position within the Committee of Imperial Defence dealt a crushing blow to any remaining hopes that the C.I.D. might function as a center of strategic planning for the British Empire. One of the major recommendations of the Esher Committee in 1904 had been to establish a permanent nucleus of the C.I.D. (see chapter VI) headed by a permanent secretary. Lord Esher "wanted it to take the form of a joint general staff that was to supersede the planning and intelligence functions of the Admiralty and the War Office, and directly to control naval and military attachés abroad."[39] Had Esher's goal to construct a general staff for the cabinet been realized, the secretariat of the C.I.D. eventually would have replaced the Directorate of Military Operations in both operational and intelligence matters. In fact, if the control of naval and military attachés had been wrested from the Foreign Office, the C.I.D.'s control of strategic intelligence—collection, production, and dissemination—would have been far more extensive than that exercised by either the War Office or the Admiralty in previous years. Lord Esher's dream was not to be. Instead, the events of January 1906 convinced Sir John Fisher and the Admiralty that Sir George Clarke and the C.I.D. had betrayed them. From that point, the Admiralty refused to provide leadership to the organization it had once nurtured and loyally supported. Despite the best efforts of Sir George Clarke, the crippled C.I.D. never recovered, at least in the vital area of strategic planning. The Admiralty simply ignored the C.I.D., while "the War Office adhered only to those decisions which it found to its liking."[40] Strategic military intelligence, except for the control of military attachés, remained entirely in the hands of the director of military operations and his staff.

Britain's military attachés were a more important source of intelligence than ever before, during the decade prior to World War I. On the Continent they had been vital to the War Office's collection effort since 1864, when the Foreign Office first appointed military attachés to Berlin, Vienna, and St. Petersburg.[41] After 1902, growing Anglo-German hostility, increasing British involvement in the affairs of Europe, the Russo-Japanese War, and the blossoming military entente with France all contributed to a heavier workload for the attachés and to the closer scrutiny given their reports by the

Foreign Office and the Admiralty, not to mention by the Directorate of Military Operations. In certain capitals the work of British military attachés was not limited to the observation of the host country's armed forces and to the collection of intelligence. The role of the British military attaché in Brussels in the initiation of staff talks with the Belgian General Staff in 1906 has already been mentioned. Sir George Clarke had contemplated a similar assignment for the British attaché in Paris in December 1905, until Repington's timely offer to act as an intermediary between Clarke and the French attaché in London solved the C.I.D.'s problem of how to initiate direct contacts with the French General Staff.[42] Though the duties of the British attaché in St. Petersburg were confined to the more traditional work of furnishing information about the Russian Army, his job was probably the most challenging of any of London's military attachés, except for the one in Berlin. The signing of the Anglo-Russian Convention in August 1907, which completed the Triple Entente and sent shock waves through the German Foreign Office, changed little in this regard.[43]

During the years 1904-14, the British attaché in Berlin was in the most critical position for the collection of strategic military intelligence. Reports written by the several officers who served in this post were read with particular interest in London. In the Foreign Office, Eyre Crowe, a specialist in German affairs who was also keenly interested in military tactics, paid close attention to the observations of Col. Edward Gleichen (attaché in Berlin from 1903 to 1906) and his successors.

> Crowe's interest in military matters led him to read and comment on almost all the reports of the service attachés in Germany. There is hardly one of these despatches which escaped Crowe's amplifications or corrections and his comments were read with interest and approval by both Hardinge [permanent undersecretary] and Grey.[44]

The Directorate of Military Operations provided the reports of the military attachés to the Admiralty's Naval Intelligence Department in exchange for reports from naval attachés. Within the N.I.D., the naval and marine officers of the Intelligence Division read and collated attaché reports with other information. Those sent from Berlin found their way to the Intelligence Division's busy German Section.[45]

The reports of Britain's military attachés certainly were of interest to the Foreign Office and to the Naval Intelligence Department, but they were absolutely essential to the work of the Foreign Intelligence Section (MO 2). MO 2 was, after all, charged with the

> Collection, Preparation, and Distribution of information concerning the Military Geography, Resources, and Armed Forces of all Foreign Countries. Supply of information regarding India and Adjoining territories. Questions relating to the defence of India, other than those concerning coast defences. Correspondence with Military Attachés. Examination of Foreign Journals and Literature generally.[46]

Information from the attachés was analyzed and collated with information from all other available sources by the various subsections. Questions and requests for more information from the attachés were formulated within the

Foreign Intelligence Section and dispatched back overseas. In the words of Charles à Court Repington, military attaché at Brussels and The Hague after the South African War, "The War Office overwhelmed me with subjects for reports, mainly of a technical character. . . ."[47] To be effective as a collector of intelligence, a military attaché had to spend a good deal of time outside of the capital. Among other things, he was expected to attend army maneuvers and to produce detailed reports on them for MO 2. Most or all of the material used in compiling handbooks on foreign armies was provided by attachés.

Though Britain's military attachés in the pre-World War I era were heavily tasked to gather information, they were not expected to engage in "secret service" and were warned to avoid even the slightest involvement in covert collection. Repington's views on "secret service" were in accord with official British policy.

> I would never do any secret service work. My view is that the Military Attaché is the guest of the country to which he is accredited, and must only see and learn that which is permissible for a guest to investigate. Certainly he must keep his eyes and ears open and miss nothing, but secret service is not his business, and he should always refuse a hand in it. An ambitious young officer revels in secrets and secret information out of sheer keenness, but he is quite sure to get into a mess if he indulges in it.[48]

With the exception of Russia, beginning in the 1890s, practically all of the European powers had ordered their military and naval attachés to stay clear of espionage. Before 1914 Russia's espionage system was "more under the immediate direction of her service attachés than that of any other great power."[49] German attachés were strictly prohibited from using "illegal sources of information" and apparently had "at last taken to heart Caprivi's instructions against spying, as patently more honest and certainly more practical."[50] For Britain's attachés, as well as those of other countries, the opportunities to get involved in "secret service" were ample. It was "quite common for agents to be sent to a new Military Attaché in order to tempt and test him, or for letters to be sent to him offering him important information on payment."[51]

Because the British military attaché traveled extensively outside of his assigned capital, he often was more in touch with the mood of his host country and sometimes better informed about political and economic developments in the country at large than anyone else at the embassy. Repington observed the staff of a British Embassy or Legation

> had no responsibility except for chancery work and routine, seldom travelled much in the countries where they lived, and were hardly ever ordered to use their brains and report upon movements of opinion, trade affairs, and all the manifold interests of the country. . . . I thought it indispensable to get the secretaries out of the narrow diplomatic and official circles of the capitals, where they tended to become cavemen. . . . The Military Attaché was not uncommonly the man who knew the most about the country, because he travelled about and saw all classes of society.[52]

From the perspective of the Foreign Office, military attachés provided valuable information to British ambassadors, not all of which was of interest to the War Office and the General Staff—all the more reason for the Foreign Office to retain firm control of the attachés.

Probably more than at any time in the half century since the first British military attachés were posted in Turin and Paris at the end of the Crimean War, between 1904 and 1914 London's attachés had to satisfy two masters. They remained under Foreign Office control, as always, and their reports had to be cleared by an ambassador before they could be released for transmittal via telegraph or courier back to England. The Foreign Office had the final say in all service attaché appointments, and an ambassador who was displeased with an attaché, for whatever reason, could demand his recall. At the same time, the specific intelligence collection requirements for military attachés normally originated in MO 2 and were approved by the DMO. As the likelihood of a European war increased during these years, the assignments received by the attachés, especially those in Berlin, Vienna, and St. Petersburg, grew more numerous and more demanding.

Although the Foreign Office had to approve all military attaché appointments, officers were nominated for attaché posts by the DMO. The DMO, in turn, only had to gain the concurrence of the chief of the General Staff before forwarding a nomination to the Foreign Office. Generally, it was mandatory that a prospective attaché be fluent in the language of the country to which he was being assigned, and it was highly desirable that he had served a tour in the Directorate of Military Operations, or its predecessor, the Intelligence Department. Unfortunately, even after a thorough discussion of the need for more care in the selection of military attachés by the Hardwicke Committee in 1903 (see chapter VI), some poorly qualified officers still managed to obtain attaché assignments. Sir William Robertson, head of MO 2 until 1907, recalled officers selected as military attachés

> who, besides being unsuitable on military grounds, had no knowledge of the language of the country to which they were sent, or of any other except their own. . . . In the case of more than one military attaché the lack of a reasonable knowledge of the language of the country was responsible for many ludicrous as well as alarming reports being sent to us, and it was no doubt answerable for our not receiving much information that ought to have been sent.[53]

Two nineteenth-century prerequisites for service attachés of all countries, "social qualities" and "private means," remained important considerations in the selection of British officers for attaché duty prior to 1914. Britain's military attachés "were for the most part underpaid, and all were paid at the same rate, irrespective of the particular capital to which they were accredited." Unfortunately, the Treasury was "unmoved" by the fact that "Paris life was infinitely more expensive than life at Peking, and that the amount of information procurable by a military attaché was largely governed by the amount of money he could spend in entertaining those from whom he might hope to procure it. . . ." Consequently, in some cases otherwise well-qualified officers were judged ineligible for attaché assignments simply because they were not independently wealthy. Colonel Robertson "tried to ensure that only properly qualified officers should be selected, but the exterior influences mentioned sometimes proved to be too strong for me."[54]

A special group of British military attachés, including three generals, was appointed in 1904 to function as observers on both sides during the Russo-Japanese War (1904-05). This was the last major conflict before 1914 during which observers from all of the world's great powers were present on both sides. Japan and Great Britain were allies, but the latter remained neutral throughout the war and was thereby able to send military and naval attachés to both the Russians and the Japanese. Twenty-seven foreign attachés were sent to the headquarters of the Russian Army in Manchuria. Two of the three British military attachés with the Russians, Lt. Gen. Sir Montagu Gerard and Col. W.H.H. Waters, had served previously as attachés in St. Petersburg, and, like the majority of British officers, both expected a Russian victory. Gerard and Waters were surprised when the Russians lost battle after battle, but they interpreted the results differently. General Gerard thoroughly revised his once favorable opinion of the Russian Army. Colonel Waters, on the other hand, criticized Russian weaknesses, but generally portrayed the losing side as a highly potent fighting force which had suffered from inept leadership. Waters and the third British attaché, Maj. J.M. Home, downplayed the magnitude of Russia's defeats on land in the Far East. In their view, the Russian Army emerged from the war with a tarnished reputation, but still posed a major threat to the British Empire. Gerard's death in Siberia during his return voyage to to England and the loss of all his notes on the war greatly reduced the impact of his assessments of the Russian Army, as compared with the notes of Waters and Home, which were published several years after the war. British military attachés furnished William Robertson's Foreign Intelligence Section with a mass of useful information about the Russian Army in action in 1904-05, but they underestimated the severity of the Russian defeats at the hands of the Japanese.[55] In contrast, Britain's naval attachés tended to be overly generous in praising the Japanese Navy's performance. The differences in the reporting of military and naval attachés in the Far East pointed to an increasing need to attain balance in overall national assessments.

While British military attachés overestimated Russian military power both before and after the Russo-Japanese War, there was also a tendency to underestimate the Japanese Army, particularly before the conflict. The British attaché in Tokyo, Col. A.G. Churchill, was typical in this regard and was a principle contributor to the prewar appraisal. Churchill was critical of the crude assault tactics used by the Japanese during peacetime maneuvers and suggested that their success in the Sino-Japanese War (1894-95) and the Boxer Rebellion (1900) had given them an undeserved reputation. There were several notable dissenters who expected the Japanese to do well against the Russians. They included Lord Roberts, then commander-in-chief, and Sir Ian Hamilton, one of the senior military attachés who joined the Japanese at the outset of the war and an officer of considerable talent who later commanded the ill-fated Dardanelles expedition in World War I. Both Roberts and Hamilton predicted a Japanese victory.[56]

The large contingent of British military attachés who accompanied the Japanese army in 1904-05 was headed by Lt. Gens. Sir William Nicholson and Sir Ian Hamilton.[57] The decisive victories of the Japanese on land and sea vindicated the confidence of Lord Roberts and Sir Ian Hamilton in Japanese military power and impressed all British observers with the Japanese in the theater of war. Taken as a whole, the British military attachés' reports reflected an admiration for the fighting qualities of the Japanese soldier and the professionalism and leadership of Japanese officers. For a variety of reasons, however, Japan's prestige in England declined rapidly after the war and British officers reverted to their old criticisms of the Japanese Army's performance on maneuvers. In British eyes, after 1905 the Japanese appeared to have discarded what they had learned in combat. During peacetime maneuvers, the tactics of the Japanese Army most closely resembled those of the Germans; they demonstrated little imagination or tactical innovation. In contrast, many British officers (including even Sir Ian Hamilton, who visited Russia in 1908 and 1909) were sufficiently impressed with what they saw of the Russian Army on maneuvers to report that "remarkable progress" had been made since 1905. Only the French Army rated higher marks from British observers for its performance on maneuvers.[58]

The success of an army during maneuvers was not necessarily indicative of how it would fare in actual battle. This was amply demonstrated in 1904-05 and again in 1914. The French Army of these years rarely failed to impress the British officers who witnessed its annual maneuvers. The French were dashing and encouraged initiative in their officers. By comparison, the Germans appeared to be stolid and unresourceful, their tactics obsolete. The British General Staff's 1906 *Report on Foreign Manoeuvers* stated,

> of the great continental armies it would appear that the German is still the most conservative. . . . There is no doubt that the impression left on the mind after attending German Manoeuvres is the excellence of the staff work. . . . the material—men and horses—is excellent; the officers good, with a striking level of efficiency. . . . But it is evident that a long period of peace has produced its effect on the methods of actual fighting adopted, so that very heavy losses are likely to be incurred in war unless more attention is paid to invisibility, rapidity of movement under fire, head cover and defilading devices in entrenchment, and the avoidance of movements to a flank under fire.[59]

In the same report, the following comments were offered about the French army:

> The admirable staff arrangements, from the army corps down to those of battalions, were striking. . . . In fact, the French staff can now compare with the best in Europe. . . . Such a thing as a conventional formation for attack or defence seems now to be entirely eliminated from the military mind. This has taken some years to effect, but the gospel of independence and of adaption of formations to the ground has been so long and carefully preached that it has at any rate in the 2nd Army Corps, at length borne fruit.[60]

Most British officers failed to appreciate the different attitudes of the French and Germans with respect to maneuvers. Like the British, the French saw them as an opportunity to evaluate the initiative of officers and men, while the Germans used them to test plans developed by the General Staff. British officers who read about the results of foreign maneuvers, either in the annual reports produced by the War Office or in professional journals, hardly could be blamed for concluding that the French Army alone was a match for the German Army, despite French inferiority in heavy artillery and other equipment. Overly optimistic assessments of both the French and Russian armies, based solely on their annual autumn extravaganzas, led many British officers to expect France and Russia could defeat Germany and Austria without help from England.[61] The prevailing opinion among British soldiers about the pre-1914 European strategic balance should not, however, be confused with the official intelligence estimates developed by MO 2 and circulated within the General Staff and other branches of the government. After all, the Military Operations Directorate's Foreign Intelligence Section had many other sources of information, upon which its officers were able to draw when preparing reports and estimates.

MO 2's chief sources of information differed little from those used by the Intelligence Branch/Department during the final quarter of the nineteenth century. All have been discussed in earlier chapters and by now will be quite familiar. They are as follows: British officers (excluding attachés and officers from MO 2) and civilians traveling or living abroad; British and foreign periodicals, newspapers, books, and other publications; espionage directed by the Secret Intelligence Service (SIS) and usually funded by the Foreign Office; covert or semicovert collection operations ("secret service") run by MO 3, the Administration and Special Duties Section; material made available by other departments of the British government, mainly the Foreign Office, the Admiralty, the Colonial Office, and the India Office; and special reconnaissance conducted by officers of MO 2 inside the countries for which they were responsible.[62]

Beginning in December 1905, there was one important new reservoir of military intelligence. As a consequence of Britain's diplomatic realignment with respect to the Continent, the intelligence services of friendly powers became available, particularly those of France. French military intelligence had been weakened by the Dreyfus affair of the 1890s, but it had recovered sufficiently by 1904 to have acquired a reasonably accurate understanding of German war plans, as mentioned earlier in this chapter. Though it is highly unlikely that the Second Bureau[63] revealed all of its sources or methods of collection, or even all of the information at its disposal, to the British, the Anglo-French military conversations, which began at the end of 1905 and continued intermittently until August 1914, certainly involved the sharing of intelligence. Colonel Huguet's willingness to discuss the Second Bureau's estimate of Germany's military capabilities and intentions with Major General Grierson during their meetings of December 1905 through May 1906 helped create an atmosphere of mutual trust and goodwill between the General Staffs of two traditional enemies. This positive atmosphere was reinforced in September 1906 when Grierson attended the French maneuvers and afterwards "had a most interesting conversation, mainly on strategical subjects and questions of organisation and defence," with the French chief of staff, General Brun.[64]

Unfortunately, the quality of the Second Bureau's estimates of German intentions declined after the first round of Anglo-French military conversations in 1905-06.[65] It was, nevertheless, valuable for MO 2 to be able to obtain an occasional glimpse of current French intelligence regarding the German Army, if only to understand better the war plans of Britain's potential ally. The exchange of military intelligence between the British and French General Staffs prior to 1914 was dependent on the status of the staff talks and the personal relationships of the three DMOs (James Grierson, John Spencer Ewart, and Henry Wilson) with various French officers. This was apparent following Grierson's departure from the War Office in 1906. During Ewart's tour as DMO (1906-10), Anglo-French staff talks were virtually nonexistent. When they were revived by his successor, Henry Wilson, in the fall of 1910, MO 2 again began receiving information from its counterpart across the Channel.

While commandant of the Staff College at Camberley (1907-10) just prior to becoming DMO, Henry Wilson had developed a lasting friendship with Gen. Ferdinand Foch, the commandant of the Ecole Supérieure de Guerre. As DMO, Wilson continued to maintain close ties with Foch and, through him, gained access to many other French military leaders and to the inner sanctums of the French General Staff. The DMO also got along very well with Colonel Huguet, still the French military attaché in London. General Wilson's numerous visits to Paris between 1910 and 1914 and his frank exchanges with Foch, Huguet, and other French officers produced obvious dividends for British intelligence. His first trip abroad, after assuming his new duties as DMO in August 1910, was a visit to France in response to an invitation from Ferdinand Foch. The visit was interrupted when Foch was called away suddenly to attend Russian maneuvers as the guest of Czar Nicholas II. Wilson was back in Paris again in October 1910 for the wedding of Foch's daughter and, during his stay, managed to spend several hours in private conversation with the bride's father, who had just returned from Russia. Foch not only offered the DMO a blunt appraisal of the Russian Army, but also revealed details from a Russian secret service report about the German General Staff.[66]

Henry Wilson also dealt directly with several chiefs of the French General Staff, who apparently were willing to share the secrets of the Second Bureau with him. Of course these men, especially Gen. Joseph Joffre (1911-14), had an ulterior motive; they wanted to secure as firm a commitment as possible from the British for the employment of the British Expeditionary Force (B.E.F.) in the event of a German attack through Belgium against France. The DMO's third trip to Paris occurred in March 1911, while he was en route to England after a visit to Berlin. Wilson's visit with the French General Staff included "half an hour's talk on secret affairs" with the chief of staff, Gen. Laffert de Ladibat. Another trip to the French capital in July 1911 brought the DMO into contact with Colonel Vignol, head of the Second Bureau. In late September Colonel Huguet told General Wilson that British intelligence, in the opinion of the French General Staff, had "overrated German numbers and dates of concentration." Wilson was also invited to attend a special meeting at the French War Office on 29 September. Present at the meeting, in addition to Wilson and Huguet, were Gen. Joseph Joffre, the new chief of the General Staff (also the wartime commander-in-chief designate) and a number of his key subordinates, including Colonel Vignol. The DMO was briefed in detail on the latest French intelligence estimates of German intentions and on the revision of Plan XVI, completed at Joffre's insistence earlier in September. Wilson recorded in his dairy,

> They were most cordial and open. They showed me papers and maps, copies of which they are giving me, showing the concentration areas of their northern armies. Intensely interesting. Then they showed me papers and maps . . . showing in detail the area of concentration for all our Expeditionary Forces.[67]

Joffre, later the architect of the Allied victory against the Germans in the First Battle of the Marne in 1914, was deeply concerned about the dangers to the French Army of a powerful German drive into Belgium, but the Second Bureau was unable to provide definitive information about the probability and extent of such a maneuver.[68] General Joffre also showed far more interest in the role of the B.E.F. than had his predecessors, and he quickly realized Henry Wilson would serve as a strong advocate for the French cause within the British General Staff and at Whitehall in general. For these reasons, it is doubtful any information of significance about Germany's military capabilities or intentions obtained by the Second Bureau between September 1911 and the outbreak of World War I was not passed on to MO 2 in London.

Strategic communications intelligence, derived primarily from the intercept and decoding of telegraphic and wireless radio messages, was a vital facet of French intelligence over which the Second Bureau exercised little or no control. This form of intelligence was, incidentally, an area in which Britain was a relative latecomer. France gained a "commanding lead in cryptology"[69] in 1883 with the publication of Auguste Kerckhoff's classic, *La Cryptographie militaire*,[70] a lead which she retained for thirty years and carried into the First World War. According to David Kahn, France had "a preponderant cryptologic superiority in 1914." There were two important centers of cryptology in France during this period: the Military Cryptography Commission, consisting of "approximately ten officers chosen from among all arms who had shown an aptitude for cryptanalysis," and the secret section of the Bureau de Chiffre (Cipher Office) at the Quai d'Orsay, also known as the *cabinet noir*. The former evaluated cipher systems used by other nations, particularly those of Germany. The latter was successful in at least partially breaking the diplomatic codes and ciphers of Italy, England, Germany, Turkey, and Japan, and probably those of the United States and Spain as well. The information it supplied to Théophile Delcassé and his successors "exercised an important and continuing . . . influence on the foreign policy of the Third Republic." The cryptanalysts of the *cabinet noir*

> continued to open diplomatic correspondence when the opportunity arose until at least 1914. From the time of the Second Empire onwards, however, its work had been immensely simplified by the increasing use of the telegraph for the transmission of diplomatic messages. Copies of all telegrams sent by foreign diplomats and newspaper correspondents

were passed on to the Quai d'Orsay as a matter of course by the French post office. The *cabinet noir* was thus increasingly able to concentrate on the important business of decipherment without wasting time on the complicated art of letter opening.[71]

During the 1890s there was frequent liaison between the Foreign Ministry's *cabinet noir* and the head of the Second Bureau,[72] and it is probable that this continued after 1900. The extent to which intelligence obtained by France's excellent pre-World War I cryptanalysis was passed on to the British is unknown. If, indeed, the information was passed, either directly from the Quai d'Orsay to the Foreign Office or from the Second Bureau to MO 2, it is almost certain that the recipients were not informed of the source.

Britain enjoyed great success in communications intelligence and cryptology during World War I, particularly in breaking Germany's diplomatic and naval codes. So well known are some of the exploits of the Admiralty's Room 40, including the decoding of the famous Zimmermann telegram in 1917, that it is often forgotten that Britain had no organized cryptanalytic effort until after the war began.[73] Throughout the decade before 1914 Britain was as weak in cryptology as France was strong. In Britain there was nothing comparable to the Military Cryptography Commission or the *cabinet noir*. In fact, France and Austria-Hungary were the only nations which had organized military cryptanalytic bureaus before the war. From May 1902 until August 1914, the War Office and the Admiralty focused their interest in cryptology solely on cryptography, the development of codes and ciphers for their own use.[74]

During the South African War (1899-1902), "cable censorship" was a euphemism for Britain's communications intelligence effort against the Boer Republics and their supporters or sympathizers in Europe. In October 1899, shortly after the beginning of the war,

> the War Office therefore obtained from the Home Secretary, who, in such cases, usually issues the warrant, authority for the Post Office to produce, for the information of the Intelligence Department of the War Office, until further notice, any telegrams passing through the Central Telegraph Office, which there is reason to believe are sent with the object of aiding, abetting, or assisting the South African Republic or the Orange Free State.[75]

Throughout the war, the intercept of telegrams between South Africa and Europe was accomplished by censorship stations at Aden, Durban, and Cape Town (see chapter VIII). In London as well as overseas, the Post Office, which administered the telegraph system, cooperated closely with the War Office and the Foreign Office in this sensitive area. At the War Office, Section H, under Maj. James E. Edmonds, was responsible for cable censorship and the development of ciphers for use in the field. The covert intercept and decoding of international telegraphic communications by British officials was halted when hostilities with the Boers were formally ended in May 1902, and the authorized officer strength of Section H was reduced accordingly. One year later, the Special Duties Section (now I. 3 instead of Section H) was still charged with the "study of cipher, composition and issue of new ciphers,

. . . Questions of censorship and organisation of censor department for war. Submarine cables . . . Government telegraph code," and various other duties unrelated to cryptology.[76]

When the Directorate of Military Operations was formed in 1904, the Special Duties Section (MO 3) retained responsibility for cryptography and for planning wartime intercept of telegrams. The first head of MO 3, Col. James K. Trotter, was firmly convinced that the staff of his section "must be experts at cipher, and must have a good knowledge . . . of the cable systems of the world, of Secret Service, and of other matters." Furthermore, a new War Office code was considered "very desirable" and cryptography, "a matter hitherto neglected," needed to be "taken up at once."[77] Trotter's successor as head of MO 3 was none other than the former head of Section H, Lt. Col. James Edmonds (1906-10). In the chapter of his uncompleted memoirs discussing MO 3, Edmonds had a good deal more to say about secet service and counterespionage than about cryptology. He did allow that one of the section's first tasks after his arrival was to devise a special code for communications with the Japanese. Also, the section adopted a new cipher for use by British Army units in the field. Colonel Edmonds took seriously his responsibility to plan for the "organisation of the censor department for war." To insure capable cryptanalysts would be available in wartime, Edmonds assembled a list of "experts in decyphering" and suggested selected junior officers be taught "cipher and other matters" in order to build up "a reserve of officers for intelligence duties in war time."[78]

The Special Duties Section was redesignated MO 5 in early 1907.[79] Though its functions basically were unchanged, it was now responsible for "wireless telegraphy" in addition to submarine cables, censorship, and ciphers. MO 5 was authorized two more officers in 1911 in the subsection charged with these responsibilities. The duties of the section relating to cryptology and communications intelligence remained the same from 1907 until 1914.[80] Had there been a peacetime cryptanalytic effort in the British General Staff in the pre-World War I era, it would surely have been conducted by, or under the direction of, MO 5. The available evidence indicates that, although officers of MO 5 studied foreign codes and ciphers, they did not engage in an organized code-breaking operation against the encrypted communications of any foreign power before the beginning of the Great War.

Until 1911, MO 5 was authorized only two officers: the head of the section and one assistant. Even after three more officers were added that year, the Special Duties Section was still the smallest section in the Directorate of Military Operations, as it had been since the creation of the Directorate in 1904. Yet, this tiny branch of the British General Staff was responsible for espionage, counterespionage, and various administrative duties, in addition to its function in the fields of cryptology and censorship. The significance of the pre-World War I Special Duties Section is perhaps best understood in terms of its future importance. Between 1914 and 1918 it gave birth to two famous British intelligence organizations, MI 5 and MI 6.[81]

As mentioned previously, the involvement of MO 5 (MO 3 from 1904 to 1907) in secret service activities may be traced back to its predecessors, Section H (1899-1901) and Section I. 3 (1901-04), during and immediately after the South African War. In 1902 the "secret section," as it was sometimes called, handled the "control and disbursement of secret service funds" and the "arrangements with officers and others employed on special service." Secret agents were hired to obtain the sort of information overseas which Britain's military attachés were unable to collect. Practically all of the section's resources were devoted to South Africa, until the end of the war. Only six months after the Treaty of Vereeniging (May 1902), the head of I. 3 informed the Hardwicke Committee, "the larger part of the expenditure of Secret Service money controlled by the section did not relate to South Africa."[82]

Some consideration was given to removing the secret service functions from the Special Duties Section at the end of the South African War. This move was resisted successfully by Trotter, Robertson, and others, but the three temporary officers added to the section to assist in secret service matters during the war were later released back to their regiments.[83] From the summer of 1902 until 1911, the Special Duties Section was insufficiently manned to be able to recruit spies overseas and direct their activities, except on a very limited basis. Instead, it appears most of the secret service funds it controlled were used to finance the travels of officers from the foreign intelligence sections (MO 2 and MO 3) to the Continent and to other areas of interest. The extensive traveling of officers of these sections to collect intelligence is amply documented in the memoirs of William Robertson, Edward Gleichen, James Edmonds, and others.

For example, Colonel Gleichen, who took over MO 2 from William Robertson in 1907, recalled "another little spy journey" to Holland in the fall of 1907 with his old friend, George Aston of Naval Intelligence. Their objective was to discover "what sort of resistance the Dutch would be able to put up against the Germans if attacked by them." From Holland, they continued on to Denmark and Sweden before returning to England. During the following year, Gleichen visited Spain, Morocco, and France. The tense situation in the Balkans attracted the DMO's attention in 1909. In the summer of 1909 Colonel Gleichen took a long journey through the Balkans. After an initial stop at Vienna, he proceeded to Belgrade and then along the Danube through Rumania and Bulgaria. Gleichen reached Constantinople via a Black Sea steamer from Constanta, Bulgaria, and then spent ten days in the Turkish capital, "making the acquaintance of numerous Turkish big-wigs and trying to acquire as much information as I could." It was apparent to the head of MO 2 that, in Turkey, "our British star was sinking and the German one beginning to shine brightly."[84]

"Spy journeys" of Edward Gleichen and other officers of the foreign intelligence sections aside, the secret service activities of the Special Duties Section remained in decline until at least 1909. When Col. James Edmonds became head of the section in October 1906, he found little resemblance to the bustling hub of wartime clandestine intelligence which Section H had been in 1899-1900. Instead, he discovered that "its activities had been allowed to die down."[85] The Secret Intelligence Service, not MO 5, directed most of Britain's espionage operations on the Continent and elsewhere during these years. The revival of the SIS, which began just prior to the South African War, was due largely to one man, the extraordinary Russian-born spy Sidney Reilly (see chapter VI). Between 1902 and 1914, the intrepid Reilly carried out danger-ous missions for the SIS in Persia, China, Germany, and Russia.[86]

It was not Britain's lack of an espionage organization, but her lack of a counterintelligence agency which enabled Edmonds to inject new life into MO 5. Even before moving to MO 5, he suspected Germany had already established a formidable spy network inside the United Kingdom. As soon as he was appointed head of the Special Duties Section in 1906, he quietly began to collect information regarding the identities and activities of German spies in England and "even found out the channel through which these agents were paid." At first Edmonds encountered skepticism among his superiors on the General Staff and in the War Office, including Richard B. Haldane, the secretary of state for war. Nevertheless, he persisted in reporting German covert intelligence activities.

> Eventually, Mr. Haldane sent for me and told me that he was at last convinced that Germany had an espionage network in this country. I think what turned the scale was a letter from the Mayor of Canterbury, which related that he had found two Germans wandering in his park, had talked to them and invited them in to dinner; when, their tongues loosened by his port, they told him they were reconnoitring the country for an advance on London from the ports of Folkestone, Dover, Rams-gate, and Margate.[87]

The discovery of a German spy network in England prompted the govern-ment to establish a subcommittee of the Committee of Imperial Defence in 1909 to examine Britain's existing counterintelligence system. The subcom-mittee, chaired by Haldane, concluded a coordinated system to deal with foreign espionage did not exist and recommended an organization for this purpose be established without delay.[88]

The new organization, created in August 1909, was called the Special Intelligence Bureau. Colonel Edmonds nominated a trusted former subordi-nate, Capt. Vernon Kell, to be its head. The Special Intelligence Bureau was part of MO 5, but Kell answered directly to the DMO. He moved into a tiny office on the first floor of the War Office and, "for a year, he was alone, with no records, no clerk, and hardly any furniture." Kell proved to be a superb choice. His surveillance of German agents was so thorough, all but one of the German spies residing in the United Kingdom were immediately arrested when Britain entered World War I in August 1914.[89] Capt. (later Col. Sir) Vernon Kell served for thirty years as head of the agency, which was renamed MI 5 during World War I, and which has also been known as the Security Service in more recent times.

The same 1909 subcommittee also reviewed Britain's own espionage apparatus. Despite the strong desire of General Ewart, the DMO, to elimi-nate entirely any connection between the General Staff and espionage activi-ties, the subcommittee did not concur with his recommendation that a single bureau be set up to control all British spies. Not until 1912 was the Special Intelligence Section (later MI 6) formed to coordinate the actions of all British agents overseas. Eventually MI 6 absorbed the SIS as well as the espionage machinery of the two fighting services.[90]

The government's decision to establish a domestic counterintelligence office in 1909 was indicative of the growing concern for the protection of state secrets—military, naval, and diplomatic—during the years before World War I. Britain's Official Secrets Act was passed in 1911 at the height of the German spy hysteria.[91] At the War Office in 1910, a special committee was created under the chairmanship of General Ewart, the DMO, to review procedures for the handling and control of secret documents. The committee's conclusions included the following:

> The distribution of books marked "Secret" and "Confidential" is at present too wide. . . . The regulations regarding the treatment of "Secret" and "For official use only" books are at present not sufficiently definite. . . . The absence in certain cases of proper means of safeguarding secret books . . . involves a serious risk of loss and puts the officer holding them in a false position.[92]

As a result of the committee's recommendations, classified documents were more carefully controlled and disseminated inside and outside of the War Office. Despite the gradually increasing security awareness within the Directorate of Military Operations in the final years before 1914, some of the intelligence products of MO 2 and MO 3 (the foreign intelligence sections) were not classified "secret" or even "for official use only."

The products of the foreign intelligence sections included handbooks on virtually every important army in the world[93] and "Military Reports" which addressed the "geography, topography, ethnography, defences, trade, resources, communications, political conditions, &c., of foreign countries. These . . . contain the bulk of the information to be put in the hands of the troops in the event of war."[94]

> A military report was compiled for any country or territory in South-East Europe, Asia, or Africa in which it was considered likely that British troops would be employed. Such reports were also compiled for some of our Colonial possessions and the colonial possessions of foreign countries.[95]

Though most were classified "For official use only," the handbooks of foreign armies were widely circulated in the officer corps of the British Army. In order to keep these handbooks up-to-date, an annual *Report on Changes in Foreign Armies* was produced and disseminated from 1904 until 1910.

The fourth (and last) edition of the *Handbook of the German Army* to appear before World War I was published in 1912. Unfortunately, substantial portions of this comprehensive, 345-page handbook were invalidated almost immediately by an ongoing reorganization of the Germany Army. Amendments published in January 1914, however, brought the 1912 handbook up-to-date, and gave the British Army a "fairly accurate standard handbook which described most aspects of the military force it was about to meet in combat."[96] Of course, British officers could also obtain information about the German Army by reading the annual *Report of Foreign Manoeuvres*, assembled and published by the foreign intelligence sections.

In contrast, the documents produced by MO 2 in the "Military Resources" series were intended primarily for the use of officers on the General Staff. Relatively few copies were printed, and distribution was strictly limited.

This series had been initiated by Charles Repington's *Military Resources of France* in 1895 (see chapter V), and consisted of secret strategical studies "of the principal countries and their powers for waging war." During the final three years prior to World War I, MO 2 produced "Military Resources" reports on France (1911, 1912), Belgium (1912, 1913), the Netherlands (1911), Bulgaria (1911), and the German Empire (1911, 1912).[97] In writing these reports, the officers of MO 2 were able to use the information that had been collected from all sources, even sensitive covert sources.

The 1912 "Military Resources" study of Germany provides an excellent example of the high quality of analytical intelligence work of which MO 2 was capable on the eve of World War I. *Special Military Resources of the German Empire* (1912) also offers a fascinating view of Germany's military capabilities and her probable wartime course of action as seen by the DMO little more than two years before Britain found herself at war with Germany. As explained in the preface,

> This work has been prepared with the object of setting forth in readily accessible form the most recent information regarding the German Empire: its military resources, national characteristics, power of offence and defence, and possible strategic action under certain broadly defined conditions. It is intended for the use of certain specially selected officers in the Military Operations Directorate of the General Staff, but it may also be issued to certain selected General Officers. . . .[98]

The authors had no illusions about the likelihood of a quick French victory over Germany in the event of a Franco-German war and conceded that the German Army might "in the long run prove more than a match for the elasticity, good staff work, and gallant *elan* of the French troops."[99]

The decade prior to World War I presented many challenges to Britain's strategic military intelligence system. Though necessary and significant changes in the priorities, collection methods, and organizational structure of the system were made during this critical period, the overall quality of work remained at a high level throughout. The handbooks, special reports, strategical studies, and estimates prepared by the foreign intelligence sections generally were both timely and reliable. The excellent record of the Directorate of Military Operations may be attributed to experienced and capable officers such as William Robertson, James Grierson, Edward Gleichen, James Trotter, James Edmonds, Henry Wilson, Charles Callwell, and others in key positions.

The changes to War Office Intelligence priorities after 1903 resulted primarily from the perception that Germany, not Russia or France, was Britain's most dangerous and likely enemy. Threats to Britain's overseas interests in Asia and Africa—especially to Afghanistan, Egypt, the Sudan, South Africa, and the Northwest Frontier of India—were still of concern, but the top priority for intelligence collection shifted to the Continent and to Germany. The successes that the British General Staff enjoyed in the collection and production of intelligence about the German Army during the pre-World War I years may be attributed not only to the reporting of Britain's military attachés and to those officers from the foreign intelligence sections who visited the Continent, but also to the Entente Cordiale and the military conversations with France which began in 1905. The personal friendships of two DMOs, James Grierson and Henry Wilson, with various French officers greatly enhanced the flow of military intelligence across the Channel from the Second Bureau in Paris.

The most dramatic structural changes in War Office Intelligence occurred when the British General Staff was established at the outset of the century. Still, the redesignation of the Intelligence Department as the Directorate of Military Operations in 1904 had little effect on the ways in which military intelligence actually was collected and produced at the national level. The establishment of a general staff did facilitate a closer relationship between intelligence and strategic planning. Furthermore, it gave the DMO authority which the DMI never had in the area of strategic plans and operations. Far less visible, but of greater significance in the long run for British intelligence, was the increasing attention paid to cryptology, espionage, and counterespionage by the Special Duties Section. The creation of a national counterintelligence agency and the attempt to bring greater centralization to all of Britain's overseas espionage operations were important developments which contained many implications for the future.

NOTES

1. The South African War cost the British Empire 22,000 deaths and approximately £200 million. Nearly one million soldiers of the British Empire died in World War I. The economic cost of the war for Britain is difficult to calculate precisely. During World War I, Britain borrowed heavily from the United States and made substantial loans to her other allies. At the end of the conflict, Britain owed about £850 million to the U.S. and was owed more than £1.7 billion by Allied governments. The war cost the British exchequer £9 billion, and the national debt rose to a level fourteen times higher than it had been in 1914. A.J.P. Taylor, *English History, 1914-1915*, pp. 120-24.

2. Most notable were Colonial Secretary Joseph Chamberlain and First Lord of the Treasury Arthur J. Balfour. Chamberlain and Balfour believed that Prime Minister Lord Salisbury was unduly suspicious of Germany.

3. C.J. Lowe, *The Reluctant Imperialists*, 1: 230-33.

4. Lord Lansdowne succeeded Salisbury at the Foreign Office in the autumn of 1900 when Prime Minister Salisbury finally was convinced that the burden of two offices at once was too great. Arthur Balfour replaced his uncle as prime minister in the summer of 1902.

5. In the Intelligence Department, the changing perception of Germany had been spurred by the reporting of Col. James M. Grierson, the British military attaché in Berlin from 1896 to 1900, and by strongly pro-Boer sympathies of Germany evidenced before and during the South African War. Col. William Robertson, head of the Foreign and Indian Subdivision (1901-04), became convinced that Germany was England's number one enemy, in 1901. At the Foreign Office, Thomas Sanderson, the permanent under secretary (1894-1906), did not trust the policymakers in Berlin and tried to convince Foreign Minister Lansdowne in 1900-01 that Germany was not a suitable ally against the Russians in the Far East. Even more strongly opposed to the idea of an Anglo-German agreement was Assistant Under Secretary Francis Bertie (1894-1903), who was instrumental in persuading Lansdowne to seek an alliance with Japan. See Zara S. Steiner, *The Foreign Office and Foreign Policy, 1898-1914*, pp. 37-40, 60-65.

6. The regularization of Britain's relations with the United States in regard to a future Panama Canal was the first (though not decisive) break with "splendid isolation." Britain rejected the first May-Pauncefote Treaty, ratified by the U.S. Senate in December 1900. The second version, drawn up during the summer of 1901 (during a critical period of British and Russian negotiations with Japan) and ratified by the Senate in December 1901, provided that the U.S. might construct a canal and have full control of its management and regulation.

7. George E. Monger, *The End of Isolation*, pp. 43-44, 62; Samuel R. Williamson, *The Politics of Grand Strategy*, pp. 2-3. See also Ian H. Nish, *The Anglo-Japanese Alliance: The Diplomacy of Two Island Empires, 1894-1907* (London: Athlone, 1946).

8. Christopher Andrew, *Théophile Delcassé and the Making of the Entente Cordiale*, p. 91. See also chapter 1, "The Formation of the Entente Cordiale" in Williamson, *The Politics of Grand Strategy*.

9. The third directorate of the General Staff was the Directorate of Staff Duties.

10. From the diary of Field Marshal Sir Henry Wilson, quoted in Maj. Gen. Sir C.E. Callwell, *Field-Marshal Sir Henry Wilson*, 1: 55.

11. Lt. Col. Isaac, "History of the Directorate of M.I.," pp. 11-15.

12. From October 1901 until the reorganization of 1904, the Strategical Section was headed by an assistant QMG. It had only two subsections, one responsible for "offensive and defensive operations" and "consideration of defence schemes abroad," and the other for "collection and distribution of information regarding resources and armed forces of the Empire." It had eleven personnel assigned, including seven officers. The four subsections of the expanded Strategical Section of 1904 were (1) Imperial Defence and Operations in War, (2) Strategical Distribution of the Army, (3) Dominions and Colonies, (4) Egypt, Sudan, and British Possessions in Africa. Isaac, "History of the Directorate of M.I.," pp. 12, 14.

13. According to Lt. Col. Brian Parritt, "special duties" referred to "the controlling of spies and agents," although the conduct of espionage operations had not been officially sanctioned by the General Staff. *The Intelligencers*, pp. 223-24.

14. Isaac, "History of the Directorate of M.I.," p. 10. Maj. (later Brig. Gen. Sir) James E. Edmonds returned to War Office Intelligence in 1904 after two years in South Africa and was assigned to MO 2 as head of a new subsection formed to follow the Russo-Japanese War. From 1907 to 1911, he served as head of MO 5—Special Duties Section (formerly MO 3). He probably is best known as author of those volumes of the British official history of World War I dealing with the Western Front: *History of the Great War, Military Operations France and Belgium* (London, 1922-30), 5 vols.

15. Ibid., pp. 12, 15. Of the thirty-seven personnel authorized in the Topographical Section of 1904, twenty-four were civilians: fifteen draftsmen, six printers, two map curators, and a photographer. MO 3 and MO 4, whose combined functions were identical to those of the Special Duties Section prior to February 1904, had a total strength of forty-five personnel, compared to forty-three in the old Special Duties Section. The net gain of two is attributed to the addition of two officers, raising officer strength from nine to eleven.

16. Officer strength in the Foreign Intelligence Section rose from fourteen to twenty-one, total personnel from twenty-one to thirty.

17. The geographical areas of responsibility for the eight subsections of MO 2 in 1904 were: (a) France and Belgium; (b) Austria-Hungary, Near East, Balkans, Abyssinia, and Liberia; (c) Germany, Holland, and the Scandinavian countries; (d) Russia and Manchuria; (e) Japan, China, and Korea; (f) USA and Mexico; (g) Italy, Spain, Portugal, and Central and South America, and (h) Indian Empire and Persia. Each subsection was headed by a deputy assistant QMG and included at least one additional officer (a staff captain) and a military clerk.

18. Field Marshal Sir William Robertson, *From Private to Field-Marshal*, pp. 129-37.

19. As discussed in chapter V, Grierson was the British Army's leading expert on the German armed forces and had twice served in the Intelligence Department prior to his tour as military attaché in Berlin (1896-1900). During his years in Berlin, Grierson had become increasingly concerned about Germany's intentions toward Britain.

20. Robertson, *From Private to Field-Marshal*, p. 139.

21. Admiral Fisher wanted to send Germany an ultimatum demanding that she halt the buildup of her fleet. If she refused, Fisher wanted to "Copenhagen" the German Navy, that is, sink it inside Kiel.

22. D.S. Macdiarmid, *Grierson*, p. 212; J.E. Tyler, *The British Army and the Continent, 1904-1914*, p. 18. Williamson, *The Politics of Grand Strategy*, p. 46.

23. Britain was obligated to come to the defense of Belgium by the 1839 Treaty of Neutrality.

24. Tyler, *The British Army and the Continent*, p. 18.

25. Williamson, *The Politics of Grand Strategy*, pp. 46-47; Sir George Aston, "The Entente Cordiale and the Military Conversations," pp. 367-69.

26. Robertson, *From Private to Field-Marshal*, p. 140.

27. Aston, "The Entente Cordiale and the Military Conversations," pp. 372-75.

28. Williamson, *The Politics of Grand Strategy*, pp. 52-55. The Schlieffen Plan did not go into effect until late 1903. It is significant that independent British and French intelligence estimates of German military strength and intentions in 1903 were remarkably similar.

29. Christopher Andrew, *Théophile Delcassé and the Making of the Entente Cordiale*, pp. 253-54; Williamson, *The Politics of Grand Strategy*, pp. 56-58.

30. On 20 December 1905, the same day that Huguet and Grierson first met, Ambassador

Cambon called upon King Edward VII and the new foreign secretary, Sir Edward Grey. With the Algeciras Conference scheduled to start in January, the French were anxious to determine whether or not the new Liberal government of Sir Henry Campbell-Bannerman would continue the strong support for France which had been offered by the Conservatives since the outset of the First Moroccan Crisis. Meanwhile, yet another Anglo-French contact was initiated by Sir George Clarke, secretary of the C.I.D. Using *Times* military correspondent Charles à Court Repington as intermediary, Clarke posed a number of questions to the French General Staff. These were passed from Repington to Huguet and carried to Paris by the attaché on 7 January 1906. See Lt. Col. Charles à Court Repington, *The First World War, 1914-1918*, 1: 2-10.

31. Repington had served a five-year tour in the Intelligence Department (1889-94), including several years as head of Section A (the French section). After service in the Sudan he was appointed military attaché for Belgium and Holland in 1898. His appointment as attaché (1898-1902) was interrupted by a brief combat tour in South Africa (1899-1900). Lieutenant Colonel Repington's military career ended "owing to personal indiscretion" in 1902. Edmonds, "Repington, Charles à Court," *D.N.B., 1922-1930*, p. 717. See also chapter IV.

32. Macdiarmid, *Grierson*, pp. 215-17; Williamson, *The Politics of Grand Strategy*, pp. 76-87. See also Michael D. Krause, "Anglo-French Military Planning, 1905-1914, Before the First World War."

33. As Samuel R. Williamson has written, "In the final analysis Ewart's unglamorous work on the Expeditionary Force made it easier, despite the numerous problems still unresolved, for Henry Wilson to devote his attention to strategy, mobilization and the military conversations." *The Politics of Grand Strategy*, p. 113.

34. General Wilson, who had served a three-year tour in the Intelligence Department at Queen Anne's Gate in the 1890s (1894-97) firmly believed in the necessity for reliable intelligence and preferred to collect it firsthand whenever possible. Even while DMO he continued his long-time habit of spending part of his holidays touring the French and Belgian frontiers by bicycle and train. In his biography of Wilson, Sir Charles Callwell describes the DMO's December 1911 visits to the Franco-Belgian and Franco-German border areas. He paid special attention to "the stretch of country between the Sambre and the Moselle, cycling backwards and forwards across the border-line so as to familiarize himself with such roads as he had not yet inspected." Callwell, *Field-Marshal Sir Henry Wilson*, 1: 17-22, 105. Major-General Lord Gleichen, *A Guardsman's Memories*, pp. 340-41.

35. Krause, "Anglo-French Military Planning, 1905-1914," pp. 328-32. "While the plans were being perfected, Wilson was in almost constant touch with the French General Staff." In August 1913 he attended French Army maneuvers and returned to London via Mezieres, Treves, Aachen, and the Ardennes in order to examine the railway capacity of these areas. In July 1914 the DMO joined French generals in a staff ride at Amiens. See also Williamson, *The Politics of Grand Strategy*, p. 299.

36. These included, most notably, Thomas Sanderson, the permanent under secretary, (1894-1906); Francis Bertie, the assistant under secretary (1898-1914); and Eyre Crowe, an assistant clerk in the African Department, who became senior clerk in 1906 and "rapidly became the Foreign Office's chief authority on German problems." Steiner, *The Foreign Office*, pp. 109-12.

37. The Committee of Imperial Defence was created in December 1902 by the Balfour government as a successor to the Defence Committee of the Cabinet, which had been etablished by the Salisbury government in 1895. Balfour's 1902 reorganization did not provide a permanent staff for the C.I.D., but service members were added and the prime minister began to attend meetings regularly. Lord Hankey, *The Supreme Command*, 1: 45.

38. Williamson, *The Politics of Grand Strategy*, pp. 66, 71, 77-80. The idea of a Baltic or coastal raid was abandoned by Clarke and an informal "preparedness" group of the C.I.D. at a meeting on 6 January 1906. Fisher was absent, but Capt. Charles L. Ottley, director of naval intelligence, was present and apparently concurred. Fisher did attend another meeting of the same ad hoc group on 12 January and, discovering that he was out of tune with the others, including Ottley, he became very angry with Clarke. On 18 January he forbade Ottley to attend future C.I.D. meetings.

39. Nicholas d'Ombrain, *War Machinery and High Policy*, p. 4.

40. Ibid., p. 12.

41. The British "liaison officers" who had continued to reside in Paris and Turin after the

Crimean War were redesignated military attachés in 1857. Thus, by the late 1860s British military attachés were stationed in five European capitals. Alfred Vagts, *The Military Attaché*, pp. 27-29. By 1904 British military attachés had been assigned to a number of additional posts, including Rome (via Turin), Constantinople, Washington, Madrid, Tokyo, Peking, the Low Countries (one attaché for Brussels and the Hague) and the Balkans (at times, one attaché for Sofia, Bucharest, Belgrade, etc.).

42. Williamson, *Politics of Grand Strategy*, p. 67.

43. As they had been in the 1890s when Col. W.H.H. Waters had been British military attaché in St. Petersburg (see chapter V), the Russians remained inordinately suspicious of all foreign military attachés, except possibly the French attaché. Their sensitivity to foreign observers was heightened after 1905 by their defeat in the war with Japan and by the Revolution of 1905. It was, no doubt, also related to the fact that "Russian attachés were the most unscrupulous buyers of secrets on the eve of 1914." Vagts, *The Military Attaché*, pp. 224-28. Unlike the Entente Cordiale of 1904, which soon developed into a military entente, the Anglo-Russian agreement of 1907 was a marriage of convenience rather than an alliance in disguise. No Anglo-Russian military conversations of substance materialized before 1914. Although the essential bargaining in 1907 was for Persia, the division of Persia into spheres of influence did not put an end to Russian ambitions there. Russia and Britain continued to distrust one another in central Asia and the Far East, as well as in Persia. K.W.B. Middleton, *Britain and Russia*, pp. 86-93.

44. Steiner, *The Foreign Office and Foreign Policy*, pp. 110-11.

45. An excellent description of the Naval Intelligence Department in 1903 is included in the evidence presented by Captain Prince Louis of Battenberg, director of naval intelligence (1900-05), to Lord Hardwicke's Committee. See "Minutes of Evidence," *Report of the Committee Appointed to Review the Permanent Establishment of the Mobilization and Intelligence Division*, pp. 49-55. Eighteen marine and naval officers were assigned to the N.I.D. in 1903. In addition, there were five naval attachés assigned. The officer strength and internal organization of the N.I.D. had not changed significantly by 1910. In 1913 there were seven British naval attaché posts: Washington, Berlin, Paris, Rome, Tokyo, St. Petersburg, and Stockholm.

46. Description of the responsibilities of MO 2 in the *War Office List* for 1905.

47. Repington, *Vestigia*, p. 182.

48. Ibid.

49. Vagts, *The Military Attaché*, pp. 224, 227-28.

50. *Ibid., pp. 217, 224-25. Chancellor Count van Caprivi had issued clear-cut instructions against espionage by Germany's service attachés in 1890. During the 1890s several German military attachés "simply disregarded the prohibition as contrary to what they had come to consider their most important activity." The last known German attaché recalled for espionage prior to 1914 was a naval attaché in the Russian capital in 1893.*

51. Repington, *Vestigia*, p. 182.

52. Ibid., pp. 247-48.

53. Robertson, *From Private to Field-Marshal*, p. 131. In its report, published in March 1903, the Hardwicke Committee had recommended the head of War Office intelligence should "exercise a preponderating influence in the selection of these Officers" and officers selected for attaché duty who had not already served in the Intelligence Department should be attached to it for a year's training before going overseas. War Office, *Report of the Committee Appointed to Review the Permanent Establishment of the Mobilization and Intelligence Department*, pp. 9-10. Henceforth it will appear as "Hardwicke Committee Report."

54. Ibid., pp. 131-32.

55. Philip Towle, "The European Balance of Power in 1914," pp. 333-35.

56. Lt. Gen. Sir Ian Hamilton, *A Staff Officer's Scrap Book*, 1: 10-12; Philip Towle, "The British Armed Forces and Japan before 1914," *Army Quarterly*, pp. 67-68.

57. The reports of British attachés on both sides of the war were published in *The Russo-Japanese War: British Officers' Reports*. The sole contributors to volume 3, *Reports from British Officers Attached to the Russian Forces in the Field*, were Maj. J.M. Home and Col. W.H.H. Waters. In contrast, seventeen officers, including Generals Nicholson and Hamilton, contributed to volumes 1 and 2, *Reports from British Officers Attached to the Japanese Forces in the Field*.

58. Philip Towle, "The British Armed Forces and Japan before 1914," pp. 68-70; "The European Balance of Power in 1914," pp. 336-37.

59. Great Britain, War Office, General Staff, *Report on Foreign Manoeuvers, 1906* (London, 1906), pp. 133-34. The annual reports of foreign maneuvers for the years 1905-13 may be seen at the Ministry of Defence Library in London. The 1906 edition contains chapters on the 1906 maneuvers in Austria-Hungary, Belgium, Bulgaria, China, France, Germany, Holland, Italy, Spain, Sweden, and Switzerland. Beginning in 1910, commentary was included on maneuvers of the Japanese, Russian, and United States armies.

60. Ibid., pp. 91-92.

61. Towle, "The European Balance of Power in 1914," pp. 333, 339-42.

62. General Staff, "Notes with Regard to the Collection of Intelligence in Peace Time," p. 4. In a discussion of the intelligence sources of MO 2 and the Military Operations Directorate in part 2 ("Organisation and Work of the Military Operations Directorate of the General Staff") of this interesting document "a regular correspondent on the spot" was thought to be the most valuable source.

63. Le Deuxième Bureau had been responsible for intelligence since the establishment of the French General Staff in March 1874. In late 1902 and early 1903, over fifty officers were assigned to the Bureau; twenty-three were permanent, the remainder were attached. See the Hardwicke Committee Report, p. 38.

64. Letter from Maj. Gen. James M. Grierson to King Edward VII, 10 September 1906, quoted in Macdiarmid, *Grierson*, pp. 220-22.

65. The problems of French military intelligence before 1914 were not entirely of their own doing. The enthusiasm of the offensive school in the French Army "tended to minimize the importance of intelligence to French planners. Before 1914, French intelligence and many French officers recognized that Germany would violate Belgian neutrality but they refused to believe that the Germans would cross the Meuse or Sambre." This miscalculation proved costly to France in 1914. Two leading proponents of the *offensive à outrance* were Gen. Ferdinand Foch, head of the Ecole Supérieure de Guerre, and Lt. Col. Loyzeau de Grandmaison, chief of the Third Bureau (operations) and an ardent disciple of Foch. Williamson, *The Politics of Grand Strategy*, pp. 121-22, 126-27.

66. Diary of Brig. Gen. Henry Wilson, 13 October 1910, quoted in Callwell, *Field-Marshal Sir Henry Wilson*, 1: 88. Foch's revelations of Russian secret service work to Wilson were particularly significant. Despite the Anglo-Russian Convention of 1907 and the gradual thawing of relations between Britain and Russia, at no time prior to 1914 did Britain's military or diplomatic ties with Russia approach the closeness of those with France. Yet France and Russia had been allies since 1894 and regularly exchanged military intelligence with each other. Only through the French could the British General Staff hope to gain access to Russian military intelligence. To what extent it had regular access to the information the Second Bureau obtained from the Russian General Staff is unknown, but the French apparently were willing to share a great deal of sensitive information with Henry Wilson.

67. Ibid. (Wilson's diary entries of 28 and 29 September 1911), pp. 94, 104-05. See also Williamson, *The Politics of Grand Strategy*, pp. 174-78, 180-81, 206-09. Although Wilson and MO 2 had estimated eighty-four German divisions would be used in the west, the French General Staff anticipated only seventy to seventy-five German divisions.

68. Field Marshal Joseph Jacques Césaire Joffre, *The Personal Memoirs of Joffre*, 1: 15-23.

69. Cryptology is the science that embraces both cryptography (the art of secret writing—the translation of messages into cipher or code) and cryptanalysis (the science of breaking codes and ciphers without the key).

70. David Kahn has written that *La Cryptographie Militaire* "stands perhaps first among the great books of cryptology." Its author, August Kerckhoff, was a naturalized French citizen, born in Holland in 1835. He wrote "the most concise book on cryptology ever written" while professor of German at the Ecole des Hautes Etudes Commerciales in Paris. France was fortunate to have had several other great cryptologists in the pre-World War I era, the most important of whom was an army officer, Etienne Bazeries. After his retirement from the French Army in 1899, Bazeries was hired as a cryptanalyst by the Quai d'Orsay. David Kahn, *The Codebreakers*, pp. 230-33, 239, 244-47.

71. Ibid., p. 262; Andrew, *Théophile Delcassé and the Making of the Entente Cordiale*, pp. 69-72.

72. Though French cryptanalysts, particularly the brilliant Bazeries, were remarkably successful

at breaking German codes, France was not the only country with such knowledge before 1914. Russia, too, was able to read some enciphered German messages. By 1900 her "knowledge of German ciphers was having an important influence on her foreign policy. There is also evidence that there may have been at least an occasional interchange of information obtained from deciphered German telegrams between the French and Russian Foreign Ministries." Andrew, *Théophile Delcassé*, pp. 73-74.

73. A small group of bright but inexperienced cryptanalysts, headed by Sir Alfred Ewing, began working at the Admiralty on 5 August 1914 in an attempt to decode German naval radio traffic. Their eventual success was made possible by two developments: (1) the British managed to cut Germany's transatlantic cables at the outset of the war, forcing her to communicate overseas via radio or by cables controlled by her enemies, and (2) within four months after the start of the war, the Royal Navy had gained physical possession of copies of all three of the principal codes used by the German Navy. In mid-November 1914, the Admiralty's codebreakers moved to Room 40 in the Old Buildings of the Admiralty. Kahn, *The Codebreakers*, pp. 266-69; Patrick Beesly, *Room 40: British Naval Intelligence 1914-18* (London, 1982), pp. 2-7.

74. The Germans were probably no better off in cryptology prior to 1914 than the British were. David Kahn writes, "And so German cryptology goose-stepped toward war with a top-heavy cryptography and no cryptanalysis." *The Codebreakers*, pp. 262-63.

75. War Office, "Telegraphic Censorship during the South African War, 1899-1902," p. 8.

76. Hardwicke Committee Report, p. 15.

77. Ibid., p. 23.

78. Edmonds Papers, 3/5, chapter 20, "General Staff, War Office Intelligence Division 1906-10," p. 7.

79. The reorganization of the Directorate of Military Operations in February 1907 resulted in the addition of two sections. The Foreign Intelligence Section (MO 2) was split into two sections: the European Section (MO 2) and the Asiatic Section (MO 3). The four subsections of the European Section were (a) France and Belgium; (b) Austria-Hungary, Near East, and Balkans; (c) Germany, Holland, and Scandinavian countries; and (d) Italy, Spain, Portugal, and South America. Those of the Asiatic Section were (a) USA, Mexico, and Central America; (b) Russia; (c) India and Persia; and (d) Far East. MO 4 was still the Topographical Section. An entirely new section, MO 6, was set up for "Foreign Medical Information and Statistics." Isaac, "History of the Directorate of M.I.," p. 17.

80. Ibid., pp. 20-22; *War Office List*, 1907-14. Detailed descriptions of the duties of the sections of the Military Operations Directorate were omitted from the annual *War Office List* beginning in 1909 "for security reasons." In the copies of the *War Office List* for these years at the M.O.D. Library in London, special supplements containing these descriptions, classified "for official use only," have been inserted.

81. Britain's national counterintelligence organization was established in 1909 as part of MO 5. When a separate Directorate of Military Intelligence was formed within the Imperial General Staff in January 1916, MO 5 became MI 5. From then until the present, the Security Service (the British equivalent to the counterespionage segment of the American F.B.I.) has been known as MI 5. Also, in January 1916, all duties of the old MO 5 not related to counterespionage were transferred to the new MI 6. Eventually MI 6 took complete control of the British Secret Service, combining the espionage operations of the armed services with those of the Secret Intelligence Service (SIS). The director of MI 6 today reports directly to the Foreign Office, although he may bypass the normal chain of command and go directly to the prime minister. The head of MI 5, who reports to the Home Office, also may go directly to the prime minister.

82. Hardwicke Committee Report, pp. 15, 21, 24, 39.

83. Ibid., pp. 10, 15.

84. Gleichen, *A Guardsman's Memories*, pp. 314-16, 330-32.

85. Edmonds Papers, 3/5; chapter 20, "General Staff, War Office Intelligence Division, 1906-10," p. 1.

86. Robin Bruce Lockhart, *Ace of Spies*, pp. 32-39, 48-55. Reilly's assignment in Russia (1911-14) was "not to spy on Russia but to collect, through Russian sources, all the intelligence he could on German military and naval power."

87. Edmonds Papers, 3/5, pp. 1-5.

88. Ibid., p. 5.

89. Parritt, *The Intelligencers*, p. 226. See also John Bulloch, *M.I. 5.*

90. Ibid.

91. Still on the books, the Official Secrets Act has faced mounting attacks in recent years, not only from the press, but from various special government inquiries as well. Basically, it states that no government official can disclose, and no reporter or other citizen can receive or publish, any information not specifically authorized for disclosure by higher authority. The violators of the Official Secrets Act can be sent to prison.

92. War Office, "Report of the Committee on the Issue and Custody of Secret Documents," pp. 3-6.

93. Between 1902 and 1914 handbooks were published by the British General Staff on the armies of the Austro-Hungarian Empire (1902, 1905, 1908, 1914); Italy (1913); Japan (1908); Belgium (1906); France (1906, 1914); Germany (1906, 1912); Turkey (1904, 1906, 1912); the Balkan States (1904); and various other nations. Although several of these were not classified, most were marked "For official use only." Copies of these handbooks are located in locked cabinets in the hall near the main entrance to the Ministry of Defence (MOD) Library, London.

94. Hardwicke Committee Report, p. 37.

95. Isaac, "History of the Directorate of M.I.," p. 15. The following are examples of "Military Reports" produced by the directorate between 1902 and 1914: "Military Report on Eastern Turkey-in-Asia" (1903, "Secret"); "Military Reports on Martinique" (1902, "Secret"); "Belgium, Road and River Reports" (1912, "F.O.U.O.," For official use only); "Report on the Tonkin Delta" (1905, "Secret"); and "Report on the Defences of Constantinople" (1908, "Secret"). All of these reports and many more were located in K Refuge, MOD Library.

96. From the introduction, by David Nash of the Imperial War Museum, to a recent reprint of *German Army Handbook April 1918.*

97. Isaac, "History of the Directorate of M.I.," p. 15. For a list of "Military Resources" reports, see "A" Paper Register, 1886-1921, in MOD Library, London. Some of these reports (on France, Belgium, and the German Empire) may be seen at the MOD Library.

98. War Office. General Staff. *Special Military Resources of the German Empire*, preface.

99. Ibid., p. 28.

Chapter XI

Conclusion: British Military Intelligence on the Eve of the Great War

> I made a map of England showing the position of the various spy
> locations which had considerable effect upon the Committee of Imperial
> Defence. I was opposed to the arrest of even undoubted espionage
> agents; it was better to let Germany live in a fool's paradise that we had
> no counter-espionage system. This was accepted: the agents were
> marked down, and all but one (on leave) seized on declaration of war.
>
> Brig. Gen. James E. Edmonds,
> from his unpublished memoirs,
> *Edmonds Papers*, III, chapter 20

The expansion and improvement of Britain's military intelligence system during the crucial years between the South African War and World War
I, together with the highly productive, often superb work of the Directorate
of Military Operations and of individual officers performing intelligence
duties throughout the British Army, yielded immediate dividends for the
nation and her soldiers in the summer and fall of 1914. Not the least of these
was the spectacular coup achieved by Vernon Kell's Special Intelligence
Bureau, the forerunner of MI 5, in bringing about the total destruction of the
German espionage network in England, in August 1914. In Belgium during
the latter part of the same month, pilots of David Henderson's Royal Flying
Corps flew aerial reconnaissance missions and provided the commander of
the British Expeditionary Force with timely and accurate information concerning German Army dispositions which, in his view, "proved of the
greatest value" and helped him "to avert danger and disaster" in the B.E.F.'s
first encounter with the enemy in the Battle of Mons.[1] The activation of the

Intelligence Corps on the day after Great Britain's declaration of war against Germany, and its immediate deployment to France, placed fifty skilled intelligence specialists at the disposal of B.E.F. commanders and their staffs by the end of August. The exchange of military intelligence between the Directorate of Military Operations in London and the Deuxième Bureau in Paris, which began with the Anglo-French military conversations of 1905-06 and which was rejuvenated by Henry Wilson and Joseph Joffre during the four years immediately prior to the outbreak of World War I, continued when hostilities began in August 1914, and was quickly and effectively established in Belgium between the B.E.F. and the French Fifth Army on its right flank before the Battle of Mons.[2] The generally excellent intelligence products—handbooks, special reports, strategical studies, estimates, and so on—prepared by the foreign intelligence sections of the Directorate of Military Operations before the war, especially those dealing with the military forces and terrain of Belgium, France, and Germany, were valuable not only in prewar planning and preparation, but also for immediate use by commanders and staff officers of the B.E.F. in the field. Other War Office products, for example, those about Turkey and the Near East, and reports provided by the Indian Intelligence Branch about Mesopotamia and Persia, were useful to British Army commanders on other fronts as well, beginning in October 1914 with the landings in Mesopotamia and continuing in April 1915 with the landings in the Dardanelles.

Despite the pre-World War I development of British military intelligence in both the tactical and strategic spheres and its impressive contributions to the war effort during the first months of the conflict, it cannot be claimed that it was superior in all respects to the military intelligence systems of the other European powers on the eve of the Great War. In some important areas, quite the opposite was true. The British Empire, Britain's extensive commercial ties abroad, and the continued supremacy of the Royal Navy on the high seas gave the British a definite advantage in strategic intelligence collection throughout the world beyond the European continent in 1914, just as they had during the nineteenth century. On the Continent, where the most important battles of the war would be fought, and where, ultimately, the war would be won, Great Britain enjoyed no comparable natural advantages over her potential enemies, Germany and Austria-Hungary, over her partners in the Triple Entente, France and Russia, or even over tiny Belgium. Nevertheless, the Directorate of Military Operations did very well in collecting strategic military intelligence on the Continent in the years before the war, thanks largely to the work of British military and naval attachés and other British military observers and the calculated generosity of French military intelligence.

On the other hand, in the increasingly important area of strategic communications intelligence, the British were far behind France and Austria-Hungary when the war began. Only after Britain's declaration of war on 4 August 1914 was an organized code-breaking effort established within the Special Duties Section (MO 5) of the Directorate of Military Operations, and, simultaneously, within the Admiralty.[3] Strategic aerial reconnaissance, employed as it was during World War II to photograph enemy installations and provide targets for long-range (strategic) bombers and for poststrike assessments—or as we know it today in the form of the sophisticated, expensive strategic reconnaissance programs of the superpowers, which rely on supersonic, high-flying manned aircraft like the SR-71 and unmanned, globe-circling satellites—was virtually nonexistent in 1914 and was only gradually developed during World War I. At the beginning of the war, the main role of visual reconnaissance from the air and aerial photography was in producing tactical, not strategic, intelligence. This was due not only to the limited range of airplanes in 1914, but also to the general lack of a concept of strategic air power. One aerial platform, the rigid airship or dirigible, had demonstrated considerable potential before 1914 for long-range aerial reconnaissance. The majestic and slower-moving airship was far more stable in the air than the airplane, and was, therefore, a better platform for the primitive cameras available in the prewar years. Also, wireless equipment had been mounted on airships prior to the war, to permit immediate reporting of information gained from visual reconnaissance. In the development and construction of rigid airships, Germany was the undisputed leader in 1914. Although some British Army officers recognized the long-range reconnaissance potential of the rigid airship before the war, and although by 1912 an airship unit with two dirigibles had been formed at the Royal Aircraft Establishment at Farnborough, the British capability to conduct strategic reconnaissance using airships in 1914 was insignificant when compared with Germany's.[4]

In contrast to their prewar weakness in communications intelligence and long-range reconnaissance, the British were relatively effective in the use of covert human sources for strategic intelligence collection. As difficult as it is to believe that they avoided detection on their periodic "spy journeys" to sensitive areas on the Continent, in North Africa, in the Balkans, and in the Near East, army officers such as William Robertson and Edward Gleichen, from the foreign sections of the Directorate of Military Operations, were able to collect a good deal of valuable information during the years before the Great War. The SIS also made significant contributions. The famous SIS spy Sidney Reilly was assigned to Russia during the years 1911-14 and was successful in obtaining intelligence about Germany's Army and Navy through Russian sources. In the Middle East, SIS operatives like the well-known Oxford archaeologist, David Hogarth, and his young protégé, T.E. Lawrence, helped make British Intelligence superior to all other intelligence services in this strategically vital area on the eve of World War I.[5] The successes of officers from the foreign sections, Sidney Reilly and T.E. Lawrence notwithstanding, it is difficult to assess with any degree of accuracy the relative strengths of the various secret services of the European powers in 1914. The Russian secret service was certainly the world's largest, both in terms of its budget and in the number of its agents, but was not necessarily its best. Although the German espionage apparatus in Great Britain was badly crippled in the first weeks of the war, the German General Staff's Intelligence Bureau, also known as "IIIb," was extraordinarily successful in penetrating the inner sanctums of the prewar French General Staff with "Agent 17," who remained under cover in Paris from 1870 to 1914 and furnished his superiors in Berlin with portions of Plan XVII, used by France at the outset of the war.[6] The French and Austrian secret services were not without their own successes in this era.

In certain respects, Britain's military intelligence system in 1914 was quite similar to the system that existed when the Franco-Prussian War began in 1870. Some of the most important sources of military intelligence, both strategic and tactical, were no less important in 1914 than they had been nearly half a century before. Military attachés, for example, were still the heart of the army's strategic collection effort on the European continent in peacetime. In the non-European areas of the world, especially in the Middle East, Africa, and India, the administrative machinery of the British Empire continued to function as an invaluable source of intelligence, including military intelligence. In the realm of tactical intelligence, the South African and Russo-Japanese wars had shown, once again, the great need for thorough reconnaissance and the value of well-placed secret agents operating behind enemy lines or within the ranks of the enemy force. Although armies in 1914, including the British Army, paid little attention to long-range strategic reconnaissance, horse cavalry was still believed, by many soldiers, to have an important role in performing short-range reconnaissance. As already mentioned, aerial reconnaissance provided B.E.F. commander Sir John French with timely information about the enemy in the opening battles of 1914, but so did his cavalry. The two branches worked in tandem at the Battle of Mons and during the subsequent withdrawal by the B.E.F., and, in the words of Sir John, "by working together as they did, the two arms gained much more accurate and voluminous knowledge of the situation."[7]

Despite these and other similarities, the size, structure, methods, and relative importance of British military intelligence on the eve of World War I had changed so much over the preceding four and one half decades that it would have been almost unrecognizable to an army officer who had known the Topographical and Statistical Department of the 1860s, or to one who had served as a field intelligence officer on the staff of a British expeditionary force sent overseas during the 1870s. Only two officers were authorized for the entire T&S Department in 1869; one was the head of the Department. By contrast, the Directorate of Military Operations had forty-three officers assigned in 1914; approximately three-fourths were performing military intelligence duties. Within the British Army of 1914, there was still a restriction against the formation of intelligence units in peacetime, but detailed plans had been made by the Directorate of Military Operations for the activation of the B.E.F.'s Intelligence Corps immediately upon the declaration of war. Methods of reconnaissance changed dramatically in the five years prior to 1914, thanks mainly to the military applications of the airship and the airplane. For dramatic evidence of the change in the relative importance of British military intelligence in the half-century before World War I, one needs only to compare the dormant T&S Department of the post-Crimean War period with the vital role played by the Directorate of Military Operations in British preparations for war between 1904 and 1914.

The growth and modernization of British military intelligence between 1870 and 1914 brought significant changes to most aspects of tactical and strategic intelligence. The cumulative effect of these alterations gave the British Army an intelligence system, on the eve of the Great War, which had acquired (or was in the process of acquiring) many of the characteristics commonly associated with "modern" intelligence organizations. The strategic portion of the British military intelligence system began to change in 1870, and, although there were several periods of relative inactivity, this process continued right down to 1914. On the other hand, the tactical or field intelligence system of the nineteenth century survived pretty well intact until the South African War. Most modifications in the size, methods, and structure of field intelligence occurred from 1899 on.

In what ways was the army's strategic intelligence system "modernized" before World War I? One absolutely essential feature of the modern national intelligence organization, whether military or civilian, is a balance between the ability to collect information and the ability to analyze it and produce intelligence. This quality was totally lacking in the T&S Department of 1869 and was a general weakness of British intelligence in the mid-nineteenth century. For the British War Office, this shortcoming was recognized at the time of the Crimean War, but was not corrected, permanently, until after the Franco-Prussian War, nearly twenty years later. The inability to process incoming information and arrange it in an orderly manner for those in the War Office hierarchy who required it had been, in Charles Wilson's view, the most serious defect of the T&S Department in 1870. His initial efforts to upgrade the statistical side of the Department, and to give it a meaningful analytical capability, initiated a process of improvement and expansion of this crucial function which continued after the creation of the Intelligence Branch in 1873 and even after the subordination of the intelligence sections to the Directorate of Military Operations during the final decade before 1914.[8]

The heads of national intelligence agencies in the twentieth century normally enjoy regular and frequent access to the highest councils of state. This access is necessary so that they may disseminate their product directly to military and political leaders and insure that the best available information is considered when policies are debated or important strategic or foreign policy decisions are made. In this area also, the T&S Department of 1869 was crippled. Until the arrival of Captain Wilson, the director had little or no access to the secretary of state for war or the commander-in-chief. The appointment of Maj. Gen. Sir Patrick Macdougall as the first head of the Intelligence Branch in 1873 partially solved this problem. As capable and respected as Sir Patrick was, however, he was subordinate to the quartermaster general, and, therefore, did not have the degree of access to the commander-in-chief he might have desired. The real breakthrough for the head of War Office Intelligence came in 1887, when Sir Henry Brackenbury was authorized to report directly to the commander-in-chief, rather than having to go through the adjutant general. The prestige and access of the head of War Office Intelligence was enhanced still further, in 1901, by the decision to upgrade the Intelligence Division to the Intelligence Department and to make the director general of military intelligence a member of the War Office Council. The establishment of the General Staff in the post-Boer War period insured the regular inclusion of military intelligence estimates and reports in the formulation of strategy and the conduct of operations. The director of military operations, who was responsible for both operations and intelligence, enjoyed easy access to the highest officials in the War Office, although, officially, he was subordinate to the chief of the General Staff.

The gradually increasing involvement of War Office intelligence personnel in planning for and actually conducting covert collection operations may be viewed as another indicator of modernization. Except in time of war, the War Office had shown little interest in covert collection until the late 1880s. British military attachés were strictly prohibited from engaging in secret service or dealing with secret agents, and the Secret Intelligence Service was collecting little or nothing of value to the army. Yet, in certain countries, military information from open sources had become more difficult to obtain. In order to fulfill its collection requirements in such areas (France, the Ottoman Empire, and most of all, Russia), the Intelligence Division began to obtain special funds to send its own officers, as well as selected volunteers from the officer corps at large, on "secret service" missions. During the South African War, a special section was formed in the Intelligence Division to control secret service funds and to oversee another aspect of secret intelligence, the intercept and decoding of communications. In the years between the South African War and the First World War, the Special Duties Section of the Directorate of Military Operations grew more and more involved in counterespionage operations, coordination of British espionage operations, and planning for a wartime code-breaking effort. This work was not only an important aspect of the preparation for the challenges of 1914; it was, at the same time, leading toward the formation of effective national intelligence organizations for counterintelligence (MI 5), clandestine collection/espionage (MI 6), and signals intelligence (GCHQ).[9]

The field intelligence system of the nineteenth century, which was basically the system used by Wellington in the peninsula, did not really begin to modernize until the South African War. The most glaring deficiencies in the system, several of which contributed to Black Week and other British defeats at the hands of the Boers in the early months of the war, were corrected in the field during the first year of the conflict. A whole series of additional problems, however, arose when the Boers reverted to guerrilla warfare. Although the Field Intelligence Department was disbanded immediately after the end of hostilities, Col. David Henderson preserved the tactical intelligence lessons of the war, and, in the process, provided an excellent manual for field intelligence officers of the future, his landmark publication of 1904, *Field Intelligence, Its Principles and Practice*. The one major unsolved problem of British field intelligence after the war was the lack of trained intelligence officers in the army (except in India). Some limited attempts were made to train intelligence officers, but far too few were ready in 1914.

Some British intelligence officers were concerned about the unique problems of tactical intelligence in a war on the Continent. Their ideas supplemented David Henderson's manual and helped to update the tactical intelligence system in the years before 1914. The most important changes in tactical intelligence methods in this period were, of course, brought about by technological advances. The development of the airship and the airplane revolutionized reconnaissance, and steady improvements in the techniques of aerial photography offered British military intelligence a means of enhancing the intelligence collection ability of aerial platforms. The rapid advance of aerial photography in World War I, as a means of collecting tactical intelligence, heralded the debut of imagery intelligence (IMINT). The potential of tactical communications intelligence (COMINT) was opened by the growing military use of wireless. Wireless mounted on aerial platforms, first on airships and later on airplanes, gave aerial observers the ability to communicate instantly with ground stations. British military intelligence had no monopoly on technical collection methods in 1914. In fact, the British lagged behind the French Army in both COMINT and IMINT at the beginning of the war. The B.E.F. possessed the capability to intercept German wireless communications from the time of its arrival in the field in August 1914, but little thought had been given to doing so in an organized fashion, for the purpose of intelligence gathering. The British observed the French Army's COMINT success, and, before the end of 1914, had established a fairly extensive tactical COMINT operation of their own, employing cavalry elements equipped with wagon-mounted wireless receivers. With help from the Marconi Wireless Telegraph Company, they had also carried out experiments in radio direction-finding (DF). In aerial photography, the French were also ahead in August 1914, but the British caught up quickly, and, in early 1915, surpassed their ally by constructing a superior aerial camera. Though behind in some respects in 1914, British intelligence officers were quick to capitalize on the potential of these new sources of battlefield information.

British military intelligence failed in one very important respect in 1914, as did the intelligence services of all of the European powers. With some important assistance from the Second Bureau of the French General Staff, it had learned a great deal about the organization, tactics, weapons, leadership, and war plans of the German Army. Yet, it was unable to accurately forecast the nature and duration of the coming European war. This was not, of course, a simple matter of underestimating the strength and staying power of the German Army or of overestimating the capabilities of its partners in the Triple Entente. Nor was it due to a lack of funds made available during the prewar years for the conduct of secret services or for military intelligence activities generally. Despite their own firsthand experience in the South African War, the presence of British military observers on both sides during the Russo-Japanese War, and the remarkably accurate predictions about the nature of World War I offered by Ivan S. Bloch around the turn of the century,[10] British military intelligence officers working in the Directorate of Military Operations believed that the next war would be a short, decisive conflict with the armies of France, Russia, and the British Empire prevailing over the Central Powers in a matter of weeks or months. Since miscalculations of this sort were practically universal among professional soldiers before August 1914, it would be unfair to single out British intelligence officers for a particular lack of vision or a dereliction of duty.

The British Army had no special branch for intelligence officers in 1914. In World War I, as in South Africa, many officers served for a time as field intelligence officers with no prospects of ever having an intelligence assignment again. Still, there were, before 1914, a group of exceptional officers who had served repeatedly in intelligence billets, both in London and in the field in India or South Africa. These officers—William Robertson, James Grierson, James Edmonds, Charles Callwell, Edward Gleichen, W.H.H. Waters, David Henderson, and others—constituted a select group of intelligence specialists. Their value as intelligence officers in peacetime was most fully realized when they served in the Directorate of Military Operations in London or in a military attaché post in one of the European capitals. Henderson, a field intelligence expert, was the exception. He, of course, found his niche as director general of military aeronautics. The idea of allowing regular officers to specialize in intelligence work was unheard of prior to 1870, except possibly for engineer officers doing survey work. The existence of a small corps of intelligence officers before World War I was yet another portent of the future.

NOTES

1. Field-Marshal Viscount Sir John French, *1914*, pp. 43-44.

2. The direct correlation between the prewar Anglo-French exchange of military intelligence, and the ease with which this exchange was accomplished in the field in Belgium in August 1914, is readily apparent in the fact that the principal liaison officer from the French Army to the B.E.F. at this critical juncture was Col. Victor Huguet, the former military attaché in London, who played a key role in the initiation of the Anglo-French military conversations in December 1905. The B.E.F. liaison officer to Gen. Charles Lanrezac's Fifth Army was Capt. Edward Spears of the Eleventh Hussars. For their personal accounts, see Gen. Victor Marie Huguet, *Britain and the War* (London, 1928) and Maj. Gen. Sir Edward Spears, *Liaison 1914*.

3. Given the prewar responsibility of MO 5 for "submarine cables, wireless telegraphy, and ciphers," it was natural for the Special Duties Section to be assigned the additional mission of breaking German military codes in August 1914. Subsection MO 5(C), which was added to perform this function, was headed by a GSO 2 and included three attached officers and three "civil officials." The original three civilians in MO 5(C) were: J. St. Vincent Pletts, a radio engineer from the Marconi Wireless Telegraph Company; J.D. Crocker, a young scholar from Cambridge University; and Oliver Strachey of the Indian Civil Service. Later designated MI 1(b), the War Office's codebreakers numbered eighty-four by the end of the war and had moved to a large private house at 5 Cork Street, several blocks from the rest of the Directorate of Military Intelligence in the War Office Building in Whitehall. Isaac, "History of the Directorate of M.I.," p. 23, and Kahn, *The Codebreakers*, pp. 309-10. The codebreakers of MO 5(C) were notably unsuccessful until mid-September 1914, when "the French provided the Army with the method and key of the German military ciphers and actual deciphering became possible for the first time." As described in chapter X, the Admiralty's codebreakers began their work on 5 August 1914. Room 40 was set up as an independent entity within the Admiralty and was not subordinated to Adm. Sir William Hall, the director of naval intelligence, until May 1917. Beesly, *Room 40: British Naval Intelligence, 1914-1918* (London, 1982), pp. 13, 169.

4. Count Ferdinand von Zeppelin, a retired German Army officer, invented the rigid airship and built the first one in 1900. By 1906, he had built an airship that could attain an air speed of thirty miles per hour. In 1908, he established the Zeppelin Foundation for the manufacture of airships and the development of aerial navigation at Friedrichshafen. When the First World War began, Germany used her Zeppelins for both long-range reconnaissance, especially for maritime reconnaissance in support of the German Navy, and strategic air raids against military installations and cities in France and England. At about the time the war began, Zeppelin's plant at Friedrichshafen had started to produce a larger version of the rigid airship, the so-called super-Zeppelin, which was approximately 140 meters long and carried a crew of twenty-five to thirty men. Although the Zeppelin raids on London and other English cities were at first very frightening to the civilian population and caused some damage and casualties, Zeppelins proved vulnerable to airplanes and antiaircraft fire from the ground and never really fulfilled the German's expectations of them.

5. The future Lawrence of Arabia joined David Hogarth, who had been elected to the prestigious post of keeper of the Ashmolean Museum at Oxford in 1908, as an archaeologist's assistant at Carchemish (the site of an ancient Hittite city on the Euphrates River in northern Syria) in

March 1911 and remained there until the spring of 1914. The Carchemish "dig" was a genuine cover for Hogarth and Lawrence while they carried out their secret missions for the SIS: to provide a continual assessment of the progress of the German-engineered Berlin to Bagdad Railway and to keep watch on the sentiments of the local population with respect to the Turks, the Germans, and the British. Lawrence's three years at Carchemish before the war, in addition to his walking tours of Syria, Lebanon, Palestine, and Mesopotamia, proved an excellent preparation for his famous wartime roles: providing intelligence to British authorities in the Middle East and helping to lead an Arab revolt against the Turks. Stewart, *T.E. Lawrence*, pp. 40-41, 78, 84-87, and 123-24.

6. Baron August Schluga, designated "Agent 17" by the IIIrd Oberquartiermeister (IIIb) of the General Staff, became a German agent in 1866. David Kahn, *Hitler's Spies: German Military Intelligence in World War II* (New York, 1978), pp. 32-34.

7. French, *1914*, p. 44. In fact, the reconnaissance role of horse cavalry on the Western Front in World War I was very limited. As Sir John French, himself an old cavalryman, admitted in 1919, one of the lessons of World War I was, "the duty of collecting information and maintaining touch with an enemy in the field will in future fall entirely upon the air service. . . ."

8. On 29 December 1915, Brig. Gen. Frederick B. Maurice assumed duty as DMO, replacing Maj. Gen. Charles E. Callwell, who had served as DMO since the beginning of the war in August 1914, when he had been called out of retirement to relieve Henry Wilson. Significantly, however, Maurice was charged only with the responsibility for directing MO 1 (Strategy, Plans, Operations), leaving the intelligence sections, which had been under the DMO since 1904, temporarily without an overall director. The separation of the intelligence and operations branches of the War Office General Staff was confirmed on 3 January 1916, when Maj. Gen. George M.W. Macdonogh assumed duty as DMI. The reestablishment of a separate Directorate of Military Intelligence, which continued through the rest of the war and into the postwar era as an independent directorate, occurred immediately following Field-Marshal Sir William Robertson's arrival as chief of the Imperial General Staff in December 1915.

9. MI 5 and MI 6 were established during World War I, the latter being the successor to the old SIS. The Government Communications Centre (GCHQ), Britain's equivalent to the National Security Agency, was not established at its current headquarters, Cheltenham, until after World War II. Its predecessor (1918-1945) was the Government Code and Cipher School (GCCS), formed when the Admiralty's Room 40 was transferred to the Foreign Office after World War I. GCCS moved from the London headquarters of MI 6, at No. 54 Broadway, in August 1939 to a red-brick mansion in Bletchley Park, about fifty miles north of London, where it remained throughout World War II.

10. Bloch's six-volume work, *The Future of War in Its Technical, Economic, and Political Relations*, was first published in St. Petersburg in 1897-98. It was translated into German in 1899. The Russo-Japanese War (1904-05) appeared to confirm many of his predictions, but his warnings about an inevitable, bloody stalemate resulting from the next major European war were largely ignored by military men.

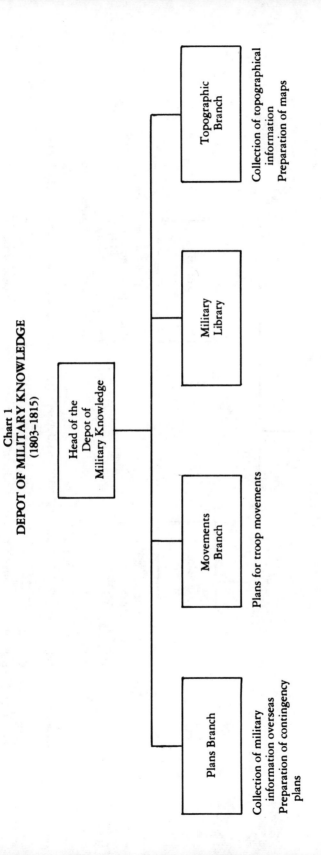

Chart 1
DEPOT OF MILITARY KNOWLEDGE
(1803–1815)

Head of the Depot of Military Knowledge

- **Plans Branch**
  Collection of military information overseas
  Preparation of contingency plans

- **Movements Branch**
  Plans for troop movements

- **Military Library**

- **Topographic Branch**
  Collection of topographical information
  Preparation of maps

Location: Horse Guards, London.

Subordination: The Depot of Military Knowledge was a branch of the Quartermaster General's Department.

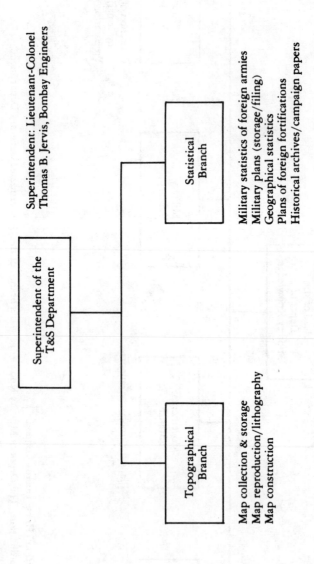

Chart 2
TOPOGRAPHICAL & STATISTICAL DEPARTMENT
(1855–1857)

Superintendent: Lieutenant-Colonel
Thomas B. Jervis, Bombay Engineers

Superintendent of the
T&S Department

Topographical
Branch

Map collection & storage
Map reproduction/lithography
Map construction

Statistical
Branch

Military statistics of foreign armies
Military plans (storage/filing)
Geographical statistics
Plans of foreign fortifications
Historical archives/campaign papers

Location: 9 Adelphi Terrace, Whitehall from March 1855 until August 1856 when it moved to No. 4 New Street, Spring Gardens, London.

Subordination: Created by the Secretary of State for War as a branch of the War Department in March 1855.

Personnel: Two military and twenty-six civilians (lithographers) for a total of twenty-eight personnel.

Chart 3
TOPOGRAPHICAL & STATISTICAL DEPARTMENT
(1871–1873)

Director: Capt. Charles W. Wilson, Royal Engineers

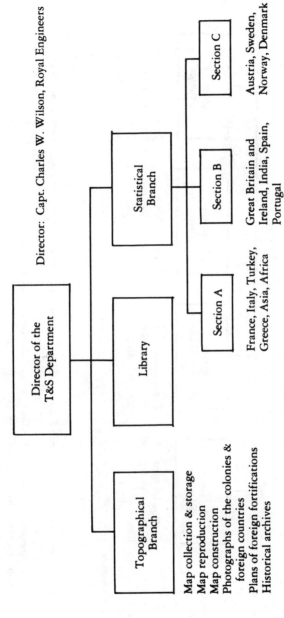

Director of the T&S Department

- **Topographical Branch**
  - Map collection & storage
  - Map reproduction
  - Map construction
  - Photographs of the colonies & foreign countries
  - Plans of foreign fortifications
  - Historical archives
- **Library**
- **Statistical Branch**
  - **Section A**
    - France, Italy, Turkey, Greece, Asia, Africa
  - **Section B**
    - Great Britain and Ireland, India, Spain, Portugal
  - **Section C**
    - Austria, Sweden, Norway, Denmark

Location: No. 4 New Street, Spring Gardens, London.

Subordination: The T&S Department of 1871–73, though very small, was a separate department of the War Office.

Personnel: Following the publication of the Northbrook Committee's Report in January 1871, the civilian strength of the T&S Department was sharply reduced and three officers were added. By late 1872, the Department's total personnel strength was twelve: five officers (including the Director), one military clerk, and six civilians.

Chart 4
INTELLIGENCE BRANCH
(1873–1875)

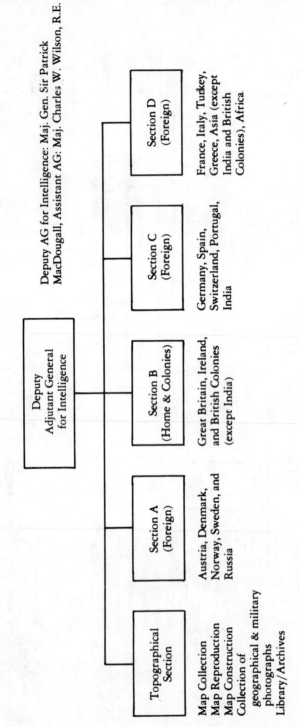

Deputy AG for Intelligence: Maj. Gen. Sir Patrick
MacDougall, Assistant AG: Maj. Charles W. Wilson, R.E.

Deputy
Adjutant General
for Intelligence

Topographical
Section

Map Collection
Map Reproduction
Map Construction
Collection of
geographical & military
photographs
Library/Archives

Section A
(Foreign)

Austria, Denmark,
Norway, Sweden, and
Russia

Section B
(Home & Colonies)

Great Britain, Ireland,
and British Colonies
(except India)

Section C
(Foreign)

Germany, Spain,
Switzerland, Portugal,
India

Section D
(Foreign)

France, Italy, Turkey,
Greece, Asia (except
India and British
Colonies), Africa

Location: No. 4 New Street, Spring Gardens from 1 April 1873 until January 1874 when it moved to Adair House in St. James
Square.

Subordination: The Intelligence Branch was subordinate to the Adjutant General's Department from 1 April 1873 until July 1374
when it was placed under the Quartermaster General's Department.

Personnel: Military and civilian personnel strength at the Intelligence Branch in 1873 was twenty-seven, including eight officers.

Foreign Sections: A fourth foreign section (Section E) was added to the Intelligence Branch in April 1875.

Other Officers (DAAGs) at the Intelligence Branch in 1874: Maj. Charles Brackenbury, Capt. Thomas Jessop, Capt. William
Smith, Capt. Francis C.H. Clarke, Lt. J.W.F. Burton.

Chart 5
INTELLIGENCE BRANCH
(1877–1879)

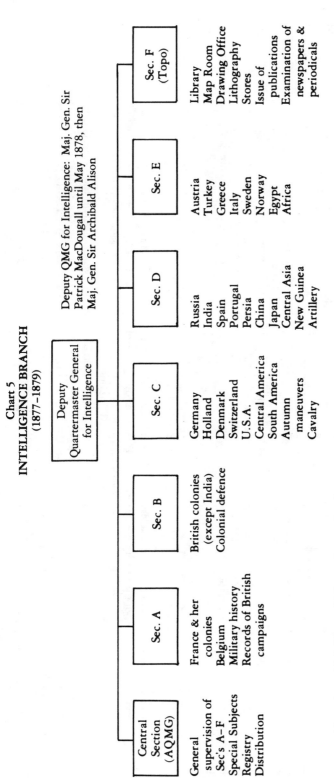

Deputy QMG for Intelligence: Maj. Gen. Sir Patrick MacDougall until May 1878, then Maj. Gen. Sir Archibald Alison

Deputy Quartermaster General for Intelligence

Central Section (AQMG)
General supervision of Sec's A–F
Special Subjects
Registry
Distribution

Sec. A
France & her colonies
Belgium
Military history
Records of British campaigns

Sec. B
British colonies (except India)
Colonial defence

Sec. C
Germany
Holland
Denmark
Switzerland
U.S.A.
Central America
South America
Autumn maneuvers
Cavalry

Sec. D
Russia
India
Spain
Portugal
Persia
China
Japan
Central Asia
New Guinea
Artillery

Sec. E
Austria
Turkey
Greece
Italy
Sweden
Norway
Egypt
Africa

Sec. F (Topo)
Library
Map Room
Drawing Office
Lithography
Stores
Issue of publications
Examination of newspapers & periodicals

Location: Adair House, St. James Square, London.

Subordination: Quartermaster General's Department.

Personnel: In August 1878, there were forty-one personnel working at the Intelligence Branch. Twenty of these were officers: eight on long tours and twelve attached.

Section Heads in August 1878 were: Col. Robert Home, AQMG, Central Section; Maj. C.J. East, DAQMG, Section A; Lt. Col. A.H. Wavell, DAQMG, Section B; Lt. Col. H.T. Butler, DAQMG, Section C; Capt. Francis C.H. Clarke, DAQMG, Section D; Capt. John C. Ardagh, DAQMG, Section E; Capt. G.E. Grover, DAQMG, Section F (Topographical).

Chart 6
INTELLIGENCE DIVISION
(1887–1895)

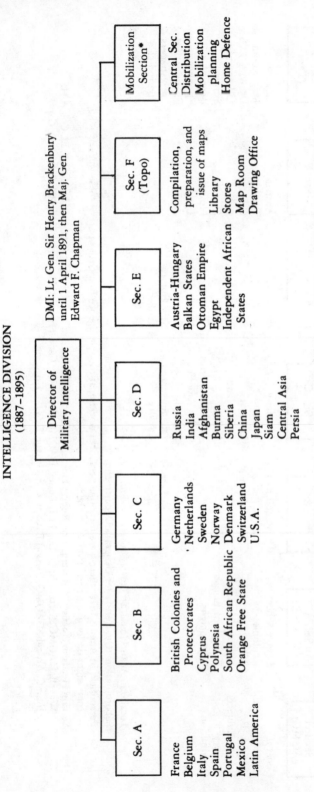

Director of
Military Intelligence

DMI: Lt. Gen. Sir Henry Brackenbury
until 1 April 1891, then Maj. Gen.
Edward F. Chapman

Sec. A

France
Belgium
Italy
Spain
Portugal
Mexico
Latin America

Sec. B

British Colonies and
Protectorates
Cyprus
Polynesia
South African Republic
Orange Free State

Sec. C

Germany
Netherlands
Sweden
Norway
Denmark
Switzerland
U.S.A.

Sec. D

Russia
India
Afghanistan
Burma
Siberia
China
Japan
Siam
Central Asia
Persia

Sec. E

Austria-Hungary
Balkan States
Ottoman Empire
Egypt
Independent African
States

Sec. F
(Topo)

Compilation,
preparation, and
issue of maps
Library
Stores
Map Room
Drawing Office

**Mobilization
Section***

Central Sec.
Distribution
Mobilization
planning
Home Defence

Location: 16 and 18 Queen Anne's Gate, London, where it had moved in December 1884 from Adair House, St. James Square.

Subordination: Though the Intelligence Branch was shifted from the Quartermaster General's Department to the Adjutant General's Department in June 1887, the DMI reported directly to the Commander-in-Chief rather than through the Adjutant General. The Intelligence Branch was redesignated the Intelligence Division in January 1888.

Personnel: In April 1889 (after the separation of the Mobilization Section from the Intelligence Division) thirty-nine personnel were assigned to the Division. There were now fourteen officers serving long tours.

Section Heads in January 1888 were: Col. John Ardagh, DAG, Mobilization Section; Lt. Col. W.R. Fox, DAAG, Section A; Col. C.W.B. Bell, DAAG, Section B; Maj. W.S. Cooke, DAAG, Section C; Capt. J.W. Murray, DAAG, Section D; Lt. Col. L.A. Gregson, DAAG, Section E; Capt. J.J. Leverson, DAAG, Section F.

*Note: This section was created in November 1887 and was moved to the Adjutant General's Office in 1888.

Chart 7
INTELLIGENCE DIVISION
(1896–1901)

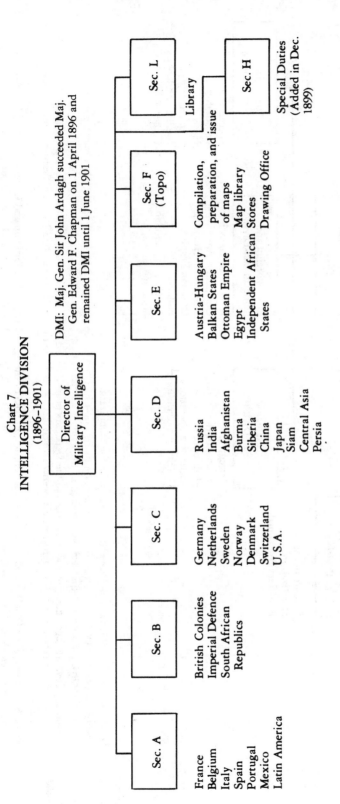

DMI: Maj. Gen. Sir John Ardagh succeeded Maj.
Gen. Edward F. Chapman on 1 April 1896 and
remained DMI until 1 June 1901

Director of Military Intelligence

Sec. A

France
Belgium
Italy
Spain
Portugal
Mexico
Latin America

Sec. B

British Colonies
Imperial Defence
South African
Republics

Sec. C

Germany
Netherlands
Sweden
Norway
Denmark
Switzerland
U.S.A.

Sec. D

Russia
India
Afghanistan
Burma
Siberia
China
Japan
Siam
Central Asia
Persia

Sec. E

Austria-Hungary
Balkan States
Ottoman Empire
Egypt
Independent African
States

Sec. F (Topo)

Compilation,
preparation, and issue
of maps
Map library
Drawing Office

Sec. L

Library

Sec. H

Special Duties
(Added in Dec.
1899)

Location: 16 and 18 Queen Anne's Gate until November 1901 when the Intelligence Division of the newly formed Mobilization and Military Intelligence Department moved to Winchester House, St. James Square.

Subordination: The DMI responded directly to the Commander-in-Chief throughout this period. The DMI was not a member of the War Office Council.

Personnel: Exact figures are not available, but total personnel strength of the Intelligence Division reached approximately forty-five prior to the South African War. This included eighteen officers on long tours.

Section Heads in this period were usually Deputy Assistant Adjutant Generals (DAAGs). DAAGs in charge of sections were provided at least one Staff Captain as an assistant. Staff Captains who served in the Intelligence Division between 1896 and 1901 included Capts. Henry H. Wilson, William R. Robertson, and Edward Gleichen.

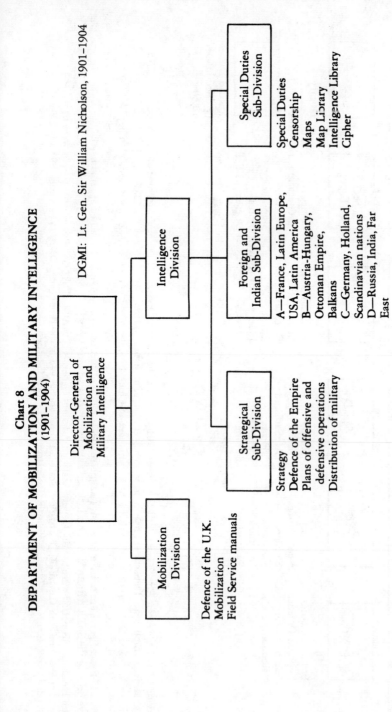

Chart 8
DEPARTMENT OF MOBILIZATION AND MILITARY INTELLIGENCE
(1901–1904)

DGMI: Lt. Gen. Sir William Nicholson, 1901–1904

Director-General of Mobilization and Military Intelligence

Mobilization Division

Defence of the U.K.
Mobilization
Field Service manuals

Intelligence Division

Strategical Sub-Division

Strategy
Defence of the Empire
Plans of offensive and defensive operations
Distribution of military

Foreign and Indian Sub-Division

A—France, Latin Europe, USA, Latin America
B—Austria-Hungary, Ottoman Empire, Balkans
C—Germany, Holland, Scandinavian nations
D—Russia, India, Far East

Special Duties Sub-Division

Special Duties
Censorship
Maps
Map Library
Intelligence Library
Cipher

Location: Winchester House, St. James Square except for the Mobilization Division.

Subordination: The DGMI responded directly to the Commander-in-Chief and the Secretary of State for War. He was a member of the War Office Council and attended the meetings of the Cabinet's Defense Committee.

Personnel: Seventy-seven personnel were assigned to the Department in 1903. Of these, thirty-three were officers: twenty on long tours and thirteen attached. The Department's twenty-five civilians were all in the Special Duties Sub-Division: draftsmen, map curator, librarian, etc.

Key subordinates of the DGMI in 1903 were: Col. J.K. Trotter, AQMG of the Special Duties Sub-Division and Deputy Director of the Department; Col. P.H.N. Lake, AQMG of the Mobilization Division; Lt. Col. E.A. Altham, AQMG of the Strategical Sub-Division; Brevet Lt. Col. W.R. Robertson, AQMG of the Foreign and Indian Sub-Division.

Chart 9
DIRECTORATE OF MILITARY
OPERATIONS (1904–1907)

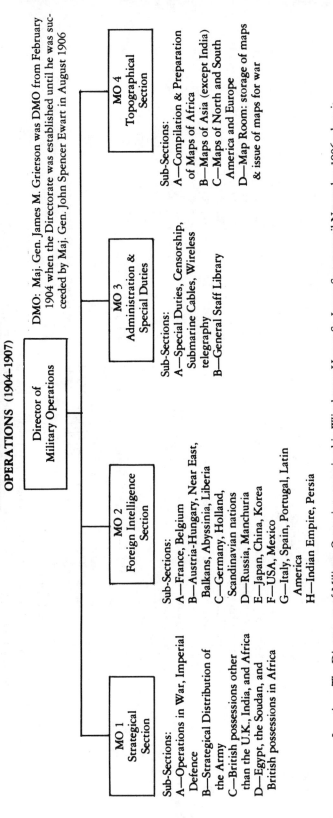

DMO: Maj. Gen. James M. Grierson was DMO from February 1904 when the Directorate was established until he was succeeded by Maj. Gen. John Spencer Ewart in August 1906

Director of Military Operations

MO 1
Strategical Section

Sub-Sections:
A—Operations in War, Imperial Defence
B—Strategical Distribution of the Army
C—British possessions other than the U.K., India, and Africa
D—Egypt, the Soudan, and British possessions in Africa

MO 2
Foreign Intelligence Section

Sub-Sections:
A—France, Belgium
B—Austria-Hungary, Near East, Balkans, Abyssinia, Liberia
C—Germany, Holland, Scandinavian nations
D—Russia, Manchuria
E—Japan, China, Korea
F—USA, Mexico
G—Italy, Spain, Portugal, Latin America
H—Indian Empire, Persia

MO 3
Administration & Special Duties

Sub-Sections:
A—Special Duties, Censorship, Submarine Cables, Wireless telegraphy
B—General Staff Library

MO 4
Topographical Section

Sub-Sections:
A—Compilation & Preparation of Maps of Africa
B—Maps of Asia (except India)
C—Maps of North and South America and Europe
D—Map Room: storage of maps & issue of maps for war

Location: The Directorate of Military Operations remained in Winchester House, St. James Square until November 1906 when it moved to the new War Office in Whitehall. The DMO and the heads of MO 1, MO 2, and MO 3 had their offices on the second floor. The foreign sections of MO 2 were on the third floor of the new War Office, along with part of MO 4.

Subordination: The Directorate of Military Operations was one of the three directorates of the General Staff and the DMO was directly subordinate to the Chief of the General Staff, Lt. Gen. Sir N. Lyttleton.

Personnel: Ninety-four military and civilian personnel were assigned to the Directorate in late 1904. There were now forty-three officers.

Heads of the Sections: Col. Charles E. Callwell, ADMO, MO 1; Col. William R. Robertson, ADMO, MO 2; Brevet Col. F.J. Davies, ADMO, MO 3; Maj. C.F. Close, DAQMG, MO 4.

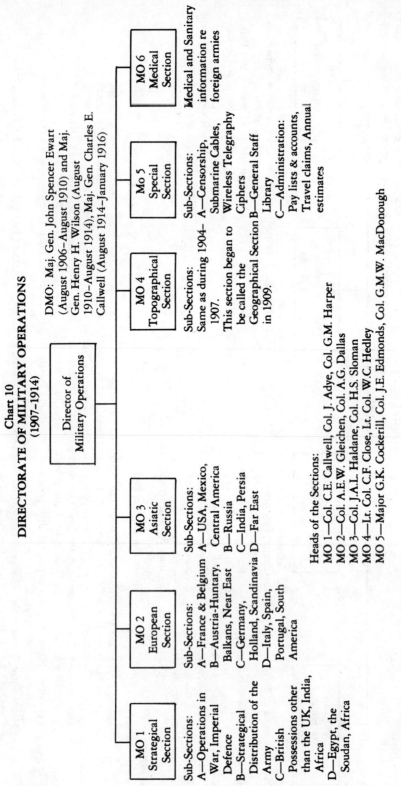

Chart 10

DIRECTORATE OF MILITARY OPERATIONS (1907–1914)

DMO: Maj. Gen. John Spencer Ewart (August 1906–August 1910) and Maj. Gen. Henry H. Wilson (August 1910–August 1914), Maj. Gen. Charles E. Callwell (August 1914–January 1916)

Director of Military Operations

MO 1 Strategical Section

Sub-Sections:
A—Operations in War, Imperial Defence
B—Strategical Distribution of the Army
C—British Possessions other than the UK, India, Africa
D—Egypt, the Soudan, Africa

MO 2 European Section

Sub-Sections:
A—France & Belgium
B—Austria-Huntary, Balkans, Near East
C—Germany, Holland, Scandinavia
D—Italy, Spain, Portugal, South America

MO 3 Asiatic Section

Sub-Sections:
A—USA, Mexico, Central America
B—Russia
C—India, Persia
D—Far East

MO 4 Topographical Section

Sub-Sections:
Same as during 1904–1907.
This section began to be called the Geographical Section in 1909.

Mo 5 Special Section

Sub-Sections:
A—Censorship, Submarine Cables, Wireless Telegraphy Ciphers
B—General Staff Library
C—Administration: Pay lists & accounts, Travel claims, Annual estimates

MO 6 Medical Section

Medical and Sanitary information re foreign armies

Heads of the Sections:
MO 1—Col. C.E. Callwell, Col. J. Adye, Col. G.M. Harper
MO 2—Col. A.E.W. Gleichen, Col. A.G. Dallas
MO 3—Col. J.A.L. Haldane, Col. H.S. Sloman
MO 4—Lt. Col. C.F. Close, Lt. Col. W.C. Hedley
MO 5—Major G.K. Cockerill, Col. J.E. Edmonds, Col. G.M.W. MacDonough

Location: New War Office building.

Subordination: DMO subordinate to the Chief of the General Staff.

Personnel: In early 1910, ninety-eight personnel were assigned to the DMO: forty-three officers, sixteen NCOs, and thirty-nine civilians (librarian, clerks, map curators, printers, draftsmen, photographers).

Additions to MO 5: In 1909, the Special Intelligence Bureau was added to MO 5 to perform a counterintelligence function. Similarly, the Special Intelligence Section was created in 1912 to coordinate British covert intelligence operations overseas.

Bibliography

I. Primary Sources
A. Manuscripts
1. Intelligence Corps Museum, Templer Barracks, Ashford, Kent, England:
   Burge Papers, A268
   Collen's Report on the Intelligence Branch, QMG's Department, A.011.14
   Downton's Notes on the History of Photographic Intelligence, A176
   Haig's Diary, 1916-18, A175
   Hawker's Notes for a History of the Intelligence Corps
   Kirke Papers, A58, A266, A253, A260
   Marshall-Cornwall Papers, A33
   Miscellaneous Papers and Reports of the General Staff, War Office, 1904-14
2. Liddell Hart Centre for Military Archives, King's College, University of London:
   Edmonds Papers, III, IV, V, VII
   Hamilton Papers, 7/3, 19/11
   Robertson Papers, I/1, I/2, I/3, I/5
3. Ministry of Defence Library (Central and Army), Old War Office Building, Whitehall:
   Isaac's Paper on the History of the Development of the Directorate of Military Intelligence, 1855-1939
   War Office Intelligence Branch/Division/Department and Directorate of Military Operations Papers, Reports, Handbooks, Manuals, Regulations, including:
      Armed Strength of Foreign Powers, 1875-83
      Handbooks on Foreign Armies, 1886-1914
      Military Resources of Foreign Powers, 1895-1914
      Reports on Foreign Manoeuvers (annual), 1905-14
      Reports on Changes in Foreign Armies (annual), 1904-10
4. Public Records Office, London:
   Committee of Imperial Defence Papers
   Directorate of Military Operations and Intelligence Papers, 1870-1925, W.O. 106

Field Intelligence Department, W.O. 108/75, 108.18

Roberts Papers, W.O. 105

War Office Reports and Miscellaneous Papers, 1853-1939, W.O. 33

World War I Intelligence Summaries, W.O. 157

B. British Public Documents

Great Britain. Cabinet. *Cabinet Papers, 1880-1914.* London: HMSO, 1964. Microfilm.

_____ . Cabinet. Committee of Imperial Defence. *Report of the Sub-Committee on Aerial Navigation.* (January 1909), Cab. 4/3/1/106B, PRO.

_____ . Cabinet. Committee of Imperial Defence. *Report of the Sub-Committee on Aerial Navigation.* (July 1912), Cab. 4/4/33/159B, PRO.

_____ . Cabinet. Committee of Imperial Defence. *Report of the Sub-Committee on Foreign Espionage in the United Kingdom.* (July 1909), Cab. 3/2/1/47A, PRO.

_____ . Cabinet. Committee of Imperial Defence. *Report of the Sub-Committee on the Military Needs of the Empire.* (October 1908), Cab. 4/3/1/109B. PRO.

_____ . Cabinet. Committee of Imperial Defence. *Report of the Sub-Committee on Press and Postal Censorship in Time of War.* (January 1913), Cab. 4/5/2/167, 168B, PRO.

_____ . Parliamentary Papers. *Memorandum of the Secretary of State Relating to the Army Estimates, 1887-88.* (Cd. 4985, 1887), 50.8-9.

_____ . Parliamentary Papers. *Memorandum showing the duties of the principal officers and departments of the War Office and details of office procedure, under the Order in Council dated 21st November 1895.* (Cd. 7987, 1896), 51.

_____ . Parliamentary Papers. *Order in Council defining the duties of the principal officers of the War Department.* (Cd. 794, 1901), 58, 1902.

_____ . Parliamentary Papers. *Order in Council of 21 November 1895.* (1896), 51.

_____ . Parliamentary Papers. *Order in Council of 10th August 1904 defining the duties of the Army Council.* (Cd. 2251, 1904), 46, 1905.

_____ . Parliamentary Papers. *Report of the War Office (Reconstitution) Committee,* part 1 (Cd. 1932, 1904), part 2 (Cd. 1968, 1904), part 3 (Cd, 1002, 1904), 8.

_____ . Parliamentary Papers. *Reports of the Royal Commissioners Appointed to Enquire into the Civil and Professional Administration of the Naval and Military Departments and the Relation of These Departments to Each Other and to the Treasury (Hartington Report).* (Cd. 5979, 1890), 19.

_____ . Royal Commission on the War in South Africa. *Report.* (Cd. 1789, 1903), 40, 1904.

_____ . Royal Commission on the War in South Africa. *Minutes of Evidence I.* (Cd. 1790, 1903), 40, 1904.

_____ . Royal Commission on the War in South Africa. *Minutes of Evidence II.* (Cd. 1791, 1903), 41, 1904.

_____ . Royal Commission on the War in South Africa. *Appendices to Evidence.* (Cd. 1792, 1903), 42, 1904.

_____ . War Office. *Abstract of the Recommendations of the Principal Commissions and Committees which have Reported on Army Matters 1806-1900.* London: War Office, 1901.

_____. War Office. *Final Report of the Committee on Military Ballooning.* (1904), A.845.

_____. War Office. *Interim Report of the Committee on Wireless Telegraphy.* (1913), W.O. 33.616.

_____. War Office. *Report of the Committee Appointed to Review the Permanent Establishment of the Mobilization and Intelligence Division (Hardwicke Report).* (March 1903), W.O. 7606/1246.

_____. War Office. General Staff. *Memorandum on the duties and requirements of the Army in India at the present time with special reference to the proposed reduction of Military Expenditure in India.* (1911), "secret," K Refuge, MOD Library.

_____. War Office. General Staff. *Report of the Committee on the Issue and Custody of Secret Documents.* (1910), A1390.

C. Published Documents and Official Histories

German General Staff. *German Official Account of the War in South Africa*, 2 vols. Translated by Col. W.H.H. Waters. London: John Murray, 1904.

Great Britain. Committee of Imperial Defence. *History of the Great War, based on Official Documents: Military Operations.* Vol. 1, J.E. Edmonds, *France and Belgium, 1914*, 3d ed. London: Macmillan, 1933.

Gooch, G.P. and Temperley Harold, eds. *British Documents on the Origins of the War 1898-1914*, 11 vols. London: HMSO, 1927-38.

Grant, Capt. Maurice H. and Maj. Gen. Sir Frederick Maurice. *History of the War in South Africa*, 4 vols. London: Hurst & Blackett, 1906-10.

Raleigh, Sir Walter and H.A. Jones. *The War in the Air* (official history of the Royal Air Force in World War I), 6 vols. London: Oxford University Press, 1922-37.

D. Contemporary Material (manuals, regulations, lectures, notes, articles, and books) having to do with the Organizational Structure and/or Operational Doctrine of British Military Intelligence

Brackenbury, Maj. C.B. "The Intelligence Duties of the Staff Abroad and at Home." *Journal of the Royal United Services Institution* 19 (1875): 242-67.

Brackenbury, Lt. Gen. Sir Henry, DMI. "Notes for the Information of Officers attending Foreign Manoeuvres." Intelligence Division (May 1889), K Refuge, MOD Library.

_____. "Rules to be observed by Officers Travelling, who are endeavoring to obtain Information for the Intelligence Division." Intelligence Division (n.d., probably written between 1888 and 1890), K Refuge, MOD Library.

Callwell, Maj. Charles E. *Small Wars, Their Principles and Practice.* London: Intelligence Division, War Office, 1896, revised 1899, 1906.

Clarke, Maj. Francis C.H. *Staff Duties: A Series of Lectures Addressed to Officers at the Staff College.* London: HMSO, 1884

Collen, Capt. E.H.H. *Report on the Intelligence Branch, Quarter-Master-General's Department, Horse Guards.* London: HMSO, 1878. Intelligence Corps Museum, A.011.14.

East, Col. C.J. "Short Account of the Formation and Present Organization of the Intelligence Branch, Horse Guards London." It was provided to Capt. G.M. Wheeler, U.S. Army Corps of Engineers, on a confidential basis on 9 September 1882. U.S.M.H.I., Carlisle Barracks, Pa.

Edmonds, Lt. Col. James E. "Intelligence in European Warfare." Lecture (January 1908). Edmonds Papers, 4/1.

Elliot, Maj. W.J. "The Military Intelligence Departments of England and Germany in Contrast." *United Service Magazine* 113 (June 1885): 529-59.

Frith, Capt. G.R. *The Topographical Section of the General Staff.* Written by direction of Maj. Gen. J.M. Grierson, Director of Military Operations. Chatham: School of Military Engineering, 1906.

Furse, Col. George A. *Information in War: Its Acquisition and Transmission.* London: William Clowes & Sons, 1895.

Gleichen, Lord Edward. "Intelligence Duties in the Field." Lecture (15 March 1908). Edmonds Papers, 7/3.

Great Britain. Army. General Staff in India. *Scouting and Patrolling.* Calcutta: Government Printing, 1918.

_____ . War Office. General Staff. *Field Service Regulations,* part 1, *Operations, 1909.* (Reprinted with amendments, 1914.) London: Harrison & Sons, 1914.

_____ . War Office. General Staff. *Field Service Regulations,* part 2, *Organization and Administration, 1909.* (Reprinted with amendments, October 1914.) London: Eyre & Spottiswoode, 1914.

_____ . War Office. General Staff. "Regulations for Intelligence Duties in the Field." (1904), MOD Library.

_____ . War Office. General Staff. *Staff War Manual (Provisional), 1912.* (1912), "for official use only," Intelligence Corps Museum.

_____ . War Office. General Staff. Directorate of Military Operations. "Notes with Regard to the Collection of Intelligence in Peace Time." (April 1907), "for official use only," K Refuge, MOD Library.

_____ . War Office. General Headquarters, Home Forces. *Intelligence Manual for Home Defence,* part 1, May 1917, part 2, August 1917.

Henderson, Lt. Col. David. *Field Intelligence, Its Principles and Practices.* London: HMSO, "for official use only," 1904. MOD Library.

_____ . Director of Military Intelligence, South Africa. "Intelligence Organisation and Administration (South Africa), Revised Instructions." (August 1901) MOD Library.

_____ . *The Art of Reconnaissance.* London: John Murray, 1907.

_____ . *The Art of Reconnaissance.* 2d ed. London: John Murray, 1908.

_____ . *The Art of Reconnaissance.* 3d ed. London: John Murray, 1914.

Patterson, Lt. Col. William. *Notes on Military Surveying and Reconnaissance.* London: Turner & Co., 1882.

Rothwell, Lt. Col. J.S., ed. *Staff Duties: A Series of Lectures for the Use of Officers at the Staff College.* London: HMSO, 1890.

Russell, Maj. Gen. F.S. "The Intelligence Department." *Blackwood's Edinburgh Magazine.* (May 1900): 725-35.

Simpson, Charles Napier. *The Eyes and Ears of the Artillery: Hints on the Education and Training of Artillery Observation Patrols and Ground Scouts.* London: Hugh Rees, 1905.

Vaughan, A.O. "Some Scouts—but not Scouting." *Longman's Magazine* (February 1904): 227-41.

White, R. Murray. "Scouting." *The National Review* (May 1903): 474-79.

Wilson, Capt. Charles W. "Memorandum on the Topographical Department, the Library, Army Statistics, &c." London: War Office, 30 April 1870. Printed in full in Lt. Col. Parritt, *The Intelligencers*, pp. 97-98.

Wolseley, Sir Garnet. *The Soldier's Pocket-Book for Field Service*. London: Macmillan, 1869.

_____ . *The Soldier's Pocket-Book for Field Service*. 3d ed. London: Macmillan, 1874.

_____ . *The Soldier's Pocket-Book for Field Service*. 4th ed. London: Macmillan, 1882.

_____ . *The Soldier's Pocket-Book for Field Service*. 5th ed. London: Macmillan, 1886.

E. War Office Intelligence Products

Brackenbury, Maj. Gen. Sir Henry. "Mobilization Reports 1, 2, and 3." War Office (14 April, 23 September, and 14 October 1886), A.47. W.O. 33/46.

Clarke, Maj. G.S. "Report on the Defences of Belgium, 1890." Intelligence Division (1890), "secret." K Refuge, MOD Library.

Great Britain. War Office. *Handbook of the Austro-Hungarian Army*. (1891, 1902, 1906, 1909), MOD Library.

_____ . War Office. *Handbook of the Belgian Army*. (1893, 1899, 1906), MOD Library.

_____ . War Office. *Handbook of the French Army*. (1906, 1914), "for official use only," MOD Library.

_____ . War Office. *Handbook of the German Army*. (1897, 1900, 1906, 1912, with amendments in January 1914), "for official use only," MOD Library.

_____ . War Office. *Handbook of the Italian Army*. (1891, 1902, 1913), MOD Library.

_____ . War Office. *Handbook of the Japanese Army*. (1886, 1908) "confidential," MOD Library.

_____ . War Office. *Handbook of the Russian Army*. (1882, 1887, 1889, 1894, 1898, 1902, 1905, 1908, 1914), MOD Library.

_____ . War Office. *Handbook of the Turkish Army*. (1892, 1900, 1904, 1906, 1912), MOD Library.

_____ . War Office. *Handbook on the Armies of Bulgaria, Greece, Montenegro, Roumania, and Servia*. (1895, 1904), MOD Library.

_____ . War Office. General Staff. *Field Notes on the Belgian, French, and German Armies*. (1914), MOD Library.

_____ . War Office. General Staff. *German Army Handbook April 1918*. New York: Hippocrene Books, 1977.

_____ . War Office. General Staff. *Handbook of the German Army in War*. (January 1917, April 1918).

_____ . War Office. General Staff. "Memorandum Regarding Railways in China and Adjoining Countries." (March 1905), "confidential," K Refuge, MOD Library.

_____ . War Office. General Staff. *Military Resources of the German Empire*. (1911), "for official use only," MOD Library.

_____ . War Office. General Staff. *Records of a Strategic War Game*. (1905), "confidential," K Refuge, MOD Library.

_____ . War Office. General Staff. *Report on Certain Landing Places in Turkey in Europe*. (1909), "secret," MOD Library.

_____ . War Office. General Staff. *Report on Changes in Foreign Armies During ----*. (Annually, 1904-10), MOD Library.

_____ . War Office. General Staff. *Report on Foreign Manoeuvres*. (Annually, 1905-13), "for official use only," except 1912 and 1913 editions, which were "confidential"; MOD Library.

_____ . War Office. General Staff. "Report on the Eastern Command Intelligence and Reconnaissance Course, 1907." Intelligence Corps Museum.

_____ . War Office. General Staff. "Report on the Eastern Command Intelligence and Reconnaissance Course, April, 1908." Intelligence Corps Museum.

_____ . War Office. General Staff. *Special Military Resources of the German Empire*. (1912), "secret," MOD Library.

_____ . War Office. General Staff. *The Military Resources of Belgium*. (Dec. 1906), "secret," MOD Library.

_____ . War Office. General Staff. *The Military Resources of France*. (1905), "secret," MOD Library.

_____ . War Office. General Staff. *The Military Resources of France*. (1911), "for official use only;" (1912), "secret," MOD Library.

_____ . War Office. General Staff. *The Russo-Japanese War: Reports from British Officers Attached to the Japanese and Russian Forces in the Field*, 3 vols. London: HMSO, 1908.

_____ . War Office. Intelligence Department. "Telegraphic Censorship during the South African War, 1899-1902." Preface by W.G. Nicholson, DGMI. (June 1903), "secret," K Refuge, MOD Library.

_____ . War Office. Intelligence Department. "War Office Systems of Foreign Countries and India" (March 1903), "confidential," MOD Library.

_____ . War Office. Intelligence Division. "Military Notes on the Dutch Republics of South Africa." (1898, 1899), "secret."

_____ . War Office. Intelligence Division. *Military Report on Martinique*. (8 December 1902), "secret," MOD Library, A758.

_____ . War Office. Quartermaster General's Department, Intelligence Branch. *Armed Strength of Foreign Powers*. Series (1875-1883).

_____ . War Office. Quartermaster General's Department. Intelligence Branch. "General Sketch of the Situation Abroad and at Home from a Military Standpoint." (3 August 1886) W.O. 33/46.

_____ . War Office. Quartermaster General's Department. Intelligence Branch. *Military Cryptography or Cipher Writing*. Prepared by Maj. F.S. Rothwell. London: HMSO, 1894.

_____ . War Office. Quartermaster General's Department. Intelligence Branch. *Notes on the Government Surveys of the Principal Countries*. London: HMSO, 1882.

_____ . War Office. Quartermaster General's Department. Intelligence Branch. *Persia*. London: HMSO, 1880, "confidential."

Jervis, Thomas Best. "The Krima or Crimean Peninsula." Reproduced from the original Russian military map. London: HMSO, 1854. USMA Library, West Point, N.Y.

Murray, Maj. James Wolfe. "Russia's Power to Concentrate Troops in Central Asia." Intelligence Division (May 1888), "secret," K Refuge, MOD Library.

Repington, Maj. Charles à Court. *The Military Resources of France.* Intelligence Division, (1895) "secret," MOD Library.

Talbot, Col. R.A.J. *Report of a Trip Through Transcaspia and Turkestan in October 1888.* London: HMSO, 1899. "confidential," MOD Library.

F. Other Contemporary Works

Arnold-Forster, H.O. *The Army in 1906: A Policy and a Vindication.* New York: E.P. Dutton, 1906.

Brackenbury, Sir Henry. *The Ashanti War.* 2 vols. Edinburgh: William Blackwood & Sons, 1874.

Bronsart von Schellendorff, Paul. *The Duties of the General Staff.* London: HMSO, 1907.

Callwell, Col. C.E. *Military Operations and Maritime Preponderance: Their Relations and Interdependence.* London: William Blackwood & Sons, 1905.

——————. *The Tactics of Today.* Edinburgh: William Blackwood & Sons, 1910.

——————. "War Office Reminiscences." *Blackwood's Edinburgh Magazine* 190 (August 1911): 154-70.

Colomb, Capt. J.C.R. "Naval Intelligence and Protection of Commerce in War." *Journal of the Royal United Services Institution* 25 (1881): 553-90.

French, Field Marshal Sir John. *1914.* New York: Houghton Mifflin, 1919.

Goodenough, Lt. Gen. W.H. and Lt. Col. J.C. Dalton. *The Army Book for the British Empire.* London: HMSO, 1903.

Griffiths, Maj. Arthur. "The War Office—Past, Present, and to Come." *Fortnightly Review* (April 1903).

Henderson, Col. G.F.R. *The Science of War: A Collection of Essays and Lectures 1891-1903.* London: Longmans, Green, & Co., 1906.

Home, Col. Robert. *A Precis of Modern Tactics.* London: HMSO, 1878.

Rawson, Lt. H.D., "Staff Tours of Foreign Armies." *Journal of the Royal United Services Institution* 21 (1878): 1050-63.

Repington, Col. Charles à Court. "The Airship Menace." *Blackwood's Edinburgh Magazine* 188 (July-December 1910): 3-13.

"Revue Militaire de L'Etranger." *Journal of the Royal United Services Institution* 23 (1880): 675-76.

Swinton, Maj. Gen. Sir Ernest. *The Defence of Duffer's Drift.* Oxford: George Ronald, 1949. (Originally published in *United Service Magazine* under the pseudonym "Backsight Forethought" in 1904).

Upton, Emery. *Armies of Asia and Europe.* New York: Appleton and Co., 1878. Reprint. New York: Greenwood Press, 1968.

"The War Operations in South Africa." *Blackwood's Edinburgh Magazine* (January 1900).

Wilkinson, Spencer. *Lessons of the War.* Westminster: Constable & Co., 1900.

——————. *The Brain of an Army: A Popular Account of the German General Staff.* London: Constable & Co., 1890.

——————. *The Brain of the Navy.* London: Constable & Co., 1895.

II. Memoirs, Diaries, and Biographies

Arthur, Sir George. *Life of Lord Kitchener*, 3 vols. New York: Macmillan, 1920.

Ash, Bernard. *The Lost Dictator; A Biography of Field-Marshal Sir Henry Wilson.* London: Cassell, 1968.

Aston, Maj. Gen. Sir George. *Memoirs of a Marine: An Amphibiography.* London: John Murray, 1919.

—————— . *Secret Service.* London: Faber & Faber, 1930.

Barnett, Corelli. *The First Churchill: Marlborough Soldier and Statesman.* New York: G.P. Putnam's Sons, 1974.

Blake, Robert, ed. *The Private Papers of Douglas Haig 1914-1919.* London: Eyre & Spottiswoode, 1952.

Bonham-Carter, Victor. *Soldier True: The Life and Times of Field-Marshal Sir William Robertson.* London: Frederick Muller, 1963.

Brackenbury, Gen. Sir Henry. *Some Memories of My Spare Time.* London: William Blackwood & Sons, 1909.

Brett, Maurice V. and Viscount Esher, eds. *Journals and Letters of Reginald Viscount Esher*, 4 vols. London: Ivor Nicholson & Watson, 1934-1938.

Briggs, Sir John Henry. *Naval Administrations 1827 to 1892: The Experiences of 65 Years.* London: Sampson, Low, Marston & Co., 1897.

Callwell, Maj. Gen. Sir Charles E. *Field-Marshal Sir Henry Wilson*, 2 vols. London: Cassell, 1927.

—————— . *Stray Recollections*, 2 vols. London: Edward Arnold, 1923.

Chandler, David. *Marlborough as Military Commander.* New York: Charles Scribner's Sons, 1973.

Charteris, Brig. Gen. John. *At GHQ.* London: Cassell, 1931.

—————— . *Field-Marshal Earl Haig.* New York: Charles Scribner's Sons, 1929.

Churchill, Winston S. *London to Ladysmith and Ian Hamilton's March.* New York: Harcourt, Brace & World, 1962.

Collier, Basil. *Brasshat: A Biography of Field-Marshal Sir Henry Wilson.* London: Secker & Warburg, 1961.

De Wet, Christiaan R. *Three Years War.* New York: Charles Scribner's Sons, 1902.

Edmonds, Brig. Gen. Sir James E. "Memoirs." Unpublished memoirs, 1890-1914. Edmonds Papers, 3, Liddell Hart Centre for Military Archives, Kings College.

Ellison, Lt. Gen. Sir Gerald. "From Here and There: Reminiscences," a series of articles which appeared in *The Lancashire Lad* between October 1931 and August 1936.

Esher, Viscount Reginald. *The Tragedy of Lord Kitchener.* London: John Murray, 1921.

Fuller, Maj. Gen. J.F.C. *Memoirs of an Unconventional Soldier.* London: Ivor Nicholson & Watson, 1936.

—————— . *The Last of the Gentleman's Wars.* London: Faber & Faber, 1937.

Gleichen, Maj. Gen. Lord Edward. *A Guardsman's Memories.* London: William Blackwood & Sons, 1932.

Haldane of Cloan, Lord Richard. *An Autobiography.* Garden City, N.Y.: Doubleday, Doran & Co., 1929.

Hamilton, Ian B.M. *The Happy Warrior: A life of General Sir Ian Hamilton.* London: Cassell, 1966.

Hamilton, Lt. Gen. Sir Ian. *A Staff Officer's Scrap Book During the Russo-Japanese War*, 2 vols. London: Edward Arnold, 1905 and 1907.

Hankey, Lord. *The Supreme Command, 1914-1918*, 2 vols. London: George Allen & Unwin, 1901.

Hannah, W.H. *Bobs, Kipling's General: The Life of Field-Marshal Earl Roberts of Kandahar, VC.* London: Leo Cooper, 1972.

Hibbert, Christopher. *The Destruction of Lord Raglan: A Tragedy of the Crimean War.* Boston: Little, Brown & Co., 1961.

James, Adm. Sir William. *The Eyes of the Navy: A Biographical Study of Admiral Sir Reginald Hall.* London: Methuen & Co., 1955.

James, David. *Lord Roberts.* London: Hollis & Carter, 1954.

Jervis, William P. *Thomas Best Jervis.* London: Elliot Stock, 1898.

Joffre, Field Marshal Joseph Jacques Césaire. *The Personal Memoirs of Joffre*, 2 vols., translated by Col. T. Bentley Mott. New York: Harper & Brothers, 1932.

Lawrence, T.E. *Seven Pillars of Wisdom: A Triumph.* New York: Doubleday, Doran & Co., 1935.

Lehmann, Joseph H. *All Sir Garnet: A Life of Field-Marshal Lord Wolseley.* London: Jonathan Cape, 1964.

Lockhart, Robin Bruce. *Ace of Spies.* New York: Stein & Day, 1968.

Lord, John. *Duty, Honor, Empire: The Life and Times of Colonel Richard Meinertzhagen.* New York: Random House, 1970.

Lyttelton, Gen. Sir Neville. *Eighty Years: Soldiering, Politics, Games.* London: Hodder & Stoughton, 1927.

Macdiarmid, D.S. *The Life of Lieut. General Sir James Moncrieff Grierson.* London: Constable & Co., 1923.

Magnus, Philip. *Kitchener: Portrait of an Imperialist.* London: John Murray, 1958.

Malmesbury, Susan Countess of. *The Life of Major-General Sir John Ardagh.* London: John Murray, 1909.

Marder, Arthur J., ed. *Fear God and Dread Nought: The Correspondence of Admiral of the Fleet Lord Fisher of Kilverstone*, 3 vols. London: Jonathan Cape, 1952-59.

Marshal-Cornwall, Gen. Sir James. "Experiences of an Intelligence Officer in World Wars 1 and 2." Marshall-Cornwall Papers, Intelligence Corps Museum, A33.

——————. *Haig as Military Commander.* New York: Crane, Russak & Co., 1973.

Maurice, Maj. Gen. Sir Frederick and Sir George Arthur. *The Life of Lord Wolseley.* London: William Heinemann, 1924.

Melville, Col. C.H. *Life of General the Rt. Hon. Sir Redvers Buller.* Vol. 2. London: Edward Arnold, 1923.

Pienaar, Philip. *With Steyn and De Wet.* London: Methuen & Co., 1902.

Preston, Adrian, ed. *In Relief of Gordon: Lord Wolseley's Campaign Journal of the Khartoum Relief Expedition, 1884-1885.* London: Hutchinson & Co., 1967.

Reitz, Deneys. *Commando: A Boer Journal of the Boer War.* London: Faber & Faber, 1929.

Repington, Lt. Col. Charles à Court. *The First World War, 1914-1918: Personal Experiences*, 2 vols. Boston: Houghton Mifflin Co., 1920.

——————. *Vestigia: Reminiscences of Peace and War.* Boston: Houghton Mifflin Co., 1919.

Roberts, Field Marshal Lord. *Forty-One Years in India: From Subaltern to Commander-in-Chief*, 2 vols. London: Macmillan, 1902.

Robertson, Sir William. *From Private to Field Marshal*. Boston: Houghton Mifflin Co., 1921

_____. *Soldiers and Statesmen, 1914-1918*. Vol. 1. London: Cassell, 1926.

Roskill, S.W. *Hankey: Man of Secrets*. Vol. 1. London: Collins, 1970; Annapolis, Md.: Naval Institute Press, 1970.

Spears, Maj. Gen. Sir Edward. *Liaison 1914: A Narrative of the Great Retreat*. London: Eyre & Spottiswoode, 1968.

Sternberg, Count Adalbert W. *My Experiences of the Boer War*. London: Longmans, Green & Co., 1901.

Stewart, Desmond. *T.E. Lawrence*. New York: Harper & Row, 1977.

Swinton, Maj. Gen. Sir Ernest D. *Over My Shoulder*. Oxford: George Ronald, 1951.

Sydenham of Combe, Lord (Sir George Clarke). *My Working Life*. London: John Murray, 1927.

Terraine, John. *Douglas Haig: The Educated Soldier*. London: Hutchinson & Co., 1963.

Viljoen, Gen. Ben. *My Reminiscences of the Anglo-Boer War*. London: Hood, Douglas & Howard, 1903. Reprint. Cape Town: C. Struik, 1973.

Waters, Brig. Gen. W.H.H. *"Private and Personal."* London: John Murray, 1928.

_____. *Russia Then and Now*. London: John Murray, 1935.

_____. *"Secret and Confidential": The Experiences of a Military Attaché*. London: John Murray, 1926.

Watson, Sir Charles M. *The Life of Major-General Sir Charles William Wilson*. London: John Murray, 1909.

Wolseley, Field Marshal Viscount. *The Story of a Soldiers Life*, 2 vols. New York: Charles Scribner's Sons, 1904.

III. Secondary Sources

A. Books

Addington, Larry H. *The Blitzkrieg Era and the German General Staff, 1865-1941*. New Brunswick, N.J.: Rutgers University Press, 1971.

Amery, L.S. ed. *The Times History of the War in South Africa*, 7 vols. London: Sampson, Low, Marston & Co., 1900-09.

Andrew, Christopher. *Théophile Delcassé and the Making of the Entente Cordiale*. London: Macmillan, 1968.

Barnett, Corelli. *Britain and Her Army, 1509-1970: A Military Political, and Social Survey*. Harmondsworth, England: Penguin Books, 1970.

Beesly, Patrick. *Room 40: British Naval Intelligence 1914-18*. London: Hamish Hamilton, 1982.

Biddulph, Gen. Sir Robert. *Lord Cardwell at the War Office: A History of His Administration, 1868-1874*. London: John Murray, 1904.

Bond, Brian. *The Victorian Army and the Staff College 1854-1914*. London: Eyre Nethuen, 1972.

Bond, Brian, ed. *Victorian Military Campaigns*. London: Hutchinson & Co., 1967.

Bulloch, John. *M.I. 5: The Origin and History of the British Counter-Espionage Service*. London: Arthur Barker, 1963.

Bywater, Hector and H.C. Ferraby. *Strange Intelligence: Memoirs of Naval Secret Service*. London: Constable & Co., 1931.

Carroll, John M. *Secrets of Electronic Espionage*. New York: E.P. Dutton & Co., 1966.

Deacon, Richard. *A History of the British Secret Service*. London: Frederick Muller, 1969.

_____ . *A History of the Russian Secret Service*. New York: Taplinger Publishing Co., 1972.

_____ . *The Silent War: A History of Western Naval Intelligence*. London: David & Charles, 1978.

D'Ombrain, Nicholas J. *War Machinery and High Policy: Defence Administration in Peacetime Britain, 1902-1914*. London: Oxford University Press, 1973.

Dunlop, Col. John K. *The Development of the British Army, 1899-1914*. London: Methuen & Co., 1938.

Dupuy, Col. T.N. *A Genius for War: The German Army and General Staff, 1807-1945*. Englewood Cliffs, N.J.: Prentice-Hall, 1977.

Ehrman, John. *Cabinet Government and War, 1890-1940*. Cambridge: Cambridge University Press, 1958.

Farwell, Byron. *Queen Victoria's Little Wars*. New York: Harper & Row, 1972.

_____ . *The Great Anglo-Boer War*. New York: Harper & Row, 1976.

Falstead, Sidney T. *German Spies at Bay*. New York: Macmillan, Brentano's, 1920.

Fortescue, Sir John William. *A History of the British Army*, 13 vols. London: Macmillan, 1902-30.

Gardner, Brian. *Mafeking: A Victorian Legend*. London: Cassell, 1966.

Gibbs, Norman H. *The Origins of Imperial Defence*. Oxford: Oxford University Press, Clarendon Press, 1955.

Glover, Michael. *Wellington's Army in the Peninsula, 1808-1814*. New York: Hippocrene Books, 1977.

Glover, Richard. *Peninsular Preparation: The Reform of the British Army, 1795-1809*. Cambridge: Cambridge University Press, 1963.

Goerlitz, Walter. *History of the German General Staff, 1657-1945*. Translated by Brian Battershaw. New York: Praeger Publishers, 1953.

Gooch, John. *The Plans of War: The General Staff and British Military Strategy c. 1900-1916*. London: Routledge & Kegan Paul, 1974.

Goodwin-Austen, A.R. *The Staff and the Staff College*. London: Constable & Co., 1927.

Gorce, Paul Marie de la. *The French Army: A Military-Political History*. Translated by Kenneth Douglas. New York: George Braziller, 1963.

Gordon, Donald C. *The Dominion Partnership in Imperial Defense 1870-1914*. Baltimore: Johns Hopkins University Press, 1965.

_____ . *The Moment of Power: Britain's Imperial Epoch*. Englewood Cliffs, N.J.: Prentice-Hall, 1970.

Gordon, Hampden. *The War Office*. London: Putnam, 1935.

Graves, Dr. Armgaard Karl and Edward L. Fox. *The Secrets of the German War Office*. New York: McBride, Nast & Co., 1914.

Hahn, Maj. J.E. *The Intelligence Service Within the Canadian Corps 1914-1918*. Toronto: Macmillan of Canada, 1930.

Hamer, W.S. *The British Army: Civil Military Relations, 1885-1905*. Oxford: Oxford University Press, Clarendon Press, 1970.

Haswell, Jock. *British Military Intelligence*. London: Weidenfeld & Nicolson, 1973.

Heathcote, T.A. *The Indian Army: The Garrison of British Imperial India, 1822-1922.* London: David & Charles, 1974.

Higham, Robin. *The British Rigid Airship, 1908-1931: A Study in Weapons Policy.* London: G.T. Foulis & Co., 1961.

Hittle, J.D. *The Military Staff: Its History and Development.* Harrisburg, Pa.: Stackpole Books, 1961.

Holt, Edgar. *The Boer War.* London: Putnam, 1958.

Howard, Christopher. *Britain and the Casus Belli, 1822-1902: A Study of Britain's International Position from Canning to Salisbury.* London: Athlone, 1974.

_____ . *Splendid Isolation.* New York: St. Martin's Press, 1967.

Howard, Michael. *The Franco-Prussian War: The German Invasion of France, 1870-1871.* London: Rupert Hart-Davis, 1968.

Howarth, David. *Sovereign of the Seas: The Story of Britain and the Sea.* New York: Atheneum Publishers, 1974.

James, Adm. Sir William M. *The Code Breakers of Room 40.* New York: St. Martin's Press, 1956.

Jeffries, Sir Charles. *The Colonial Office.* London: George Allen & Unwin, 1956.

Johnson, Franklyn A. *Defence by Committee: The British Committee of Imperial Defence, 1885-1959.* London: Oxford University Press, 1960.

Jones, Ray. *The Nineteenth-Century Foreign Office: An Administrative History.* London: Weidenfeld & Nicolson, 1971.

Kahn, David. *The Codebreakers: The Story of Secret Writing.* New York: Macmillan, 1967.

Knightley, Phillip. *The First Casualty; From the Crimea to Vietnam: The War Correspondent as Hero, Propagandist, and Myth Maker.* New York: Harcourt Brace Jovanovich, 1975.

Kruger, Rayne. *Good-bye Dolly Gray: The Story of the Boer War.* London: Cassell, 1959.

Landau, Capt. Henry. *All's Fair: The Story of the British Secret Service behind the German Lines.* New York: G.P. Putnam's Sons, 1934.

Lowe, C.J. *The Reluctant Imperialists: British Foreign Policy 1878-1902,* 2 vols. London: Routledge & Kegan Paul, 1967.

Luvaas, Jay. *The Education of an Army: British Military Thought 1815-1940.* Chicago: University of Chicago Press, 1964.

_____ . *The Military Legacy of the Civil War: The European Inheritance.* Chicago: University of Chicago Press, 1959.

Mackintosh, John P. *The British Cabinet.* London: Stevens & Sons, 1968.

Marder, Arthur J. *The Anatomy of British Sea Power: A History of British Naval Policy in the Pre-Dreadnought Era, 1880-1905.* London: Frank Cass & Co., 1940.

Mason, Philip. *A Matter of Honour: An Account of the Indian Army, Its Officers and Men.* New York: Holt, Rinehart & Winston, 1974.

Middleton, K.W.B. *Britain and Russia: An Historical Essay.* London: Kennikat Press, 1947.

Monger, George E. *The End of Isolation: British Foreign Policy, 1900-1907.* London: Thomas Nelson, 1963.

Morris, Donald R. *The Washing of the Spears: A History of the Rise of the Zulu Nation under Shaka and Its Fall in the Zulu War of 1879.* New York: Simon & Schuster, 1965.

Morrow, John Howard, Jr. *Building German Airpower, 1909-1914.* Knoxville: University of Tennessee Press, 1976.

Newman, Bernard. *Spy and Counter-Spy.* London: Robert Hale, 1970.

Nicolai, Col. W. *The German Secret Service.* Translated by George Renwick. London: Stanley Paul & Co., 1924.

Pakenham, Thomas. *The Boer War.* New York: Random House, 1979.

Parritt, Lt. Col. B.A.H. *The Intelligencers: The Story of British Military Intelligence up to 1914.* Templer Barracks, Ashford, Kent: Intelligence Corps, 1971.

Preston, Richard A. *Canada and "Imperial Defense": A Study of the Origins of the British Commonwealth's Defense Organization, 1867-1919.* Durham, N.C.: Duke University Press, 1967.

Preston, Richard A. and Sydney F. Wise. *Men in Arms: A History of Warfare and Its Interrelationships with Western Society.* 2d ed. New York: Praeger Publishers, 1970.

Ralston, David B. *The Army of the Republic: The Place of the Army in the Political Evolution of France, 1871-1914.* Cambridge: MIT Press, 1967.

Ropp, Theodore. *War in the Modern World.* New York: Collier Books, 1962.

Rothenberg, Gunther E. *The Art of Warfare in the Age of Napoleon.* London: B.T. Batsford, 1967.

Rowan, Richard W. *The Story of Secret Service.* New York: Literary Guild of America, 1937.

Schurman, Donald M. *The Education of a Navy: The Development of British Naval Thought 1867-1914.* London: Cassell, 1965.

Steiner, Zara S. *The Foreign Office and Foreign Policy, 1898-1914.* Cambridge: Cambridge University Press, 1969.

Strong, Maj. Gen. Sir Kenneth. *Men of Intelligence.* London: Cassell, 1970.

Sweeney, Walter C. *Military Intelligence, A New Weapon in War.* New York: Frederick A. Stokes Co., 1924.

Taylor, A.J.P. *English History, 1914-1945.* New York: Oxford University Press, 1965.

——————. *The Struggle for Mastery in Europe, 1848-1918.* Oxford: Oxford University Press, 1954.

Taylor, John W.R. and David Mondey. *Spies in the Sky.* New York: Charles Scribner's Sons, 1972.

Terraine, John. *Mons: The Retreat to Victory.* New York: Macmillan, 1960.

Tyler, J.E. *The British Army and the Continent, 1904-1914.* London: Edward Arnold, 1938.

Vagts, Alfred. *The Military Attaché.* Princeton, N.J.: Princeton University Press, 1967.

Ward, S.G.P. *Wellington's Headquarters: A Study of the Administrative Problems in the Peninsula, 1809-1814.* London: Oxford University Press, 1957.

Wheeler, Capt. Owen. *The War Office Past and Present.* London: Methuen & Co., 1914.

Williamson, Samuel R., Jr. *The Politics of Grand Strategy: Britain and France Prepare for War, 1904-1914.* Cambridge: Harvard University Press, 1969.

Woods, David L. *A History of Tactical Communication Techniques.* Orlando, Fla.: Martin Marietta Corp., 1965.

Younghusband, Col. G.J. *The Story of the Guides.* London: Macmillan, 1908.

B. Articles

Aston, Sir George. "The Entente Cordiale and the Military Conversations." *Quarterly Review* 258 (April 1932): 363-83.

Bond, Brian. "Richard Burdon Haldane at the War Office, 1905-1912." *Army Quarterly and Defence Journal* 86 (April 1963): 33-43.

——————— . "The Effect of the Cardwell Reforms in Army Organization, 1874-1904." *Journal of the Royal United Services Institution* 105 (November 1960): 515-24.

D'Ombrain, Nicholas J. "The Imperial General Staff and the Military Policy of a 'Continental Strategy' during the 1911 International Crisis." *Military Affairs* 34 (1970): 88-93.

Ellison, Lt. Gen. Sir Gerald. "Lord Roberts and the General Staff." *The Nineteenth Century and After* 112 (December 1932): 722-32.

Hammerton, M. "The Military Predictions of E.D. Swinton." *Journal of the Royal United Services Institution* 120 (December 1975): 31-32.

Hargreaves, J.D. "The Origin of the Anglo-French Military Conversations in 1905." *History* 36 (October 1951): 244-48.

Horward, Donald D. "The Archives de la Guerre: Its History and Importance in Napoleonic Scholarship." *The Journal of Library History*. (1969): 66-72.

Howard, Christopher. "The Policy of Isolation." *Historical Journal* 10 (1967): 77-88.

Irvine, Dallas D. "The Origin of Capital Staffs." *Journal of Modern History*, no. 2 (June 1938): 161-79.

Lockhart, John Bruce. "The Relationship between Secret Services and Government in a Modern State." *Journal of the Royal United Services Institute for Defence Studies* 119 (June 1974): 3-8.

Mackintosh, John P. 'The Role of the Committee of Imperial Defence before 1914." *English Historical Review* 77 (July 1962): 490-503.

McMunn, Maj. Gen. Sir George. "The Quarter-master-General's Department and the Administrative Services in India from the Mutiny to the Present Time." *Journal of the Royal United Services Institution* 70 (1924): 101-26.

Preston, Adrian W. "British Military Thought, 1856-90." *Army Quarterly* 89 (October 1964): 57-74.

——————— . "The Eastern Question in British Strategic Policy During the Franco-Prussian War." *Historical Papers 1972*. Ottawa: Canadian Historical Association, 1973.

Roskill, Capt. S.W. "Lord Hankey—the Creation of the Machinery of Government." *Journal of the Royal United Services Institute for Defence Studies* 120 (September 1975): 10-17.

Sixsmith, Maj. Gen. E.K.G. "Kitchener and the Guerillas in the Boer War." *Army Quarterly* 104 (January 1974): 203-14.

Steiner, Zara S. "Great Britain and the Creation of the Anglo-Japanese Alliance." *Journal of Modern History* 31 (March 1959): 27-36.

——————— . "The Last Years of the Old Foreign Office, 1898-1905." *Historical Journal* 6 (1963): 59-60.

Thurbon, Wing Commander M.T. "The Origins of Electronic Warfare." *Journal of the Royal United Services Institution* 122 (September 1977): 56-63.

Towle, Philip. "The British Armed Forces and Japan Before 1914." *The Army Quarterly* 104 (June 1974): 67-71.

_____ . "The European Balance of Power in 1914." *The Army Quarterly* 104 (April 1974): 333-42.

Tucker, Albert V. "Army and Society in England, 1870-1900: A Reassessment of the Cardwell Reforms." *Journal of British Studies* 2 (May 1963): 110-41.

Williams, Beryl J. "The Strategic Background to the Anglo-Russian Entente of August 1907." *Historical Journal* 9 (1966): 360-73.

C. Unpublished Manuscripts

Downton, W.O. II G., Intelligence Corps. "Notes and Pictures on the Hisotry of Photographic Interpretation." n.d. (material does not go beyond 1945.) Intelligence Corps Museum. A,176.

Harpin, Paul H. "The British War Office: From the Crimean War to Cardwell, 1855-1868." Master's thesis, University of Massachusetts, 1976.

Hawker, Maj. D.S. "Working Notes for a History of the Intelligence Corps." n.d. (appears to have been completed between 1962 and 1965), Intelligence Corps Museum.

Isaac, Lt. Col. W.V.R. "Field-Marshal Sir William Robertson when Head of the Foreign Military Intelligence Section, War Office." 1960, MOD Library, A011.14.

_____ . "The History of the Development of the Directorate of Military Intelligence, the War Office, 1855-1939." A paper prepared to mark the centenary year of British Military Intelligence, 1955. Ministry of Defence Library, A.O.11.14.

Krause, Michael Detlef. "Anglo-French Military Planning, 1905-1914, Before the First World War: A Study in Military Diplomacy." Doctoral dissertation, Georgetown University, 1968.

Scales, Robert H., Jr. "Artillery in Small Wars: The Evolution of British Artillery Doctrine, 1860-1914." Doctoral dissertation, Duke University, 1976.

Summerton, N.W. "The Development of British Military Planning for a War Against Germany, 1904-1914." Doctoral thesis, London, 1970.

IV. Reference Books

Brassey's *Naval Annual* (1900-14)
Dictionary of National Biography
Hart's *Annual Army List* (1874-96)
War Office List (1903-18)
Who Was Who?

INDEX